The Secret Teachings of the Masonic Lodge

The Secret Teachings of the Masonic Lodge

A CHRISTIAN PERSPECTIVE

John Ankerberg
John Weldon

MOODY PRESS

CHICAGO

All Scripture quotations, unless noted otherwise, are from the *New American Standard Bible,* © 1960, 1962, 1963, 1968, 1971, 1972, 1973, 1975, and 1977, by The Lockman Foundation, and are used by permission.

Library of Congress Cataloging in Publication Data

Ankerberg, John, 1945-
 The secret teachings of the Masonic Lodge : a Christian
perspective / by John Ankerberg & John Weldon.
  p.   cm.
 Includes bibliographical references.
 ISBN 0-8024-7695-3
 1. Freemasonry—Religious aspects—Christianity. 2. Freemasonry-
-Religious aspects. 3. Freemasons—United States. I. Title.
HS495.A64   1990
366'.1'0242—dc20   90-33075
                                                        CIP

17 19 20 18 16

Printed in the United States of America

Contents

Hear us with indulgence, O infinite Deity.... Help us to perform all our Masonic duties, to ourselves, to other men, and to Thee. Let the great flood of Masonic light flow in a perpetual current over the whole world and make Masonry the creed of all mankind.

Prayer given in the opening ceremonies
31st Degree of the Scottish Rite
J. Blanchard, *Scottish Rite Masonry Illustrated*, 2:320

Introduction

In the 1990s, the teachings of Masonry (also known as Freemasonry or the Masonic Lodge) continue to affect American society and many of its institutions, including the church. The purpose of this volume is to discuss the influence, teachings, and consequences of Masonry.

In Part 1 many important facts concerning Masonry are examined. We look at some official definitions of Masonry and show how one determines authoritative Masonic teachings. The relationship between the various branches of Masonry is presented (the Blue Lodge, the Scottish Rite, and the York Rite). Further, we document the great influence of modern Masonry, including the claims of Masonry toward other religions and its influence in the church. We also discuss the origins of Masonry, appendant organizations, why Masonry is attractive to so many people, and the real goals of Masonry—showing why it is more than simply a fraternal organization. Full documentation is given that Masonry is a religion and that its rites are incompatible with Christian belief. Then, too, we discuss the importance of symbolism to the Craft and why secrecy is so critical to its interests. We also question whether or not its humanitarian activities are a form of recruitment.

In Part 2 we proceed to document the theological beliefs of the Lodge. Authoritative Masonic sources are cited to reveal what the Lodge teaches concerning God, Jesus Christ, salvation, man, the Bible, and the afterlife. These are the concerns most critical to an evaluation of Masonic religion.

Part 3 covers some Masonic religious practices that we are particularly concerned about. These practices flow naturally from the beliefs exposed in Part 2. We examine the frightening oaths that every Mason must swear by. The Masonic claim that it truly unites all religions is evaluated, and we answer the question, "Should a Christian church allow members who are Masons to be leaders in the church?"

In Part 4 we examine the connections between the Masonic Lodge and the world of the occult. We show how the teachings of Masonry support the occult and can lead individual Masons in this direction. We also document that the spirit world itself is interested in promoting Masonry in order to secure its own goals. Next, we cite the connections between modern Masonry and a particular form of ancient occultic belief: the pagan mystery religions. Finally, we show how a common characteristic of occultic religion is also found in the Masonic Lodge. This concerns the deliberate deception of the "profane" —those who are considered "unworthy" to receive the carefully guarded secrets.

Many people buy a book about Masonry because a friend, relative, or family member is already in the Lodge. They want to know what Masonry believes and teaches and whether there are spiritual or other implications of those teachings. Many also want to know if Masonry, as a religion, conflicts with their own particular religion—the Christian faith, for example. We urge these readers to turn to Part 2. This is a self-contained unit designed specifically to answer such questions. But such readers may profit from a prior look at chapters 3 and 4. It is the authors' hope that this text will serve a useful purpose to anyone having a need for authoritative information on the Masonic Lodge.

Note: Some note references in this book represent a series of citations by the same author or dealing with similar subject matter. If a quotation is not immediately referenced, therefore, the source information will be listed in the notes under the next-occurring reference.

Part 1

The Masonic Lodge

1

Masonic Nature and Influence

Masonry (also known as Freemasonry or "The Lodge") is a powerful, old fraternal order that began early in the eighteenth century. According to most Masonic authorities, modern Masonry (also called "speculative" Masonry) can be traced to the founding of the first Grand Lodge in London in 1717.[1]

The Lodge is also a secret society. In fact, the *Encyclopaedia Britannica* classifies it as the largest secret society in the world. To maintain its secrets, Masonry uses symbolism, secret oaths, and secret rituals to instruct new members called "Initiates." Each new member swears during these secret ceremonies to remain loyal to the Lodge and its teachings. The teachings instruct each new candidate how he is to serve and the rewards he can expect.

In addition, Masonry views its mission in life as helping to bring the beliefs of all men into harmony—a harmony based primarily on Masonic teachings.[2] Two of these teachings form the foundation of all Masonry.

First is their belief in the universal fatherhood of God and brotherhood of man. By this, Masons teach that all men—Muslims, Jews, Hindus, Mormons, Buddhists, and Christians—regardless of their personal religious views, are the spiritual sons of God. Masonry's second foundational belief is that reforming personal character and practicing good works will secure God's favor. In other words, the Masonic Lodge clearly teaches that the good character and good works of a Mason will earn him a place in the "Celestial Lodge Above" (i.e., heaven).

THE NATURE OF MASONRY

Several leading Masons have defined Masonry. According to Albert G. Mackey in *Revised Encyclopedia of Freemasonry*, "All [Masons] unite in declaring it to be a system of morality, by the practice of which its members may advance their spiritual interest, and mount by the theological ladder from the Lodge on earth to the Lodge in heaven."[3] Other respected Masonic authorities define Masonry in the following ways:

"Masonry is the realization of God by the practice of Brotherhood."[4]

"It is a science which is engaged in the search after Divine Truth, and which employs symbolism as its method of instruction."[5]

"[Masonry is] that religious and mystical society whose aim is moral perfection on the basis of general equality and fraternity."[6]

"Freemasonry, in its broadest and most comprehensive sense, is a system of morality and social ethics, a primitive religion and a philosophy of life. . . . Incorporating a broad humanitarianism, . . . it is a religion without a creed, being of no sect but finding truth in all. . . . It seeks truth but does not define truth."[7]

A man who becomes a Mason is defined by Masonic authorities as "one who has been initiated into the mysteries of the Fraternity of Freemasonry."[8]

On the other hand, defining Masonry presents us with a dilemma. No single definition of Masonry is accepted by all Masons. This is because the practice of Masonry means many different (and sometimes contrary) things to individual Masons. For some of its members, Masonry has become little more than a social club; for others, Masonry dominates their life and work.

This point is well stated by leading Masonic authority Henry Wilson Coil in *A Comprehensive View of Freemasonry*:

> Nobody knows what Freemasonry is, or, if that statement be deemed too strong, at least no one has been able to demonstrate that he knows the answer to the question. What one [Mason or Masonic authority] asserts another of apparently equal ability doubts or denies.... Nor is this divergence of opinion due to ignorance or lack of investigation, for conflicts arise principally among the most zealous and erudite of Masonic students. The Fraternity has no central authority to declare its creed and no censor of books to check aberrations. Anyone, either within or without the Society, may speak or write about it what he wills, and many have taken advantage of that liberty.[9]

Coil proceeds to discuss the basic problem of definition presented by Freemasonry:

> Freemasonry has spread so widely, has expanded into so many degrees [more than 1,100 degrees according to *Coil's Masonic Encyclopedia*, p. 600; cf. *Encyclopaedia Britannica, Micropaedia*, 15th ed., s.v."Freemasonry"], and has undergone so many changes, to say nothing of having been subjected to so many diverse interpretations, that the question: What is Freemasonry? must first be answered by another question: When, where, and what phase of it? Though much of Masonic doctrine has remained remarkably well fixed and stable, its laws have changed, its degrees have changed, its ceremonies have changed, its religion has changed, and doubtless the concepts of it by its members have changed.[10]

Through its history Masonry has changed, and even today Masonry worldwide is not uniform. This characteristic of Masonry presents an important issue that needs to be resolved at the outset: Does Masonry's lack of a central authority make it incapable of being subject to legitimate criticism? The answer is no. The mere fact that Masonry has evolved historically or that Masons disagree among themselves is irrelevant to the production of a factual analysis. Some Masons imply that because Masonry has no "official voice," some Masonic writers are only voicing personal opinions that have no authority. Consider the argument of Masonic historian Alphonse Cerza. Cerza claims that some Masons have advanced theories or made statements that merely express personal views, implying that such views are not Masonic and therefore irrelevant to Masonry:

> Some Masonic authors have unintentionally supplied oppo-
> nents of the Craft with some of their arguments. Dr. Albert
> Churchward, J. S. N. Ward, W. L. Wilmshurst, Arthur Waite,
> and others have advanced theories and made statements that
> express personal views. Some of their statements are not
> based on fact, are mere theories, and are not generally ac-
> cepted by Masons. But the anti-Masons pick up these state-
> ments and hold them up to ridicule by stating that they are
> from books of "Masonic authority." These anti-Masons have
> difficulty in understanding that Freemasonry has no "official
> voice" and that freedom of thought and expression is one of
> the fundamental principles of the Order.[11]

Cerza cites the lack of a central authority in Masonry as a reason critics have been able to quote Masons in their so-called unfounded attacks. But the issue is, "Are what these Masonic writers say true for Masonry?" It is not the fault of one who ana-lyzes Masonry that Masonry has no central authority. But Ma-sonry clearly has a specific history. Masonry clearly has a gen-eral consensus as to its world view. Even the leading Masonic authority, Albert Mackey, has admitted "the doctrine of Freema-sonry is everywhere the same."[12] As we have seen above, Coil himself admits that much of Masonic doctrine "has remained remarkably well fixed and stable."

The real issue is whether or not the statements made by these Masonic authorities are in harmony with what Masonry represents and constitutes, both historically and in terms of its world view. That is the only issue that needs to be decided. Ma-sonry may not have a single human authority, but few Masons will dispute that Masonry *itself* provides *the* authority. In *The Newly-Made Mason*, H. L. Haywood refers to the obligations placed upon the new Mason:

> I hereby solemnly and sincerely promise and swear that as a
> beginning Craftsman in the Masonry of the mind and as a
> Newly-Made Mason I will not permit myself to be led into

making hasty conclusions. I promise and swear that I will not listen to those who are not competent to teach me. There will be nothing binding on me except the truth. If there be those who say one thing and if there be others who say the opposite thing, I will consider that it is Freemasonry itself which finally is to decide between them.[13]

What we present in this book, therefore, is an analysis of Masonry itself, as stated by Masonic authorities recommended by at least half of the Grand Lodges in the United States. We recognize that all of what is presented may not necessarily coincide with the individual beliefs of a given Mason. Some Masons have no interest in the history and doctrines of Masonry. Some are unfamiliar with its occult aspects. But for others, Masonry is a religious world view that dominates their life and their work.

Regardless of the fluid and sometimes historically contradictory nature of Masonry, there remains a solid core of belief that is central to the majority of Masonry and to which almost all Masonic writers appeal.[14] We have examined this core belief, but we have done a great deal more. In examining Masonry in some depth, we have tried to show that the implications of Masonry extend far beyond what the average Mason might suspect.

Before an individual supports Masonry with his oaths, vows, time, and money, he should acquire sufficient information as to the teachings and implications of his craft. It is only then that a rational decision can be made as to whether or not one can indeed support Masonry in good conscience. We have written this text in the hope that it will perform a genuine service to Masons so that this decision can be made intelligently. Further, we believe the material presented in this volume will be a considerable help to everyone outside the Lodge who needs authoritative information on Masonry.

DETERMINING THE AUTHORITATIVE SOURCES IN MASONRY

Mr. Bill Mankin, a 32d Degree Mason, admitted on national television that "The authoritative source for Masonry is The Ritual. The Ritual—what happens in the Lodge, what goes on."[15] He was correct.

But Coil points out "the misconception that originally there was somewhere one authorized ritual. The Masonic rituals were not created: they grew [historically] and there never was only one Masonic ritual; there have always been many."[16] The question then becomes, "Who determines what the ritual will consist of in each Masonic Lodge?" The answer is, the Grand Lodge of each state has the power to regulate the ritual practiced in that Lodge. As Coil writes, it is "well understood that Grand Lodges are the highest Masonic authorities in both law and doctrine."[17]

What must be recognized here is that, historically and worldwide, Masonic ritual varies. But in contemporary American Masonry, it is highly uniform. Thus, if one examines Masonry historically, he will find that the Grand Lodges of each state have disagreed on many of the landmarks (principles of Masonry) and precisely what should be included in the ritual. However, when one examines the different manuals containing the current ritual for each state in America, it is apparent that the ritual and interpretations given are very close, if not identical. Therefore, the ritual in the Masonic manuals can be considered the authoritative teachings of the Lodge. Former Worshipful Master Jack Harris reveals: "In [all] other states . . . the principle and the doctrines are exactly the same. The wording only varies slightly."[18]

In addition, the ritual itself is but the *reflection* of Masonic doctrine. State by state the rituals may vary slightly, but the doctrines they are intended to convey are everywhere uniform. For example, Mackey states in his encyclopedia on Masonry that

> in each Masonic Jurisdiction it is required, by the superintending authority, that the Ritual shall be the same; but it more or less differs in the different Rites and Jurisdictions. But this does not affect the universality of Freemasonry. The Ritual is only the external and extrinsic form. The doctrine of Freemasonry is everywhere the same. It is the Body which is unchangeable—remaining always and everywhere the same. The Ritual is but the outer garment which covers this Body, which is subject to continual variation. It is right and desirable that the Ritual should be made perfect, and everywhere alike. But if this be impossible, as it is, this at least will con-

sole us, that while the ceremonies, or Ritual, have varied at different periods, and still vary in different countries, the science and philosophy, the symbolism and the religion, of Freemasonry continue, and will continue, to be the same wherever true Freemasonry is practised.[19]

A vast amount of Masonic literature is available to the researcher. This includes at least 100,000 volumes, among which are a minimum of 600 analytical works giving a broad treatment of the subject of Masonry.[20] Also in print are numerous exposés of Masonry by former members who have revealed virtually all the secrets of the Craft (e.g., Byers, Harris, McQuaig, Ronayne, and Shaw). Thus, Masonry is a "secret society" only to those who have not read this literature.

Which authors and books do Masons themselves recommend to outsiders as authoritative? In order to answer this question, a letter was sent to each of the fifty Grand Lodges in America. We addressed this letter to the Grand Master of each Lodge and asked him to respond to the following question: "As an official Masonic leader, which books and authors do you recommend as being authoritative on the subject of Freemasonry?"

Twenty-five of the Grand Lodges in the United States responded.[21] A response of fifty percent is sufficiently high to suggest that the responses of other states would not have varied significantly. In other words, we may assume that these responses are normative for U.S. Masonry as a whole. Remember, for each state, no higher jurisdictional authority than its Grand Lodge exists.

Which authors were recommended by the Grand Lodges as being authoritative for Masons?

44 percent recommended Henry Wilson Coil
36 percent Joseph Fort Newton
32 percent Albert G. Mackey
24 percent Carl H. Claudy
24 percent H. L. Haywood
20 percent Alphonse Cerza
20 percent Robert F. Gould
20 percent Allen E. Roberts
16 percent Albert Pike

Other authors recommended included W. R. Denslow, R. V. Denslow, Charles C. Hunt, Bernard Jones, Roscoe Pound, James Anderson, Henry C. Clausen, D. Darrah, Manly Hall, W. Hutchinson, M. M. Johnson, Karl C. F. Krause, W. Preston, G. Steinmetz, J. H. Van Gorden, T. S. Webb, and Louis Williams.

What individual books were recommended by the Grand Lodges as being authoritative interpreters of Freemasonry?

44 percent *Coil's Masonic Encyclopedia*, by Henry Wilson Coil

36 percent *The Builders*, by Joseph Fort Newton

32 percent *Mackey's Revised Encyclopedia of Freemasonry*, by Albert G. Mackey

24 percent *Introduction to Freemasonry*, by Carl H. Claudy

24 percent *The Newly-Made Mason*, by H. L. Haywood

20 percent *A Masonic Reader's Guide*, by Alphonse Cerza

20 percent *History of Freemasonry*, by Robert F. Gould

20 percent *The Craft and Its Symbols*, by Allen E. Roberts

16 percent *Morals and Dogma*, by Albert Pike

Notice that the Grand Lodges recognize Coil, Newton, and Mackey as the three leading Masonic authorities.[22] For example, Masonic scholar Oliver D. Street observes that all Masons "will admit that Dr. Albert G. Mackey was one of the leading scholars of the Masonic world."[23]

Albert Pike should also be listed among leading Masonic authorities. The current Sovereign Grand Commander, C. Fred Kleinknecht, relates the following about this Masonic scholar in *The House of the Temple of the Supreme Council* (a text extolling the headquarters of the Supreme Council, 33d Degree): "Albert Pike remains today an inspiration for Masons everywhere. His great book *Morals and Dogma* endures as the *most complete exposition* of Scottish Rite philosophy. He will always be remembered and revered as the *Master Builder of the Scottish Rite*" (italics added).[24] Because of the Sovereign Grand Commander's lofty estimate, when considering the meaning of the higher degrees in the Scottish Rite, we often include what Albert Pike wrote. Masons cannot claim that Pike was only teaching his "own opinions."

Because of the high esteem in which these authors are held by the Grand Lodges, they are typically the most frequently quoted in our analysis of Masonry. At the same time, we have tried not to neglect the other Masonic authors recommended by the Grand Lodges. We have tried to quote fairly from as many as possible. Masons must acknowledge that these authors and books do represent their most authoritative interpreters of Freemasonry. So if we are wrong, then the ritual itself and Masonry's highly esteemed authors are also wrong and should be discarded by those in the Lodge.

THE BLUE LODGE, THE SCOTTISH RITE, AND THE YORK RITE

The Blue Lodge is the parent, or mother, Lodge of Freemasonry. In the Blue Lodge are conferred the first three degrees: (1) the Entered Apprentice, where a man is initiated into the beginning mysteries of the fraternity of Freemasonry; (2) the degree of Fellow Craft; and (3) the Master Mason Degree. Before they may proceed to the higher degrees, all men must go through the first three degrees of the Blue Lodge. But it is possible to go through only the first one or two degrees.

After passing the three degrees of the Blue Lodge, the candidate may choose not to proceed any further. Many, and probably most, Masons do stop with the first three degrees. But the candidate may choose to proceed higher along one or both of two branches in Masonry.

One branch is known as the Scottish Rite, which advances by numerical degrees, beginning with the Fourth and ending with the 32d, the 33d Degree being either active or honorary. The other major branch is the York Rite, which goes through what are called the "Chapter," "Council," and "Commandery" degrees ending with the degree of Knights Templar.

Anyone who passes the first three degrees and becomes a Master Mason may visit other Blue Lodges. If a Mason is suspended or expelled from his Blue Lodge, that automatically severs his connection with all other Masonic bodies.

Below we present a diagram of the three Blue Lodge degrees that every Mason must take, plus the optional degrees of the York and Scottish Rites:[25]

Blue Lodge
1. Entered Apprentice
2. Fellow Craft
3. Master Mason

York Rite

Chapter (Capitular Degrees)

Mark Master

Past Master (Virtual)

Most Excellent Master

Royal Arch Mason

Council (Cryptic Degrees)

Royal Master

Select Master

Super Excellent Master

Commandery (Chivalric Degrees)

Order of the Red Cross

Order of the Knights of Malta

Order of Knights
Templar Commandery

Scottish Rite

Lodge of Perfection

4. Secret Master
5. Perfect Master
6. Intimate Secretary
7. Provost & Judge
8. Intendant of the Building
9. Elu of the Nine
10. Elu of the Twelve
11. Elu of the Fifteen
12. Master Architect
13. Royal Arch of Solomon
14. Perfect Elu

Chapter Rose Croix

15. Knight of the East or Sword
16. Prince of Jerusalem
17. Knight of the East & West
18. Knight Rose Croix

Council of Kadosh

19. Grand Pontiff
20. Master of the Symbolic Lodge
21. Noachite or Prussian Knight
22. Knight of the Royal Axe
23. Chief of the Tabernacle
24. Prince of the Tabernacle
25. Knight of the Brazen Serpent
26. Prince of Mercy
27. Knight Commander of the Temple
28. Knight of the Sun
29. Knight of St. Andrew
30. Knight Kadosh

Consistory

31. Inspector Inquisitor
32. Master of the Royal Secret
33. (Active or Honorary)

Besides the above degrees, numerous side degrees of Masonry may be sought, and many affiliated, or appendant, organizations exist. These are orders with specific memberships (youth, women, relatives, collegians) or goals (such as the Shriners, the Ancient Arabic Order of Nobles of the Mystic Shrine). These will be discussed later.

THE RELATION OF THE BLUE LODGE TO THE HIGHER DEGREES

Most Masons believe that Blue Lodge Masonry makes one as full or complete a Mason as one can (or needs to) be. But an important fact must be noted. Although the Blue Lodge is Masonry, and although it is the Masonry of most Masons, it is not all that Masonry constitutes. Some Masons would view Blue Lodge Masonry—at least as it is usually interpreted—as an initial or beginning form of Masonry. They maintain that the real substance of Masonry—its lifeblood—lies only in the higher degrees and in the initiate's search for their true meaning. Some Masons would even consider Blue Lodge Masonry as merely the cover of the book. These Masons would say that to understand Masonry truly, one must open the book and read what lies *within* the cover. But what one finds there will shock even most Masons (see chapter 19).

Sovereign Grand Commander Henry C. Clausen admits, "It must be apparent that the Blue Lodge . . . degrees cannot explain the whole of Masonry. They are the foundation. . . . An initiate may imagine he understands the ethics, symbols and enigmas, whereas a true explanation of these is reserved for the more adept."[26] Another leading Masonic scholar admits:

> If you have been disappointed in the first three Degrees, *as you have received them*, . . . remember . . . that these antique and simple Degrees now stand like the broken columns of a roofless Druidic temple, in their rude and mutilated greatness; in many parts, also, corrupted by time, and disfigured by modern additions and absurd interpretations. They are but the entrance to the great Masonic Temple. . . . Imagine not that you will become indeed a Mason by learning what is commonly called the "work," or even by becoming familiar with our traditions. Masonry has a history, a literature, a philosophy. Its allegories and traditions will teach you much; but

much is to be sought elsewhere. The streams of learning that now flow full and broad must be followed to their heads in the springs that well up in the remote past, and *you will there find the origin and meaning of Masonry.* (Italics added)[27]

For many Masons, the first three degrees of Masonry, then, are merely a stepping-stone to the higher "truths" of the Lodge. In fact, as in the ancient pagan mystery cults (which were also divided into the "lesser" and "greater" mysteries), many Masons will admit that the Blue Lodge teachings are purposely deceptive. They are intended to hide the real truths of Masonry from the initiate until such a time as he is "worthy" of receiving them.[28] It would seem, then, that Blue Lodge Masonry parallels the "lesser mysteries" while the York and Scottish rites parallel the "greater mysteries." Under his discussion of the Third Degree of the Blue Lodge in *Morals and Dogma*, Albert Pike observes that

> Masonry, like all the Religions, all the Mysteries, Hermeticism and Alchemy, *conceals* its secrets from all except the Adepts and Sages, or the Elect [the worthy], and uses false explanations and misinterpretations of its symbols to mislead . . . to conceal the Truth, which it calls Light, from them, and to draw them away from it. Truth is not for those who are unworthy.[29]

In other words, according to Pike, many Masons are uninformed about Masonry because the Craft has purposely kept the truth from them. And lest Masons claim that Pike was only asserting his own opinions, remember the words of C. Fred Kleinknecht affirming that Pike's *Morals and Dogma* "endures as the most complete exposition" of Scottish Rite Masonry.

The Influence of Masonry

Masonry exists in 164 countries of the world.[30] According to the *Encyclopaedia Britannica*, its membership of 6 million qualifies Masonry as "the largest worldwide secret society."[31] At least 15,300 Lodges operate in the U.S., and more than 33,700 Lodges exist around the world.[32]

For example, in the Philippines there are 211 Lodges and 15,037 Masons. England has more than 8,000 Lodges with a membership of more than 600,000. West Germany has 388 Lodges with 21,000 members, and Italy has 562 Lodges with 24,000 members. Even Communist Cuba has 324 Lodges and 19,728 members! In Canada, there are 183,000 members in 1,600 Lodges, and the U.S. boasts at least 4 million Masons in 15,300 lodges. More Masons live in California (188,535) than in Canada. There are 90,000 Masons in Georgia, 83,000 in Florida, 146,000 in Illinois, 88,000 in Massachusetts, 111,000 in Michigan, 220,000 in Ohio, 206,000 in Pennsylvania, 75,000 in South Carolina, 206,000 in Texas, and 96,000 in Tennessee.[33]

These large numbers is one reason Masonry has exerted such a considerable influence in American society and the church:

> One member of the Craft pointed out that there are at least 160 organizations (which he did not identify) that require their members to also be initiates into the Masonic Fraternity. In 1948, *The New Age* boasted that some ten million adults were linked directly, or were indirectly associated with the nation's three million Master Masons. The Scottish Rite publication estimated that "between one in five and one in 10 of the adult thinking population come directly within the circle of Masonic influence."[34]

Even in 1912 scholar Martin Wagner could observe in his critical treatment on Masonry that "Masonry, with its numerous offsprings, is a powerful factor in our civilization. It is influencing our civic, our social, our family, and our moral and religious life far more than is generally realized."[35] Wagner's assessment remains true.

Critic Paul A. Fisher, who has had considerable experience in military intelligence and has been active in political life, refers to Masonry's "enormous influence in the world media" and lists several founders, publishers, and editors of American papers who are Masons. In the U.S., according to the leading Masonic magazine, *The New Age*, many members of the National Press Club are Masons. Historian Mildred Headings claims Masonry has influenced almost half of French periodicals, off and on, during the late nineteenth and early twentieth centuries.[36] A standard source on religions, *Hastings' Encyclopedia of Religion and Ethics*, has correctly pointed out that "with the spread of Freemasonry over the whole world, . . . [it] has become a potent factor in promoting a feeling of universal brotherhood among mankind."[37]

Finally, Fisher observes that Masons have dominated the U.S. Supreme Court from 1941-1971. From 1941-1946 the ratio was 5 to 4; from 1949-1956 it was 8 to 1; from 1957-1967 it was 6 to 3 and from 1969-1971 it was again 5 to 4.[38] He concludes that such influence may have contributed to the high court's "determination to move the nation away from an emphasis on Judeo-Christian values in public life," helping to further secularize society and sustain "an epoch of revolutionary liberalism" with far reaching consequences.[39]

If Fisher's claims contain any substance, then addressing the religious views, content, and goals of Freemasonry is not an idle task but is relevant to each of us. In the 13th Degree of the Scottish Rite the oath reads, "I furthermore promise and swear to use every means in my power . . . to contribute with all my might to the . . . propagation of liberal ideas wheresoever I may be."[40]

According to Masonic and Congressional records, as many as fourteen U.S. Presidents have been Masons: George Washington, James Monroe, Andrew Jackson, James Polk, James Buchanan, Andrew Johnson, James Garfield, William McKinley, Teddy Roosevelt, William Howard Taft, Warren Harding, Franklin Delano Roosevelt, Harry Truman, and Gerald Ford. An additional fourteen Masons have been Vice Presidents.[41]

The influence of Masonry in contemporary government was revealed by the Senate Congressional record of September 9, 1987.[42] In those proceedings, some members of the Senate Judiciary Committee had questioned the propriety of appointing Judge David Sentelle as a U.S. Circuit Judge for the District of Columbia. The objection was raised on the grounds that he was a Mason.

In response to this, a number of Senators who were Masons vigorously protested. They felt it was unthinkable to question an appointee merely because he was a member of the

Lodge. They considered it "extraordinary," "totally unwarranted," "most absurd," and "galling and preposterous." These Senators were "astounded" and "aghast."

In the debate, Masonic Senators Strom Thurmond and Alan Simpson, and Senate Majority Leader Robert Byrd, all of whom admitted pride of membership, revealed that Masons constituted

- Forty-one members of the Federal Judiciary

- Half the membership of the Senate Judiciary Committee

- Eighteen Senators, including Lloyd Bentsen, Sam Nunn, Bob Dole, Jesse Helms, John Glenn, and Mark Hatfield

- Seventy-six members of the House of Representatives, including former Speaker of the House Jim Wright, Claude Pepper, William Ford, Dan Glickman, and Trent Lott

- At least two Senators were 33d Degree Masons: Bob Dole and Senate Majority Leader Robert Byrd

Objections from other Congressional members were raised against questioning Masonry because "Masonry in this country is the bedrock" and because being a Mason "simply means people who believe in God and love their fellow man." It is clear that Masonic influence extends to the highest levels of American government.

Many famous and influential persons from all walks of life have been Masons: Protestant minister Norman Vincent Peale,[43] former Senator Howard H. Baker,[44] former Congressman Jack Kemp,[45] Irving Berlin, actor Ernest Borgnine, William Jennings Bryan, famous scientist Luther Burbank, comedian Bob Burns, Christopher "Kit" Carson, Sir Winston Churchill, Samuel Clemens (Mark Twain), Tyrus (Ty) Cobb, William "Buffalo Bill" Cody, motion picture producer Cecil B. DeMille, Thomas E. Dewey, Major General James R. Doolittle, and Sir Arthur Conan Doyle (author of the Sherlock Holmes books).

Mention could also be made of Edward VIII (Duke of Windsor), Douglas Fairbanks, Sr., comedian W. C. Fields, Henry Ford, Benjamin Franklin, Arthur Godfrey, Johann Wolfgang von Goethe, Barry M. Goldwater, astronaut Virgil E. Grissom, Oliver

Hardy (of "Laurel and Hardy"), composer Franz Joseph Haydn, J. Edgar Hoover, magician Harry Houdini, John Paul Jones, King Kamehameha V (king of Hawaii), Rudyard Kipling, and Colonel Charles A. Lindberg.

Also Masons were such notables as General Douglas Mac-Arthur, Chief Justice of the Supreme Court John Marshall, Presbyterian clergyman and chaplain of the U.S. Senate Peter Marshall, motion picture producer Lewis B. Mayer, Charles H. Mayo (founder of the Mayo Clinic), Wolfgang Amadeus Mozart, Admiral Robert E. Peary, James C. Penney (founder of J. C. Penney Company), General John J. Pershing, Paul Revere, all seven of the Ringling Brothers, cowboy hero Roy Rogers, Will Rogers, Sir Walter Scott, comedian Richard "Red" Skelton, French writer and philosopher Francois Voltaire, General Jonathan M. Wainwright, Lou Wallace (author of *Ben Hur*), Chief Justice of the Supreme Court Earl Warren, and Booker T. Washington.[46] Given such facts, who can doubt the influence and power of modern Masonry?

RELATED MASONIC ORGANIZATIONS

The Lodge also exerts considerable influence through affiliated or appendant organizations, which usually espouse similar beliefs. Masonry is generally considered to be the "mother" organization of these groups, whose rituals, secrets, or goals may have similar characteristics to those of Freemasonry.[47] In 1912 Martin Wagner observed, "The whole secret society system with its countless lodges and their organizations, is an outgrowth of Masonry. All the secret societies, even the so-called minor orders, have assimilated and incorporated more or less of the fundamental principles of Masonry. A comparison of their various rituals with the rituals of Masonry demonstrates this fact."[48]

Concerning the modern situation, J. W. Acker, who was a member of the Lutheran Church—Missouri Synod's Commission on Fraternal Organizations, discloses that Masons themselves have characteristically prepared the rituals of the lesser fraternities:

Masonry's religion has become the pattern for the religious philosophy of all other lodges. In fact, prominent Masons have almost without exception prepared the rituals of the lesser fraternities. So intimate are the ties between the larger orders that lurking in the background there seems to be a virtual interlocking directorate in this secret empire. Words, entire phrases, and allegorical passages of the Masonic ritual are reproduced, perhaps subconsciously, in the rituals of practically all other lodges. It is for that reason that the identical false doctrines of Masonry are found ingeniously interwoven into the texture of such rituals, although not in so coarse or offensive a manner, as a rule. In the rituals of some lodges, particularly recently revised rituals, the parent influence of Freemasonry has become quite remote, and offensive expressions are less frequently found.[49]

Some of these organizations are officially Masonic and others are not, but all of them have, characteristically, been influenced by Masonry to some degree.

THE ORDER OF THE EASTERN STAR

The Order of the Eastern Star is specifically intended for the wives, daughters, and female relatives of Master Masons.[50] Its rituals were prepared by Dr. Rob Morris, a leading Mason. Dr. Morris is considered the "Master Builder" of the Order of the Eastern Star. Thus, the *Ritual of the Order of the Eastern Star* published by the authority of the General Grand Chapter Order of the Eastern Star (1970) gives the history of Dr. Morris.

Dr. Morris became a Master Mason in Oxford, Mississippi March 5, 1849. . . . He soon became interested in an idea that the female relatives of Master Masons should share, in a measure, the benefits from knowledge of this great fraternal Order. . . . He worked with zeal writing a Ritual of the Order of the Eastern Star. . . . In 1855 he organized a Supreme Constellation with himself as the Most Enlightened Grand Luminary, with headquarters in New York City. . . . He was an author of great ability and wrote numerous and valuable works on Masonry and its kindred subjects. . . . In 1858-59 Dr. Morris served as Most Worshipful Grand Master of Masons in Kentucky. In 1860 he drafted the Constitution of the Grand Lodge. . . . Having spent most of the stretch, thought and wisdom of his early manhood in a close study of the Rituals, codes, principles and tenets of Masonry, he was conceded to be one of the most versatile and learned Masons of his day. In 1880 the General Grand Chapter conferred on Dr. Morris the title of "Master Builder of the Order of the Eastern Star."[51]

When one reads through the ritual of the Order of the Eastern Star, the claim is made that "the Order is no part of that Ancient Institution" (i.e., Masonry). Yet there can be no doubt that the Order of the Eastern Star supports both the causes and doctrines of Masonry. This is evident throughout the ritual itself where the Order is stated to uphold Masonry.[52]

In addition, a similar emphasis is laid upon various Masonic beliefs: 1) faith in (the Masonic) god; 2) secrecy and solemn oaths; 3) personal character building and the immortality of the soul which presuppose salvation by works. However these are not as forcefully or clearly stated as in the rituals of Masonry itself. It is as if the Order of the Eastern Star exists to *introduce* the daughters, wives and other relatives of Master Masons to a basic Masonic world view with the understanding that the Master Mason himself as head of the household will fill in any remaining gaps. In other words, Masonic appendant organizations function as a preliminary introduction into Masonry, which is designed to support the Mason himself. Such appendant organizations ensure that the personal environment of the Mason (mothers, wives, children, etc.) becomes a support and encouragement for his own involvement in Masonry. [53]

The following points illustrate similarities of the Order of the Eastern Star to the Masonic Lodge. They can be compared to the corresponding Masonic teachings in parts 2 and 3.

The Masonic god:

> Life is a labyrinth through which we would wander blindly were it not for an All Seeing Eye that watches over us and an All Powerful Hand that guides us on our way. This Order is founded on a belief in the existence of a Supreme Being that rules the universe for good, and no one can become a member Order who does not hold this belief. . . . Do you believe in the existence of a Supreme Being?[54]

Masonic secrecy and solemn oaths:

> The Obligation you are about to take is a solemn pledge which you must give to this Chapter before you can participate in the privilege of our Order. By it you bind yourself to the most solemn secrecy respecting the work of the Order and to that performance [of its goals]. . . . When the Conductress reaches the Altar she causes the candidate to kneel and places the Bible in her hands.[55]

The "landmarks" of the Order of the Eastern Star state:

> Five. Its obligations are based upon the honor of those who obtain its secrets, and are framed upon the principle that whatever benefits are due from Masons to the wives, daughters, mothers, widows, and sisters of Masons, reciprocal duties are due from them to Masons.
> Six. The Obligation of our Order voluntarily assumed, is perpetual, from the force of which there is no release.[56]

The building of personal character:

> When you have entered our portals, listen closely to all that you hear for your initiation is a symbol of the road of life. The lessons which you receive are given to assist you in building your own individual character.

> The color appropriate to this degree is white, a symbol of Light, Purity and Joy which teaches us that a pure and upright life is above the tongue of reproach.[57]

The immortality of the soul:

> [From the installation ceremony:] Thus may we confidently hope that, in the good providence of God, each of us will be brought, through a useful, and happy life, to a blissful close and triumphant entrance upon the joys of celestial life.

> Beyond the grave, the loved ones gone before are waiting to welcome us to our eternal home.

> [A prayer of the order:] Enlarge our powers to benefit mankind and to honor thee, our God. And when, one by one, each link [person] shall fall away in death, may the parting be

temporary and the meeting eternal. In the world where death comes not, may we realize the full happiness of loving and serving thee forever. Amen.[58]

A claim to obey the Bible:

"The open Bible is appropriate to Jephtha's Daughter as a symbol of Obedience to the Word of God."[59]

Funeral ceremonies that presuppose works salvation and universalism:

> Sisters and Brothers, we have gathered here to pay love's tribute to the memory of Sister _____ ... who has now passed into the fullness of immortal life and now abides in the mercy and care of our Heavenly Father.... We thank Thee for the assurance that Thou has given us in the eternal life which lies beyond death.

> Our God is just. We know that, as our Sister was faithful to her convictions of right and duty; as she was obedient to the demands of honor and justice; as she was loyal to kindred and friends; as she was guided by a trustful faith in the hour of trial; as she lived in the spirit of charity and love of truth, so shall be her reward.[60]

The above statements reflect the doctrine of works salvation taught in the Masonic Lodge. Thus, not once in the entire rituals of initiation, installation of officers, or funeral ceremonies is it ever stated that personal faith in the biblical Jesus Christ is necessary to salvation. Although several biblical events, characters, and illustrations are cited, they are cited in such a manner as to support the beliefs of Masonry, not Christianity. For example,

> Green is an emblem of nature's life and beauty. The evergreen is a symbol of Immortal Life and teaches us that in the economy of God there is no death; forms change, but the spirit survives. [The biblical character] Martha, beside the grave of her beloved brother [Lazarus], avowed her trustful faith and hope of immortal life. The Greenery of our Star

shines here to assure us of our Sister's entrance into a glorious immortality.[61]

OTHER RELATED ORGANIZATIONS

The so-called animal lodges reflect Masonic influence but are not, strictly speaking, Masonic organizations. Among these are the Fraternal Order of Eagles (FOE), the Benevolent and Protective Order of Elks (BPOE), and the Loyal Order of Moose (LOOM). Other affiliated or appendant organizations include the Independent Order of Odd Fellows, the Woodsmen of the World, the Knights of Pythias, Tall Cedars in Lebanon, the Mystic Order of Veiled Prophets of the Enchanted Realm (Grotto), Acacia Fraternity, and the Knights of the Red Cross of Constantine.[62]

Other masonically affiliated female organizations also exist, such as Daughters of the Nile, the Order of Amaranth, the White Shrine of Jerusalem, and the Daughters of Mokanna. Numerous affiliated youth organizations add to the list, such as the Order of DeMolay, Order of Job's Daughters, Order of the Builders, and Order of the Rainbow. Finally, the Lodge has exerted a considerable influence in the history of Mormonism[63] and in liberal religion, such as Unitarian Universalism.[64]

Occasionally, the Kiwanis, Rotary, Lions Club, American Legion, and Veterans of Foreign Wars are incorrectly associated with Masonry or its affiliated organizations. But unlike Masonry, these are not religious groups having religious goals[65] and should not be confused with Masonry.

WHY MASONRY IS A SECRET SOCIETY

Masonry stresses the importance of secrecy for at least two principal reasons. The first is that the element of secrecy itself is something that attracts men and makes them feel important. They have access to what they believe are vital secrets and truths that other men do not share. The second reason is because it offers the Craft a stabilizing influence. Men who swear extremely solemn oaths of secrecy to the Lodge not only conclude that the information received is important but that it must be protected at all costs (see chapter 14). For example, the *Guide to the Royal Arch Chapter* observes, "Mystery has charms as well as power. 'The entire fabric of the universe is founded on secrecy; and the great Life-force which vivifies, moves, and beautifies the whole, is the profoundest of all mysteries. . . . The first obligation of a Mason—his supreme duty—his chief virtue—is that of silence and secrecy.'"[66]

Masonic historian Alphonse Cerza further believes:

> The secrecy of our ceremonies of initiation are intended to meet a natural human characteristic. What is open is often overlooked, but what is hidden attracts attention. It is hoped that the new member, because of the element of secrecy and interest in discovering what it is all about, will come to the meeting with an alert mind giving the matter greater attention than he otherwise would do if he knew what was about to happen.[67]

Thus, as Albert Pike confesses, "Secrecy is indispensable in a Mason of whatever degree."[68]

But there are other reasons for Masonry's secrecy, both religious and, apparently, sometimes political. By maintaining secrecy, Masonry can hide its religious nature from the outside world and secure converts who would not otherwise join. In addition, some believe secret political goals of the Lodge exist. Paul A. Fisher, formerly active in both military intelligence and political life, claims that "Freemasonry in America and elsewhere is far more than a fraternal organization. It never hides its charitable endeavors. But its secret work is something else entirely."[69] Fisher documents that, at least on occasion, its "secret work" may have involved the attempt to undermine a particular social or political order to further its own liberal agenda.[70]

THE GOALS OF MASONRY:
WHY MASONRY IS MORE THAN A FRATERNAL FELLOWSHIP

For some Masons, Masonry is merely a fraternal fellowship. But for many, Masonry is a vital worldwide organization that they hope will help bring peace and universal brotherhood to all mankind. To begin with, Masonry sees itself as a "World Fraternity":

There is no such thing as "Lodge Masonry." The Masonic Fraternity is a single, indivisible fellowship which is neither divided nor affected by local or by national boundaries. . . . It has one set of Landmarks, one set of Degrees, one teaching for the whole world. . . . The one World Fraternity is everywhere one and the same thing.[1]

The goals of Masonry are to unite the world under the umbrella of Masonic doctrine that teaches the fatherhood of God, the brotherhood of man, and the immortality of the soul. Masons foresee the day when all religious division and sectarianism (i.e., what Masonry views as specific or exclusivistic, and therefore "divisive," religious beliefs) will be wiped away, and a new era of universal peace, brotherhood, and religious faith will emerge.

But this new worldwide religious faith will be equivalent to the fundamental teachings of Masonry. In this sense, Masonry is far more than merely a fraternal brotherhood. It seeks to remold the world after its own image. In other words, it wants to transform the world.

Masonic author H. L. Haywood sets forth the objectives of Masonry. He asserts that Masonry will bring about a new world order: "It [Masonry] is a world law, destined to change the earth into conformity with itself, and as a world power it is something superb, awe inspiring, godlike."[2] Another Masonic writer declares that "the doctrines of Masonry will ultimately rule the intellectual world."[3]

Masonic scholar Albert Pike affirms that the "hope" of the Mason is "in the ultimate annihilation of evil in the universe; [and] in the final triumph of Masonry, that shall make of all men one family and household."[4] *Mackey's Revised Encyclopedia of Freemasonry* illustrates this goal when it discloses that "the mission of Masonry is . . . to banish from the world every source of enmity and hostility," "to destroy the pride of conquest and the pomp of war," and "to extend to [all] nations" the principles of Masonry.[5]

The most widely read and influential book in Masonry is Joseph Fort Newton's *The Builders.* In one of his chapters, Newton explains what Masonry "is trying to do in the world":

- "To bring about a universal league of mankind"

- "To form mankind into a great redemptive brotherhood"

Newton declares that as Masonry expands, all religious dogmas will "cease to be." All individual creeds and doctrines will be done away with, and what remains will be what is termed "the one eternal religion—the Fatherhood of God, the brotherhood of man, the moral law, the golden rule, and the hope of a life everlasting!" Because of this, Newton defines Masonry as "a great order of men, selected, initiated, sworn, and trained to make sweet reason and the will of God [i.e., Masonry] prevail!" Newton claims that Masonry will not become "only one more factor in a world of factional feud" but that "it seeks to remove all hostility which may arise from social, national or religious differences."[76]

Why does Masonry seek to change the world? Because Masonry teaches that all non-Masons are living in spiritual darkness. The ritual of Masonry for the First Degree of Entered Apprentice teaches the candidate that he "has long been in darkness, and now seeks to be brought to light."[77] The Lodge teaches that only true Masons are enlightened and live in the Truth. Masonry claims that "each member is a living stone in this Holy House"—the Masonic temple.[78] It refers to itself as a "Holy Empire" whose mission is "to dispel darkness."[79] Thus, it is the mission and "duty of its initiates to diffuse among men its ideals, without which error, superstition, and spiritual subjugation *must be eternal*" (italics added).[80]

The result of this premise is that, if true world brotherhood is ever to be achieved, it demands for its success a worldwide religion of Masonry. Thus, informed Masons partake in "the glorious privilege which belongs to Masonry as the precious jewel of its prerogative, to be the *chiefest of human agencies used by God* to bring forward the rosy dawn of this magnificent future" (italics added).[81]

But if Masonry is to one day rule the world, then all non-Masonic beliefs must either be abandoned or absorbed into Masonry. "Sectarian" religions with exclusive teachings, such as the Christian faith (John 14:6; Acts 4:12), simply cannot be permitted if Masonry is to succeed. Masonry then, claims that the Lodge is the light of the world and that only "its ideals" can save the world from its errors and superstition.

All of this is why Masonry is far more than simply a worldwide fraternal brotherhood. Masonry desires to change the world. As we have seen, one means by which it hopes to change the world is to influence and remold the church. In the following chapters, we will take a closer look at the history, world view, religion, and morality of Masonry. In Part 2 we will provide detailed documentation revealing how the religious world view of Masonry distorts, dismantles, and replaces the Christian faith with Masonic doctrine.

Freemasonry may rightfully claim to be called a religious institution.
Albert Mackey

2

Masonic Religion

The origins of Masonry (at least its historical antecedents) are shrouded in antiquity. As Henry Wilson Coil observes in *Freemasonry Through Six Centuries*, "The origin of Freemasonry, its early development and character, are unknown, and are likely to remain so."[1] Most scholars believe it is difficult to trace the origins of Masonry (as it is known today) to before the early 1700s. We do know that in 1717, four Lodges combined to form the first Grand Lodge in London, England. Today, all Masonic Grand Lodges in the world trace their origin to this first Grand Lodge. The first U.S. Lodge began in 1729, and the first Canadian Lodge started in 1745.[2]

However, an older type of Masonry, the operative or working Masons (essentially itinerant craftsmen), can be traced back to the Middle Ages. These persons formed primitive trade unions (lodges) for protection and professional credibility. These lodges became the foundation for modern Masonry, which is termed "speculative Masonry," to contrast it from their older "operative Masonry." But the ritual, symbolism, and many teachings of Masonry can be traced even further back in history to ancient paganism—in particular, the ancient mystery religions of Egypt, Rome, Greece, and other cultures (see chapter 19).

THE DEVELOPMENT OF SPECULATIVE MASONRY

In the transitional phase from operative to speculative (or modern) Masonry, membership was not restricted to stone masons. The doors swung open to anyone seeking membership. Interest in the Lodge mushroomed, and a wide diversity of membership resulted. Among the members of the Lodges were clergymen, politicians, and scientists, as well as astrologers and other occultists. These individuals then became involved in formulating the ritual, doctrine, degrees of advancement, and other important aspects of Masonry: "In fact, men in all ranks of life became actively engaged in manufacturing degrees and arranging rites to advance their particular interests, theories, dogmas, or ambitious pretensions."[3] This is why more than 1,100 degrees were eventually produced.[4]

In particular, modern Masonry owes a great deal to several medieval occult practices and religions. Many of its teachings were derived from these as Haywood admits in *The Great Teachings of Masonry*:

> All our historians, at least nearly all of them, agree that Freemasonry owes very much to certain occult societies or groups that flourished—often in secret—during the late Middle Ages, and even into the after-Reformation times. Chief among these were the Rosicrucians and the Knights Templar.[5]

But another form of influential medieval occultism known as kabbalism also exerted great influence upon Masonry, as virtually all Masonic historians also admit.[6]

Scholar Dr. Shildes Johnson lists such groups as the Rosicrucians, and two other occult orders, the Golden Dawn and the Illuminati, as having influenced Masonry. He further observes, "Today, the chief religious influence of Masonry may be observed in the Unitarian-Universalist Church, in the Church of Jesus Christ of Latter-Day Saints (Mormons), and in witchcraft."[7] Three basic influences are responsible for the modern teachings of the Masonic Lodge:

Ancient paganism. The ancient pagan mystery religions practiced in Egypt, Asia Minor, and later in Greece appear to have formed the religious basis of much Masonic teaching, symbol, and ritual, although no direct link can be established.

Medieval Stonemasonry. Much of the symbols of modern Masonry were derived from the tools of the trade of the "operative" or "working" Masonry of the Middle Ages (1200-1700), the itinerant craftsmen known as stone masons. During that period, Masonry was also influenced by various occult sects of the age.

Modern Masonry. A gradual change took place in operative Masonry through the infusion of medieval occultism and other elements, and this transformation resulted in the development of modern Masonry. Thus, modern Masonry combines elements of both of its earlier counterparts. For example, the working tools of the stone masons have been changed into symbols expressing moral and spiritual lessons (such as the square and compass), and the teachings and rites of the ancient mystery religions (found variously in medieval occultism) can also be found in Masonry, although they have sometimes undergone considerable modification.

THE DEFINITION OF RELIGION

Masonic authority Silas H. Shepherd writes: "There is nothing better understood among Masons than that [Masonry] is not a religion. . . ."[8] But even though respected Masons such as Charles Lacquement, the Grand Chaplain of Masonry in Pennsylvania, bluntly say, "Freemasonry is not a religion, it is a philosophy,"[9] this can easily be proved false.

Writing in *The Encyclopedia of Philosophy*, William Alston, professor of philosophy at the University of Michigan, cites the following characteristics of religion:

- A belief in supernatural beings (God or gods)
- A distinction between sacred and profane objects
- Ritual acts that are focused upon such sacred objects
- A moral code that has supernatural sanction
- Religious feelings that are aroused by sacred objects or ritual, and connected in idea with God or gods
- Prayer

- A particular world view that encompasses the individual's place within the world

- The more or less total organization of one's life based on such a world view

- A social group that is bound together by the above traits[10]

Space does not allow a detailed discussion of these characteristics, but Masonry exhibits all nine of them. This is why the most respected Masonic authorities who have written on this issue have admitted that Masonry is a religion, or at least religious.

A simpler standard definition of religion from *Webster's New World Dictionary* reads, "(1) (a) belief in a divine or super human power . . . to be obeyed and worshipped as the Creator and ruler of the universe; (2) [an] expression of . . . [this] belief in conduct and ritual."[11]

THE RELIGIOUS NATURE OF MASONRY

The Lodge fits Webster's definition of religion in that it requires belief in a supreme being, obedience to this supreme being, and worship of him as the creator and ruler of the universe.

MASONRY REQUIRES THAT ALL ITS MEMBERS BELIEVE IN A SUPREME BEING

Masonry does require that every member of the Lodge believe in God. According to Masonry's own respected authors, belief in God is so fundamental to Masonry that without it there simply is no Masonry.[12] In the very first degree of Masonry, the Entered Apprentice Degree, the ritual requires each candidate to swear that he believes in God:

> THE CANDIDATE'S ASSENT IS REQUIRED TO THE FOLLOW-ING DECLARATIONS:
>
> Do you seriously declare upon your honor, that you believe in a Supreme Being to whom all men are accountable?
>
> Answer: I do.[13]

Not only is each Mason required to swear that he believes in God, but the ritual requires each candidate be dedicated in prayer to the "Almighty Father of the Universe." He is also dedicated through "the secrets of our [Masonic] art" to be better "enabled to display the beauties of godliness to the honor of God." Here is the prayer that is said in every lodge for candidates being initiated into the Entered Apprentice Degree:

> Vouchsafe Thine aid, Almighty Father of the Universe, to this our present convention; and grant that this candidate for Freemasonry may dedicate and devote his life to Thy service, and become a true and faithful brother among us. Endue him with a competency of Thy divine wisdom, that by the secrets of our art [Masonry] he may better be enabled to display the beauties of godliness to the honor of Thy holy name. Amen.
>
> Response: So mote [may] it be.[14]

Thus, Masonry clearly fulfills the first requirement of Webster's definition of religion, namely, that the candidate and each person in the Lodge must believe in a Supreme Being.

MASONRY REQUIRES EACH OF ITS MEMBERS TO OBEY GOD

The entire ritualistic system of Masonry from the First Degree to the 33d Degree instructs Masons that they must obey God (i.e., by performing their Masonic duties). The First Degree states,

> The 24-inch gauge is an instrument . . . to measure and lay out their work: but we, as free and accepted Masons, are taught to make use of it for the more noble and glorious purposes of dividing our time . . . it being divided into 24 equal parts is emblematic of the 24 hours of the day, which we are taught to divide into three parts, whereby *we find a portion for the service of God.* (Italics added)[15]

In the Second Degree a prayer is said over the candidate asking God to help the initiate serve God "all the days of his life." In addition, it is said, "By speculative Masonry, we learn to subdue the passions, . . . [to] keep a tongue of good report. . . . [Masonry] is so far interwoven with religion as to lay us under obligations to pay that rational homage to the Deity, which at once constitutes our duty and our happiness."[16]

In the Master Mason, or Third Degree, we are told in the ritual,

> In youth, [as] Entered Apprentices, we ought industriously to occupy our minds in the attainment of useful knowledge; in manhood, as Fellow Crafts, we should apply our knowledge to the discharge of our respective duties to God, our neighbors, and ourselves; so that in age, as Master Masons, we may enjoy the happy reflections consequent on a well spent life, and die in the hope of a glorious immortality.[17]

In the Mark Master Degree of the York Rite, the ritual outlines the prayer at the closing of a Mark Master's Lodge as follows: "Supreme Grand Architect of the Universe, who sittest on the throne of mercy, deign to view our labors in the cause of virtue and humanity with the eye of compassion; purify our hearts, and cause us to know and serve thee aright."[18]

Whether it be the First, Second, Third, or any of the other Masonic degrees, each candidate is instructed that he is to obey God. The Masonic Monitor offers this closing prayer for the Entered Apprentice degree: "Supreme Architect of the Universe, . . . Make us sensible of *our obligations to serve Thee* and may all our actions tend to Thy glory and our advancement in knowledge and virtue" (italics added).[19]

The evidence shows that Masons who practice and follow their ritual ceremonies are fulfilling Webster's second requirement of religion, namely, obedience to God. Many Masons assume that it is the God of the Bible to whom they are praying and swearing oaths. But this is not so (see chapter 9).

MASONRY REQUIRES ITS MEMBERS TO WORSHIP GOD AS CREATOR AND RULER OF THE UNIVERSE

Webster's dictionary defines *worship* as "a prayer . . . or other rite showing reverence or devotion for a deity."[20] Masonry is full of worship to God as the creator and sustainer of the universe. Masonic authority Allen E. Roberts affirms that

Masons walk in [God's] presence continually.... [In Masonic ritual the candles] formed a triangle about the altar at which you knelt in reverence. They symbolized the presence of Deity. ... The Masonic altar can be said to be one of sacrifice.... You have taken the obligations [to God] that have sacrificed your self interest forevermore.[21]

The standard Masonic *Monitor* issues this command to every Mason: "Let no man enter any great or important undertaking without first evoking the aid of Deity.... The trust of a Mason is in God."[22]

Respected Masonic author Carl H. Claudy frankly confesses that "Freemasonry worships God": "Freemasonry's lodges are erected to God.... Symbolically, to 'erect to God' means to construct something in honor, in worship, in reverence to and for him. Hardly is the initiate within the West Gate before he is impressed that Freemasonry worships God."[23]

Do all of the worshipful rites in Masonry show reverence and devotion to a deity? There is no doubt about this. In fact, every Mason, by his good works, is worshiping the Masonic deity and is said to be actually erecting a divine temple that this deity himself will inhabit. All Masonic *Monitors* give the following instruction to initiates of the First Degree:

> My brother... the ceremony has the following significance: As the operative Mason [the medieval stone Masons] has a corner stone usually placed in the northeast corner, upon which to erect his temporal building, so should the speculative [modern] Mason have a corner stone upon which to erect his spiritual temple. This corner stone is his initiatory instruction. You have this night commenced the great task, which in your future Masonic life should never be discontinued, *that of erecting in your heart a temple for the indwelling of God.* (Italics added)[24]

The 13th, or Royal Arch, Degree of the Scottish Rite offers this prayer for the opening ceremonies:

> Great Architect of the Universe, adorable God in all, be so kind and exact our desires in this moment when we beg thy divine goodness. In thyself is the true wisdom to which we

aspire, and by the strength of thy favor we may hope for thy wisdom which shall make the beauty we dare to consecrate to them [initiates]: That is to say, [that] its beauty may purify our hearts in which we desire continually that you may reside. Amen.[25]

In the 17th Degree of the Scottish Rite, the ritual tells the candidate "that Masonry is of divine origin" and that supposed Masonic forerunners "took an oath to spend the last drop of their blood to establish the true religion of the most high God."[26] Joseph Fort Newton explains that "everything in Masonry has reference to God, implies God, speaks of God, points and leads to God. Not a degree, not a symbol, not an obligation, not a lecture, not a charge but finds its meaning and derives its beauty from God the Great Architect, in whose temple all Masons are workmen."[27]

From all of this evidence it should be clear to all that Freemasonry fits Webster's definition of religion in every point. Even Henry Wilson Coil's *A Comprehensive View of Freemasonry* agrees that "religion is espoused by the Masonic ritual and required of the candidate."[28] Coil's discussion of religion, encompassing some fifteen thousand words, argues that "Freemasonry is undoubtedly religion."[29] The other premier Masonic authority, Albert Mackey, says that

> *Freemasonry may rightfully claim to be called a religious institution.* . . . The tendency of all true Freemasonry is toward religion. . . . Look at its ancient landmarks [doctrines], its sublime ceremonies, its profound symbols and allegories—*all inculcating religious doctrine, commanding religious observance, and teaching religious truth,* and who can deny that it is eminently a religious Institution? . . . We open and close our Lodges with prayer; we invoke the blessing of the Most High upon all our labors; we demand of our neophytes a profession of trusting belief in the existence and the superintending care of God. . . . It is impossible that a Freemason can be "true and trusty" to his Order unless he is a respecter of religion and an observer of religious principle. (Italics added)[30]

Masonic scholar Albert Pike declares that "every Masonic Lodge is a temple of religion; and its teachings are instruction in religion." He further explains that the Mason's "reward is the knowledge of the True God" and that "Masonry is a *worship*. . . . It is the universal, eternal, immutable religion, such as God planted it in the heart of universal humanity."[31] In his *Introduction to Freemasonry* Carl H. Claudy teaches that "God is the very warp and woof of Freemasonry. . . . Take God out of Freemasonry and there is, literally, nothing left."[32] Other sources could be listed that describe Freemasonry as a religion. Numerous Christian writers, secular researchers, dozens of independent investigations by church committees, and many other Masonic authors all conclude that Masonry is a religion.[33]

If Freemasonry is a religion (as even Masonic scholars admit), why then do almost all Masons claim that Masonry is *not* a religion? The reason is this: the Lodge could not gain as many converts to Masonry if it were known to be another religion. It would seem that deception is necessary in order to keep old members and gain new ones.

THE CLAIMS OF MASONRY TOWARD OTHER RELIGIONS

Masonry claims that it in no way interferes with any person's religious faith. Masonic authority George Oliver asserted that Masonry "exists to assist or to support the church."[34] Charles H. Lacquement, D.D., the Grand Chaplain of Pennsylvania, forcefully teaches that Masonry enforces, supplements, and supports the Christian church.[35] Leading Masonic scholar Albert Pike claims, "We utter no word that can be deemed irreverent by anyone of any faith."[36] As the initiate progresses up the Masonic ladder, over and over again he is promised and reassured before God and men that nothing in Masonry will conflict with his religious beliefs.

This is the pledge of the Second Degree: "I assure you there is nothing therein [the Fellow Craft Degree] that is incompatible with your civil or religious duties, or with those higher and nobler duties which you owe to God, your country, your neighbor, your family, or yourself. With this assurance, do you still desire to proceed?"[37] This pledge is repeated in the Third Degree: "The third degree is the cement of the whole [Blue Lodge]. . . . Yet I will give it to you with the assurance that in all its solemn words there is not one incompatible with your civil or religious duties, or with those higher and nobler duties which you owe to God, your country, your neighbor, your family, or yourself. *With this assurance*, do you still desire to proceed?"[38] *Mackey's Revised Encyclopedia of Freemasonry* states that "there is *nothing* in [Masonry] repugnant to the faith of a Christian" (italics added).[39]

In the Sixth Degree of the York Rite (Most Excellent Master), the initiate is told, "I assure you, as before, [this oath] is neither to affect your religion or politics."[40]

THE INFLUENCE OF MASONRY IN THE CHURCH

As a result of such forthright claims, Masonry has infiltrated the church in ways that otherwise would not have been possible. In fact, it is sufficiently influential within the church that most major conservative Christian denominational bodies in Europe and America have issued official declarations condemning Masonry as a non-Christian and/or as an anti-Christian religion.

The Baptist Union of Scotland published an official report, endorsed by the Baptist Unions of Great Britain and Ireland, that stated a "clear conclusion": "that there is an inherent incompatibility between Freemasonry and the Christian faith" and that "there is great danger that the Christian Mason may find himself compromising his allegiance to Jesus."[41] Appendix 3 of this report included similar statements from the Church of Scotland Panel on Doctrine (1965) and the Free Church of Scotland.

A report by the British Methodist Church presented similar conclusions:

> On the most generous reading of the evidence, there remain serious questions for Christians about Freemasonry. . . . It is clear that Freemasonry may compete strongly with Christianity. There is a great danger the Christian who becomes a Freemason will find himself compromising his Christian beliefs or his allegiance to Christ. . . . Methodists should not become Freemasons![42]

An official report issued by the Church of England, even though Freemasons sat on the committee, nevertheless concluded that there were "a number of very fundamental reasons to question the compatibility of Freemasonry with Christianity."[43] In his book *Darkness Visible*, Walton Hannah has observed that virtually every Christian church that had studied Masonry came to the conclusion that Masonry and Christianity were incompatible. Whether it is the Greek Orthodox Church, Lutheranism, Baptists, Presbyterianism, or any other church body, all have affirmed that Masonry is not Christian.[44]

An official report issued at the Ninth General Assembly of the Orthodox Presbyterian Church meeting at Rochester, New York, June 2-5, 1942, concluded that "Masonry is a religious institution and as such is definitely anti-Christian. . . . Membership in the Masonic fraternity is inconsistent with Christianity." The report of the Ad-Interim Committee to the 15th General Assembly of the Presbyterian Church in America, meeting in Grand Rapids, Michigan, in June 1987 stated that "participation in Masonry seriously compromises the Christian faith and testimony."[45] Finally, the Commission on Organizations of the Lutheran Church–Missouri Synod concluded that "the Lodge is a religion—a Christless religion—and thus . . . totally incompatible with Christianity and to be avoided by every Christian."[46]

These represent only a narrow sampling of official declarations issued by Christian churches censuring the Masonic religion. Most of these reports acknowledge that the principal reason many Christians have joined Freemasonry is out of simple ignorance—they do not know the contradictions between Masonry and Christianity.[47] This indicates that the church must do a better job in educating her members concerning both Christian doctrine and the teachings of the Craft. For example, former Mason Jack Harris observes that "many ministers, elders, deacons, trustees and Sunday school teachers" are Masons.[48] Another former Mason and pastor confesses that "many preachers whom I had known and loved and respected were Masons."[49]

In the South, in particular, but throughout the entire nation, literally thousands of Masons are active within the local church. They are in positions of leadership. One Masonic text notes that as teachers of Bible classes and Sunday school, these Masons "are bringing to the interpretation of the Bible many of

Masonry's great revelations" on religion (such as salvation by personal merit, the fatherhood of God, and the brotherhood of man)—but without doctrine or theology.[50] In other words, the Bible is being reinterpreted by Masons to conform to Masonic doctrine. But interpreting the Bible "without attention to doctrine and theology" is like interpreting a book without attention to the characters and plot. As we shall see, a logically applied Masonic approach to the Scriptures undermines virtually every distinctive Christian teaching. In the end, one is left with, at best, liberal religion.

Masonic influence can be felt in many places throughout the Christian world. Masonic author Cerza divulges that many officers of the Salvation Army are Masons.[51] Investigator Stephen Knight documents why it is no longer accurate "to assume that Roman Catholic professional men are not Freemasons." And he supplies evidence that "the Vatican itself is infiltrated [in some degree] by Freemasons."[52]

In Europe, the Presbyterian Church of Wales is "strongly influenced" by Masonry. Again, Knight observes that "thousands of practicing Christians in Britain today worship the Freemasonic God believing it to be precisely the same as the Christian God." He expands further on this: "Despite overwhelming evidence of Masonry's incompatibility with Christianity, the Church of England has been a stronghold of Freemasonry for more than 200 years. Traditionally, joining the Brotherhood and advancing within it has always been the key to preferment in the church."[53]

Although Knight is neither a Christian nor a Freemason, he does note that "Freemasonry is extremely anxious to have— or appear to have—good relations with all Christian churches." In fact, Masonic power within the church is so strong that "the church . . . dares not offend or provoke thousands of influential and often financially substantial laymen by inquiring into the religious implications of Freemasonry."[54]

Freemasonry is anxious to maintain good relations with the church for one principal reason. As is true for many modern cults as well, the church can provide a large number of converts. This is one reason a particular oath is offered specifically for Christian ministers who are joining the Lodge. This oath pledges them to accept the idea that true Christianity, by its very nature, must safeguard the interests of Masonry: "You, brother, are a preacher of [Christian] religion. . . . You cannot, therefore, but be fond of the [Masonic] Order, and zealous for the interests of Freemasonry. . . . Whoever is warmed with the spirit of Christianity, must esteem, must love Freemasonry."[55]

Why has Masonry infiltrated the church? One reason is that Masonry asserts everywhere (quite falsely) that it is not a religion or a substitute for religion. Instead, it claims to be merely a fraternal brotherhood seeking to better the world. It asserts that it is fully compatible with all religions and that there is absolutely nothing in Masonry that is in any way opposed to Christian belief. In addition, Masonry speaks openly of the importance of belief in God and claims that each member is free to interpret God in any manner he wishes. Finally, many Masons openly proclaim that the institution of Freemasonry "exists to assist or to support the church."[56]

THE SYMBOLS AND RITUAL OF FREEMASONRY

The symbols and ritual in Masonry are important because they are used as a principal method of teaching Masonic ideals. In Masonic authority Allen E. Roberts's text, *The Craft and Its Symbols: Opening the Door to Masonic Symbolism*, the author observes that "symbolism is the lifeblood of the Craft. . . . It is the principal vehicle by which the ritual teaches Masonic philosophy and moral lessons."[57] Mackey asserts that "Freemasonry is . . . a system of doctrines which [is] taught . . . by allegories and symbols."[58] This is why use of symbols is interwoven throughout Masonic Ritual.

The rituals themselves are tied to ancient legends and myths that are replete with symbolic content. Like an onion, the symbols in Masonry may have layers of meaning. At one level of initiation a symbol may mean one thing, and at a higher level of initiation it may mean something else entirely.[59] In the beginning, most Masonic symbols have certain more or less universally accepted meanings. But in the end, after a Mason is "enlightened," each symbol can mean virtually anything a Mason wants it to mean.

Below are a few brief illustrations of Masonic symbols and their meaning.[60] These are used during the ritualistic initiations of the Blue Lodge:

- The *square and compass* (sometimes with a capital "G" in the middle): the square symbolizes morality, the compass symbolizes spirituality, and the "G" represents God or geometry. (For some Masons, the "G" symbolizes gnosticism.)

- The *cable tow* with which the Mason is tied up during the ritual symbolizes the tie of Masonic brotherhood. The candidate's removal of his shoes symbolizes humility.

- The *apron* the candidate wears symbolizes innocence, purity, and honor.

- The *three burning tapers* symbolize the sun, moon, and Masonic Worshipful Master.

- The *sword pointing to a naked heart* symbolizes justice and the knowledge that God will reward men according to their works.

- The candidate's *walking in a circle* (circumambulation) symbolizes the spiritual (e.g., mystical and occult) links to the past that represent man's dependence upon man.

- The *sprig of acacia* symbolizes faith in the promises of God in the "Volume of the Sacred Law" (e.g., depending on the culture, the Bible, Koran, Upanishads, etc.).

That the Masonic Rituals are composed of myths and legends, even pagan myths and legends, is irrelevant; Masons consider it unimportant whether they are true or false. What is important is whatever meaning they give to the candidate in his never-ending search for Masonic "light" and "truth."[61]

Here the subjectivism of the Craft is plain: there is no "final word" on the Masonic symbols because "there is no limitation to what a person can find in this or any other symbol." Thus, the "symbols [of Masonry] have a variety of meanings for everyone." Each person brings a unique perspective to the lessons and secrets of Freemasonry.[62]

THE ATTRACTION OF FREEMASONRY

Masonry is attractive to people for many reasons. Masonry claims to be divinely instituted and therefore appeals to man's search for God.[63] For example, the ritual of the Scottish Rite teaches the candidate that "Masonry is of divine origin."[64]

Others are curious and are allured by the secrecy of the Lodge. They enjoy the idea of belonging to a society in which only they have access to the inner mysteries of Masonry. For example, such persons "love [the] ritual and are held enthralled by the wonder and mystery of the Masonic work and rituals."[65] Allen E. Roberts describes how many Masons feel during the ritual of the First Degree of Masonry: "You could not have helped but to be thrilled and full of pride when you reached the Northeast Corner of the Lodge. There you stood, a just and upright Mason! Every brother present exulted with you. You were about to complete the first step of the most meaningful journey of your life."[66] Some people are fascinated by the symbolism and pagan mysteries of Masonry, noting its similarities to many of the older "mystery religions."

Masonry enjoys a measure of respect in society. Many are attracted by its lofty ideals and its humanitarian works. Others are drawn to Masonry because they are impressed by the idea of a worldwide brotherhood encompassing idealistic goals to better the world.

Some are allured by the power of Masonry. For example, the Worshipful Master exercises absolute control over his Lodge.[67] Still others see in Masonry the ability to seek occult power: it is "a secret order which can have great power if properly developed."[68] Others are charmed simply by its social fellowship.

All in all, Masonry offers brotherhood, social prestige, a sense of mystery, lofty ideals, the lure of secrecy, and the hope of religious quest. For these and other reasons, Masonry is attractive to many people. But as we will later see, Masonry also has hidden motives for its lofty ideals, its humanitarianism, and all else that makes the Craft attractive to outsiders.

The average Mason is lamentably ignorant of the real meaning of Masonic symbology and knows as little of its esoteric teaching.
George H. Steinmetz
Freemasonry—Its Hidden Meaning

3

Masonic World View

A world view is a set of assumptions about life through which men interpret themselves, their universe, and their place in the universe. Because Masonry is a religion (see previous chapter), it offers a comprehensive view of man and man's place in the world. This is why Master Mason W. L. Wilmshurst states, "Masonry, then, is a system of religious philosophy in that it provides us with a doctrine of the universe and of our place in it. It indicates whence we are come and whither we may return."[1] Allen E. Roberts confesses, "Freemasonry is many things, but most of all, FREEMASONRY IS A WAY OF LIFE."[2]

If we understand the world view of Masonry, then we will understand how Masonry influences the life of an individual Mason and how it can be expected to influence the church. Five principal characteristics of Masonry help to form its world view: Masonry is a *subjective philosophy* (with no validated, objective, absolute authority to which a Mason may appeal); Masonry is *liberal religion* (a humanistic religion stressing the inherent divinity and universal brotherhood of mankind); Masonry is a *hierarchical system* (offering different levels of practice, interpretation, and belief); Masonry is a *syncretistic faith* (it draws upon the beliefs of various ancient and modern religions, and yet it offers itself as the true core of all other faiths); Masonry is a form of *"New Age" mysticism* (offering an individual Mason the potential for cultivating altered states of consciousness and developing occultic powers).

MASONRY OFFERS A SUBJECTIVE PHILOSOPHY OF LIFE

Although Masonry claims objective and even divine authority for its practices and beliefs, it offers no independently validated authority to substantiate either its claims or any of its beliefs. Its principal sources of authority are fundamentally subjective. The Worshipful Master is one major source of authority in the Lodge, but he rules his Lodge in an autocratic fashion. "The power of the Worshipful Master is that of an absolute Monarch."[3]

Another principal source of authority in Masonry is, as previously discussed, the *symbolic ritual* of the craft. These rituals are generally uniform both in the ceremonies and in the interpretations given them. But the symbols used in Masonry have various subjective levels of meaning. "There is no limitation to what a person can find in this or any other symbol."[4]

A third source of Masonic authority is the Masonic Landmarks or basic principles of Masonry. Leading authority Albert Mackey asserts that for a Masonic doctrine to be a Landmark, it must have "(1) immemorial antiquity; (2) universality; (3) absolute irrevocability and immutability."[5] The *Ceremonies of Installation and Dedication* charge the initiate with, "You admit that it is not in the power of any man, or body of men to make innovations in the essential and fundamental principles of Freemasonry."[6] Several authoritative definitions have been given to the Landmarks:

> Those fixed tenets by which the limits of Freemasonry may be known and preserved.
>
> The Landmarks of Masonry are those ancient principles and practices which mark out and distinguish Freemasonry.
>
> A Landmark, to be a landmark, must command the universal respect and observance of all Masons.
>
> The Ancient Landmarks are those fundamental principles . . . without which the institution cannot be identified as Masonry.[7]

In their encyclopedias, Coil and Mackey list some twenty-five Landmarks that have been variously accepted by the Masonry of the last three centuries. But Masonic authorities like Coil, Mackey, and Shepherd have never agreed upon the definition, number, classification, or meaning of the Landmarks.[8] As Masonry has evolved and changed throughout the centuries, so have its basic principles:

> [Masonic] authorities have never agreed on the definition, classification or enumeration of the "Ancient Landmarks."... Jurists and scholars express widely divergent opinions about them—nor has any Grand Lodge ever promulgated a list that would be acceptable to all.... The last word has not here been said—perhaps never will be said—on a subject which from its very nature is fluid, therefore constantly changing.[9]

Although Masonry does have certain universally accepted doctrines, it offers no objective evidence for them. They are simply the inventions and opinions of men, which have evolved historically into their present form. Masonry has no revealed canon or scripture, no necessarily absolute source of authority, no developed systematic theology. On an individual level Masonic writers, including their authorities, may and often do contradict one another. Thus, "Each man, as will appear, sees in Masonry the thing nearest to his own nature and need, his own heart and thought."[10]

Such contradiction is especially prominent when a Mason views the basic teachings of Masonry through the particular religious world view he brings to Masonry. For example, a Christian Mason may interpret Masonry through Christian eyes and see in the symbols and rituals of Masonry something never intended. But while there is no objective standard or authority for Masonic belief, we need to remember that Masonry does contain a general core of more or less accepted teachings.

There are at least three basic Landmarks of Masonry that are required belief, at least for modern Masons. These fundamental doctrines are (1) the universal fatherhood of God, (2) the universal brotherhood of man, and (3) the immortality of the soul. For example, Carl H. Claudy asserts that "the ultimates of truth are immutable and eternal: the Fatherhood of God; the immortality of the soul."[11] H. L. Haywood asserts that Masonry is equivalent to the "one universal religion . . . belief in one God as the Father of all, in the immortality of the soul, and in the brotherhood of man."[12] These required Landmarks of Masonry take us to our next characteristic of the Masonic world view.

MASONRY OFFERS THE VIEWPOINT OF LIBERAL RELIGION[13]

Liberal religion has long stressed the fatherhood of God, the brotherhood of man, and salvation by character. It typically teaches unitarianism (God is one person, not three) and universalism (all men will be saved). This is why many liberal ministers have taken notice of Masonry. "The Relation of the Liberal Churches to the Fraternal Orders" is a pamphlet published by the American Unitarian Association and written by E. A. Coil, a Unitarian minister and Mason. In that article he pleads for a closer cooperation between Masonry and liberal religion because of their similar beliefs about God, man, and salvation by character. The following definition of Masonry, given in the *Iowa Quarterly Bulletin*, illustrates the similarity:

> Masonry is a Divinely appointed institution, designed to draw men nearer to God [by character], to give them a clearer conception of their proper relationship to [a unitarian] God as their Heavenly Father [the universal fatherhood of God], to [all] men as their brethren [the universal brotherhood of man] and the ultimate destiny of the human soul [the immortality of the soul, i.e., universalism].[14]

THE FATHERHOOD OF GOD

Masonry teaches the idea of a universal fatherhood of God (see chapter 7). God is the father of all men, regardless of their individual religious beliefs. This underscores the influence of deism in Masonry. (In the lower degrees Masonry has elements of deism; in the higher degrees it is both deistic and pantheistic.) *Deism* stresses God as the Creator of the world, but teaches a belief in God apart from any specific canon of divine revelation. Deism is also known as natural religion or the religion of nature because it stresses the revelation or "word" of God in nature and the human conscience.[15]

By stressing the "word of God" in nature, Masonry can more easily offer the "same" God to men of conflicting religions. Masonry teaches that (at least, apart from the principal teachings of Masonry) God has not given men a personal canon of revelation concerning theological truth. If it were important to do so, He would have done this. Because He has not, Masonry does not need to concern itself with the specific and contradictory theological teachings in the world religions and can safely ignore them.

In this manner, God becomes the father of all men because their specific religious beliefs are of little concern to Him. Thus, any given religious belief *cannot* become a requirement for His acceptance. God accepts everyone because they are all His children. Believing in Jesus, Buddha, Allah, or Krishna makes little difference to the God of Masonry. (At least, this is what Masons are told is true at one level of Masonic belief.)

Although Masonic authorities have objected to classifying Masonry as deistic, the influence of deism is unmistakable. Many non-Masonic researchers agree on this: "In short, the Masonic concept of God is deism,"[16] and, "Modern Freemasonry owes much to the thought of the eighteenth century, and this [Masonic] concept of God reflects the prevalent Deism, in which God is the Supreme Being, the Creator who has set the world in motion, laid down His moral laws for men to obey, but does not continue to act personally in the world in mercy or in judgment."[17]

The deism of Masonry denies both the personal revelation of God in the Bible and, defined biblically, His ongoing personal involvement in the world of men. Again, the reason for this is that, in order to promote "universal brotherhood," Masonry requires a deity that is nonspecific—unknowable, unapproachable, and far away—a deity that men can say very little about. If there is little men can say about God, there is very little to disagree over. It is because of this belief that Masonry rejects the God of Christian faith who has given specific revelation of Himself in the Bible.

THE BROTHERHOOD OF MAN

Masonry teaches that all men are spiritual brothers because they share the same universal Father, the God of Masonry (see chapter 11). This central teaching of Masonry underscores the essentially "humanistic" nature of the Lodge. In Masonry, man himself is divine. Masonry is, therefore, a distinct form of religious humanism. Leading English Mason Wilmshurst observes that "the study of man leads to knowledge of God, by revealing to man the ultimate divinity at the base of human nature."[18] Thus, as Masonic leader Henry Clausen emphasizes, "We must return to a faith in man himself."[19]

It is because of these two beliefs, the universal fatherhood of God and the brotherhood of man, that Masonry rejects the Christian teaching that God is the true spiritual father only of those who accept His Son, Jesus Christ (John 1:12).

THE IMMORTALITY OF THE SOUL

Masonry teaches that all men possess an immortal soul. This third central Landmark of Masonry also teaches what is known as theological *universalism*: the belief that all men will go to heaven (or however the afterlife is conceived) regardless of their actions or beliefs. It is based upon the previous two Landmarks: (1) God is the spiritual Father of all men and accepts them indiscriminately; (2) all men are spiritual brothers who possess an immortal soul. It logically follows that all men are already saved and guaranteed eternal life with God. It is because of this belief that Masonry rejects the Christian concept that salvation comes only by faith in Jesus Christ who died on the cross to deliver us from God's wrath against human sin.

MASONRY OFFERS DIFFERENT LEVELS OF INTERPRETATION AND BELIEF

Within Masonry there exists different levels of initiation and spiritual "enlightenment." This is why some Masons refer to a "lower" and a "higher" Masonry, the first three degrees being introductory and the higher degrees being more advanced.[20]

LEVELS OF INITIATION

Those who have completed only the first three degrees in Masonry are often unaware of what occurs in the higher levels. Even for Masons at the higher levels, variations exist. For example, a Scottish Rite Mason may be ignorant of the teachings of the York Rite and vice versa. When confronted with the blasphemous secret name for God (Jabulon), as given in the Royal Arch Degree of the York Rite, evangelical Christian Mason Bill Mankin responded, "I know nothing of that. The Royal Arch is a York Rite. I'm not a York Rite Mason; I'm a Scottish Rite Mason. . . .That's part of the York Rite. That's not part of the Scottish Rite."[21]

LEVELS OF SPIRITUAL ENLIGHTENMENT

The nominally religious Mason. This Mason has been through the Masonic rites stressing the importance of Masonic religion, but for him Masonry has become merely a social club and secular brotherhood. This member sees Masonry as an assistance to social standing and advance in his community or a means to assist his business or employment through contacts with other Masons. He is content in his view of Masonry as it is. For this Mason, the entire subject of religion is largely irrelevant. Many Masons fall into this category. But it is important to note that many leaders in Masonry see a trend within the Lodge toward the next two categories.

The humanistically religious Mason. This Mason accepts, lives, and promotes the religious nature of Masonry—but largely at its face value. He accepts the literal or "outer" meaning of Masonry. He is committed to Masonic truth as he sees it and seeks to live his life according to Masonic ideals: the fatherhood of God, the brotherhood of man, the immortality of the soul, salvation by character, and Masonry as the hope of the future. This Mason would probably view the first category of the nominal Mason as an apostate who has denied and dishonored the "sacred" truths of Masonry. For this Mason, the outward claims of Masonry concerning religion are accepted at face value: e.g., Masonry truly honors all religions and seeks genuine religious brotherhood where men of all faiths may unite in worship to

God. He does not consider the matter further and therefore never understands the real intent and nature of Masonry. The Mason who lives at this level of Masonry has still not understood Masonry in its totality.

The mystically religious (gnostic) Mason. This Mason looks at Masonry at a deeper and more esoteric level. He finds in Masonry, correctly so, a thorough-going system of mysticism, offering occult enlightenment for those who seek it. He sees almost everything in Masonry as part of the tradition of the ancient mystery schools, as a gnostic religion whose "outer form" preserves the genuine secrets of "true" Masonry from the profane (the unenlightened, whether non-Mason or Mason). This Mason views Masons in the above categories as somewhat ignorant and naive: they are unenlightened as to the real nature of Masonry. For this Mason, Masonry is the one true religion on earth whose mystical core constitutes the alleged inner truths of all religions. The "genuine" Mason thus seeks the ancient *gnosis* or secret knowledge—an ultimate spiritual enlightenment through both ritual and consciousness.

This is why many Masons confess that other Masons live in spiritual ignorance. Allen E. Roberts comments, "There is much that is still unknown to even the ardent Masonic student."[22] Masonic authority Rollin C. Blackmer complains, "It is a lamentable fact that the great mass of our membership are . . . densely ignorant of everything connected with Masonry."[23] An official Masonic text for Georgia confesses, "The majority of Masons are sadly lacking in the knowledge of the height, breadth and depth of Masonic teachings as contained in the meanings of the many symbols of Masonry."[24] Ronayne states that "those who know the least about Freemasonry are the Masons themselves."[25] The Reverend William M. Russell declares that "nearly every Mason thinks he knows all about Masonry, and also what Speculative [modern] Masonry is. As a matter of fact, however, he does not."[26]

George H. Steinmetz summarizes the condition of the majority of Masons when he writes, "Most of the truly great Masonic writers have deplored the lack of esoteric Masonic knowledge among the Craft in general. . . . The average Mason is lamentably ignorant of the real meaning of Masonic symbology and knows as little of its esoteric teaching."[27] The individual Mason may be unaware of the *religious nature* of Masonry, unaware of the teachings of the *higher degrees* of Masonry, and unaware of the true *inner meaning* and *intent* of Masonry.

MASONRY OFFERS THE ONE TRUE RELIGION

A simple definition of syncretism is the belief that the teachings of one's own religion are really the "true" core teachings of every other religion, whether or not the followers of those religions realize it. Most of the criticisms of syncretistic religions, such as the Baha'i World Faith, are directed at their claims to contain the true essence of all religions—in complete disregard of the individual facts taught by those religions. Masons have made the following statements:

> There is under all the creeds one universal religion.[28]

> This one true religion . . . is the very soul of Masonry.[29]

> The true disciple of ancient Masonry has given up forever the worship of personalities. . . . As a Mason his religion must be universal: Christ, Buddha or Mohammed, the names mean little, for he recognizes only the light and not the bearer [the personality]. He worships at every shrine, bows before every altar, whether in temple, mosque or cathedral, realizing with his truer understanding the oneness of all spiritual truth. . . . No true Mason can be narrow, for his Lodge is the divine expression of all broadness. There is no place for little minds in a great work.[30]

Masonry is, allegedly, the genuine friend of all religions.[31] But Masonry teaches that it alone contains the true inner meaning of all religions. It alone safeguards genuine religious truth. Thus, the specific doctrines and dogmas of all other religions are wrong and false. "Masonry seeks to free men from a limiting conception of religion, and thus to remove one of the chief causes of sectarianism."[32] This is why Masonry is not the friend of religion but actually the enemy. It seeks to do away with all religions (as they exist) by absorption into Masonry.[33] Thus, Masons who are aware that Masonry is the one true religion can hope to "strip from all religions their orthodox tenets, legends, allegories and dogmas."[34]

Unless such dogmas can be done away with, true universal brotherhood cannot exist. Masonry hopes to accomplish this by educating members of all faiths that the true teachings of their religion are the teachings of Masonry. What this means is the Masonic claim to tolerance and respect for all religions is false. It *offers* to all religions tolerance and respect—but it does not *deliver* them. And it only offers religions tolerance and respect so that it may finally replace them with Masonry. In this sense, Masonry is a Trojan horse. With one hand it comes bearing gifts and offers friendship. But in the other hand it conceals a deadly weapon.

Masonry Offers a Mystical World View

Our fifth and final characteristic of Masonry is to note its similarity to New Age beliefs. In many ways Masonry, especially certain elements of it, may be classified as a New Age mystical religion. Some Masons even speak in classic New Age terms. Clausen, for example, claims that once men learn to use higher consciousness to recognize the divinity within them and apply it to the world, then the world will experience a true New Age.[35]

In general, Masonry (at least its "enlightened" portion) has certain characteristics in common with New Age religion.

- It stresses universal brotherhood and is working for a new world order.

- It offers an esoteric enlightenment stressing "higher" states of consciousness.

- It believes that all men are in some sense divine.

- It accepts occult philosophy and practice, including spiritism (see chapters 17-19).

Another characteristic of the New Age is eclecticism. Masonry is religiously eclectic in that it draws from many different sources. Manly P. Hall, a 33d Degree Mason, says, "A hundred religions have brought their gifts of wisdom to its altars."[36] Masonry has been influenced by ancient paganism (e.g., the mystery religions of Rome and Greece). Pythagoras was a famous sixth-century B.C. philosopher and occultist. But modern Freemasonry hails Pythagoras as "an ancient friend and brother" because his ancient school of occultism bears considerable organizational and doctrinal resemblance to modern Masonry.[37]

Masonry also has been influenced by medieval mysticism and occultism (e.g., Rosicrucianism, alchemy, hermeticism), by modern liberal religion (e.g., Unitarian Universalism), and by orthodox Christianity.

Like the New Age movement, Masonry (collectively) is polytheistic and stresses the importance of the "religion of Nature." Although theoretically it claims to offer belief in the one true God, practically speaking it must, worldwide, be classified as a *polytheistic* religion. Masonry accepts the worship of many different gods (at least for its "unenlightened" initiates who have not yet comprehended the ultimate meaning of Masonry): "in his private devotions a Mason will pray to Jehovah, Mohammed, Allah, Jesus, or the deity of his choice."[38]

A Mason may, in his ignorance, worship the god of his religion, but according to "higher Masonry," this is a false god. As the Mason becomes instructed in the truths of Masonry and is reeducated along the lines of Masonic religion, he will realize that the one true religion lies far beyond the limiting doctrines of the religion and gods most men know. This is why many Masons see the work of Masonry as that of "rebuilding the temple of fallen humanity" and that Masonry "has a world mission in aid of all men everywhere in the world, and that this mission is spiritual."[39]

The five characteristics of Masonry—its subjectivism, its liberal religious perspective, the various levels of initiation and spiritual "enlightenment," its religious syncretism, and its New Age mysticism—combine to form a distinctive perspective and world view that is fundamentally incompatible with, and even hostile to, Christian faith.

What is moral to one man may be immoral to another. Each man must decide for himself what the
word encompasses.
Allen E. Roberts
The Craft and Its Symbols

4

Masonic Morality

M asonry claims it is an institution designed to promote morality. But certain values held by Masonry give cause for
concern.

THE FIRST DUTY OF THE MASON IS TO MASONRY

When Masonic secrets or vital interests are at stake, the
rights of Masonry are apparently placed above duty to country,
family, church, and possibly even law.[1] The *Mentor's Manual of
Masonry* admits, "The obligation is the heart of the degree, for
when it is assumed by the candidate, he has solemnly bound
himself to Freemasonry and assumed certain duties which are
his for the rest of his life."[2] In his covenant with Masonry, the
candidate solemnly promises that he "will forever conceal and
never reveal" the secrets of Masonry.[3] According to Past Master
Edmond Ronayne, page 196 of "Webb's Monitor" reads that
"the first duty of the reader of this synopsis is to obey the edicts
of his Grand Lodge. Right or wrong, his very existence as a Mason hangs upon obedience to the powers immediately set
above him. The one unpardonable crime in a Mason is contu-
macy or disobedience."[4]

The ritual of the 17th Degree of the Scottish Rite divulges
that "a Mason should not hesitate to spill his blood for the sup-

port of Masonry."⁵ This ritual discusses the symbolic meaning of certain items:

> The bow, arrows and crown signify that the orders of this re-spectable Council should be executed with as much quick-ness as the arrow flies from the bow, and be received with as much submission as if it came from a crowned head or a chief of a nation. The sword [signifies] that the Council is al-ways armed to punish the guilty. . . . The skull is the image of a brother who is excluded from a lodge or Council. The cloth stained with blood, that we should not hesitate to spill ours for the good of Masonry.⁶

Masons are sworn to protect fellow Masons, right or wrong. The Georgia *Monitor* teaches, "Secrecy is an essential element of Freemasonry, and every Mason is bound by irrevo-cable ties to keep inviolate its private ceremonies, signs, words, the business of the lodge, and (excepting treason and murder) never to divulge any secret that may be confided by a brother if accepted as such."⁷ The Tennessee *Monitor* states that a secret communication from a brother Mason, "when communicated to and received by you specifically as such, are to be kept by you sacred and inviolable under all circumstances unless he voluntarily releases you."⁸

The Mason swears: "I will obey all regular signs, sum-mons, or tokens, given, handed, sent, or thrown to me from the hand of a brother Master Mason,"⁹ and, "A companion Royal Arch Mason's secrets, given me in charge as such, and I know-ing them to be such, shall remain as secure and inviolable in my breast as in his own, without exception."¹⁰

The moral problem with such standards should be ob-vious. Suppose a man is a witness in a criminal case involving anything but murder or treason. The one charged with the crime is a brother Master Mason. What if the witness receives a sign from the brother Mason charged with the crime? He is sworn to retain the secrets of his brother Mason. The standard Masonic *Monitor* states, "I furthermore promise and swear, that I will assist a companion Royal Arch Mason when I see him en-gaged in any difficulty, and will espouse his cause so far as to

extricate him from the same, *whether he be right or wrong*"
(italics added).[11]

The previous oath cited two exceptions: "murder and treason." But here no exceptions are given. Apparently, the Mason
is free to decide the issue for himself. Former Mason Ronayne
believed that by its absolute stress upon secrecy, keeping of the
oaths, and the belief in Masonry as the highest good, in effect
Masonry taught the following:

> Whenever you see any of our signs made by a brother Mason,
> and especially the *Grand Hailing sign of distress,* you must
> always be sure to *obey* them, even at the risk of your own life.
> If you're on a jury, and the defendant is a Mason, and makes
> the Grand Hailing sign, you must obey it; you must disagree
> with your brother jurors, if necessary, but you must be very
> sure not to bring the Mason guilty, for that would bring dis-
> grace upon our order. It may be perjury, to be sure, to do
> this, but then you're fulfilling your obligation, and you know
> if you "live up to your obligations you'll be free from
> sin." . . . You must conceal all the crimes of your brother Ma-
> son, except murder and treason, and these only at your own
> option, and should you be summoned as a witness against a
> brother Mason be always sure to shield him. Prevaricate,
> don't tell the whole truth in this case, keep his secrets. (Italics
> added)[12]

Masons may deny that such things have ever happened,
but given the biblical teachings concerning human nature (the
sinfulness of man), can we suppose that such things have never
happened? This is why many persons express concern in areas
of potential conflict between the duties the Mason owes first to
Masonry and secondarily to any other institution, military or political. Cerza himself admits, "Occasionally individual Masons in
European countries have used their Lodge connections to promote their political ambitions."[13] This is why the Baptist Union
of Scotland observed:

> Allegations of unfair advantage, of the distortion of justice
> and even of corruption, have often been made and as often
> strenuously denied. Because the movement works largely in
> secrecy and uses secret signs and code words, it is often diffi-

cult to pinpoint specific instances. Some who have recently investigated some of the allegations at depth appear to be convinced that they have some foundation. For example, Sir Kenneth Newman in his guidelines issued to the metropolitan police leaves no doubt that in his view, Freemasonry and police service are incompatible.[14]

Dr. R. A. Torrey, a founder of what later would become Biola University and Talbot School of Theology in La Mirada, California, and superintendent of the Moody Bible Institute, had personal experience on this issue. In his tract "My Reasons for Not Joining the Masonic Fraternity" he explains: "To my own personal knowledge, Masonry has been used to protect criminals and other evil doers from the just consequences of their wrong doing."[15]

Pastor John R. Rice confesses, "My father told me of cases of violence by Lodge action, which he justified. The spirit of vengeance is inseparably connected with the horrible oaths and penalties of the secret orders."[16] In his exposé of Freemasonry Paul Fisher reveals similar findings:

> Yet, some become disillusioned and separate themselves from the Craft, only to find Masons often "retaliate against members who quit by trying to get them fired from their jobs and otherwise harassing them." Several former members of the Fraternity said they moved from their residences after leaving the lodge, and some asked that their names not be used by newspaper reporters because they feared reprisals. . . .
>
> Anokan Reed, a former top-level York Rite Mason pointed [out] the morality of such oath by commenting: "It's okay to seduce another man's daughter, or steal his car, as long as he's not a Master Mason. . . . In the higher degrees, Masons deny the reality of evil."
>
> Reed, a former 13th Degree York Rite member, said he joined a lodge in Kokomo, Indiana when he was in his 20s, because his boss, a Mason, guaranteed he would "move up in the steel mill" if he joined. After becoming a Mason, Reed was promoted to a supervisory position, for which, he admits, he was not qualified.[17]

Author Stephen Knight spent seven months investigating Masonry in Britain. In spite of the "disinformation tactics" of several Freemasons,[18] he developed an extensive network of contacts within Freemasonry. He was able to "establish within a few months an entire network of moles" and interviewed "hundreds of Masons."[19] "There can be no doubt," he said, "that many others have suffered because of Freemasonry entering into areas of life where, according to all its publicly proclaimed principles, it should never intrude. The abuse of Freemasonry causes alarming miscarriages of justice."[20]

Knight provides a number of illustrations. He cites the police corruption in Scotland Yard exposed in 1974 and 1975. The problem was that Scotland Yard was "heavily Masonic":

> And despite A-10's [a special unit set up to weed out corruption] success in ridding the Yard of suspect detectives—nearly 300 have been forced to resign by spring 1975—it was constantly obstructed in its attempts to obtain evidence solid enough to make charges stick. Even in cases of obvious criminality, fellow officers whose evidence was vital clammed up and obstinately refused to make statements, or cooperate in any other way. Some would not speak at all. It rapidly became clear why. The "honest" men needed as witnesses were members of the same Brotherhood as the "bent" officers. Many shared the same lodges.[21]

These Masons were only obeying the oaths they had sworn in Masonry. The candidate is told that "Masonry is of divine origin."[22] The *Guide to the Royal Arch Chapter* asserts that the Mason owes his duty primarily to God. But this is "God" as Masonry conceives Him, which is really a duty to Masonry itself, because it is Masonry that, principally, represents God on earth.

Further, the candidate is told that the political power of the land ("the king") is subordinate to the Masonic High Priest:

> The institutions of political society teach us to consider the King as the chief of created beings, and that the first duty of his subjects is to obey his mandates; but the institutions of our sublime degrees, by placing the King in a situation subordinate to the High-Priest, teaches us that our duty to God [i.e., Masonry] is paramount to all other duties, and should ever claim the priority of our obedience to man.[23]

Perhaps this is why President Ulysses S. Grant once observed, "All secret, oathbound, political parties are dangerous to any nation."[24] President John Quincy Adams was more severe. After an impartial investigation of Freemasonry, he concluded in his "Address to the People of Massachusetts,"

> I saw a code of Masonic legislation adapted to prostrate every principle of equal justice and to corrupt every sentiment of virtuous feeling in the soul of him who bound his allegiance to it. I saw the practice of common honesty, the kindness of Christian benevolence, even the abstinence of atrocious crimes, limited exclusively by lawless oaths and barbarous penalties, to the social relations between the Brotherhood and the Craft. I saw slander organize into a secret, widespread and affiliated agency.... I saw self-invoked imprecations of throats cut from ear to ear, of hearts and vitals torn out and cast off and hung on spires. I saw wine drunk from a human skull with solemn invocation of all the sins of its owner upon the head of him who drank it.[25]

But the response of Masonry to all of this is simply to remain silent. The Mason is charged in the First Degree, "Neither are you to suffer your zeal for the institution to lead you into argument with those who through ignorance may ridicule it."[26] Alphonse Cerza urges, "Let us not dispute, or argue, or engage in discussion on this subject of Anti-Masonry.... Let us continue to maintain a discreet silence."[27]

Cerza and all Masons would probably deny the above charges. They would claim that Masonry is harmless and innocent. But this would make the above testimonies lies, and what motive would respected leaders such as John Quincy Adams have to lie? The problem with a secret society is precisely in its secrecy. And if the secret society has no absolute standard of morality, what then? Given human nature, one cannot be optimistic.

Masonic Morality Is Subjective and Self-determined

Masonic authority Allen E. Roberts observes that when Masons are told that their rituals are intended to teach morality, they often ask, "What *is* morality?" Perhaps they are confused by the fact that Masonic morality is "taught by symbol and illustrated in allegory."

> [Morality] is difficult to define. What is moral to one man may be immoral to another. Each man must decide for himself what the word encompasses, taking into account the moral standards of the society in which he lives. . . . He must set his own standards, his own principles. It can be dangerous to apply his standards in judging another person.[28]

Because Masonry is a worldwide institution one wonders what an individual Mason might think of this relative assessment of morality, given, for example, the pervasive corruption that exists in such countries as Mexico and India or in an adulterous and pornographic society like our own. If something evil in one country is socially accepted in another, can a Mason logically condemn it?

In *The Great Teachings of Masonry*, Haywood defends an experiential and largely pragmatic, humanistic, and pleasure-oriented morality.

> When a man is in moral predicament, and does not know whether or not a given course of action is right or wrong, to what final authority can he refer his problem? In the writer's opinion there can be but one answer. Human experience, both individual and racial, is the one final authority in morals. . . . Wrong is whatever hurts human life, or destroys human happiness; right is whatever helps human life, and tends to sustain or increase human happiness. There is but one way to learn what it is that hurts or helps and that is by experience. . . . *Acts are not right or wrong intrinsically*, but according as their effects are hurtful or helpful. The purpose of right living is not in order to render obedience to some code, or to some supposed authority, but to enable a man to live richly, healthfully, happily. (Italics added)[29]

Perhaps such an attitude is what has led some Masons into fraudulent practices, and worse.[30] As long as an issue is one that remains a matter of private experience, a person "has no right to decide for another."[31] But human experience is not necessarily a sound standard of what is right or moral. For example, it is precisely this kind of "morality," determined by experiential "logic," that has brought upon America the AIDS plague. As long as homosexuals are happy, and allegedly not hurting anyone, we must not say that their actions are wrong. Appealing merely to "human happiness" as an absolute standard can pervert the interest of morality in dozens of ways.

If there is a more or less "official" morality in Masonry, it is the morality of *nature*.[32] In his *Textbook of Masonic Jurisprudence*, Mackey contrasted this law of nature with the Ten Commandments:

> Every Mason is obliged by his tenure to obey moral law. Now this moral law is not to be considered as confined to the decalogue of Moses, within which narrow limits the ecclesiastical writers technically retain it, but rather as alluding to what is called the *lex naturae* or the law of nature. . . . No law less universal could have been appropriately selected for the government of an institution whose prominent characteristic is its universality.[33]

Wagner has revealed how it was under the powerful influence of deism in the eighteenth century that Masonry adopted its moral law of nature.[34] But what is this law of nature? Is nature necessarily moral? What offends nature? Can we ever think of nature permitting an act that would offend her? Is even *human* nature intrinsically moral? Wagner shows why the law of nature that Masonry adopts is not the same as the "law of nature" spoken of by theologians nor the moral law of Christianity:

> This law of nature is simply the natural inclination of human nature acting without let or hindrance as expressed or exhibited in the free life of nature. . . . This law of nature is not a command. . . . It is not addressed to creatures, but exists rather as instinct. It is substantially identical with the "divine nature" as conceived of in the Phrygian and other ancient mysteries, the ancient Freemasonry, to whose ethical ideas and symbolism Masonic writers frequently refer as illustrations and warrants for their moral ideas and practices.[35]

> The standard of Masonic morality is the law of nature, and so long as he obeys it, he is a moral man. He may steal, lie, deceive, and commit adultery outside of the circumscribed

sphere of the fraternity, and not be guilty of any immorality, Masonically viewed. He is under a *different* moral government, bound by a *different* moral law, and guided by a *different* system of ethics. *Masonry by its covenant makes the essence of morality consist in the relation of the individual to Masonry.* (Italics added)[36]

MASONRY MAY BE RACIST OR OTHERWISE PREJUDICED

The *Encyclopedia Britannica* observes, "In practice, some lodges have been charged with prejudice against Jews, Catholics, and non-whites. U.S. lodges rejected the legitimacy of Negro Masonic Lodges, the Prince Hall lodges."[37] Another researcher concludes that, "It appears that most lodges, especially the Masonic Lodge, discriminate racially (even as they freely admit 'unanimous consent' is necessary for any candidate to be 'entered' into the craft)."[38] This is further documented by Fisher.[39]

Masons are also told to exclude the unintelligent and the handicapped from their Lodges:

> You agree to be cautious to admit none but good men into your lodge, to receive no one who does not do his duty as a Blue [Lodge] Mason, and who is not a good character, intelligent and respectable.

> A candidate for initiation must be a man, free born, unmutilated and of mature age. . . . These landmarks can never be changed.[40]

MASONRY ENCOURAGES FAVORITISM

L. James Rongstad was part of an official Lutheran inquiry into Masonry. He asserts that "favoritism is often practiced in employment, letting of contracts, business deals, and other functions in society."[41] This, too, is contrary to the teachings of Scripture (James 2:1-3). Even the Roman Catholic church concluded that "it is unchristian to join any secret organization which systematically benefits its own members to the detriment of the legitimate interests of non-members."[42]

MASONRY PERMITS AN EXTREMELY WIDE LATITUDE OF ETHICAL BELIEFS

"Inasmuch as the only religious doctrines that operate in Masonry are belief in a personal God, in immortality, and in brotherhood, the man who holds them is, for Masonry, sufficiently equipped, and Masonry has no reason to find fault with whatever he may further believe."[43] But someone's "further beliefs" may involve racism, bigotry, moral relativism, fascism, Marxism, cultism, and many other beliefs not necessarily moral or good.

MASONRY REJECTS GOD AND HIS LAW

In that the biblical Scriptures are only "symbolic" and in that Masonry denies every Christian doctrine and offers its members a false and deistic god, Masonry has no logical basis for establishing morality, except a morality defined as Masonry itself or that of personal preference. Masonry may make claim to morality, but this does not necessarily mean it is speaking of morality in a Christian sense. For these reasons, and a great deal more, Wagner concluded that the claims of Masonry concerning morality were false:

> The ethics of Masonry when the veil is removed, is decidedly immoral, and subversive of the divine order.... If these principles were to animate mankind, the state, the family and the church, and all the moral relations, ties and duties now universally recognized as right and proper would be overthrown and broken down, and society again would wallow in the styles of paganism.
>
> We admit that this is a serious charge, but we make it only after a prolonged and careful study of the "covenant," and of the language of Masonic authorities. We make this charge against Masonry, and not against Masons as individuals, but with the conviction that when men assume a name they also assume the obligations of that name. Men cannot honestly accept or subscribe a confession, or enter into a covenant unless they believe its contents and agree to live and practice its principles.... We hold, therefore, that if a Mason is a moral man, he is such not because of the covenant, but in

spite of it, for some men are better than the system to which they adhere."[44]

MASONRY USES HUMANITARIAN ACTIVITIES TO FURTHER COVERT GOALS

Masons, particularly groups like the Shrine, are known primarily for their humanitarian activities, e.g., children's hospitals. Certainly we can all be thankful for such activities on behalf of these children and all needy persons. But, unfortunately, this is not the whole issue, and a number of sources have questioned the use of funds donated for such causes.

The Southaven, Michigan, *Daily Tribune* of April 24, 1987, revealed that even though the Shrine is the richest charity in the nation, it gave its twenty-two hospitals for children less than one-third of the total amount collected from the public in 1984. The remainder was spent on travel, entertainment, fraternal ceremonies, fund-raising, food, and so on. In other words, the Shriners allegedly kept 71 percent of $21.7 million raised.

Circuses sponsored by the Shrine generated $23 million in 1985, but less than 2 percent went to the medical care of children. The *Orlando Sentinel*, June 29, 1986, ran a special four-part series on its six-month investigation into Shrine charity expenditures, confirming the above statistics through IRS records. Also in 1984, the Shrine hospitals received only *1 percent* of an estimated $17.5 million collected from Shrine circuses.

It is a common characteristic of many cults to make extravagant claims touting their funding of charitable causes. But investigation often reveals that far more money is kept to promote the organization's own religious goals. This raises the question as to the motive underlying Masonry's humanitarian activities. What are their motives? Unfortunately, Freemasonry is not the benign and charitable fraternity it claims to be. That it engages in charitable causes cannot alter the fact that it leads millions of people astray spiritually. That great men are counted among its membership shows only that great men can also be deceived. That Masonry wants to be best known for its charitable works is, like its "secrecy," often a cloak to hide its real teachings and goals from the undiscerning.

Concerning this point we quote the analysis of Fisher at some length, for his own experience is typical:

> The Shriners are well known for their ability to evoke laughter and spread happiness among young and old. They also are universally admired and respected for sponsoring hospitals which specialize in caring for children. My own experience at a 1965 Shriner's parade in Washington, D.C. left my wife and me so impressed . . . we were strongly persuaded to believe the Catholic Church's age-old condemnation of the Masonic Fraternity must certainly be misguided.
>
> Consequently, it was shocking later to learn that behind the festive facade and the children's charities lurked a more profoundly selfish purpose. Adam Weishaupt suggested the reason for such activities nearly 200 years ago when he instructed his Illuminees: "We must win the common people in every corner. This will be obtained chiefly by means of the schools, and by open, hearty behaviour. Show condescension, popularity, and toleration of their prejudices, which we, at leisure, shall root out and dispel."
>
> In 1945, a member of the Craft put it this way: "the major job of the Masonic Fraternity is the creation of a healthy and enlightened public opinion." And, he added: All other Masonic activities are "incidental" to the real purpose of Freemasonry, which is "the creation and maintenance of a public opinion that will sustain the kind of world that we all wish to live in."
>
> Public relations activities are the life-blood of Masonry, because the Craft's policy ostensibly forbids extending invitations to join the Fraternity. Rather, men who are attracted to the Craft must themselves request entry into the Lodge. . . .
>
> In 1968, the Scottish Rite Grand Commander clearly explained the technique for luring men into the Fraternity. . . . "tact, diplomacy, and skillful salesmanship will bring opportunities." . . . Commenting further [in "How to Create a Favorable Opinion of Freemasonry in the World of the Profane," *New Age,* October 1968], the Grand Commander said: "Crippled children's hospitals throughout the country, and the knowledge that Masons are largely responsible for them, has induced many outsiders to petition for the degrees of Masonry. The same can be said about education programs of the Supreme Council in support of the public schools a..d Americanism." . . .

Pressing home the need for luring men into the Fraternity, the Commander said the Brethren must be "recognized as strong advocates of Masonic participation" in such publicly accepted entities "as public schools, scouting, youth organizations, YMCA, Salvation Army, and libraries." . . .

It is truly surprising that thousands of men are lured into joining an organization about which they know almost nothing. Advertising experts call it "selling the sizzle and not the steak." . . .

A . . . *New Age* editorial remarked on the phenomenon by observing that the applicant for membership in the Craft "does not know in advance the vows he must take or the principles to which he will pledge allegiance. Yet, in spite of such a handicap, hundreds of persons every year make application to join a Masonic Lodge."

Why do they do so? The editorial explains that the major reason is because a man's acquaintances and friends are members of the Fraternity, "and, if they have found Masonry in accordance with its reputation for good in the community, then he feels justified in the faith that nothing will be asked of him which could not be proclaimed to the world with propriety."

But the editorial did not find it necessary to report that, once inside, the initiates are bound by solemn oaths, and stern promises of mutilation and death if they reveal Masonic secrets. However, even if the Brotherhood's secrets are revealed, they are dismissed as untrue by the general public, because so many honorable men are associated with the Fraternity.

But what are the Fraternity's secrets? Why must members bind themselves so solemnly and agree to accept mutilation and death if the secrets are revealed? If the organization is simply fraternal, charitable and dedicated to good works, surely such extreme measures are totally uncalled for.

The obvious conclusion is that the Secret Brotherhood is hiding something so serious that decent men would never join it if they were fully informed in advance of its activities and purposes.[45]

One must wonder about the real reason for Masonry's support of charitable causes. In other words, does Masonry utilize charitable causes primarily to promote Masonry? After reading every page of every monthly issue of *New Age* magazine from 1921-1981, Fisher concluded,

It is evident that international Freemasonry historically has been a revolutionary world-wide movement organized to advance Kabbalistic Gnosticism; [and] to undermine and, if possible, to destroy Christianity; to infuse Masonic philosophy into key government structures. . . . All evidence points to the fact that most members of the Masonic Fraternity are largely ignorant of its . . . [real] designs.[46]

Citing a study by a Catholic theologian, Fisher observed:

The ultimate aim of the Craft, Fr. Gruber said, is the overthrow of all spiritual and political "tyranny" and class privileges, so that there will be established a universal social republic in which will reign the greatest possible individual liberty and social and economic quality [cf. chapters 7 and 15 in this book]. To accomplish their goal, Masons believe the following is necessary: 1. The destruction of all social influence by the Church and religion generally . . . [including by] so-called separation of Church and State. 2. To laicize or secularize all public and private life and, above all, popular education. 3. To systematically develop freedom of thought and conscience in school children, and protect them, so far as possible, against all disturbing influences of the Church, and even their own parents—by compulsion if necessary.[47]

What is significant about such comments is not their lack of credibility in light of the benign public *perception* of Masonry, but how closely they parallel the trend of modern American life as reflected in public education, Supreme Court decisions, and other areas. The extent of Masonic responsibility for this state of affairs may be unknown—but it cannot be denied that Masonry intends to exert some influence in this direction.

Those Masons who believe that the Craft is merely a social and fraternal order are, in the words of the Grand Commander, operating under an "erroneous impression" and are in fact "a distinct liability" to the organization. Most men are lured into Masonry by promises of brotherhood, charity, and advancement in employment or public life. But at what cost?

Part 2

Religious Secrets: Beliefs

The purpose of this section is to compare the authoritative teachings of the Masonic Lodge and its higher degrees with those of traditional orthodox Christianity. If you are interested in knowing the real teachings of Masonry, or if you are a Christian with friends or relatives who have participated in the Lodge, and especially if you are a Mason who is a Christian, this section was written for you.

For almost three hundred years Masonry has influenced the Christian church. Today, however, such influence is perhaps greater than ever before. But most people, Christians included, have little knowledge of Masonry and little understanding of its implications or of how deeply unchristian it is. Indeed, the very reason that Masonry continues to find an influence within the church is Christian ignorance as to its real teachings and not just its claims. Once it is understood what Masonry really teaches, a great deal of the confusion over this subject will be dissipated.

Individual Masons may have a number of responses to the content of this section. For those who say (incorrectly), "This is not what the Lodge officially teaches," we have documented each statement from the authoritative rituals of each state and from the Masonic authorities recommended to us by at least half the Grand Lodges in the fifty states (see chapter 1). So if we are wrong, then the ritual itself and Masonry's highly esteemed authors are also wrong and should be discarded by those in the Lodge. For those who say, "This is not what I gathered from my years of experience in the Lodge," the only way to gauge if one's experience is accurate is to compare it with the ritual and accepted Masonic authorities. For whatever reason, some Masons may never have correctly understood their own accepted authorities.

For example, some Christian Masons tend to interpret the ritual and teachings of the Lodge through Christian eyes. They have imposed their own Christian world view on the teachings of Masonry in spite of the Lodge's stated beliefs. Such persons ignore what the Lodge really teaches. But this does not change the facts. The real question is whether or not a person is acting in accord with orthodox Christianity or traditional Masonry. A Christian might possibly belong to a Buddhist shrine, participate in Buddhist ritual and ceremony, and claim such practices were Christian. But it is inconsistent and contradictory for a Christian to practice, believe, and support the ritual and ceremonies of Buddhism and call it Christian. Christian belief and practice have definite content, and Christian belief and practice are different from Masonry.

Although Masonry may not properly be classified as a cult per se, we have documented the following cultic characteristics displayed by Masonry in varying degrees:

- Parallels to ancient religious cultic themes and beliefs (chapter 19)

- The deliberate deception of the "profane" or unworthy, whether Mason or non-Mason (chapter 20)

- Spiritual intimidation or secrecy reinforced by penalty (chapter 14)

- An element of authoritarianism (chapter 14)

- The justification, intended or otherwise, of certain unethical practices (chapter 4)

- The occasional attempt at suppression of critical literature (Stephen Knight, *The Brotherhood: The Explosive Exposé of the Secret World of the Freemasons*, pp. 9-12)

- A relationship to paganism and the promotion of the occult (chapters 17-19)

- The distortion of Scripture and, theologically, the denial and rejection of Christian faith (Parts 2 and 3)

We will reveal what both the authoritative ritual and official authorities of Masonry teach. We will uncover what Masonry truly believes and compare it with Christian belief. In this way the reader will be free to judge whether or not he is in step with the beliefs and teachings of Masonry or Christianity.

> We beseech thee that our thoughts may be engaged
> in the grand work of our perfection, which when
> attained will be an ample reward for our labor....
> Grant that all our proceedings may tend to our glo-
> ry.... Bless and prosper our works, O Lord.
>
> Opening prayer Thirteenth Degree of the Scottish Rite
> J. Blanchard, *Scottish Rite Masonry Illustrated*, 1:297-98

5

The Plan of Salvation

Did you know that the Masonic Lodge teaches a way to heaven that is not taught in the Bible? Masonry teaches exactly what God condemns as a false gospel, namely, that a man will be saved and go to heaven as a result of his good works and personal self-improvement. The Bible places such a teaching under God's curse: "But even though we, or an angel from heaven, should preach to you a gospel contrary to that which we have preached to you, let him be accursed. As we have said before, so I say again now, if any man is preaching to you a gospel contrary to that which you received, let him be accursed" (Galatians 1:8-9).

GRACE VS. WORKS

Masonry denies and opposes the biblical teaching of "salvation by grace alone" (Ephesians 2:8-9) and replaces it with a teaching that stresses salvation by good deeds and self-improvement. In each of the first three degrees, the Lodge promises the candidate that God will reward him if he does good deeds and improves his character. To prove that Masonry teaches a "works salvation" in each of the first three degrees, we only need read the standard Monitors (official textbooks containing Masonic ritual), which are more or less uniform for each state.

Beginning with the First Degree (Entered Apprentice), the Lodge uses the symbol of the *lambskin* to impress upon the candidate the following instruction:

> In all ages the lamb has been deemed an emblem of innocence; he, therefore, who wears the Lambskin as a badge of Masonry is continually reminded of that purity of life and conduct which is necessary to obtain admittance into the Celestial Lodge above [heaven], where the Supreme Architect of the Universe [God] presides.[1]

But although this instruction is important to the Lodge, the Bible rejects this particular teaching. According to the Bible, Masons cannot gain entrance into the Celestial Lodge by their "purity of life and conduct." On the contrary, the Scriptures teach:

> He [God] saved us, *not on the basis of deeds which we have done in righteousness*, but according to His mercy, by the washing of regeneration and renewing by the Holy Spirit. (Titus 3:5; italics added)

> And the witness is this, that God has given us eternal life, and this life is in His son. He who has the Son has the life; he who does not have the Son of God does not have the life. (1 John 5:11-12)

How can a Christian allow himself to be initiated into Masonry when he has to swear to uphold teachings clearly rejected by the Bible? Possibly, many Masons may not realize Masonic teachings are in direct conflict with biblical teachings. If so, consider another example of the conflict between the Lodge and the Bible.

HUMAN INABILITY

In the Second Degree ("Fellow Craft" Degree) of Masonry, the ritual imparts the following instruction:

> The apron of a Mason is intended to remind him of purity of mind and morals. . . . Thus you will wear your apron while laboring among us as a speculative Fellow Craft, to distinguish you from the Entered Apprentices, ever remembering that

you are to wear it as an emblem of that purity of heart and conscience that is necessary to obtain for you the approval of the Grand Architect of the Universe.[2]

Here again the candidate is impressed with the necessity of good works to earn God's favor. He is to "ever remember" that his apron is worn as an emblem of the "purity of heart and conscience" required to gain God's approval. But the Bible clearly offers no hope in this area:

> "The heart is deceitful above all things and beyond cure. Who can understand it? I the Lord search the heart and examine the mind." (Jeremiah 17:9-10; NIV*)

> For all of us have become like one who is unclean, and all our righteous deeds are like a filthy garment; and all of us wither like a leaf, and our iniquities, like the wind, take us away. (Isaiah 64:6)

In light of what the Bible says, can any Mason really think he will stand before the gaze of the infinitely holy God who searches all hearts (Leviticus 19:2; 1 Samuel 2:2; 6:20; Isaiah 57:15) and be considered worthy of heaven? What can any Mason do to rid himself of those blots on his record? What about his sins? If the Bible reveals that God sees every man as a sinner who needs a Savior, how will a man ever be allowed into heaven without Jesus as his Savior (1 John 2:2; 4:9-10)? The Bible says this of man's standing before God:

> All have sinned and fall short of the glory of God. (Romans 3:23)

> As it is written: "There is no one righteous, not even one; there is no one who understands, no one who seeks God. All have turned away, they have together become worthless." (Romans 3:10-12; NIV)

To forgive our sins "the Father has sent the Son to be the Savior of the world. Whoever confesses that Jesus is the Son of God, God abides in him, and he in God" (1 John 4:14-15). If

* *New International Version.*

Masonry teaches a man's good works can fit him for heaven, this makes believing on Jesus as personal Savior merely optional.

THE BASIS FOR DIVINE ACCEPTANCE

In the Third Degree (the degree of Master Mason), the Lodge promises each candidate that, at his death, God will reward him with heavenly rewards on the basis of his "conduct," "deeds," "thoughts," and "the record of his whole life and actions." At death the Lodge places the white apron he received in the First Degree upon him as he lies in his coffin. From that day until he dies, he is to remember this:

> Let its pure and spotless surface be to you *an ever present reminder* of purity of life and rectitude of conduct, a never ending argument for nobler deeds, for higher thoughts, for greater achievements. And when those weary feet shall come to the end of their toilsome journey, and from your nerveless grasp shall drop forever the working tools of life, *may the record of your whole life and actions* be as pure and spotless as the fair emblem I have placed in your hands tonight. *And when at that last great day* your poor, trembling soul stands naked and alone before the great white throne, *may it be your portion to hear* from Him who sitteth as the Judge Supreme the welcome words, "Well done, good and faithful servant, *enter thou into the joy of thy Lord.*" (Italics added)[5]

When a Mason dies, the Lodge tells his family and friends at his funeral service that his soul went to heaven to reside in the "Celestial Lodge Above." And though it is admitted the man did not live a perfect life, the Lodge confidently states that he has been accepted into heaven based on his willingness to live by the truths and principles of Masonry. The Masonic funeral service teaches that

> Masonry has come down from the far past. It uses the tools of the builders' trade as emblems and symbols to teach Masons how to build character and moral stature.... It seeks constantly to build the temple of the soul and thus *to fit us for that house not made with hands, eternal in the heavens....* Masons believe sincerely that when life on earth comes to a

close, the soul is translated from the imperfections of this mortal sphere, to that all-perfect, glorious and Celestial Lodge Above, where God, the Grand Architect of the Universe, presides. With these truths and convictions, our brother was well acquainted. Though perfection of character is not of this world, yet we are persuaded that our brother sought to live by these truths and principles of Masonry. . . . When our brother labored with us in Masonic attire, he wore a white apron, which he was taught is an emblem of innocence and a badge of a Mason. By it, he was constantly reminded of that *purity of life and that rectitude of conduct so necessary to his gaining admission into the Celestial Lodge Above.* He will now wear that apron forever as the emblem of the virtues it represents [i.e., good works]. . . . In accordance with our custom, I now place this evergreen over the heart of our brother. (Italics added)[4]

But on what basis can the Masonic Lodge tell Masons what God will do when they die? By what authority does the Lodge so confidently assert to all who are listening that they will enter into God's presence and be accepted because of their good works? Scripture clearly teaches that this is impossible! The Bible emphasizes this again and again:

> Not by works of righteousness which we have done, but according to His mercy He saved us. (Titus 3:5; NKJV*)

> Where, then, is boasting? It is excluded. . . . For we maintain that a man is justified by faith apart from observing the law. . . . David says the same thing when he speaks of the blessedness of the man to whom God credits righteousness apart from works. (Romans 3:27-28; 4:6; NIV)

The apostle Paul told Timothy, "From childhood you have known the sacred writings which are able to give you the wisdom that leads to salvation through faith which is in Christ Jesus" (2 Timothy 3:15). None will deny that a committed Mason is zealous for his God. But even more so were the Israelites of Paul's time, and notice what he said about them:

* *New King James Version.*

> Brothers, my heart's desire and prayer to God for the Israel-
> ites is that they may be saved. For I can testify about them that
> they are zealous for God, *but their zeal is not based on
> knowledge.* Since they did not know the righteousness that
> comes from God [by faith] and sought to establish their own
> [by works], they did not submit to God's righteousness. (Ro-
> mans 10:1-3; NIV; italics added)

> For it is by grace you have been saved, through faith—and
> this not from yourselves, it is the gift of God—not by works,
> so that no one can boast. (Ephesians 2:8-9; NIV)

So you see, the Bible is absolutely clear that teaching salvation by personal merit, goodness, and works is something
that is utterly opposed to the will of God. Rather, salvation is by
grace; it is the free gift of God, provided for humanity when
Christ died and paid the penalty for our sins:

> And if [salvation is] by grace, then it is no longer by works; if
> it were, grace would no longer be grace. (Romans 11:6; NIV)

> Know that a man is not justified by observing the law, but by
> faith in Jesus Christ. So we, too, have put our faith in Christ
> Jesus that we may be justified by faith in Christ and not by
> observing the law, because by observing the law no one will
> be justified. . . . I do not set aside the grace of God, for if righ-
> teousness could be gained through the law, Christ died for
> nothing! (Galatians 2:16, 21; NIV)

> All who rely on observing the law are under a curse, for it is
> written: "Cursed is everyone who does not continue to do
> everything written in the Book of the Law." Clearly no one is
> justified before God by the law, because, "The righteous will
> live by faith." (Galatians 3:10-11; NIV)

> Tell me, you who want to be under the law, are you not
> aware of what the law says? . . . So the law was put in charge
> to lead us to Christ that we might be justified by faith. (Gala-
> tians 4:21; 3:24; NIV)

If you are a Christian Mason and know that the Bible
teaches this, how can you possibly justify being a Mason? Does
the Bible not teach that all men are sinners and that the only
way to enter into right standing with God is on the basis of plac-

ing one's complete faith in His Son, Jesus Christ? Does the Bible not promise that if a man totally relies on Jesus, admitting and turning from his sin, this results in his justification? (To be justified means that God Himself declares men perfectly righteous before Him solely on the basis of belief on Jesus and acceptance of Him as Savior and Lord of their lives.[5]) Because Christ paid the penalty for each man's sin when He died on the cross, God is now able to offer salvation as an entirely free gift. Therefore, Masonry is wrong in teaching that salvation can be earned.

That is why the apostle can write that all believers *"are justified freely* by his grace through the redemption that came by Christ Jesus" (Romans 3:24; NIV) and that in Christ "we have redemption through his blood, the forgiveness of sins, in accordance with the riches of God's grace that he lavished on us with all wisdom and understanding" (Ephesians 1:7-8; NIV).

But the Masonic Lodge denies these Scriptures and continues to promise Masons that their own righteousness will save them and make them acceptable before God. For example, in the Masonic *Monitor*, Masons are taught that the symbol for God is the All-Seeing Eye. And when they teach about God, they tell Masons that God will reward them according to their works: "[The] All-Seeing Eye . . . pervades the inmost recesses of the human Heart, and will reward us *according to our merits* [works]" (italics added).[6] Masons are also taught that they are to devote all their energies to attaining this merit before God so that they will be rewarded with heaven:

> Let all the energies of our souls and the perfection of our minds be employed in attaining the approbation [approval] of the Grand Master on high, so that when we come to die, . . . we gain the favor of a speedy entrance to the Grand Lodge on high, where the G.A. of T.U. [Grand Architect of the Universe, i.e., God] forever resides, and where, seated at his right hand, he may be pleased to pronounce us upright men and Masons.[7]

Not only does the Masonic Lodge promise Masons in the first three degrees that their own good works will make them acceptable before God, but also in the higher degrees of the

Scottish Rite and the York Rite. In all, *Masonry has forty degrees teaching its candidates salvation by personal merit.*

In the 19th Degree of the Scottish Rite, Masons are referred to "who have given proof of their attachment to the statutes and rules of the order, which in the end will *make them deserving* of entering the celestial Jerusalem [heaven]" (italics added).[8] Further, in the 28th Degree of the Scottish Rite, we are told, "the true Mason [is one] who raises himself by degrees till he reaches heaven."[9] In that same degree, the candidate is asked, "What more dost thou desire?" He replies, "To divest myself of original sin."[10]

In the Fifth Degree of the Scottish Rite, Masonry "teaches us that we cannot arrive at the Sanctum Sanctorum [heaven] but by purity of manners, righteousness of heart, and the secrets of the first degrees of which they are the school. . . . To remind me that by being dead in vice, I must hope to rise in virtue."[11]

In the Eighth Degree of the Scottish Rite, the Mason is told that "it is required in this degree . . . to show that it is only gradually [that] we can arrive at perfection."[12] In the 12th Degree of the Scottish Rite, we find the following:

> Now my illustrious brother, is the auspicious moment, place your trust in the Great Architect of Heaven and Earth, take justice for your Polar Star, prudence at the helm, temperance for your guide, let your sails fill with the gentle breeze of charity and you will in the end find yourself moored in that peaceful harbor, where the wicked cease from troubling and the weary are at rest.[13]

In the 14th Degree of the Scottish Rite, the candidate is told

> May your heart ever throb with a hope of immortality, may your lips ever invoke the true name of the Grand Architect of the Universe, and may your eyes behold him face to face and not fail when they awake in the dazzling glory of his presence. I now stamp you with the seal of the Grand Architect of the Universe, to the end that you may always live in his adorable presence and that he may always be in your heart and mind and that an ardent zeal and constancy may always be the rule of all your actions.[14]

In the 24th Degree of the Scottish Rite, the candidate is admonished, "Let it ever remind thee that none but the pure of heart can be admitted to the Holy Tabernacle in the heavens."[15] In the initiation instruction of the 17th Degree of the Scottish Rite, the candidate is told that this ritual "is supposed to represent the end of the world when all good Masons receive their reward by being conducted to a throne at the right hand of the All Puissant [God], having been purified by washing their robes in their own blood."[16]

All of this is why Sovereign Grand Commander Henry C. Clausen has stated that *each* of the thirty-two degrees of the Scottish Rite "teach by ceremony and instruction" that the "noblest purposes and duties of man" are to struggle for his own salvation, that each Mason is to overcome and win, "to reach the spiritual and divine within himself," because "man is . . . an eternal soul advancing ever nearer and nearer to perfection."[17] One of the most well-known and eminent Masonic authorities was Albert Pike, who taught that "step by step men must advance toward Perfection; and each Masonic degree is meant to be one of those steps."[18]

It is not only the Blue Lodge and Scottish Rite that teach salvation by human effort and personal righteousness. The higher degrees of the York Rite also teach this doctrine. In the Royal Arch Degree of the York Rite, the candidate is told that "white is emblematic of that purity of life and rectitude of conduct, *by which alone* we can expect to gain admission into the Holy of Holies above" (italics added).[19] In the Mark Master Degree of the York Rite, the initiate is promised Divine acceptance for good works:

> As a Mark Master Mason we learn the great truth that the Eternal Father is no respecter of persons, but will bestow the gifts of his beneficent hand alike to each one who sincerely labors to obey his righteous law. . . . If we but do our duty, if we are faithful and earnest, we shall receive our wages in a clear conscience, and in the commendation "well done good and faithful servant."[20]

> If we are victorious in our endeavors to reach the goal set · before us, we shall receive for our reward . . . the passport for our admission into the Celestial Lodge above.[21]

All of Masonry is actively committed to teaching "works salvation," opposing itself to the gospel of Jesus Christ. Over and over again, Masonry teaches that a man must be "worthy of life after death,"[22] and entrance into the Celestial Lodge is possible if the candidate is willing to give "service and obedience" to Masonry[23] and live his life regulated by "morality, faith and justice."[24]

Through the Lodge or Through Christ?

Masonry feels itself superior to Christianity because of its confidence in its way of "works salvation." As former 33d Degree Worshipful Master Jim Shaw recalls:

> Never in all my years of dedicated service to Masonry did anyone in the lodge witness to me about the love and saving grace of Jesus. The lodge attended a church once each year as a group. Each time the pastor (who was himself a Mason) would introduce us to the congregation and then exalt the craft, telling them about all our wonderful works. We usually left the church thinking of how wonderful we were and feeling sorry for all those in the church who were not Masons, participating in all our good deeds.[25]

The *Guide to the Royal Arch Chapter* charges the chaplain of the Order to instruct men in the Lodge to believe that "by refining our morals, strengthening our virtues, and purifying our minds, [this will] prepare us for admission into the society of those above whose happiness will be as endless as it is perfect."[26] Even in the Masonic edition of the Bible (published by Holman) one can find listed under the "Masonic Creed" the bold assertion that "character determines destiny."[27] Likewise, the Masonic symbol of the ladder teaches each Mason that he can climb his way to heaven by his own good deeds:

> As to the modern Masonic symbolism of the ladder, it is, as Brother Mackey has already said, a symbol of progress, such as it is in all the old initiations. Its three principal rounds, representing Faith, Hope, and Charity, *present us with the means of advancing from earth to heaven*, from death to life —from the mortal to immortality. Hence its foot is placed on

the ground floor of the Lodge, which is typical of the world, and its top rests on the covering of the Lodge, which is symbolic of heaven. (Italics added)[28]

All of the examples from Masonic ritual cited above are why Masonic authorities everywhere—including Coil, Mackey, and Clausen—teach that men are saved by their good works. Masonic publications agree. In *The Pennsylvania Freemason*, Pennsylvania Grand Chaplain Charles H. Lacquement writes:

> Freemasonry has been teaching for centuries . . . the capability of man to reach a higher level of perfection through education and training. . . . The philosophy of Freemasonry is to make man the master of his own destiny, to show him that there also is an immortality on earth brought by his actions; that he can, *through his own efforts, . . . inscribe his name in the "Book of Life."* (Italics added)[29]

Masons consider that their deeds are so good they deserve God's favor. "Freemasons worship the creator through acts deserving of divine approval."[30] Masons are told, "By . . . a pure and blameless life . . . [God] will be pleased to pronounce us just and upright Masons."[31] Leading Masonic authority Henry Wilson Coil describes how many Masons depend solely on the teachings of the Masonic Lodge to get them into heaven: "Freemasonry has [its] religious service to commit the body of a deceased brother to the dust whence it came, and to speed the liberated spirit back to the Great Source of Light. Many Freemasons make this flight with *no other guarantee of a safe landing than their belief in the religion of Freemasonry*" (italics added).[32]

If you were to hear all of this taught to you in the Lodge, would you not think that you can go to the "Celestial Lodge Above" if you live a pure life and engage in good deeds? Is this not teaching a person he can be saved by his own works and personal righteousness? When the Lodge teaches a man that by his good life, and by his good deeds, God will admit him into heaven, is that not contrary to Christian teaching? Is that not "another gospel"(Galatians 1:6-8)?

But in spite of all this evidence, Masons officially deny that Masonry teaches salvation by works. In a debate on "The John Ankerberg Show," Mason William Mankin, a professing Christian, looked straight into the eyes of the audience and told them:

> [Masonry] is not a religion. *It offers no system of salvation.* . . . Our symbols are related to the development of character, of the relationship of man to man. They are working tools to be used in the building of life. These working tools have been used from time immemorial to build buildings, and all we are saying is that if you as an individual adopt the principles represented [in Masonry], . . . you will be a better person. *Not that you're going to go to heaven.* (Italics added)[33]

In a similar fashion, the Board of General Purpose of the United Grand Lodge of England published a tract in 1985 entitled *Freemasonry and Religion.* It baldly asserts that Masonry "does not claim to lead to salvation by works, by secret knowledge, or by any other means."[34] But former Worshipful Master Mason Jack Harris flatly contradicts such statements:

> In all the rituals that *I* taught for eleven years, *Masonry did teach how to get to heaven.* They taught it with the apron that I wore, by my purity [of] life and conduct. They taught it in the Hiram Abiff legend in the third degree [symbolizing] the immortality of the soul. Through all their writings they say they are teaching the immortality of the soul to the Mason. But the Word of God tells me that the only way to have immortal life is through the Person of Jesus Christ. Never at any Masonic ritual did they point out that Jesus is the way of salvation. (Italics added)[35]

The evidence is clear. Masonry is promising men in the Lodge that they can get to heaven by being good. But we have seen that God pronounces a curse upon such a false and destructive teaching (Galatians 1:6-8). No Christian should ever join such a non-Christian fellowship, swear his allegiance to such nonbiblical teachings, support it with his time and efforts, contribute financially to its welfare and promotion, and claim that this false gospel is the true teaching of Jesus Christ and the Bible.

Jesus told us that a bad tree could not bear good fruit (Matthew 7:18). A testimony from the days of the Civil War is perhaps sufficient to illustrate the real problem of the "fruit" of Masonry. Steven Merritt was Master of the largest Lodge in New York. He left Masonry because, "I found the tendency of the whole thing evil, . . . so I protested and left."[36] In particular, he left Masonry because of the agony of a dying friend:

> One incident helped to open my eyes. I have always preached that there is no other name but Christ by which we can be saved. But again and again I found Masons dying without God and without hope. I was called to the bedside of one member of my lodge who was thought to be dying. He gave me the grip as I sat down by him. He said he was dying and was in great distress for his soul. I tried to have him look to Christ. But he reproached me, saying I had led him astray. I had told him in the lodge, as Master, that a moral life was enough. He said, "You told me then that it was all right if I was an upright man, and obeyed the precepts of the lodge, but I am leaning on a broken reed; and now I am dying without God. I lay this to your charge, Worshipful Master. I leaned on you and now I am dying."[37]

Dying apart from Christ: this is the "fruit" and real testimony of Masonry. And only eternity shall be able to judge its true weight. Merritt warns that when "ministers and other good men are in the Lodge, they help to make it a delusion and a snare."[38] In other words, men are drawn by the alleged outward goodness of Masonry and caught in a system that will lead to their eternal destruction. This is the very reason that Scripture warns, "See to it that no one takes you captive through hollow and deceptive philosophy, which depends on human tradition and the basic principles of this world rather than on Christ" (Colossians 2:8; NIV).

Frighteningly, the apostle Paul warns that it is the same devil who lied to Adam and Eve in the garden who is behind false gospels, such as the one found in the Lodge. He says,

But I am afraid that just as Eve was deceived by the serpent's cunning, your minds may somehow be led astray.... For if someone comes to you and preaches ... *a different gospel* from the one you accepted, you put up with it easily enough. ... And no wonder, for Satan himself masquerades as an angel of light. It is not surprising, then, if his servants [those teaching a different gospel] masquerade as servants of righteousness. Their end will be what their actions deserve. (2 Corinthians 11:3, 4, 14-15; italics added; NIV)

Again, we stress that Masonry's plan of salvation is so contrary to God's way of salvation that Scripture places it under a divine curse (Galatians 1:6-8). The following Scriptures plainly state the biblical position on how a man can gain eternal life:

And there is salvation in no one else [other than Jesus Christ]; for there is no other name under heaven that has been given among men, by which we must be saved. (Acts 4:12)

To the man who does not work but trusts God who justifies the wicked, his faith is credited as righteousness. (Romans 4:5; NIV)

The verses quoted in this chapter demonstrate the scriptural truth that salvation is a *gift* of God. Salvation comes solely by the grace (unmerited favor) of God, not by anything we can do to earn God's favor or by personal righteousness. By being a part of the Lodge, a Christian Mason is supporting "another gospel," a false system of salvation that lies to people about how they may be saved.

If you are a true believer in Jesus Christ, realizing what the Lodge believes and teaches, should you not obey the biblical admonition in 2 Corinthians 6:14-17 and leave the Lodge?

Do not be yoked together with unbelievers. For what do righteousness and wickedness have in common? Or what fellowship can light have with darkness? What harmony is there between Christ and Belial? What does a believer have in common with an unbeliever? What agreement is there between the temple of God and idols? For we are the temple of the living God. As God has said: "I will live with them and walk among them, and I will be their God, and they will be my people. Therefore come out from them and be separate," says the Lord. "Touch no unclean thing, and I will receive you." (NIV)

Those pastors or Christian leaders who have Masons on the church board or staff should express their genuine concern and take whatever action is necessary to safeguard the purity of God's church.

Make then the Holy Bible, that Great Light in Masonry, the man of your counsels, and the meditation of your heart.
From the Past Master Degree of the York Rite
Sheville and Gould, *Guide to the Royal Arch Chapter*, p. 93.

6

The Rule of Faith and Practice

Even as Masonry claims that it does not teach a system of salvation, but does, and as it teaches that it is not a religion, but is, Masonry also claims that it honors the Bible as God's Word, but does not. Masonry does "affirm" the Bible. The standard Masonic *Monitor* claims that the Bible is "the great light in Masonry" and even advises Masons to study it diligently:

> I particularly direct your attention to the Great Light in Masonry, the Holy Bible. Howsoever men differ in creed or theology, all good men are agreed that within the covers of the Holy Bible are found those principles of morality which lay the foundation upon which to build a righteous life. Freemasonry therefore opens this Book on its altars, with the command to each of its votaries that he diligently study therein to learn the way to everlasting life.[1]

The Masonic *Monitor* declares the following: "The three great lights in Masonry are the Holy Bible, Square and Compass, and are thus explained: the Holy Bible is given us as the rule and guide for our faith and practice."[2] Masonic authorities teach that "with us, the Bible is supreme. . . . Its truth is inwrought in the fiber of our being."[3]

THE BIBLE AS SYMBOL

But Masonry really believes the Bible is merely a *symbol*, a symbol for the will of God. In the Masonic Bible, the *Holman Temple Illustrated Edition of the Holy Bible*, Masonic scholar Joseph Fort Newton wrote the following in a preface:

> *The Bible*, so rich in symbolism, *is itself a symbol*. . . . It is a sovereign symbol of the Book of Faith, the will of God as man has learned it in the midst of the years—that perpetual revelation of himself which God is making to mankind in every land in every age. Thus, by the very honor which Masonry pays to the Bible, it teaches us to revere [honor and respect] every book of faith . . . *joining hands with the man of Islam* as he takes oath on the Koran, *and with the Hindu* as he makes covenant with God upon the book that he loves best. For Masonry knows, what so many forget, that religions are many, but Religion is one—perhaps we may say one thing. . . . Therefore it invites to its altar men of all faiths knowing that, if they use different names for "the Nameless One of a hundred names," they are yet praying to the one God and Father of all; knowing, also, that while they read *different volumes*, they are in fact reading *the same vast Book of the Faith of Man*. (Italics added)[4]

This makes it clear that, for Masonry, the Bible is not a "rule and guide for faith and practice," but only a symbol. We all know what a symbol is. The American flag is a symbol of freedom. The flag itself is not freedom; it is a piece of cloth symbolizing freedom. In the same way, Masonry teaches that the Bible itself is not God's Word; it is only words on paper symbolizing God's Word. This is why the Bible is officially designated as a piece of "lodge furniture." That's all the Bible is—furniture. The flag is cloth, the Bible is furniture. They are important only because they represent or symbolize something else.

This symbol points Masons to another source of information. The Bible and the scriptures of all other faiths really point to Masonic doctrine.[5] That's why Masonry does not object to Masons in Utah placing the *Book of Mormon* upon the Masonic altar instead of the Bible. That's why Masonry does not object to Masons placing the *Vedas* or *Upanishads* on their Masonic altar in India. That's why Masons in Muslim lands can place the *Koran* on their altar. None of these books are to be followed literally as truth; they are only to be honored as symbols of truth.

THE BIBLE AS FURNITURE

But what value is the Bible to the Lodge if it is only a symbol? One of the greatest of Masonic scholars, Albert Pike, explains how Masonry *uses a candidate's reverence for the Bible* to commit him to the Lodge:

> The Bible is an indispensable part of the furniture of a *Christian* Lodge, *only because* it is the sacred book of the Christian religion. The Hebrew Pentateuch in a Hebrew Lodge, and Koran in a Mohammedan one, belong on the Altar. . . . The obligation of the candidate is always to be taken on the sacred book or books of his religion, *that he may deem it more solemn and binding*; and therefore it was that you were asked of what religion you were. *We have no other concern with your religious creed.* (Italics added)[6]

Thus, in the obligation (oath) of the 10th Degree of the Scottish Rite, the candidate states, "I, _____, do promise and swear upon the Holy Bible . . . to keep exactly in my heart all the secrets that shall be revealed to me."[7] In the initiation of the 14th Degree of the Scottish Rite, the Thrice Puissant says to the candidate, "My brother, you are now in the most sacred and secret place in Masonry, the sacred mysteries of which are now going to be revealed to you as we repose the utmost confidence in your discretion. Come, my brother, add to our satisfaction by swearing (upon your holy book) fidelity to us."[8]

From this we can see that the only purpose Masonry has for recognizing the scriptures of all faiths is to get men to swear allegiance to Masonry on the authority of the scriptures they hold dear. Men swear upon their sacred scriptures to obey Masonic religious beliefs that deny and distort what their sacred scriptures really teach. In doing so, Masonry mocks and profanes each faith's holy "symbol."

This leads us to a startling conclusion: the Christian and those of other faiths have been callously deceived. Masonry has only used the Christian's respect for the Bible to get him to swear allegiance to Masonry. Why? Obviously, Masonry cannot ask a Christian to swear his allegiance on the Koran or the Upanishads when he does not believe these are authoritative scriptures. But since Christians believe the Bible is holy and sacred, Masonry asks him to swear upon it. Masonry practices the same in regard to other faiths and their respective holy books. Put simply, Masonry has no real respect for the *contents* of holy books, only an appreciation of their motivating power to secure one's commitment to Masonry. As Pike has said, "We have no other concern for your religious creed."

FIVE DISTINCT TEACHINGS

Masonry never intended that Christians would keep and follow their Bibles, for to do so would be to deny the distinctive teachings of Masonry. Proof of this may be seen in the following statements by Masonic authorities Coil, Mackey, and others. From these men we learn that Masonry has at least five distinct teachings about the Bible:

The Bible is only a piece of Lodge furniture, a great "light" upon which the candidate obligates himself to Masonry.

Mackey's Revised Encyclopedia of Freemasonry teaches that "in the American system, the Bible is both a piece of furniture and a great light."[9]

The Bible is not really to be believed; it is only a symbol of the will of God.

Masonry teaches that the actual contents of the Bible are not the Word of God. In *Coil's Masonic Encyclopedia* we read, "The prevailing Masonic opinion is that the Bible is only a symbol of Divine Will, Law, or Revelation, and not that its *contents* are Divine Law, inspired, or revealed. So far, no responsible authority has held that a Freemason must believe the Bible or any part of it" (italics added).[10]

Masonic authority Silas H. Shepherd admits, "When our rituals and Monitors tell us the Bible is one of the Great Lights of Masonry and that as such it is the rule and guide to our faith, it can only be speaking symbolically, as it certainly is when speaking of the other two Great Lights, the square and the compass."[11]

Masonry considers the Bibles of other faiths equally authoritative or, more to the point, equally unauthoritative.

Mackey's Revised Encyclopedia of Freemasonry explains: "The Bible is used among Freemasons as a symbol of the will of God, however it may be expressed. Therefore, *whatever to any people expresses that will* [of God] *may be used as a substitute for the Bible in a Masonic Lodge. . . .* Whether it be the Gospels to the Christian, the Pentateuch to the Israelite, the Koran to the Musselman [Muslim] or the Vedas to the Brahman [Hindu], it everywhere Masonically conveys the same idea—that of the symbolism of the Divine Will revealed to man." (Italics added)[12]

Because the Bible is not the literal Word of God, it is not to be literally obeyed.

Masonic scholar Oliver D. Street frankly confesses, "The Bible is not displayed on our altars now and never has been for the reason that Masons are not required to believe its teachings. We know that there is a very large element of the Craft the world over who do not believe the teachings of the New Testament. . . . Hence, unless we are perpetrating a grim mockery, we do not employ the Bible as a profession that we as a Society accept all its teachings and doctrines."[13]

Masonic doctrine itself is the literal (true) Word of God.

Martin L. Wagner, an authority on Masonry, reveals, "The eminent Masons all contend that there is a veil upon the scriptures, which when removed, leaves them clearly in accord with Masonic teachings and in essential harmony with other sacred books."[14] Logically then, Masonry is the only divine truth that is to be obeyed.

In the higher degrees of Masonry we also find taught that Christians cannot properly interpret their own Bible. In the 28th Degree of the Scottish Rite, Albert Pike declares, "The Hebrew books [the Bible] were written in Symbols *unintelligible to the Profane* [i.e., the ignorant or the non-Mason]" (italics added).[15] In other words, only Masons can "properly interpret" the Bible. Martin L. Wagner comments:

> Charles Sotheran speaks of the Bible as a pseudo-revelation. ... Many Masonic writers ridicule the Christian doctrine that the Bible is a supernatural revelation from God. They say it is a book written for the vulgar, by the ancient priests, and that they concealed under its exoteric [outer or normal] language, the secret doctrine, which is the true Freemasonry.[16]

The Masonic view of the Bible is especially clear in Chase's *Digest of Masonic Law*, where he asserts:

> To require that a candidate profess a belief in the divine authority of the Bible is a serious innovation [violation] in the very body of Masonry. The Jews, the Chinese, the Turks, each reject either the Old or the New Testament, or both, and yet we see no good reason why they should not be made Masons. In fact, *Blue Lodge Masonry has nothing whatever to do with the Bible.* It is not founded on the Bible. If it were, it would not be Masonry. (Italics added)[17]

In conclusion, virtually all Masonic authorities "establish three things: (1) that the Bible is only a symbol, (2) that a Mason is not required to believe the Bible's teachings, and (3) that some other book may be substituted for the Bible."[18] This is why Masonic authority Rollin C. Blackmer, M.D., says that the Bible "is almost never read in the lodge. In thirty years of almost constant attendance at lodges in many jurisdictions, the writer has never heard the Bible read in the lodge, though portions of Scriptures are occasionally quoted in the ritualistic work."[19]

But these Masonic views concerning the Bible are in direct conflict with what the Bible claims about itself:

> All Scripture is inspired by God and profitable for teaching, for reproof, for correction, for training in righteousness; that the man of God may be adequate, equipped for every good work. (2 Timothy 3:16-17)
>
> No prophecy of Scripture is a matter of one's own interpretation, for no prophecy was ever made by an act of human will,

but men moved by the Holy Spirit spoke from God. (2 Peter 1:20-21)

Every word of God is tested; He is a shield to those who take refuge in Him. Do not add to His words, lest He reprove you, and you be proved a liar. (Proverbs 30:5-6)

Here is what Jesus taught about the Bible:

"The Scripture cannot be broken." (John 10:35)

"Sanctify them in the truth; Thy word is truth." (John 17:17)

"It is written, man shall not live on bread alone, but on every word that proceeds out of the mouth of God." (Matthew 4:4)

"The words which Thou gavest Me I have given them." (John 17:8)

"Heaven and earth will pass away, but My words shall not pass away." (Matthew 24:35)

"He who rejects Me, and does not receive My sayings, has one who judges him; the word I spoke is what will judge him at the last day. For I did not speak on my own initiative, but the Father Himself who sent Me has given Me commandment, what to say, and what to speak. . . . The things I speak, I speak just as the Father has told me." (John 12:48-50)

Christians know that the Bible is not simply to be read as a symbol or allegory—or to be ignored. The Bible is to be obeyed as the Word of God. Scripture emphasizes this repeatedly. What good does it do to talk about the Bible as the "Great Light" of Masonry if a person never turns on the switch? Masons everywhere swear the Bible is a great light but they never use it or obey it.

How can Christians who are Masons, those who claim to believe that the Bible is the literal Word of God, promote an organization that denies God's Word and denies what Jesus taught about the Bible?

Our Father who dwells in heaven [also dwells] in the hearts of all good Masons.

From the 13th Degree of the Scottish Rite
J. Blanchard, *Scottish Rite Masonry Illustrated*

7

The Fatherhood of God

Masonry believes that, because God is the Creator of all people, all people are automatically His spiritual sons, in right standing with Him. But here Masonry makes a false assumption. It assumes men are in right standing with God simply because He created them. But the Bible says all men have freely chosen to disobey God and have sinned. Therefore, they are not in right standing with God; they are sinners who justly stand under His condemnation and deserve His punishment.

God created Adam and Eve and gave them the right to obey or disobey Him. Man chose to disobey God and lost his perfect relationship—his sinless standing—before God. We today have followed in Adam's and Eve's footsteps, rebelling against God's laws, and we too deserve the righteous judgment of God. Masonry contradicts the Bible and teaches that even though we have sinned and maintain our rebellion against God, God will still honor and reward us.

THE MASONIC BELIEF

In the *Liturgy of the Ancient and Accepted Scottish Rite*, adherents are told: "Believe that there is a God; that he is our father; that he has a paternal interest in our welfare and improvement; . . . that he has destined us to a future life of endless progress toward perfection and a knowledge of himself."[1] According to Masonic authority Carl H. Claudy: "Among the most beautiful of Freemasonry's symbols, these [symbols revealing Masonic teachings] express at the very beginning the fundamental principle of Freemasonry: *the Fatherhood of God, and the brotherhood of man*" (italics added).[2]

Masonry holds that God is the Father of every man, regardless of his religious belief. There *is* a sense in which God is the Father of all men, "that the moral and emotional qualities of fatherhood remain in God toward all men."[3] We accept that the attributes of fatherhood are biblically applied to all people: God loves mankind as His special creation (Genesis 1:31; John 3:16); God is kind and benevolent to all people, even evil people (Matthew 5:44-45; Acts 14:17); God desires everyone to be saved (2 Peter 3:9); Christ died for all (1 John 2:2).

But as J. Sidlow Baxter points out, the universal fatherhood of God does *not* imply universal sonship (cf. John 1:12-13; Romans 8:14; Galatians 3:26). He makes a good point: that evangelicals, in their zeal to counter liberal theology, have denied the genuine fatherhood of God to all but a tiny minority. His biblical and logical documentation for this position is convincing.[4] What we should understand is this: although God may be the Father of all people, this does not make all people His spiritual children. This allows us to preserve the all-important concept of universal fatherhood without denying the genuine need of people to repent and have faith in Jesus Christ. When we criticize the Masonic doctrine of God's fatherhood, we are specifically taking exception to Masonry's assumption that the fatherhood of God also demands the conclusion that all Masons are thereby sons of God. Biblically, sonship comes only by personal faith in Jesus Christ.

Masonry has incorporated this doctrine into its ritual. As the Masonic *Monitor* says, "Vouchsafe thine aid, Almighty Father of the universe."[5] Contrary to biblical teaching, in the Second Degree of Masonry the Masonic initiate is told that the square, level, and plumb represent the *innate equality* of all people before God: "By them . . . we are reminded of the natural equality of the human family."[6]

Masonry teaches in the 13th Degree that "our Father who dwells in heaven [also dwells] in the hearts of all good Masons." In the initiation of this Degree of the Scottish Rite we are told, "God is infinite, he dwelleth in all, with all, and beyond all." The higher degrees even teach that "the Holy Spirit [dwells] in the hearts of [all] those that observe faithfully the laws" of Masonry.[7]

One of the strongest statements in all of the Masonic rituals concerning the true goal of Masonry polarizes the issue:

> In all the preceding degrees you must have observed that the object of Scotch Masonry is to overthrow all kinds of superstition, and that by admitting in her bosom on the terms of the strictest equality, the members of all religions, of all creeds and of all countries, without any distinction whatever, she has, and indeed can have, but one single object and that is to restore to the Grand Architect of the Universe; to the common father of the human race those who are lost in the maze of impostures, invented for the sole purpose of enslaving them. The Knights Kadosh recognize no particular religion, and for that reason we demand of you nothing more than to worship God. And whatever may be the religious forms imposed upon you by superstition at a period of your life when you were incapable of discerning truth from falsehood, we do not even require you to relinquish them. Time and study alone can enlighten you. But remember that *you will never be a true mason unless you repudiate forever all superstitions and prejudices.* (Italics added)[8]

This ritual quotation from the 30th Degree reveals four important truths concerning Masonic goals:

This citation reveals the core belief of Masonry: the doctrine of the fatherhood of God.

Masonry had promised the candidate in its earlier degrees that it would not hinder him from following his own religious beliefs (see chapter 2). But here it shows that this was only a ruse—a lie—in order to get a person started in Masonry. The goal of the Lodge was always to eventually change the person's original beliefs (see chapter 15). And notice: original religious beliefs are labeled as "superstition."

This ritual also teaches that all men are lost—in spiritual darkness—and not true Masons until they accept this premise.

This statement reveals that the true goal of the Masonic Lodge is to have its initiates finally drop and repudiate their previous religious beliefs—their "superstitions and prejudices"—and to accept the final and only truth of Masonry.

All the above is why Masonry claims that it alone is the true religion (see chapter 15). For example, in the 13th Degree of the Scottish Rite the candidate is told in his initiation, "If then we wish order and peace to prevail on earth, we must be united; we must have *but one will, but one mind.* Both we find *in the teachings of Masonry only,* and against that compact of unity, tyranny and usurpation, whether religious or political, *must fall subdued and powerless.*" Thus, the candidate is assured, "Masonry, victorious over all adverse circumstances, will become the honored medium of uniting all mankind in one vast brotherhood." In fact, the Mason swears the following oath to enforce this philosophy: "I, _____, solemnly and sincerely promise and swear wholly to devote myself to the emancipation of humanity. . . . To strive unceasingly for . . . the propagation of light and for the overthrow of superstition."[9]

THE SCRIPTURAL TEACHING

This doctrine of the universal fatherhood of God is not biblical. Scripture is clear that only those who receive and believe on Jesus Christ have a proper standing with God and are His true sons.

> But as many as received Him [Jesus Christ], to them He gave the right to become children of God, even to those who believe in His name. (John 1:12)

> While you have the light, believe in the light [Jesus Christ], in order that you may become sons of light. (John 12:36)

> Now what you worship as something unknown I am going to proclaim to you. The God who made the world and everything in it is the Lord of heaven and earth and does not live in temples built by hands. And he is not served by human

> hands, as if he needed anything, because he himself gives all
> men life and breath and everything else.... Therefore since
> we are God's offspring, we should not think that the divine
> being is like gold or silver or stone—an image made by
> man's design and skill.... But now he commands all people
> everywhere to repent. For he has set a day when he will
> judge the world with justice by the man [Jesus Christ] he has
> appointed. He has given proof of this to all men by raising
> him from the dead. (Acts 17:23*b*-25, 29, 30*b*-31; NIV)

The Bible teaches that all men are God's "offspring" by
virtue of their creation by God. But they are not His *spiritual*
children. This is obvious from the fact that Jesus gives to those
who believe on Him the right to *become* children of God. God
does not have an intimate father/son relationship with all people. It seems Masonry has forgotten, or chosen to ignore, the
account of man's Fall in Genesis. The Bible teaches that man,
through disobedience to God, sinned and broke his spiritual
relationship with God. Now God "commands all people everywhere to repent." *To repent* means that we must be willing to
turn away from our beliefs and our own way of doing things,
and turn to and act on God's promises and instructions.

The apostle Paul did not hesitate to teach that only those
persons who have placed their faith in Christ become God's
spiritual sons: "For you [believers] are all sons of God *through
faith in Christ Jesus*" (Galatians 3:26; NIV; italics added). The
Scriptures clearly teach that all those outside of Christ are spiritually cursed and under God's wrath—not blessed by God and
accepted by Him:

> Whoever believes in the Son has eternal life, but whoever re-
> jects the Son will not see life, for God's wrath remains on
> him. (John 3:36; NIV)

> For as many as are of the works of the Law are under a curse;
> for it is written, "Cursed is everyone who does not abide by
> all things written in the book of the law, to perform them."
> (Galatians 3:10)

> Among them we too all formerly lived in the lusts of our
> flesh, indulging the desires of the flesh and of the mind, and
> were *by nature children of wrath*, even as the rest.... Re-

member that you were at that time *separate from Christ* . . .
and strangers to the covenants of promise, *having no hope
and without God* in the world. . . . being darkened in their
understanding, excluded from the life of God, because of the
ignorance that is in them, because of the hardness of their
heart. (Ephesians 2:3, 12; 4:18; cf. 2 Peter 2:14-15)

The Bible's teaching on this point is strong and clear. It
cannot be ignored or dismissed. Only the believer in Christ is
God's true child: "See how great a love the Father has bestowed
upon us, that we should be called children of God; and such we
are. For this reason the world does not know us, because it did
not know Him" (1 John 3:1, cf. Romans 9:27). Those who do not
accept God's free gift of salvation, those who do not believe in
Christ, cannot possibly be God's children (John 17:3-16).

Only those to whom God has given the Holy Spirit and
who are led by the Spirit of God are God's children: "For all
who are being led by the Spirit of God, these are sons of
God. . . . The Spirit Himself bears witness with our spirit that we
are children of God, and if children, heirs also, heirs of God
and fellow heirs with Christ, if indeed we suffer with Him in
order that we may also be glorified with Him" (Romans 8:14,
16-17).

Can Masonry possibly be led by the Holy Spirit when it
denies everything the Spirit of God has inspired in the Scriptures (2 Timothy 3:16; 2 Peter 1:21)? Is the Mason willing to
identify with and suffer for Christ, or is he embarrassed by
Christ and not willing to follow Him fully? Only those who love
God (Romans 8:28) and obey Christ are God's children:

> And by this we know that we have come to know Him [Jesus],
> if we keep His commandments. (1 John 2:3)

> Therefore be imitators of God, as beloved children; and walk
> in love, just as Christ also loved you, and gave Himself up for
> us, an offering and a sacrifice to God. (Ephesians 5:1-2)

In the end, all men are either living for God or living for
self, whether they realize this or not. There are true sons of
God, but there are also rebellious sinners who are sons of the
"evil one." Jesus taught this in His parable of the sower: "And

he answered and said, 'The one who sows the good seed is the Son of Man, and the field is the world; and as for the good seed, these are the sons of the kingdom; and the tares are the *sons of the evil one*; and the enemy who sowed them is the devil'" (Matthew 13:37-39; italics added).

In His discussion with the *religious* leaders of His day, Jesus said, "Why do you not understand what I am saying? It is because you cannot hear My word. *You are of your father the devil*, and you want to do the desires of your father. . . . He who is of God hears the words of God; for this reason you do not hear them, because you are not of God" (John 8:43, 44, 47; italics added).

The apostles Paul and John describe all men who have not believed on Christ in these words:

> And you were dead in your trespasses and sins, in which you formerly walked according to the course of this world, according to the prince of the power of the air, of the spirit [Satan] that is now working in the *sons of disobedience.* (Ephesians 2:1-2; italics added)

> By this the children of God and the *children of the devil* are obvious; anyone who does not practice righteousness is not of God, nor the one who does not love his brother. (1 John 3:10; italics added)

But Masonry denies all of this when it teaches that there are no "sons of disobedience" or "children of the devil" but that all men are by nature sons and children of God. As we have seen, the ritual also teaches that *all* Masons are erecting a temple in their hearts so that God can dwell in it.[10] But Scripture teaches that only the bodies of believers in Christ can be called the temple of God (1 Corinthians 3:9, 11, 16; 6:19; 2 Corinthians 6:15-16; Ephesians 2:19-22).

Masonry denies what the Bible teaches about man's relationship to God and about how a man can become God's child. Christ alone is God's Savior for all of mankind.

> Jesus answered, "I am the way and the truth and the life. No one comes to the Father except through me. If you really

knew me, you would know my Father as well. From now on, you do know him and have seen him." (John 14:6-7; NIV)

Salvation is found in no one else, for there is no other name under heaven given to men by which we must be saved. (Acts 4:12; NIV)

For there is one God and one mediator between God and men, the man Christ Jesus, who gave himself as a ransom for all men—the testimony given in its proper time. (1 Timothy 2:5-6; NIV)

How can Christian Masons continue to participate in the Lodge when it teaches that all men are already children of God and acceptable to Him? How can they remain in the Lodge when it teaches men that they do not need to place their faith in Jesus Christ? How can Christian pastors who are Masons continue to give their influence and authority to the Lodge, when it denies the very basis by which men become Christians?

> Masonry [is that religion] around whose altars the
> Christian, the Hebrew, the Moslem, the Brahman,
> the followers of Confucius and Zoroaster, can as-
> semble as brethren and unite in prayer to the one
> God who is above all the Baalim.
>
> Albert Pike
> *Morals and Dogma*

8

The Nature of God

If you are a Christian Mason and you truly believe the god of Masonry is the God of the Bible, this chapter is written for you. The god of Masonry is not the God of the Bible but a different god altogether. There can be no doubt that the Masonic rituals teach every Mason about "God."

NO ATHEISTS ARE PERMITTED MEMBERSHIP IN THE LODGE

In the charge given to those being initiated into the First Degree of the Blue Lodge (Entered Apprentice), each new candidate is told of three great duties he must perform: to God, to neighbor, and to self. Concerning God, the candidate is told he must vow "his belief and trust in God; and it is on that avowal alone that his admission among us is based."[1]

In the Second Degree of the Blue Lodge (Fellow Craft), the Mason is given more "divine light." He is introduced to the letter "G" and told "it is a symbol for God which alludes to the sacred name of Deity." During the ritual, each of the Masonic initiates must "with reverence most humbly bow" before "this sacred name of Deity."[2]

In the Third Degree of the Blue Lodge (Master Mason), while kneeling "on his naked knees, both hands resting on the Holy Bible," the Masonic initiate is promised that "nothing in

[Masonry] will interfere with the duty you owe to your God."
(This is a totally false promise, as will be seen later.) In addition, the initiate "most solemnly and sincerely promises and
swears" to the truth of all these things: "so help me God, and
keep me steadfast in due performance of the same." He then
kisses the Bible to seal his vow. Later, the Mason is again reminded that God "will reward us according to our works," and
"if we are found worthy," He will permit us entrance into His
heaven.[3]

In Masonry, all men swear to their belief in a Supreme Being. This is an absolute requirement for admission to Masonry.
In fact, the ritual commands each Mason that he "should never
engage in any undertaking on which [he] could not invoke the
blessing of Deity."[4]

Masonry offers various names for its god. In the First De-
gree, Masonry refers to its god as "the Almighty Father of the
Universe" and "The Great Architect of the Universe"
(G.A.O.T.U.). In the Second Degree, he is called "the Grand
Geometrician of the Universe" and "the Grand Artificer of the
Universe."[5] In the Third Degree, Masonry refers to its Deity as
"the Supreme Grand Architect of the Universe," "the Ideal
Good and the Ideal Beauty," and "the Master Workman of the
Universe."[6]

In the opening prayer of most monitors, Masons are
taught to pray in these words: "Great Architect of the Universe,
in Thy name we have assembled and in Thy name we desire to
proceed in all our doings."[7] Masons of all religions—Buddhists,
Hindus, Muslims, Jews, Christians, Mormons, Taoists, Shintoists
—all are instructed to swear by and pray to this god: "Vouchsafe Thine aid, Almighty Father of the Universe, to this our present convention; and grant that this candidate for Freemasonry
may dedicate and devote his life to Thy service."[8]

The instruction of the ritual reads: "Our Masonic career
was begun with an expression of our faith in God. Step by step
we were taught that in God we live and move and have our being. We learn that He is the Great Architect of the Universe.
... These truths give us ... the assurance that he that doeth the
will of God abideth forever."[9]

According to Martin L. Wagner, an authority on Masonry, this god—the Great Architect—is the god of Masonry:

> It is faith in this deity that, as a prerequisite for membership, is demanded at the door of the lodge of every candidate for Masonic honors. It is this deity in whose name the covenant is made, and who is invoked for help to keep it inviolate. It is to him that the prayers in the lodge are addressed, . . . whose praises are sung in Masonic odes and whose divinity is extolled. It is to him that Masonic altars are built, priests consecrated, sacrifices made, temples erected and solemnly dedicated. *This Great Architect of the Universe is the "one God" in Freemasonry and besides him there is no other in that institution.* Freemasonry as such knows no deity save the Great Architect of the Universe. (Italics added)[10]

It is evident, then, that Masonry teaches its members about its god. First, they must swear belief to a single Supreme Being and give worship to that Being. Second, all Masons are given the names of this particular god, the most common one being the Great or Grand Architect of the Universe. It is this god to whom the Mason is being dedicated and to whom he swears to devote his life. Third, Masons are taught that whatever they call god, ultimately he is the one true God. Fourth, as we have seen, Masons are erecting in their hearts a temple for the dwelling of this god. For the ritual teaches, "My brother, . . . you have this night commenced the great task, which in your future Masonic life should never be discontinued, that of erecting in your heart a temple for the indwelling of God."[11]

Masonry teaches that if men call God by different names and define him differently, it is only because they do not know any better. They are doing this in ignorance because of the spiritual darkness in them.[12] Masonry claims it can remove this darkness by revealing that, however imperfectly, all men worship the one true God. In brief, the Masonic initiate swears his belief and commitment to God in each of the first three degrees of Masonry. But who is this deity to whom the Mason swears his loyalty?

Anyone who has ever read what Albert Pike taught about God in the higher degrees knows that the deity of Masonry is not the God of the Bible: "Masonry, [is that religion] around whose altars the Christian, the Hebrew, the Moslem, the Brahman, the followers of Confucius and Zoroaster, can assemble as brethren and unite in prayer to the one God who is above all the Baalim."[13]

Who are the Baalim? Pike defines the term "Baalim" as the idols and false gods that are found in all other religions outside of Masonry. These false gods are considered dim reflections of the one true Masonic god, the Supreme Architect, that Masonry reveals.[14] Pike taught that *"Every religion and every conception of God is idolatrous,* insofar as it is imperfect, and as it substitutes a feeble and temporary idea in the shrine of that Undiscoverable Being [of Masonry]."[15]

Consider what leading Masonic authority Albert Mackey says in his *Encyclopedia*: "God is equally present with the pious Hindoo [sic] in the temple, the Jew in the synagogue, the Mohammedan in the mosque, and the Christian in the church."[16] That may be true of the god of Masonry, but it is definitely not true of the God of the Bible. Jesus said, "God is Spirit, and those who worship Him must worship in spirit and *in truth*" (John 4:24; italics added). But everyone familiar with these religions knows that the "truth" about God taught in Hinduism, Judaism, Islam, and Christianity is not the same.

Nevertheless, Masonry does not care by what name the candidates refer to God. Masonry teaches (initially) that all that matters is that a person believe in *some* supreme being. Carl Claudy says,

> [The Mason] must declare his faith in a Supreme Being before he may be initiated. But note that he is not required to say, then or ever, *what* God. He may name him as he will, think of him as he pleases; make him impersonal law or personal and anthropomorphic; Freemasonry cares not. . . . God, Great Architect of the Universe, Grand Artificer, Grand Master of the Grand Lodge Above, Jehovah, Allah, Buddha, Vishnu, Shiva, or Great Geometer. (Italics added)[17]
>
> Masonry does not specify any God of any creed; she requires merely that you believe in some Deity, give him what name you will. . . . A belief in God is essential to a Mason, but . . . any god will do, so [long as] He is your God.[18]

> Freemasonry . . . asks no questions as to what God, nor even what kind of a God [men believe in]. Freemasonry cares not. That she does not care is one of her dearest symbols. . . . Men may believe in God, Jehovah or [the] Great First Cause; in Love, Confucius, Mithra [an ancient pagan deity of the Syrians] or a Cosmic Urge, and still be children of one Father, and therefore brethren in the true meaning of the word.[19]

But the God of the Bible has revealed Himself to man. God has told us of His attributes and characteristics. And the God of the Bible has revealed He is not the same as the gods described in other religions. Just as Masonry has claimed it does not teach a system of salvation but does; just as it claims it is not a religion but is; just as it claims it reverences the Bible but does not; Masonry now claims that the god of Masonry and the God of Christianity are the same god. But this, too, is false.

> While it tacitly admits the existence of other gods in allowing its disciples to hold their private views, *it does so on the theory that these god-ideas are perversions and corruptions of its own theistic conceptions and which it aims to correct.* . . . It reduces all monotheistic deities to one and the same thing as its Great Architect, and all the great religions as identical with itself.[20]

Masonry's syncretism has eclectic elements. For example, some Masons' description of God as Creator, Preserver, and Destroyer[21] is reminiscent of Hindu constructions. Masonry's stress on God's absolute unitarian nature and transcendence, over against His immanence, is similar to the Muslim concept of God, and its deism and pantheism are common to many other religions.

Thus, although Masonry initially claims it cares not which god men believe in, Masonry proceeds to teach the candidate its own unique and distinct concept of God, and it also teaches men that their gods are really false. In fact, Masonry actually believes she alone possesses the truth about God, and that every other concept of God must be false and therefore rejected. (For documentation, see chapter 15.)

That is why Masonry teaches that everyone must be reeducated to learn that their ideas of God are incorrect—that they are merely inferior reflections concerning the true Great Architect of the Universe. This is one reason that Masonry stresses the importance of education, why it stresses in the words of the Pennsylvania Grand Chaplain, "the capability of man to reach a higher level of perfection through education and training."[22] In a real sense, Masonry is *religious training and reeducation* —specifically, an *indoctrination* into the distinct and unique *theology* of Masonry, including indoctrination into its own *specific deity*, which it claims is the only true God. This conforms to Pike's confession: "there is but *one* true religion, *one* dogma, *one* legitimate belief" (italics added).[23]

There are three fundamental problems with the god of the Lodge. First, Masonic descriptions of their Great Architect of the Universe are not Christian or biblical. Second, far from accepting the Christian God, Masonry opposes and rejects the triune Christian God. Third, in the York Rite, Masonry actually defines its god as "Jabulon" (see chapter 9),[24] which clearly describes a pagan amalgamation of gods.

THE MASONIC DESCRIPTIONS OF GOD ARE NOT CHRISTIAN

In Masonry the G.A.O.T.U. is described as having *some* of the standard attributes of God—e.g., infinity, eternity, omnipotence. But Masonry's description of God conflicts with the specific description of God given by Christianity, or any other religion for that matter. Proof of this is in *Coil's Masonic Encyclopedia*, where all men in the Lodge are told they must decide between the inferior Christian God or the one true god of Masonry:

> Men have to decide whether they want a God like the ancient Hebrew *Jahweh*, a partisan, *tribal God*, with whom they can talk and argue and from whom they can hide if necessary, or a *boundless, eternal, universal, undenominational, and international, Divine Spirit*, so vastly removed from the speck called man, that He cannot be known, named, or approached. So soon as man begins to laud his God and endow him with the most perfect human attributes such as justice, mercy, beneficence, etc., the Divine essence is depreciated and despoiled. . . . The Masonic test [for admission] is *a Supreme Be-*

ing, and any qualification added is *an innovation and distortion*. (Italics added)[25]

Here the God of the Bible is clearly rejected as an inferior "tribal" deity and the universal god of Masonry is exalted as superior. Masonic scholar Albert Pike asserts, "Masonry says to its Initiates this: 'God is One; Unapproachable, Single, Eternal and Unchanging.... There is but one God, infinite and incomprehensible, to whom no human attribute can be properly assigned, even when imagined to be infinite'."[26]

Thus is the God of the Bible rejected. Masonry claims that God is "unapproachable." But the Bible teaches that God can be approached by men (through Christ), and it is God's will that people do so. In Masonry, men are told that God is "single." But the Bible presents a God who is a trinitarian Being (Acts 5:3-4; Philippians 4:20; Titus 2:13). Masonry says that God does not have personal emotions. For example, He "is incapable of anger."[27] But the Bible teaches that, not only is God angry with sin, He is also loving and merciful to those who repent.

Only two characteristics seem to be required for the Masonic deity: absolute inoffensiveness and absolute unknowability. The Masonic god cannot be offended by men, nor can He ever really be known by men. But such assertions, which are compatible with anything and everything, say nothing. Philosophers Anthony Flew and John Wisdom demonstrate the meaninglessness of such Masonic "god statements":

> Once upon a time, two explorers came upon a clearing in the jungle. In the clearing were growing many flowers and many weeds. One explorer says, "Some gardener must tend this plot." The other disagrees, "There is no gardener." So they pitch their tents and set a watch. No gardener is ever seen. "But perhaps he is an invisible gardener." So they set up a barbed-wire fence. They electrify it. They patrol with bloodhounds. (For they remember how H. G. Wells' *The Invisible Man* could be both smelt and touched though he could not be seen.) But no shrieks ever suggest that some intruder has received a shock. No movements of the wire ever betray an invisible climber. The bloodhounds never give cry. Yet still the Believer is not convinced. "But there is a gardener, invisible, intangible, insensible to electric shocks, a gardener who

has no scent and makes no sound, a gardener who comes secretly to look after the garden which he loves." At last, the
Skeptic despairs, "But what remains of your original assertion? Just how does what you call an invisible, intangible,
eternally elusive gardener differ from an imaginary gardener
or even from no gardener at all?"[28]

Masonry's assertions about God do not escape this death
by a thousand qualifications. Nevertheless, according to Masonic authors the Christian belief in God is an "inferior" view
of God that Christians hold in their ignorance.[29] As a Christian
learns more and more of Masonic teachings, he is faced with a
conflict between the so-called inferior view of God he was
taught as a Christian and the allegedly superior, more grand
and sublime, Masonic conception of Deity. The result? The
Christian begins to think that the biblical God is an inferior rep-
resentation of the "One True God"—and this impacts every
area of his spiritual life.

Contrary to the Lodge, the Bible teaches that God is Jehovah—a particular concrete Deity with a clearly defined nature
and clearly defined attributes. God is love (1 John 4:7-21), God
is holy (1 Peter 1:16; 1 John 1:5), and God can become angry.
He is a God of wrath against human sin and evil (Revelation
14:10). But in Masonry, all such particular concepts and descriptions of God are considered false. The true Masonic deity is ultimately unknowable. In Masonic literature, God is held to be
"unapproachable" and the one who "cannot be known." He is
"a boundless, eternal, universal, undenominational and international Divine Spirit."[30]

In Masonry, the reason for this is clear. If God is infinitely
beyond, and superior to, all human concepts of deity, then men
will find it impossible to argue over Him. This concept of God
is Masonry's alleged "solution" to the religious differences that
have prevented a universal worldwide brotherhood of men.
Any and all non-Masonic definitions or descriptions of God are
either useless, irrelevant, or even blasphemous in that they lim-
it and constrain the limitless and infinite God. Masonry thus
hopes that little will remain for men to argue over. This is why
Pike taught that all specific conceptions of God are idolatrous—
except Masonry's—[31] and that there is only "one true religion."[32]

But, in fact, pantheistic conceptions of the Masonic deity are implied in the higher degrees. For example, Masonry accepts a particular form of pantheism (that all is God and God is all) called Pan*en*theism (that the universe is God's "body"):

> In its doctrines concerning the divine eminence Freemasonry is decidedly pantheistic, partaking of the various shades of that view of the divine. God (the Great Architect) is the great "soul" of the universe, and the universe is the garment in which he is clothed.
>
> The Masonic view of the revelation of God, in the lower degrees, is deistic, but in the higher degrees it becomes pantheistic. The writings of Garrison, Buck, Pike, and other eminent Masons show this unmistakably. It is this particular pantheistic conception of deity which has passed from India through the secret doctrines of the Kabbalah into modern speculative Freemasonry. . . . In Masonry, a god distinct from the life of nature has no existence.[33]

Nevertheless, the God of the Bible has revealed specific things to us about Himself that flatly contradict the teachings of Masonry.

MASONRY REJECTS THE CHRISTIAN CONCEPT OF GOD'S TRIUNE NATURE

Masonry may claim that the God of the Bible is the same as the god of Masonry, but this is not so. Masonry opposes the Christian concept of the Trinity. Whenever it defines God, it defines God as "one," "single," or "unitarian." It *must* do this: otherwise, it will offend Masons who are not Christians and who reject the Trinity. For example, the *Proceedings of the Grand Lodge of Texas* (December 22, 1920) states, "No phrase or terms should be used in a Masonic service that would arouse sectarian feelings or wound the religious sensibilities of any Freemason."[34] This is also the reason Mackey refers to the "chief mission" of Masonry as "the preservation of belief in the unity of God."[35]

Some Masonic writings teach that the idea of the Trinity is of pagan origin.[36] As a result, the biblical concept of the Trinity is either deliberately rejected[37] or redefined.[38] Mason G. A. Kenderdine teaches in his article in *New Age* magazine that "Masonry holds and teaches that with all and above all there is God, *not essentially a Christian triune God*" (italics added).[39]

One Masonic source acknowledges that Christian Masons are permitted to believe in "a symbolical triune essence" but only as a "subsidiary and secondary" belief after faith in the Masonic god.[40] But, of course, a symbolical triune essence is not the Christian doctrine of the Trinity.

When Pike and other Masonic authorities state or imply that the biblical Deity is a "provincial tribal god" or that the Christian God and all non-Masonic gods are "the Baalim," meaning false gods or idols, it can hardly claim to be tolerant of others' religious beliefs let alone that it teaches such beliefs.[41]

Coil even admits, "Monotheism . . . violates Masonic principles, for it requires belief in a specific kind of Supreme Deity."[42] That is very interesting since most Christian Masons describe Masonry's belief in God as "monotheistic." Yet here Coil teaches that any belief in monotheism is not proper Masonic belief.

The god of Masonry is not the God of the Bible. Masonry teaches men in the Lodge, including Christian Masons, to believe in and worship its god. But the God of the Bible says that there is no God besides Him:

> Thus says the Lord, the King of Israel and His Redeemer, the Lord of hosts: "I am the first and I am the last, and there is no God besides Me. . . . Is there any God besides Me, or is there any other Rock? I know of none. . . . I am the Lord, and there is no other; besides Me there is no God." (Isaiah 44:6, 8; 45:5)

The entire thrust of both the Old and New Testament revelation is to warn men against false gods and the consequences of worshiping false gods, which is idolatry. Idolatry sends men to hell.

The Bible says that God is greater than all the false gods that men worship: "Greater is our God than all the gods . . . for the heavens and the highest heavens cannot contain Him" (2 Chronicles 2:5*b*-6). "Who is like thee among the gods, O Lord? Who is like Thee, majestic in holiness, awesome in praises, working wonders?" (Exodus 15:11). "For great is the Lord, and greatly to be praised; He also is to be feared above all gods. For all the gods of the peoples are idols, but the Lord made the heavens. . . . Tremble before Him, all the earth, . . . for He is coming to judge the earth" (1 Chronicles 16:25-26, 30, 33*b*).

Jesus made God's requirements very clear: "It is written, 'You shall worship the Lord your God and serve Him only'" (Luke 4:8). God Himself states, "You shall fear only the Lord your God; and you shall worship Him. . . . You shall not follow other gods, any of the gods of the peoples who surround you, for the Lord your God in the midst of you is a jealous God; otherwise the anger of the Lord your God will be kindled against you, and He will wipe you off the face of the earth" (Deuteronomy 6:13-15).

In light of all this, how can a Christian Mason justify remaining a Mason? Does he truly love God, or is his profession of faith shallow or mere hypocrisy? Should not those Masons who truly love God renounce Masonry, for it has led them into idolatry and sin?

> Jah, Bel, and On appear in the American ritual of the Royal Arch degree on the supposition that Jah was the Syriac name of God, Bel (Baal), the Chaldean, and On, the Egyptian.
> *Coil's Masonic Encyclopedia*

9

The Name of God

Did you know that Masonry refers to its deity by using the names of heathen gods that are condemned in the Bible? That Masonry has pagan concepts of God is not surprising. Masonry itself is in some ways a modern revival of the ancient pagan mystery religions. As the Texas *Monitor* confesses, "the most learned among Masonic scholars conclude that *Masonry* is of very ancient origin, and in some aspects, the modern successor of, and heir to . . . the Temples of India, Chaldea, Greece and Rome, as well as the basic doctrines of the Essenes, Gnostics and other mystic orders."[1] (See chapter 19 for a more detailed discussion.)

THE "TRUE NAME" OF GOD

For example, in the Royal Arch Degree of the York Rite, the Mason is told the "true name" of God. (Prior to this degree, the Mason has been told that the real name of God had been lost.) Masons are told that the true name for God is "Jabulon." Lodge members who have only taken the first three degrees of the Blue Lodge are not aware that the Great Architect of the Universe (G.A.O.T.U.) is later identified as Jabulon.[2]

One thing is certain: Masonry connects the one true and righteous God of the Bible with the evil and pagan deities Baal and "On" or Osiris. In the ritual of the Royal Arch Degree, every Royal Arch Mason is told that the true name for the God he has been praying to throughout the different degrees of Masonry is "Ja" (for Jehovah), joined with "Bel" or "Bul" (for Baal, the ancient Canaanite god), and "On" (possibly for Osiris, the Egyptian mystery god).[3] (For a discussion of the influence of Egyptian deities in the Old Testament, see chapter 15.) Why has Masonry combined Jehovah with gods that are condemned in the Bible? Martin L. Wagner offers an explanation:

> In this compound name an attempt is made to show by a coordination of divine names ... the unity, identity and harmony of the Hebrew, Assyrian and Egyptian god-ideas, and the harmony of the Royal Arch religion with these ancient religions. This Masonic "unity of God" is peculiar. It is the doctrine that the different names of gods, [such as] Brahma, Jehovah, Baal, Bel, Om, On, etc., all denote the generative pro-creative principle, in that all religions are essentially the same in their ideas of the divine.[4]

Coil's Masonic Encyclopedia confesses, "Jah, Bel, and On appear in the American ritual of the Royal Arch degree on the supposition that Jah was the Syriac name of God, Bel (Baal), the Chaldean, and On, the Egyptian."[5] Coil himself admits that Bel refers to the Babylonian god "Baal."

How serious is this? The god "Baal" mentioned in the composite term Ja-bul-on is the evil Canaanite nature deity.[6] This deity, whom the God of the Bible utterly hated and judged, is the god whose name appears on the Masonic altar:

> There is no dispute between Freemasons and their fiercest critics that both the word Jehovah and the composite word, Jahbulon, appear on the [Masonic] altar, on top of which is inscribed a circle, containing a triangle. Around the circle is inscribed the name JEHOVAH and on the three sides of the triangle the letters JAH BUL ON. . . . To all of this must be added the third and final feature of the top of the pedestal: the Hebrew characters set at the angles of the triangle: Alif, Beth, and Lamed, each of which is said to have reference to the deity or to some divine attribute. "Take each combination [of the letters] with the whole, and it will read thus: Ab Bal,

[meaning] Father, Lord: Al Bal, Word, Lord; Lab Bal, Spirit, Lord" [quoting a Masonic source]. The obvious result of such juggling of the Hebrew characters is to emphasize the formation of Bal, the name of a Semitic deity bitterly opposed by Elijah and the later Hebrew prophets; to associate this name in any way with that of Jehovah would have deeply shocked them.[7]

BAAL WORSHIP

Associating Baal's name with the name of Jehovah would have indeed shocked the prophets in the Bible. It would have shocked them because Baal was condemned by God as a false idol in whose name incredible evil was done. Archaeology reveals that Baalism was one of the most evil systems of idol worship found in the ancient world, leading people into the worst kinds of sin and vice, including the practice of self-mutilation (1 Kings 18:28), ritual prostitution (Judges 2:17; Jeremiah 7:9; Amos 2:7), and sacrificing of children (Jeremiah 19:4, 5, 15).[8] Yes, under this "god," people actually promoted the murder of innocent children. Such practices would have shocked the Old Testament prophets the same way it shocks us to read of certain modern cults practicing human sacrifice.

Historically, Baal has been another name for Satan. The god Baal was sufficiently Satanic that both Jesus and the New Testament used the name of Baal in an extended manner to refer to Satan himself: "Beelzebul" is a New Testament name for Satan based on the Old Testament term *Baalzebub*.[9] Consider just a few of the more than fifty Scriptures in the Old Testament that indicate how evil Baal worship was, how destructive was his influence upon the people of God, and how much God abhorred this false deity:

> Because they have forsaken Me and have made this an alien place and have burned sacrifices in it to other gods . . . and because they have filled this place with the blood of the innocent and have built the high places of Baal to burn their sons in the fire as burnt offerings to Baal, a thing which I never commanded or spoke of, nor did it ever enter My mind; therefore . . . behold, I am about to bring on this city and all its towns the entire calamity that I have declared against it, be-

cause they have stiffened their necks so as not to heed My words. (Jeremiah 19:4-5, 15; cf. 7:9-10)

The days of punishment have come. . . . Because of the gross-ness of your iniquity, and because your hostility [toward God] is so great. . . . They have gone deep in depravity . . . they came to Baal-peor [i.e., Baal] and devoted themselves to shame, and they became as detestable as that which they loved. (Hosea 9:7-11)

And the sons of Israel did what was evil in the sight of the Lord, and forgot the Lord their God, and served the Baals. (Judges 3:7)

The God of the Bible refers to Baal as "shameful" (Jeremiah 11:13), and there are many other instances in Scripture showing just how wicked a deity Baal was and of the tragic consequences that resulted from following him. One encyclopedia discusses the influence of Baal worship and reveals how the ancient Israelites joined the names of Jehovah and Baal, just as modern Masons do:

It [Baal worship] was attended by the appropriate response from the worshippers, culminating in the grossly sensuous rites accompanying the sacred marriage, in which ritual prostitution of both sexes was a prominent feature. . . . In . . . time . . . Yahweh continued to be worshipped, [but] the attributes and even the name of Baal became attached to Him. . . . The Samaria ostraca dating from c. 780 B.C., show that this tendency was particularly prominent in the northern kingdom; *for every two names in the lists compounded with the name of Yahweh, one was formed with Baal.* . . . Israel sustained the deliberate attempt by the Phoen. princess Jezebel to obliterate Yahweh worship (cf. 1 Kings 18:4) and make Baal (prob. Baal-melquart) the official god. Only 7000 Israelites remained true to Yahweh (19:18), but the crisis was averted by the decisive action of the prophet Elijah (ch. 18). The 8th cent. prophets recognized the dangers inherent in the situation and called the people back to a belief in Yahweh alone. . . . Hosea proposed that the name of Baal be no longer employed of Jahweh (Hosea 2:16, 17) and he and Jeremiah, of all the prophets, pointed out the dangers of a Canaanized Yahweh. . . . Once this was realized, the name of Baal was regarded with abhorrence. (Italics added)[10]

IDOLATRY

Masonry has chosen the worst name possible to make equal with Jehovah! If you are a Christian Mason, do you think that God is pleased when He hears you pray and swear solemn oaths to a pagan deity He has condemned? Do you not think this mocks God (Galatians 6:7)? Do you not think that such idolatry will affect your spiritual life? But many Christian Masons will typically reply, "What we do in the Lodge is not idolatry." What does the Bible say?

God condemned Israel's evil in choosing Baal and in joining Baal's name with Jehovah. God called this practice idolatry. As a result, Israel was deported to Assyria in painful judgment.

> And the sons of Israel did things secretly which were not right, against the Lord their God. . . . And they served idols, concerning which the Lord had said to them, "You shall not do this thing." Yet the Lord warned Israel and Judah, through all His prophets and every seer, saying, "Turn from your evil ways and keep My commandments. . . ." However, they did not listen, but stiffened their neck like their fathers, who did not believe in the Lord their God. And they rejected His statutes and His covenant which He made with their fathers, and His warnings with which He warned them. And they followed vanity and became vain, and went after the nations which surrounded them, concerning which the Lord had commanded them not to do like them. And they forsook all the commandments of the Lord their God and made for themselves molten images . . . and worshiped all the host of heaven [an astrological practice] and served Baal. Then they made their sons and their daughters pass through the fire [human sacrifice], and practiced divination and enchantments, and sold themselves to do evil in the sight of the Lord, provoking Him. So the Lord was very angry with Israel, and removed them from His sight; none was left except the tribe of Judah. (2 Kings 17:9, 12-18)

When Elijah opposed the 450 prophets of Baal on Mount Carmel, we all know the outcome. God's judgment was swift and decisive. The prophet asked God's people, "How long will you hesitate between two opinions? If the Lord is God, follow Him; but if Baal, follow him" (1 Kings 18:21).

The first commandment reads, "Thou shalt have no other gods before me." The biblical God will have no other gods before Him because such gods do not exist. Only Satan's demons are behind idols guiding people into evil.[11] Yet, if there are no other gods, then claiming one such as the G.A.O.T.U. or Baal as being equal with God becomes idolatry. Worshiping a false god as if he were the true God is idolatry. This is why Wagner argues:

> The Christian cannot, he dare not recognize other deities, or assent to their worship. This God is of necessity jealous of his honor, and he cannot give his glory to another.... Biblical monotheism is an absolute monotheism ... and demands a worship of him and him only and in his name only. It demands that there be neither belief in the existence, neither the recognition, nor the worship of other gods. It denies that God can be known from speculation, but only by the revelation of Himself, in His Word.[12]

In conclusion, there is absolutely no doubt that Masonry's god is not the God of the Bible. First of all, Masonry deliberately rejects Jehovah God.[13] Second, it permits, at one level, the gods of Hinduism, Buddhism, Islam, Mormonism, and Shintoism to be worshiped around its altar according to each individual Mason's belief. At a higher level, Masonry defines God as G.A.O.T.U.: a vague, absolutely unknowable and inoffensive unitarian deity whom it encourages all men to worship. Fourth, it calls this god by the secret name "Jabulon," a joining together of evil heathen deities with the God of the Bible. Because Masonry has done these things, it has rejected the God revealed in the Bible and exchanged Him for a false god. Therefore, Masonry practices idolatry and blasphemes God.

Is it any wonder that the General Synod of the Church of England concluded that "JAHBULON (whether it is a name or description), which appears in all the rituals, must be considered blasphemous: in Christian theology the name of God (Yahweh/Jehovah) must not be taken in vain, nor can it be replaced by an amalgam of the names of pagan deities."[14]

The god of Masonry is not the God of the Bible. How then can you as a Christian possibly remain a Mason when you now know Masonry has lied to you and tricked you into practicing idolatry? How can you remain a Mason knowing that Masonry is causing you to blaspheme God? If you are a Christian pastor whose divine calling is to preach and teach the truths concerning the God of the Bible, how can you continue to support Masonry, which instructs its members to worship a false god? Jesus said, "No one can serve two masters. Either he will hate the one and love the other, or he will be devoted to the one and despise the other" (Matthew 6:24; NIV).

Christian Masons and Christian pastors who presently support Masonry, must choose to whom they will give allegiance—to the God of the Bible or to the god of Masonry. It is impossible to do both.

Jesus was just a man. He was one of the "exemplars," one of the great men of the past, but not divine and certainly not the only means of redemption of lost mankind.
Former Mason Jim Shaw
Past Worshipful Master of the Blue Lodge
Past Master of all Scottish Rite bodies
Knight Commander of the Court of Honor

10

Jesus Christ

If you are a Mason who believes in and follows Jesus Christ, did you realize that you support an organization that actually leads men away from Him? This is a strong charge to make, but it is the testimony of many former Masons and the cumulative result of our detailed research in the Masonic ritual and more than a hundred Masonic texts.

WHAT MASONRY TEACHES ABOUT JESUS

Masonry turns men away from Christ in at least five ways: (1) Masonry deliberately deletes the name of Christ from its prayers and Scripture quotations; (2) Masonry requires a Christian to disobey Christ by officially prohibiting all discussion of Christ from Lodge activities; (3) Masonry blasphemously offers the titles and offices of Christ to unbelievers; (4) Masonry denies the deity of Christ; and (5) Masonry purposely downplays the unique role of Christ as Savior, e.g., by teaching that the Christian message of divine redemption is merely a revival of earlier pagan stories.

Masonry does all of this and yet still claims that "Freemasonry is far removed from all that is . . . ungodly."[1] Masonry falsely asserts, "We do not say to Christians that Christ was a mere man, whose life story is only a revival of similar older [pagan] stories. To do any of these things would be irreverent. We utter no such words."[2] These statements are simply not true.

MASONRY DELETES THE NAME OF CHRIST FROM ITS PRAYERS AND SCRIPTURE QUOTATIONS

Masonry does not allow the ritual to cite the name of Jesus Christ. Even though Jesus' name is used in many biblical passages, the Masonic ritual deletes His name when it quotes these passages. The following samples illustrate this:

Passage	Masonic Ritual	The Bible
1 Peter 2:5	To offer up spiritual sacrifices acceptable to God.	To offer up spiritual sacrifices acceptable to God *through Jesus Christ.*
2 Thessalonians 3:6	Now we command you, brethren, that ye withdraw yourselves from every brother that walketh disorderly, and not after the tradition which he received of us.	Now we command you, brethren, *in the name of our Lord Jesus Christ* that you keep aloof from every brother who leads an unruly life and not according to the tradition which you received from us.
2 Thessalonians 3:12	Now them that are such, we command and exhort, that with quietness they work and eat their own bread.	Now such persons we command and exhort *in the Lord Jesus Christ* to work, in a quiet fashion and eat their own bread.[3]

Notice how Masonry has removed the name of Jesus Christ from these Bible passages. Every Christian knows the Bible is God's Word and, therefore, not to be tampered with. God warns in Deuteronomy 4:2*a*, "You shall not add to the word which I am commanding you, nor take away from it." But Masonry not only deceptively deletes the name of Christ from the Scriptures, it also prohibits the giving of prayers in the name of Christ in the Lodge.

For the Christian, the Bible's teaching on prayer is explicit. The Christian is to pray to God the Father in the name of the Lord Jesus Christ at all times. In Christ's name, he is to labor in fervent prayer, to continue in prayer, to strive in prayer (John 14:13-14; Romans 12:12; 15:30; Ephesians 6:18; Philippians 4:6; Colossians 3:17; 4:2, 12; 1 Thessalonians 5:17).

But Masonry forbids prayer to Jesus, or to God in Jesus' name, in the Lodge. The *Maryland Master Mason* magazine of March 1973 asserts the following regulation concerning prayer in the Lodge:

> All prayers in Mason lodges should be directed to the one deity to whom all Masons refer as the Grand Architect of the Universe. . . . Prayers in the lodges should be closed with expressions such as "in the Most Holy and precious name we pray," using no additional words which would be in conflict with the religious beliefs of those present at meetings.[4]

Consider the following real life illustration of what happens to the naive Christian Mason who attempts to offer a prayer in the name of Jesus Christ:

> The Commander of the Guard called me aside and rebuked me sharply. He said . . . I had ended the prayer "in Christ's holy name." For that, he said, I would be reported! . . . I was called in to see the Secretary of the Scottish Rite (a Christian Scientist) about my unsatisfactory performance. He was nice about it, but told me that I was never to end a prayer "in Jesus' name" or "in Christ's name." He said, "Make your prayers universal."[5]

To recognize the lengths to which Masonry has gone in rejecting Christ's name from its prayers one need only examine Mackey's *Masonic Ritualist*, where there are almost thirty sample prayers given for different Masonic occasions, but not one is offered in the name of Christ.[6] In fact, in every prayer offered in the Blue Lodge and in all the prayers of the higher degrees of the York and Scottish Rites not once is a prayer offered in the name of Jesus Christ.

Masonry will not allow the name of Jesus Christ to be used in the Lodge because it cares more about what men might think than it does about what Jesus Christ taught. In this sense, Masonry is ashamed of Jesus Christ. One would think that as soon as Christians recognized this, *they* would be ashamed to remain in the Masonic Lodge. Jesus Himself and the apostle John give these warnings:

> Everyone therefore who shall confess Me before men, I will also confess him before My Father who is in heaven. But whoever shall deny Me before men, I will also deny him before My Father who is in heaven. (Matthew 10:32-33)

> Whoever denies the Son does not have the Father; the one who confesses the Son has the Father also. (1 John 2:23)

> And every spirit that does not confess Jesus is not from God; and this is the spirit of the antichrist, of which you have heard that it is coming, and now it is already in the world. . . . And we have beheld and bear witness that the Father has sent the Son to be the Savior of the world. Whoever confesses that Jesus is the Son of God, God abides in him, and he in God. . . . The one who believes in the Son of God has the witness in himself; the one who does not believe God has made Him a liar, because he has not believed in the witness that God has borne concerning his Son. And the witness is this, that God has given us eternal life, and this life is in His Son. He who has the Son has the life; he who does not have the Son of God does not have the life. (1 John 4:3, 14-15; 5:10-12)

MASONRY OFFICIALLY PROHIBITS ALL DISCUSSION OF CHRIST DURING LODGE ACTIVITY

The Christian is commanded by Jesus Christ to verbally witness of His love to all men. Jesus commanded His disciples to go into all the world and testify of Him:

> And Jesus came up and spoke to them, saying, "All authority has been given to me in heaven and on earth. Go therefore and make disciples of all the nations, baptizing them in the name of the Father and the Son and the Holy Spirit, teaching them to observe all that I commanded you; and lo, I am with you always, even to the end of the age." (Matthew 28:18-20)

The apostle Paul said, "Woe is me if I do not preach the gospel. . . . For though I am free from all men, I have made myself a slave to all, that I might win the more" (1 Corinthians 9:16, 19). But he makes the proclamation of the gospel message the task of all Christians (cf. Acts 10:42-43; Romans 10:11-15):

> I solemnly charge you in the presence of God and of Christ Jesus, who is to judge the living and the dead, and by his appearing and His kingdom: preach the word; be ready in season and out of season; reprove, rebuke, exhort, with great patience and instruction. For the time will come when they will not endure sound doctrine; but wanting to have their ears tickled, they will accumulate for themselves teachers in accordance to their own desires; and will turn away their ears from the truth, and will turn aside to myths. (2 Timothy 4:1-4)

But Masonry prohibits the Christian from talking about Christ in any fashion in the Lodge. The charges (regulations) of Freemasonry adopted in 1723 instruct the Christian Mason to keep his own personal religious opinions to himself: "Though in ancient Times Masons were charged in every Country to be of the Religion of that Country or nation, whatever it was, yet 'tis now thought more expedient only to oblige them to that Religion in which all men agree, *leaving their particular Opinions to themselves*" (italics added).[7]

In his discussion of the 10th Degree of the Scottish Rite, Masonic authority Albert Pike teaches those in the Lodge that "the Mason's creed goes further than that. No man, it holds, has any right in any way to interfere with the religious belief of another."[8] The 20th Degree teaches that "no man has the right to dictate to another in matters of belief or faith; no man can say that he has possession of truth as he has of a chattel."[9]

The Texas *Monitor*, along with many others, stresses that Masonry is correct in "forbidding all sectarian discussion within its lodge rooms."[10] In other words, Masonry absolutely prohibits all attempts by Christians to share Jesus Christ with other Masons. The Lodge prohibits all attempts at conversion—except, of course, the *subtle conversion* offered by Masonry itself. Notice that Pike was not necessarily speaking of activity within the Lodge but, apparently, in general terms. Nevertheless, in the Lodge the command of Masonry is absolute: Discussion of traditional religions is simply forbidden. Yet it is permissible to speak and teach other Masons about the god of Masonry, the G.A.O.T.U.

MASONRY OFFERS THE TITLES AND OFFICES OF CHRIST TO UNBELIEVERS

The offices and titles of Christ are actually appropriated to Masons during the ritual and used by them as Masonic passwords: for example, "I AM THAT I AM," "Immanuel," "Jehovah," "Adonai"[11] (see chapter 13). In the 19th Degree of the Scottish Rite, the "Thrice Puissant" is portrayed as a kind of rival to Christ Himself. The parallels between the "Thrice Puissant" and Christ in the Masonic ritual are described in *Scottish Rite Masonry Illustrated:*

> The Lodge Master is "Thrice Puissant," personating Christ, who has "all power." The Master is "seated on a throne and holds a Sceptre," with the blue canopy of the heavens over him. This is Christ's rival. . . . The degree itself, says Mackey, . . . "is founded on the mysteries of the Apocalypse," which is "the revelation of Jesus Christ." (Revelation 1:1) And his lodge members are "clothed in white linen robes," like attending Angels; (Revelation 15:6) and on the jewel is engraved "Alpha and Omega," which is the title of Christ.[12]

When Masonry applies the offices of Christ to unbelievers or uses them as passwords, it is engaging in blasphemy. No Christian should participate in such activities (see chapter 13).

MASONRY DENIES THE DEITY OF CHRIST

Masonry teaches that Jesus Christ was merely a man. Masonic leader Jim Shaw was a 33d Degree Mason, a Past Worshipful Master of the Blue Lodge, Past Master of all Scottish Rite bodies, and a Knight Commander of the Court of Honor. He says that official Masonic doctrine concerning Christ is "Jesus was just a man. He was one of the 'exemplars', one of the great men of the past, but not divine and certainly not the only means of redemption of lost mankind."[13]

The important Masonic ritual called the Maundy Thursday Ritual of the Chapter of Rose Croix denies the deity of Jesus

Christ when it officially states in the ceremony, "We meet this day to commemorate the death [of Jesus], not as inspired or divine, for this is not for us to decide."[14] According to Masonry, an individual Christian Mason may choose to believe that Jesus was God and Savior of the world, but this is optional for him and not Masonic truth. Those such as Albert Pike who considered themselves enlightened Masons, hoped that their "unenlightened" brethren would realize that all specific dogmas about Christ (e.g., Jesus is God) are in error.

Clausen emphasized that it is important to "strip from all religions their orthodox tenets, legends, allegories and dogmas."[15] This is why Pike asserted that Jesus was only "a great teacher of morality"—but no more.[16] J. W. Acker, a member of the Lutheran Church—Missouri Synod's Commission of Fraternal Organizations—concluded, "Masonry regards Jesus Christ as a great teacher *only*, not as the Son of God and Savior from sin, placing Him on the same level with the heathen Greek philosopher Socrates and with the prophet Mohammed" (italics added).[17]

So it is neither fair nor true for Masons to say that Masonry does not offend Christians. By teaching that Jesus was only a man, this is exactly what Masonry has done. Why does Masonry say that Christ was only a man, rather than just remaining silent on the issue? It does this because it does not wish to offend the religious sensibilities of those Masons who are members of faiths that deny that Jesus is the only incarnation of God and the Savior of the world. The unique nature and mission of Christ is denied by Hindus, Buddhists, Muslims, and Jews. In order not to offend these people, Masonry offends Christians.

Masonic writers have frequently denied Christ's specific deity in favor of Masonry's nebulous and general idea of God. In his *Symbolism or Mystic Masonry*, Masonic writer J. D. Buck wrote, "[Christian] Theologians first made a fetish of the Impersonal Omnipresent Divinity; and then tore the Christos from the hearts of all humanity in order to deify Jesus, that they might have a god-man peculiarly their own."[18]

In a similar fashion, R. Swineburne Clymer, who is a high Mason, teaches in his *The Mysticism of Masonry* that "in deifying Jesus, the whole humanity is bereft of Christos as an eternal potency within every human soul, a latent (embryonic) Christ in every man. In thus deifying one man [Jesus], they have orphaned the whole of humanity [of its divinity]."[19] Here, Buck and Clymer use the name "Christ" to refer not to the biblical Jesus but to a nebulous spirit that pervades the universe and supposedly indwells all men.

There is absolutely no doubt that Masonry denies the deity of Jesus Christ. How then is it possible for a Christian Mason to support this organization that denies his own Lord?

MASONRY DENIES THE ROLE OF CHRIST AS SAVIOR

Masonry denies the biblical teaching that Jesus Christ is the world's only Savior:

> And this is love, not that we loved God, but that He loved us and sent His Son to be the propitiation for our sins [by Christ's vicarious and expiatory death, God has dealt with sin and can now show mercy to the believing sinner]. . . . And there is salvation in no one else; for there is no other name under heaven that has been given among men, by which we must be saved. . . . And we have beheld and bear witness that the Father has sent the Son to be the Savior of the world. (1 John 4:10; Acts 4:12; 1 John 4:14)

Nowhere in Masonic literature will you find Jesus called God or see Him portrayed as the world's Savior who died for men's sin. To portray Him in such a light would offend most men in the Lodge, and this is taboo. In offending none, however, it offends God Himself by rejecting the truth about His Son: "The one who does not believe God has made Him a liar, because he has not believed in the witness that God has borne concerning His Son" (1 John 5:10*b*).

Masonry completely excludes all particular biblical teachings about Christ such as His incarnation, redemptive mission, death, and resurrection. In fact, *no* biblical truth about Jesus Christ is affirmed by Masonry. Former Mason Edmond Ronayne states:

> Freemasonry "carefully excludes" the Lord Jesus Christ from the Lodge and chapter, repudiates his mediatorship, rejects

his atonement, denies and disowns his gospel, frowns upon his religion and his church, ignores the Holy Spirit, and sets up for itself a spiritual empire, a religious theocracy, at the head of which it places the G.A.O.T.U.—the god of nature—and from which the one only living and true God is expelled by resolution.[20]

Albert Pike and other Masonic authors have held that the biblical teaching of Christ as God and Savior is merely a different version of "similar" stories in some of the earlier pagan religions.[21] They often teach that the New Testament is a corrupted version of such stories and that Christianity, as normally interpreted by the church, is false. In fact, many of them are offended that Christianity teaches that only Jesus is God. They prefer a more mystical Christ, a Christ who recognizes that all men are divine.

For example, in *Mystic Masonry and the Bible* (1975) Corinne Heline teaches an amalgamation of Christian mysticism, theosophy, and occultism. She says the "true Christ" resides within all men as higher consciousness and is the means to encourage man toward occult development.[22] Thirty-third Degree Mason Manly Hall refers to "the birth of the Christ within," which can be achieved by Masonic effort.[23]

But Masons who adopt a mystical Christ disagree with what Jesus taught about Himself and with what the church has maintained for two thousand years. If Masonry does not respect the teachings of Jesus, how can it claim to be "tolerant" of what Christians believe?

WHAT THE BIBLE TEACHES ABOUT JESUS

First, the Bible teaches that Jesus is the unique and only begotten Son of God—the only incarnation of God ever to appear (John 1:1-14; 3:16, 18; Philippians 2:5-9). The Bible teaches that Jesus is not merely another human religious teacher. God has exalted Him far above every man, prophet, or religious leader who has ever lived:

Therefore also God highly exalted Him, and bestowed on Him the name which is above every name, that at the name of

Jesus every knee should bow, of those who are in heaven, and on earth, and under the earth, and that every tongue should confess that Jesus Christ is Lord, to the glory of the Father. (Philippians 2:9-11)

For by Him all things were created, both in the heavens and on earth, visible and invisible, whether thrones or dominions or rulers or authorities—all things have been created by Him and for Him. And He is before all things, and in Him all things hold together. (Colossians 1:16-17)

Jesus said of Himself:

I am the light of the world; he who follows Me shall not walk in the darkness, but shall have the light of life. (John 8:12)

If you abide in My word, then you are truly disciples of Mine; and you shall know the truth, and the truth shall make you free. (John 8:31-32)

He who comes from above is above all. (John 3:31)

The Bible teaches that Jesus is God. His teachings carry an infallible authority. Jesus is not merely an "exemplar" or one who had "good moral teachings"—He is God Himself:

In the beginning was the Word, and the Word was with God, and the Word was God. . . . And the Word became flesh, and dwelt among us. (John 1:1, 14)

For in Him all the fulness of Deity dwells in bodily form. (Colossians 2:9)

Looking for the blessed hope and the appearing of the glory of our great God and Savior, Christ Jesus. (Titus 2:13)

Jesus Himself repeatedly claimed He was God:

He . . . was calling God His own Father, making Himself equal with God. (John 5:18)

Jesus said to them, "Truly truly, I say to you, before Abraham was born, I am." (John 8:58)

He who has seen me has seen the Father. (John 14:9)

Because Jesus Christ is God, He will one day judge all the world, including all Masons.

> For not even the Father judges anyone, but He has given all judgment to the Son, in order that all may honor the Son, even as they honor the Father. He who does not honor the Son does not honor the Father who sent Him. (John 5:22-23)

> But when the Son of Man comes in His glory, and all the angels with Him, then He will sit on His glorious throne. And all the nations will be gathered before Him; and He will separate them from one another, as the shepherd separates the sheep from the goats.... Then the King will say to those on His right, come you who are blessed of My Father, inherit the kingdom prepared for you from the foundation of the world. ... Then He will also say to those on His left, depart from Me, accursed ones, into the eternal fire which has been prepared for the devil and his angels.... And these will go away into eternal punishment, but the righteous into eternal life. (Matthew 25:31-34, 41, 46)

Both Jesus and the New Testament writers teach that Jesus alone is the Savior of the world, whose death on the cross paid the penalty for human sin (cf. John 4:42; 5:24; 6:29; 14:6):

> The Son of Man did not come to be served, but to serve, and to give His life a ransom for many. (Matthew 20:28)

> For God so loved the world, that He gave His only begotten Son, that whoever believes in Him should not perish, but have eternal life. For God did not send the Son into the world to judge the world, but that the world should be saved through Him. He who believes in Him is not judged; he who does not believe has been judged already, because he has not believed in the name of the only begotten Son of God. (John 3:16-18)

> For there is one God, and one mediator also between God and men, the man Christ Jesus, who gave Himself as a ransom for all, the testimony borne at the proper time. (1 Timothy 2:5-6)

> And there is salvation in no one else; for there is no other name under heaven that has been given among men, by which we must be saved. (Acts 4:12)

All of the above-mentioned Scripture proves that Masonry is absolutely wrong about Jesus Christ and should not be supported by Christians. Jesus warned, "Why do you call me 'Lord, Lord' and do not do what I say?" (Luke 6:46). Did not even He state, "But whoever shall deny Me before men, I will also deny him before my Father who is in heaven" (Matthew 10:33)?

Masonic Ritual and oath demand that the Christian Mason's first allegiance be to Masonry, not to Jesus Christ. The Masonic oaths force Christians to deny and disobey their Lord. Knowing this, how is it conceivable that a Christian Mason would choose to stay in the Lodge? How is it possible for Christian pastors to preach that Masonry and Christianity are compatible?

> Every spirit that does not confess Jesus is not from God; and this is the spirit of the antichrist. (1 John 4:3)

> They are from the world; therefore they speak as from the world, and the world listens to them. We are from God; he who knows God listens to us; he who is not from God does not listen to us. By this we know the spirit of truth and the spirit of error. (1 John 4:5-6)

> I have not written to you because you do not know the truth, but because you do know it, and because no lie is of the truth. Who is the liar but the one who denies that Jesus is the Christ? This is the antichrist, the one who denies the Father and the Son. Whoever denies the Son does not have the Father; the one who confesses the Son has the Father also. . . . These things I have written to you concerning those who are trying to deceive you. (1 John 2:21-23, 26)

We have now seen and documented from the Lodge's own rituals and teaching authorities Masonry's view on salvation, the Bible, God, and Jesus Christ. Masonry has claimed that it offers no plan of salvation. But this is false. It *does* offer a plan of salvation: works of righteousness. Freemasonry claims it is not a religion, but it is. Masonry claims it respects the Bible as a great light. But it perverts and prostitutes the Bible and teaches that the Bible is only a symbol, not to be obeyed literally. In fact, the Bible is of less value than the other Masonic symbols—the Square and Compass—for these are universal symbols throughout the earth. The Bible, however, is only a symbol in Christian cultures. Masonry has claimed that the God of Christianity is the God of Masonry. But this, too, is a deception and a lie. Finally, Masonry claims that it does not dishonor Jesus Christ, but this too is false. Masonry denies *everything* of importance about Jesus Christ.

In other words, the Masonic ritual has repeatedly told the Christian Mason that there is nothing in it or in Masonry that will interfere with his religion or with the duties he owes to his God (see chapters 2, 15). Contrary to this, the Texas *Monitor* claims under the heading of "TRUTH" that "to be good and true, is the first lesson we are taught in Masonry. . . . Hypocrisy and deceit are unknown among us, sincerity and plain-dealing distinguish us."[24] However, in light of what we have uncovered so far, is the Lodge telling the truth?

We are taught that if we would find God, look for his revelation within our own souls. We are a part of him and he of us.
W. L. Wilmshurst
The Meaning of Masonry

11

The Nature of Man

In its tract *Freemasonry—A Way of Life*, the Grand Lodge of the State of Maryland teaches that the purpose of Masonry is "to make good men better."[1] In other literature Masonry claims that it is *divinely designed* "to make its members wiser, freer, better and consequently happier men."[2] This illustrates that Masonry greatly overestimates the ability of man to correct his sin problem. It does this in three ways: by teaching that man is less than perfect but is capable of redemption by self-correction; by completely ignoring the biblical teaching concerning the sinfulness of man and implying that sin is of little concern to God; and by stressing that man will, in some sense, be perfecting himself forever.

THE LODGE: MAN CAN REDEEM HIMSELF

Masonry teaches that man's nature is good, not sinful, and believes it can offer the spiritual guidance by which good men may make themselves even better. Through Masonry men can prepare themselves to become spiritual vehicles fit for the dwelling of God.[3] Through Masonry men can perform good works that are "deserving of divine approval."[4] Masonry claims to be able to provide a brotherhood of men that all the world will envy.

No one will deny that telling sinful men how good they are and claiming that they can perfect themselves even more is the most appealing Masonic doctrine. But can Masonry really make good men better? In its prayers and ritual, Masonry teaches that all men are worthy before God just as they are. This is what the Texas *Monitor* teaches each candidate in its prayers:

> That all our actions may tend to Thy Glory.

> That the sublime principles of Freemasonry may so subdue every discordant passion within us, so harmonize and enrich our own hearts with thine own love and goodness ... [because] the great objects of our association are the restraint of improper desires and passions.

> Endue him with a competency of Thy divine wisdom that by the secrets of our art he may better be enabled to display the beauties of godliness to the honor of Thy holy name. Amen.[5]

But can men, through Masonry alone (the Masonry that, as we have already seen, exists and functions apart from the Bible and faith in Christ's redemptive provision), perform actions that glorify God? Can Masonry alone "subdue every discordant passion in men"? Can Masonry alone "harmonize and enrich" the Mason's own life with "God's own love and goodness"? Can Masonry alone endow the candidate with the "competency of divine wisdom"? Can Masonry alone (by "the secrets of our art") "better enable" the initiate "to display the beauties of godliness" to the glory of God? Can Masonry really supply the "sublime principles" that will permit all of this to be accomplished and justify a man before God? The teachings of the Lodge and the Bible are in conflict concerning man's nature, his condition before God, and how his faults are corrected.

THE LODGE: MAN IS NOT SINFUL

The importance of an accurate diagnosis of the human condition cannot be emphasized strongly enough. Whether in medicine, car repair, or any other field, misdiagnosis of a problem can be extremely serious. In a similar manner, if the problem of man is misdiagnosed, that will not solve it but only compound it.

THE MASONIC VIEW: ESSENTIAL GOODNESS

The Masonic ritual teaches through its symbols and emblems that man is not sinful in the biblical sense; he is merely "flawed" in a minor and temporary sense. He is in a rude and imperfect state, not in a fallen and sinful state. Masonry has no real grasp of the biblical doctrine of sin.

The Masonic ritual teaches that man is essentially good and can cooperate with God's strength to make himself righteous. The First Degree of Masonry teaches the perfectibility of man through its teaching of what it calls the Rough and Smooth Ashlars. The *Monitor* explains:

> By the Rough Ashlar we are reminded of our rude and imperfect state by nature; by the Perfect Ashlar, of that state of perfection at which we hope to arrive by a virtuous education, by our own endeavors, and by the blessing of God.[6]

In other words, Masonry is teaching that human nature is only in a rough and unpolished state. Scripture teaches, however, that human nature is in a morally fallen state: that is, every part of us has been so tainted by sin that anything we perform before God is unable to merit His notice or reward (Romans 3:10-18; 5:1-10; Ephesians 2:1-9).

But Masonry holds out hope of man's arriving at a "state of perfection" by means of "a virtuous education" (i.e., Masonic instruction), his "own endeavors" (i.e., living out Masonic instruction), and the blessing of God (i.e., the promise that God will faithfully reward men if they do their part). The *Monitor* describes the symbolic importance of the gavel:

> [The common gavel] is an instrument made use of by operative medieval Masons to break off the rough and superfluous parts of stones, the better to fit them for the builder's use; but we, as Free and Accepted Masons, are taught to make use of it for the more noble and glorious purpose of divesting our minds and consciences of all the vices and superfluities of life, thereby fitting ourselves as living stones, for that spiritual building, the house not made with hands, eternal in the heavens.[7]

But according to the Bible, man cannot simply get out the "gavel" and knock off the rough edges of human nature. Sin is far more deeply ingrained in man than that. Simply chipping off a few rough edges will not solve the sin problem or give one right standing before God. This Masonic teaching is a complete denial of what Scripture states about the fallen nature of man, the consequences of man's sin, and God's holiness and response to sin.

THE BIBLICAL VIEW: ESSENTIAL SINFULNESS

Consider what the Bible truly teaches about the nature of man in the following passages:

> For all of us have become like one who is unclean, and all our righteous deeds are like a filthy garment; and all of us wither like a leaf, and our iniquities, like the wind, take us away. (Isaiah 64:6)

> Can the Ethiopian change his skin or the leopard his spots? Then you also can do good who are accustomed to do evil. (Jeremiah 13:23)

> Truly, truly, I say to you, everyone who commits sin is the slave of sin. (John 8:34)

In the book of Job we find man described as "detestable and corrupt," as one "who drinks iniquity like water" (Job 15:16). Further, Job rhetorically asks, "How then can a man be just with God?" (Job 25:4). These Scriptures reveal that Masonry is giving its members a false teaching when it tells them that their good deeds and personal righteousness will get them to heaven.

But it is not only from the Bible that we know of the falseness of Masonry's teaching about man's nature. We know it from all of human history and experience. For example, historian John C. Green stated in *The Death of Adam: Evolution and Its Impact on Western Thought* that "the events of the twentieth century bear tragic witness to the realism of the biblical portrait of man."[8]

Even the famous agnostic Thomas Huxley, certainly no friend of Christianity, was forced to admit, "The doctrines of

. . . original sin, of the innate depravity of man . . . of the primacy of Satan in this world . . . faulty as they are, appear to me to be vastly nearer the truth than the liberal, popular illusion that babies are all born good . . . and other optimistic figments."[9] What the Bible teaches about man is confirmed daily in the newspaper and on television. Consider the reports of corporate greed, of the more than thirty sexually transmitted diseases (such as AIDS), of white collar crime, alcoholism, drug abuse, divorce, cheating on taxes, bribery, violent crime, child abuse. And we have not even scratched the surface.

According to Scripture, people, in the secret motives of their hearts, are unbelieving, self-justifying, greedy, untrustworthy, liars, and selfish, to name a few vices. If we are willing to face facts, does not Romans 1:29-32 describe people in every culture?

> Being filled with all unrighteousness, wickedness, greed, evil; full of envy, murder, strife, deceit, malice; they are gossips, slanderers, haters of God, insolent, arrogant, boastful, inventors of evil, disobedient to parents, without understanding, untrustworthy, unloving, unmerciful; and, although they know the ordinance of God, that those who practice such things are worthy of death, they not only do the same, but also give hearty approval to those who practice them. (Romans 1:29-32)

Even the "good" that men do is typically selfish, done primarily for their own welfare or profit. For example, in 1985 the popular talk show host Phil Donahue was interviewed on television. He was asked why he was so nice to the visitors who come to see his show. For example, he says "good-bye" to each one personally as they leave the studios. Here is his response: "It's really kind of selfish. . . . it's going to insure I stay competitive a little bit longer."

Perhaps the world's greatest opera tenor, Placido Domingo, was interviewed on "60 Minutes" in the summer of 1983. During the interview he was very congenial, likable, and gracious, even to his critics. When asked, "Why are you so nice to everyone?" he replied, "I do it because it's best for me."

An industry representative observed on the television program "Entertainment Tonight" for November 21, 1986: "It sounds terrible, but a lot of the celebrities go with the charity that will give them the most publicity."

The great theologian Augustine observed that the apparent good men do is really a result of the fact that, in their lives, one kind of lust is merely repressing and restraining another kind. He cited the illustration of a man whose lust for money caused him to restrain other kinds of sin in his life such as drinking and adultery. But can we really call this good? Is it good when a man forgoes one sin only to partake of another?

Most people deny the truth about themselves because it is difficult to face. So they ignore or rationalize their true selves. But as English preacher C. H. Spurgeon once said, "He who doubts human depravity had better study himself."[10] In the book of Romans the apostle Paul taught about man's natural inclinations:

> There is none righteous, not even one; there is none who understands, there is none who seeks for God; all have turned aside, together they have become useless; there is none who does good, there is not even one. Their throat is an open grave, with their tongues they keep deceiving; the poison of asps is under their lips; whose mouth is full of cursing and bitterness, their feet are swift to shed blood, destruction and misery are in their paths, and the path of peace have they not known. There is no fear of God before their eyes. (Romans 3:10-13)

Which man among Masons would be willing to accept the above statements concerning his natural motives to be true? But consider how accurate, in fact, it is. In Alexander Solzhenitsyn's address accepting the Templeton Prize for Progress in Religion in London in 1983, these were the first words out of his mouth:

> Over a half century ago, while I was still a child, I recall hearing a number of old people offer the following explanation for the great disasters that had befallen Russia: "Men have forgotten God; that's why all this has happened." Since then I have spent well nigh fifty years working on the history of our revolution; in the process I have read hundreds of books, col-

lected hundreds of personal testimonies, and have already contributed eight volumes of my own toward the effort of clearing away rubble left by that upheaval. But if I were asked today to formulate as concisely as possible the main cause of the ruinous revolution that swallowed up some sixty million of our people, I could not put it more accurately than to repeat: "Men have forgotten God; that's why all this has happened."[11]

Only the scriptural teaching on the nature of man can explain human history. Whether we wish to accept it or not, the facts of history and personal experience reveal that men are fundamentally evil. Romans mentions that men's feet were swift to shed blood, and in the last 6,000 years the world has known only 292 years of peace. A computer analysis, reported in the California *Stockton Herald*, revealed that since 3600 B.C. the world has known less than 300 years of peace. In that time, stretching over more than 55 centuries, 14,531 wars have been fought in which over 3.5 billion people have been killed. Since 650 B.C. there have been 1,656 arms races. All except sixteen of those ended in war, and those sixteen ended in the economic collapse of the countries involved.[12] To bring things up to date, Frank Barnaby, the director of the prestigious Stockholm International Peace Research Institute, revealed that, since September 1945, not a single day has passed in which one or more wars were not being fought somewhere in the world. In fact, on an 'average' day, *twelve* wars were being fought![13]

TWO VIEWS IN COLLISION

Concerning the biblical view of human nature, Masonic authority H. L. Haywood emphasizes that, though an individual Mason might rarely hold the biblical view, "the Order itself does not hold it, or countenance it, [which] is abundantly proven by the ritual, and by all our Masonic principles."[14]

Contradicting the Bible, which lies on the altar of most lodges, Masonry does not believe that man is born sinful or that he needs deliverance from his sin. There simply is no concept of the seriousness of sin, the depth of man's sinfulness, or

God's infinite wrath against sin. In a reference to belief in original sin, we find that Masonry rejects the concept outright:

> Nor does Masonry teach that human nature is a depraved thing, like the ruin of a once proud building. Many think that man was once a perfect being but that through some unimaginable moral catastrophe he became corrupt unto the last moral fiber of his being, so that, without some kind of supernatural or miraculous help from outside him, he can never [be saved].[15]

Because Masonry does not understand how serious man's sin problem is, it can offer no solution.

But even psychiatrists, such as M. Scott Peck, recognize the evil capacity man possesses. In his book *People of the Lie*, Peck describes man's sinfulness and the human capacity for self-rationalizing:

> The concept of evil has been central to religious thought for millennia. Yet it is virtually absent from our science of psychology—which one might think would be vitally concerned with the matter. . . . My own experience, however, is that evil human beings are quite common and usually appear quite ordinary to the superficial observer.
>
> The varieties of people's wickedness are manifold. As a result of their refusal to tolerate the sense of their own sinfulness, the evil ones become uncorrectable grab bags of sin. They are, for instance, in my experience, remarkably greedy people. Thus they are cheap—so cheap that their "gifts" may be murderous. In *The Road Less Traveled*, I suggested the most basic sin is laziness. In the next subsection I suggest it may be pride—because all sins are reparable except the sin of believing one is without sin. But perhaps the question of which sin is the greatest is, on a certain level, a moot issue. All sins betray—and isolate us from—both the divine and our fellow creatures. As one deep religious thinker put it, any sin "can harden into hell."[16]

Peck's entire book is a frank and uncomfortable testimony to the deep-rooted principle of evil that lives within all of us. This is why the reality of sin and evil is evidenced everywhere in the world about us (as it has been throughout history). In essence, the Masonic view of human nature is proved false every day by our own experience. As Peck observed, people will do anything to hide their own sinfulness from themselves.

Jesus taught that all people are addicted to sin. He called us "slaves of sin" (John 8:34). "That which proceeds out of the man, that is what defiles the man. For from within, out of the heart of men, proceed the evil thoughts, fornications, thefts, murders, adulteries, deeds of coveting and wickedness, as well as deceit, sensuality, envy, slander, pride and foolishness. All these evil things proceed from within and defile the man" (Mark 7:20-23).

What Jesus taught is what theologians refer to as the doctrine of human depravity. What does the doctrine of depravity teach? Depravity refers to God's moral estimation of man outside of Christ. It refers to man's condition or status before God, not his behavior before men (which is relative and may be considered good or evil). The biblical doctrine of depravity reveals that man's condition or status before God is totally helpless and hopeless (Romans 5:6; Ephesians 2:12). In fact, Scripture says clearly that unredeemed people are God's enemy (Romans 5:10), "sons of disobedience," and "by nature children of wrath" (Ephesians 2:2-3).

What this means is that man is as bad off as he can be (before God), although he is not as bad as he can be (before man). Whereas a person can perform what is considered good, before God (because he has sinned and has a nature that is sinful), he or she cannot perform what God considers good; he can never be good enough, spiritually or otherwise, to pay for his rebellion or change his nature; therefore, his depravity, his helplessness in sin before God, is total.

The doctrine of depravity is often misunderstood. It does not mean that people are as bad as they have the potential to be, or that people are equally bad. Nor does it mean that human nature itself is evil—i.e., that to be human is to be evil. Human nature was originally created good, but when man rebelled and disobeyed God, he fell from a state of purity and innocence into corruption. Nor does it mean that men are without conscience or entirely destitute of virtue or that they cannot perform actions that others consider good.

What depravity does mean is that moral and spiritual corruption has tainted every part of man's being and that the corruption is pervasive (Romans 7:14-25). This is why Scripture speaks of man as being "alienated and hostile in mind, and engaged in evil deeds" (Colossians 1:21). This is why Psalm 143:2 states, "For in Thy sight no man living is righteous," and why God warns, "'You have all transgressed against Me,' declares the Lord" (Jeremiah 2:29).

Further, the doctrine of depravity teaches that man's sinful nature actively resists God. In his fallen condition, no one wants to live for God. Jesus taught, "This is the judgment, that the light is come into the world, and men loved the darkness rather than the light; for their deeds were evil" (John 3:19). This is why an official Baptist report of Masonry concluded:

> Freemasonry teaches much about moral righteousness but almost nothing about sin and repentance. There appears to be no need for the forgiveness of sins and reconciliation to God through the shed blood of Jesus Christ. Masons are encouraged to become involved in charitable causes, and in the minds of many these good works may be their idea of earning salvation.[17]

Masonry teaches that men are good enough to perfect themselves and subsequently earn a place in heaven. Masons are so optimistic about what they can achieve because the ritual actually promises them heaven as a reward for their good works:

> [If your life is] without soil or blemish, you will be received at the pearly gates of heaven and there be presented with the pure white robe of righteousness.

> Perform the duties of your respective stations . . . and you will receive from your Almighty Father an inheritance incorruptible and undefiled, that fadeth not away.[18]

THE LODGE: MAN WILL PERFECT HIMSELF FOREVER

What's worse, some Masons actually believe that man is divine—a god of sorts: "We are taught that if we would find God, look for his revelation within our own souls. We are a part of him and he of us."[19] Masonic authorities who have passed through the higher degrees and studied their meaning and implication often teach that man is inwardly divine: "The study of man leads to knowledge of God, by revealing to man the ultimate divinity at the base of human nature."[20] Some Masons go even further, stating that "man" existed, in some sense, within God as a divine "spark" that was later born and enveloped in a body.[21]

This is why Masons speak of man as being divine or "becoming God." Leading Masonic writer Joseph Fort Newton asserts that "the great secret of Masonry" is "that it makes a man aware of that divinity within him."[22] Thus, Masonry testifies to the profound truth of "the discovery of Divinity within us" and that "God becomes man that man may become God."[23]

In fact, the above words are given verbatim and emphasized in the introduction to the *Kentucky Monitor: Complete Monitorial Ceremonies of the Blue Lodge.*[24] Another leading Masonic authority teaches in his discussion of the 25th Degree of Scottish Rite that the purpose of Masonry is to enable men to look within "to reach the spiritual and divine within himself." He further claims that because God is in all men, "we have within us an infinite, unlimited source of power."[25]

Manly Hall, a 33d Degree Mason, teaches that through Masonry "man is a god in the making" who eventually "receives . . . godhood." In fact, he describes the truly enlightened Mason as "a god-man." He tells us that the Master Mason is "entitled to definite veneration."[26] He is even worthy to have the very words that God the Father applied to Christ at His baptism:

> For him the Heavens have opened and the Great Light has bathed him in its radiance. . . . The voice speaks from the Heavens, its power thrilling the Master until his own being seems filled with its divinity, saying, *"This is my beloved Son, in whom I am well pleased. . . ."* The Master Mason is in truth a sun, a great reflector of light. . . . He, in truth, has become the spokesman of the Most High. . . . Through him passes "Hydra," the great snake and from its mouth there pours to man the light of God. (Italics added)[27]

The teachings of Masonry about the nature of man are wrong—and dramatically opposed to the Bible. How can a Christian Mason continue to support Masonry when it denies biblical truth and deceives people about their own condition before God?

THE BIBLE: JESUS CHRIST IS OUR REDEMPTION

Sometimes Masonry will admit that it cannot change human nature: "Freemasonry has magic with which to touch the hearts of men but no wizardry to make the selfish, unselfish; the brutal, gentle; the coarse, fine; the bad, good."[28] But Jesus Christ *can* change human nature. He truly regenerates, truly changes human nature, even as 2 Corinthians 5:17 states: "Therefore if any man is in Christ, he is a new creature; the old things passed away; behold, new things have come."

In 1833 Charles Darwin went to the South Sea Islands looking for the so-called Missing Link. As he studied the cannibals who lived there he concluded that no creatures anywhere were more primitive, and he was convinced that nothing on earth could possibly lift them to a higher level. Darwin believed he had truly found a lower level of humanity that could fit his theory of evolution. But thirty-four years later he returned to the same islands. To his utter amazement he discovered schools, churches, and homes occupied by some of the former cannibals. In fact, many of them wore clothes and gathered frequently to sing hymns of praise to God. The reason soon became evident. Missionary John G. Patton had been there proclaiming the truths of the gospel and salvation in Christ. Darwin was so moved by the transformation of the natives that he made a generous contribution to the London Missionary Society.[29]

During the Korean War a civilian South Korean Christian was arrested by the Communists and ordered shot. When the Communist leader learned that the prisoner was in charge of an orphanage caring for small children he decided to spare him but kill the man's son instead. In the presence of the father they shot his nineteen-year-old boy. Eventually the fortunes of war changed. The Communist leader was captured by the United Nations forces, tried, and condemned to death. But before the sentence could be carried out, the Christian, whose boy had been killed, pleaded for the life of his murderer. He forgave him because of Christ. "Give him to me," said the father, "and I'll train him." He was granted his request, and the man took the murderer of his own son into his home and cared for him. Today, that young Communist is a Christian pastor.[30]

In 1946, Czeslaw Godlewski belonged to a young gang that roamed and sacked the German countryside. On an isolated farm they brutally attacked ten members of the Wilhelm Hamelmann family. Nine of the victims died, but Wilhelm himself survived four bullet wounds. When Godlewski completed a twenty-year prison term for his brutal crimes, the state would not release him because he had no place to go. Wilhelm learned of the situation and asked the authorities to release Godlewski to his custody. He wrote in his request, "Christ died for my sins and forgave me. Should I not then forgive this man?"[31]

In the August 1983 segment of "Crossfire," the interviewer of Watergate figure Charles Colson admitted he was once an utter and total skeptic of Colson's conversion to Christ. Chuck Colson was no saint; the things he did were terrible. Yet after getting to know him, after seeing his work over the past ten years since his conversion, even this skeptic stated on nationwide television with enthusiasm in his voice that this was "one of the greatest transformations of recent history."

Christ can change human nature. No matter how low or degraded, because of His love for men, Christ will change the one who turns to Him in faith. Can Masonry offer anything like this? It does not even try. What all this means is that Masonry cannot really deliver its own promises to justify men before God and that it is leading its own people spiritually astray. It is leading them down what Jesus called the "broad road that leads to destruction" (Matthew 7:13).

Given the importance of personal salvation through Christ and given Masonry's unrelenting opposition to this by repeatedly stressing that men can save themselves, then can anyone doubt that Masonry and Christianity are at odds with each other and that a person cannot embrace both at the same time?

Scripture is emphatic as to the impossibility of moral and spiritual elevation by personal effort. Jesus taught,

> Abide in Me, and I in you. As the branch cannot bear fruit of itself, unless it abides in the vine, so neither can you, unless you abide in Me. I am the vine, you are the branches; he who abides in Me, and I in him, he bears much fruit; for apart from Me you can do nothing. (John 15:4-5)

No Mason will ever produce fruit for God apart from Jesus Christ. And no Mason will ever enter heaven apart from a spiritual rebirth through Christ. Jesus emphasized,

> Truly, truly, I say to you, unless one is born again, he cannot see the kingdom of God... [and] he cannot enter into the kingdom of God. That which is born of the flesh is flesh, and that which is born of the Spirit is spirit. Do not marvel that I said to you, "You must be born again." (John 3:3, 5-7)

Hell is as much a part of the love story of God as
heaven.
Donald Barnhouse

12

Hell

Masons staunchly declare that "the Holy Bible is given us as
the rule and guide for our faith and practice."[1] That is, the
Bible is held to be "the great light" of Masonry.[2] But if this is so,
why does Masonry never once warn men about hell? Because
Masonic authorities teach that the Bible is only a symbol. Candidates, however, are not told this in the ritual, and Christian Masons do not view the Bible in this way.

HELL IN THE LODGE

Hell is not mentioned in any of the rituals or ceremonies
of the three degrees of the Blue Lodge, the ten degrees of the
York Rite, or the thirty degrees of the Scottish Rite. Rather, the
Lodge offers Masons the false hope that they will be granted ad-
mittance to the "glorious Lodge above, where the Supreme Architect of the Universe presides." In the teachings of the Third
Degree, the Arkansas *Monitor* states:

> Let us imitate the good man in his virtuous and amiable con-
> duct, in his unfeigned piety to God, in his inflexible fidelity to
> his trust, that we may welcome death as a kind messenger
> sent from our Supreme Grand Master to translate us from
> this imperfect to that all perfect and glorious Lodge above,
> where the Supreme Architect of the Universe presides.[3]

Nothing could constitute a greater disservice than to do as the Masonic Lodge does here, to make men think they will automatically go to heaven when they die because of their good works and never warn them of the penalty for rejecting God's true salvation.

HELL IN THE BIBLE

Jesus taught plainly that hell exists (Matthew 25:46; Mark 9:47; Luke 16:19-31). Because He was the only man in all of human history to prove the truth of His teachings by rising from the dead, we must accept His word. The probability that hell exists is exactly the same as the probability that Christ rose from the dead. Because Christ's resurrection has withstood the test of time, including the critical scrutiny of leading intellects through the ages,[4] the existence of hell is certain. Jesus said He was God incarnate, and God incarnate knows what awaits men after death. Jesus not only told us about death, He approved the Scriptures' teachings about death.

Where are the dead? The Bible speaks plainly about this. It divides all past mankind into two large groups: the saved and the lost.

> When the Son of Man comes in his glory, and all the angels with him, he will sit on his throne in heavenly glory. All the nations will be gathered before him, and he will separate the people one from another as a shepherd separates the sheep from the goats. He will put the sheep on his right and the goats on his left. Then the King will say to those on his right, "Come, you who are blessed by my Father; take your inheritance, the kingdom prepared for you since the creation of the world. . . ." Then he will say to those on his left, "Depart from me, you who are cursed, into the eternal fire prepared for the devil and his angels. . . ." Then they will go away to eternal punishment, but the righteous to eternal life. (Matthew 25:31-34, 41, 46; NIV)

The Bible comments at length as to the position of the saved dead. They go to be with the Lord:

> "And if I go and prepare a place for you, I will come back and take you to be with me that you also may be where I am. You

know the way to the place where I am going. . . ." Jesus answered, "I am the way and the truth and the life. No one comes to the Father except through me." (John 14:3-4, 6; NIV)

And this is the testimony: God has given us eternal life, and this life is in his Son. (1 John 5:11; see Luke 23:43; John 12:26; 14:1-3; 17:24; 2 Corinthians 5:8; Philippians 1:21, 23; NIV)

But the unsaved dead—the lost—meet a different fate. The most unpopular passages of the Bible deal with the confinement and punishment of those who die in unbelief. Nevertheless, the Scriptures are clear:

This is how it will be at the end of the age. The angels will come and separate the wicked from the righteous and throw them into the fiery furnace, where there will be weeping and gnashing of teeth. (Matthew 13:49-50; NIV)

This will happen when the Lord Jesus is revealed from heaven in blazing fire with his powerful angels. He will punish those who do not know God and do not obey the gospel of our Lord Jesus. They will be punished with everlasting destruction and shut out from the presence of the Lord and from the majesty of his power. (2 Thessalonians 1:7*b*-9; NIV)

Jesus gave enough warnings for the entire human race to hear (e.g., "You fool! This very night your soul is required of you."—Luke 12:20; NIV). In fact, Jesus told His disciples that they need not fear murderers, "who kill the body, and after that have no more that they can do" (Luke 12:4). Those killers only bring about the first death. It is fearful enough, of course, but Jesus' point was to warn of God's righteous wrath after death. It is God who has sway over the final death: "Fear the One who after He has killed has authority to cast into hell; yes, I tell you, fear Him!" (v. 5).

It has always been a curiosity that people, like the Masons, who swear that the passages in the Bible concerning heaven are absolutely true, utterly reject the passages on hell. Hell is described in the Bible in a variety of terms: "outer darkness," "the resurrection of judgment," "the black darkness," "the punishment of eternal fire," "the place where there is weeping and gnashing of teeth," "eternal punishment," to name a few (Matthew 8:12; 22:13; 25:46; Mark 9:43, 48; John 5:29; Revelation 19:20; 20:10-15).

What bothers people is not the fact of punishment after death—most people accept the idea that there should be some punishment for those who do wrong, like purgatory—but the fact that the Bible teaches that this punishment is eternal gives them a problem. Some might admit that a person like Hitler was worthy of eternal punishment. But they cannot seem to understand why those who reject Jesus should be sentenced to hell. Actually, God punishes them for their sins as well as for rejecting Christ. But they could have escaped hell had they accepted God's gift of forgiveness through Christ.

The problem is not that hell exists—it must exist if God is infinitely holy; it must exist if there is an absolute distinction between good and evil. Our sins cannot go unnoticed or unpunished by a holy God or else He would not be holy. The problem is that people do not understand how serious a crime our sins are and that each one of them is worthy of sentencing us to eternal punishment. Why is this true?

Since God is infinitely holy, when we sin against Him we have committed an infinite crime, and an infinite crime requires an infinite punishment. That is why Jesus preached an eternal hell. Hell is not unjust; it is exactly what man deserves for his rebellion against an infinitely loving and holy God.

How serious are our sinful deeds? One only needs to remember that the Son of God Himself had to die a horribly torturous death on the cross to pay the penalty for our sins. Jesus paid the price of eternal hell for each of us. While He was dying, the judgment of all mankind's sins was placed on Him! God spared Him not (Romans 8:32). Since God provided for every man's salvation, every sin will be accounted for. Because Jesus was punished for every sin, we should never think that God will deal lightly with those who reject His Son and do not repent of their sins:

> We must pay more careful attention, therefore, to what we have heard, so that we do not drift away. For if the message spoken by angels was binding, and every violation and dis-

obedience received its just punishment, how shall we escape if we ignore such a great salvation? This salvation, which was first announced by the Lord, was confirmed to us by those who heard him. God also testified to it by signs, wonders and various miracles. (Hebrews 2:1-4; NIV)

If we deliberately keep on sinning after we have received the knowledge of the truth, no sacrifice for sins is left, but only a fearful expectation of judgment and of raging fire that will consume the enemies of God. Anyone who rejected the law of Moses died without mercy on the testimony of two or three witnesses. How much more severely do you think a man deserves to be punished who has trampled the Son of God under foot, who has treated as an unholy thing the blood of the covenant that sanctified him, and who has insulted the Spirit of grace? (Hebrews 10:26-29; NIV)

In the least, these verses teach that those who have heard the message of salvation and continue to reject it can only expect eventual judgment. If the Bible is the great light of Masonry, why are men not warned of this fearful judgment to come?

HELL IN THE TEACHING OF THE CHURCH

Serious Bible scholars have wrestled with the biblical teaching concerning hell for centuries. Donald Barnhouse once wrote,

The nature of God is justice to balance his love. The fact that God's time of patience will end and that he will strike out in justice is the hope of the sin cursed universe. If God does not act to destroy, then we face an eternity of sinfulness. But God is holy and just, and therefore he will destroy. For believers, he has already moved to destroy their sin by placing it on Christ and dealing with it for eternity, but upon those who will not enter in to Christ, the flood of his wrath must fall. Hell is as much a part of the love story of God as heaven.[5]

Greek scholar and eminent theologian Leon Morris has said,

People do not realize that it is not easy to do away with hell without at the same time getting rid of heaven. I do not mean that we are forced into an acceptance of every detail of a hell that some of an earlier day knew far too much about. They spoke more confidently about the details of the place of punishment than Scripture allows, and in reaction some others abandoned the whole concept. But if there is nothing corresponding to hell, then we all pass into the afterlife. There is then no distinction between the good and the bad, between those who have trusted Christ and those who have not. All are in the afterlife together, with the evil apparently having as much right to it as the righteous. It is this world all over again! There is no place where righteousness dwells.[6]

Lewis Sperry Chafer warned:

Men are pleased to receive the Bible revelation concerning Heaven, but do not heed its warning regarding hell. Human sentiment, opinion, and reasons are valueless concerning these eternal issues. It is wisdom to heed the voice of the Son of God, and he more than any other has stressed the woes of the lost (Mt. 5:22, 29, 30; 10:28; 18:9; 23:15, 33; Mk. 9:43, 47; Lk. 12:5). If eternal punishment cannot be comprehended, it should be remembered that infinite holiness and the sin by which infinite holiness is outraged are equally unmeasurable by the human mind. God is not revealed as one who causes good people to suffer in hell; but he is revealed as one who at infinite cost has wrought to the end that sinners, believing in Christ, may not perish, but have everlasting life.[7]

Oxford scholar C. S. Lewis has expanded on the fairness of the biblical teaching on hell:

If a game is played, it must be possible to lose it. If the happiness of a creature lies in self-surrender, no one can make that surrender but himself (though many can help him to make it) and he may refuse. I would pay any price to be able to say truthfully "all will be saved." But my reason retorts, "Without their will, or with it?" If I say, "Without their will" I at once perceive a contradiction; how can the supreme voluntary act of self-surrender be involuntary? If I say, "With their will," my reason replies, "How, if they *will not* give in?"[8]

Theologian Harold O. J. Brown has said, "Hell has been called 'the most enduring monument to the freedom of the hu-

man will',"[9] and C. S. Lewis stated, "There are only two kinds of
people in the end: those who say to God '*Thy* will be done,' and
those to whom God says, in the end, 'Thy will be done.'"[10] Jesus
Himself once said, "You are unwilling to come to Me, that you
may have life" (John 5:40). And Jesus' statement is the truth
about hell. We choose it for ourselves. It is not God who
chooses hell for us, but we ourselves. We can either choose to
receive God's gift of salvation, paid for by the death of Christ for
our sins, or we can refuse God's gift and receive the punishment we deserve in hell. Masons and all people everywhere
should take careful thought as to what our Lord Jesus and the
Bible teach concerning heaven and hell.

In his *Systematic Theology*, Chafer observed a crucial
point that is often overlooked: if God *were* to forgive sin by an
act of mere kindness, His own holiness would be compromised; but *if* He could forgive sin by an act of mere kindness,
the death of Christ would be unnecessary. Frankly, neither op-
tion is possible:

> Many are the attempts made by those who understand noth-
> ing of the real character of God to save Him from the unde-
> sirable reputation He must acquire if He does not in compas-
> sion rescue all beings from eternal retribution.... God is
> holiness and righteousness as well as love. It is the holiness
> of His Person and the righteousness of His government
> which preclude Him from any mere generosity which would
> make light of sin. In fact, sin is sufficiently sinful to require
> eternal retribution as the divine penalty for it. There is no
> field for argument at this point. The Word of God must stand
> and man must be reminded that of the two issues involved—
> sin and holiness—he knows nothing about their depth of
> meaning. Being *absolute*, divine holiness cannot be varied or
> altered in the least degree. This truth is the key to the entire
> problem which the idea of retribution engenders. If God
> could have forgiven one sin of one person as an act of mere
> kindness, He would have compromised His own holiness
> which demands judgment for sin. Having thus compromised
> Himself with sin, He would need Himself to be saved be-
> cause of the unrighteous thing He had done. He would, by
> such supposed kindness, have established a principle by
> which He could forgive all human sin as an act of divine

clemency, and thus the death of Christ . . . becomes the greatest possible divine blunder."

Masonry denies the Bible's teachings on life after death. Worse, Masonry does not warn men about hell. How then can a Christian Mason in good conscience give his time and money to an organization that teaches a lie about what happens to a man when he dies? Where then does the Christian Mason's allegiance lie? How can a Christian pastor continue to support the Lodge when the Lodge says, in effect, that Christ did not need to die for the sins of the world—that men are good enough to earn their own salvation—and that never says a word about the judgment of God in hell?

A Christian Response to Part 2

In this section we have uncovered many things about Masonry. We have seen that Masonry has not been honest about its teachings. Masonry claims that it offers no plan of salvation, but it does. It offers salvation based upon good works and personal merit, a plan the Bible condemns as a "false gospel."

As we saw in Part 1, Masonry emphatically denies that it is a religion. But it meets every criteria of religion in Webster's dictionary. Masonry claims that the Holy Bible is its great light and the rule and guide for Masonic faith and practice. But in reality, Masonry treats the Bible as merely a symbol, a piece of Lodge furniture that really does not have to be obeyed by men. Masonry distorts the Bible in its rituals and alters its teachings. In fact, Masonry recognizes the Scriptures of many other religions as being equally "valid" for Masons.

Masonry claims that the god of the Lodge is the same God Christians worship. But we have seen that this, too, is a deception. The god of the Masonic Lodge has nothing whatever to do with the God of Christianity. The god of Masonry is a pagan, foreign deity that forces members of the Lodge to engage in idolatry—the worship of a false god.

Masonry claims that it reveres Jesus Christ. But, in fact, it denies Him, blasphemes Him, and turns men away from Him. It deletes the name of Christ from its prayers and scriptural quotations; it offers the titles and offices of Christ to unbelievers;[1] it forces Christians to disobey Christ by prohibiting all discussion of Christ during Lodge activity; it denies the deity of Jesus Christ and teaches that He was only a man; and, finally, it denies the role of Christ as Savior. Some Masons even teach that the Christian message of divine redemption is a corruption of earlier pagan stories.

Masonry claims that it can make good men better. But because Masonry denies the biblical teaching on the sinfulness of man, this is an impossible task and a false hope. In God's eyes, men are not good to begin with, and apart from regeneration, it is impossible for men to do good works acceptable to God.

Masonry teaches that all men will live forever in the Celestial Lodge Above. But again, Masonry completely distorts what the Bible plainly says on the subject of the afterlife, ignoring and denying the biblical doctrines of heaven and hell.

What's more, Masonry claims that God is the spiritual Father of all men and that all people, regardless of religious belief, are the spiritual sons of God. But we have seen that this, too, is false. Only those who believe in Christ are granted the right to become true spiritual sons of God. Is it any wonder that Lutheran pastor and authority on Masonry Martin L. Wagner concluded of Masonry:

> The whole system is a giant evil. We firmly believe that it is the greatest foe that the church has to contend against. It insidiously undermines and overthrows the very foundations of evangelical Christianity. Its tendency is to make men indifferent to doctrine and hostile to the positive teachings of [the Bible].[2]

It is to the Bible that we must turn for a succinct statement on Masonry, particularly relevant to those who are "Christian Masons":

> For our transgressions are multiplied before Thee,
> And our sins testify against us;
> For our transgressions are with us,
> And we know our iniquities:
> Transgressing and denying the Lord,

And turning away from our God,
Speaking oppression and revolt,
Conceiving in and uttering from the heart lying words.
(Isaiah 59:12-13)

As a Christian, why not pray and ask God to forgive you and cleanse you from your sin? If you are a Mason who is not a Christian, we would ask you: If Masonry is a religion, is it the true religion? Will it truly lead you to heaven? Does it truly honor and glorify the God of the Bible?

The bottom line for you should be, if Masonry is true, then you should follow it and promote its teachings. But if Masonry has rejected and opposed the truth—if it has denied God and His Word, if it has denied the Lord Jesus Christ, and if it has denied God's plan of salvation, offering instead a false hope—then you should reject Masonry, receive Jesus as your Savior, and leave the Lodge.

Jesus taught, "I am the way, the truth and the life: no man cometh unto the Father, but by Me" (John 14:6; KJV*) and, "This is eternal life, that they may know Thee, the only true God, and Jesus Christ whom Thou hast sent" (John 17:3). The Bible further teaches, "And there is salvation in no one else; for there is no other name under heaven that has been given among men, by which we must be saved" (Acts 4:12).

If you know you have broken God's laws and are a sinner, and understand Jesus died and paid for your sins on the cross, and if you are willing now to confess your sins to Him and place your entire trust in Him to make you a Christian, you may receive Jesus into your life by saying the following prayer:

> Lord Jesus, I confess that I am a sinner. I believe that You died for my sins on the cross. I receive You now as my Lord and Savior and ask You to give me the resolve and strength to turn from what is evil and to live a life that is pleasing to You. I know now that Masonry does not bring honor to You, and I am willing to resign from the Lodge.

* King James Version.

If you prayed this prayer, please write us at Moody Press or "The John Ankerberg Show," and we will send you some materials to help you grow as a Christian. As a further help to those of you (whether Christian or non-Christian) who have decided to leave the Lodge, we recommend the following instructions and provide a sample letter. The rules and orders of the Lodge specify that, if your letter meets the following requirement, it must be read before the members of the Lodge. If done in this fashion, your letter will become a testimony to others in the Lodge concerning the truth of Jesus Christ.

In your letter, tell them that the reason you are leaving the Lodge is because it conflicts with the teaching of the Bible and especially the teachings of Christ. Give a few Bible verses to prove where it conflicts (e.g., you might bring up John 8:12, which asserts that the Christian is not in darkness apart from Masonry). You could refer to the nature (deity) and mission of Christ (redeeming Savior) or to the nature of salvation—by grace through faith—not works (Ephesians 2:8-9). If the letter is addressed in the following manner, according to Masonic law, it must be read before the Lodge:

The letterhead and envelope must both be addressed to the *members of the Lodge*. Never address your letter to the Lodge Master or merely to, say, "Lodge 202," because this refers to the officers, who will simply process your request without reading it to the Lodge membership. Again:

1. Your letter must be addressed (on the outside of the envelope) "To the members of Lodge number _____," then give the address.

2. The letter itself must begin with "To the members of Lodge number _____" and not to any particular person— only to Lodge members.

To help you officially sever your ties from the Lodge, we recommend the following sample letter as given by former Mason Dale Byers:

Sample Letter for Receiving a Demit

To the members of Lodge number _____:

This letter is a formal request for my demit from the Masonic Lodge. Please remove my name from your membership rolls and mail to me a copy of my demit.

Thank you for allowing me an opportunity to express my reasons for withdrawing from the Lodge. Do understand that my withdrawal has no personal bearing upon individual members or any personal conflicts with members. Those in the Lodge who are my friends know that I still treasure their personal friendships.

However, I am a Christian and must forsake the Lodge because its teachings are contrary to the true teachings of the Bible. Freemasonry rejects the Lord Jesus Christ Who is the Lord and Master of my life. I cannot with a clear conscience be a Mason because Jesus Christ is not allowed to be named or worshiped in the Lodge as it might offend another Mason. Masonry's respected authors, Albert Mackey and Albert Pike, openly claim that Masonry is a religion. They are right! It is a religion without Christ.

Many of us have heard that the Lodge is based on the Bible. However, in Freemasonry the Bible is rejected and God's Word is misused and misquoted. The Lodge's religion is universalism and the Bible is nothing more than a symbol.

Masonry promises to its members the blessings of Heaven and acceptance before God. [But] the Masonic plan of salvation is totally contrary to what the Bible teaches. Men cannot be saved apart from Jesus Christ as [their] Savior.

In closing, may I express my love for you as individuals and if you desire, I will gladly share how I became a Christian and help you to understand how you, too, may become a follower of Jesus Christ.

Your friend in Christ,[5]

Masonry . . . is not the rival of any religion, but the friend of all.

Joseph Fort Newton
The Religion of Masonry

Part 3

Religious Secrets: Practice

We first promise to love and adore God.
The initiation of the Tenth Degree of the Scottish Rite
J. Blanchard,
Scottish Rite Masonry Illustrated, 1:220

13

Blaspheming God's Name

Dictionaries define *blasphemy* as contempt for God, as irreverence toward God, or as "the act of claiming the attributes or prerogatives of deity."[1] The truth is that few things are more blasphemous, show more contempt for God, and demonstrate irreverence toward Him than Masonic rituals. In the higher degrees of Masonry—that is, in both the York and Scottish Rites—the Masonic Lodge misuses the personal name of God or the things that God alone does.

In Mark 2:5 Jesus merely said the words "Your sins are forgiven" to a man who was paralyzed. The Jewish leaders immediately accused Jesus of blasphemy because "only God can forgive sin." From the perspective of the Pharisees, Jesus, whom they considered a mere man, had identified Himself with an activity reserved for God alone.

Men in the Lodge do not realize that, when they identify themselves with the names of God or with the activities only God can do, they are committing blasphemy. In Revelation 5:1-5, for instance, only Jesus Christ is permitted to open the "seven seals." But in the 17th Degree of the Scottish Rite, the "All-Puissant" opens the seven seals in the Masonic ritual:

Senior Warden	Brother, you will examine closely everything which the All Puissant is going to show you. [Pauses a moment.] Is there [a] mortal here worthy to open the book with seven seals? (All cast their eyes down and sigh.)
All Puissant	[Opens First Seal of Bible and takes out a bow, a quiver filled with arrows and a crown which he hands to the youngest Knight saying: Depart and continue the conquest.]
All Puissant	[Opens Second Seal and removes a sword which he hands to next oldest Knight.]
All Puissant	[Opens Third Seal and takes out a balance. . . .]
All Puissant	[Opens Fourth Seal and takes out a human skull. . . .]
All Puissant	[Opens Fifth Seal and removes a cloth stained with blood. . . .]
All Puissant	[Opens Sixth Seal and at that moment the Sun (on the chart) is darkened and the Moon stained with blood.]
All Puissant	[Opens Seventh Seal and takes out incense. . . .]
All Puissant	Here is seen the fulfillment of a prophecy (Revelation vii, 3). . . .[2]

Another scriptural example illustrating the nature of blasphemy (albeit through an incorrect accusation) takes place in Mark 14. Jesus was on trial for His life. During this trial, He used an Old Testament title, "the Son of Man," from Daniel 7, and He referred this title to Himself. Then "the high priest asked him, 'Are you the Christ [Messiah], the Blessed One?' 'I am,' said Jesus. 'And you will see the Son of Man sitting at the right hand of the Mighty One and coming on the clouds of heaven'" (Mark 14:61-62). When the high priest heard this, he "tore his clothes. 'Why do we need any more witnesses?' he asked. 'You have heard the blasphemy. What do you think?' They all condemned [Jesus] as worthy of death" (Mark 14:63-64; NIV).

Here, Jesus' appropriation to Himself of a title that belonged to the Messiah was regarded by Caiaphas as blasphemy, for which the Mosaic law proscribed death by stoning (Leviticus 24:16). Masons do not realize they are committing the horrible sin of blasphemy by assigning to their members names re-served only for God. No Christian should have anything to do with such ceremonies.

BLASPHEMY IN THE YORK RITE

In the Royal Arch or Seventh Degree of the York Rite, the personal name God used in His revelation to Moses (and also correctly appropriated by Jesus in the New Testament)—namely, the "I AM"—is wrongly appropriated to mere men:

High priest	Companion Captain of the Host, are you a Royal Arch Mason?
Captain	*I am that I am.* . . .
High priest	What is the color of his banner?
Captain	White, and is emblematical of that purity of heart and rectitude of conduct which are essential to obtain admission into the divine sanctum sanctorum [heaven] above. (Italics added)[3]

Later, the "I AM" name of God is used as a Masonic password:

We were directed to use the words, "I AM THAT I AM," as a password.

Principal Sojourner	We will go up. Companions, you will follow me; our password is, I AM THAT I AM. . . .
Master of First Veil	How do you expect to enter here?
Principal Sojourner	By a password that we received in Babylon.
Master of First Veil	Give it to me.
Principal Sojourner	I AM THAT I AM.[4]

Here the special and holy name God revealed to His people is blasphemously degraded to a password. Why is this considered blasphemy? God said, "This is My name forever, and this is My memorial-name to all generations" (Exodus 3:15*b*) and "You shall not misuse the name of the Lord your God, for the Lord will not hold anyone guiltless who misuses his name" (Exodus 20:7; NIV). The Masonic Lodge has misused God's name, reducing it to a password for believer and unbeliever alike. Unbelievers in the Lodge have taken to themselves the very name of God in their response to the ritual.

In the same degree, the Masonic Lodge blasphemously combines God's name with the names of the pagan deities Baal and Osiris, resulting in the name *Jah-bul-on* (see chapters 8 and 9):

> They then rise and give all the signs, from the Entered Apprentice up to this Degree, after which they join in squads of three for giving the Grand Omnific Royal Arch Word, as follows: . . . As we three did agree, in peace, love, and unity, the Sacred Word to keep, so we three do agree, in peace, love, and unity, the Sacred Word to search; until we three, or three such as we, shall agree to close this Royal Arch. They then balance three times three, bringing the right hand with some violence down upon the left. The right hands are then raised above their heads, and the words, Jah-buh-lun-Je-ho-vah, G-o-d, are given at low breath, each companion pronouncing the syllables or letters alternately.[5]

In chapter 9 we saw saw how evil and blasphemous is this intermingling of Jehovah's holy name with the pagan god Baal. In fact, we saw that God judged the nation of Israel for identifying Him with Baal and then following after the ways of Baal. Here again, the Masonic Lodge has blasphemously used God's name in its ritual.

BLASPHEMY IN THE SCOTTISH RITE

The Scottish Rite uses several names for God in a blasphemous way. First, Masonry blasphemes *Jehovah* in the Scottish Rite by denigrating its use to a common password or secret sacred word men identify themselves by in the Lodge. In the initiation of the Sixth Degree the following exchange takes place:

Solomon	What is the great word?
Hiram	J E H O V A H mentioned by letters. . . .
Solomon	What signifies the J which you see in the window?
Hiram	Jehovah.
Solomon	What does the word signify?
Hiram	It is the third pronunciation of the great name of the Architect of the Universe. . . .[6]

In the initiation and lecture of the Fifth Degree, Jehovah is used as a password:

MARCH:	Make a square by walking four steps and bring the feet together at each step.
PASSWORD:	Acacia.
SACRED WORD:	Jehovah.[7]
Adoniram	What is the meaning of the letter "J" which is in the center of the square stone?
Stolkin	It is the initial of the ineffable name of the Grand Architect of the Universe and of the sacred word of the Perfect Masters.
Adoniram	Pronounce it.
Stolkin	Jehovah.[8]

Jehovah's name is also blasphemously used in the 13th, the 23d, and the 26th Degrees.[9]

Adonai is another of the names for God that is blasphemously used by the Lodge. In the initiation of the 14th Degree both *Adonai* and *Jehovah* are degraded by their use as secret words:

Third Covered Word	Adonai.
Third Pass Word	Bea Makeh, Bamearah, interpreted, "Thank God we have found."
SACRED WORD:	Jehovah.
GRAND WORD:	Jod He Van He [JHVH]. . . .[10]

Another example is found in the lecture of the 11th Degree:

Thrice Puissant	What is your sacred word in quality of Sublime Knight Elected?
Inspector	Adonai, which is God.[11]

Adonai is blasphemously used as a sacred word in the 12th Degree as well.[12]

In closing ceremonies of the 13th Degree of the Scottish Rite, God's name *I AM* is applied to the candidate:

Solomon	Brother Inspector, what are you?
Inspector	I am that I am.[13]

Another name for God in the Bible is *Immanuel*, which means "God with us" (Isaiah 7:14; Matthew 1:23). This name is blasphemously used in the ritual of the 18th Degree:

> SIGN OF HELP.
> Cross the legs, the right behind the left.
> ANSWER.
> Same except left leg behind the right.
> TOKEN.
> Give the sign of the Good Shepherd; face each other, bow; place reciprocally crossed hands on breast and give the fraternal kiss and pronounce the pass word.
> PASS WORD: Emanuel [*sic*].
> SACRED WORD: I. N. R. I. *Inri*; lettered by the persons giving it alternately. They are the initials of the Latin Words; *Jesus, Nazarenus, Rex, Judaeorum*, signifying Jesus of Nazareth, King of the Jews.[14]

We find the same use in the 27th Degree.[15] In the 19th Degree, God's name, *Immanuel*, is also downgraded to a password. The office of Christ Himself is given to the candidate:

> OBLIGATION
> Be thou a Priest forever, after the order of Melchizedek, virtuous, sincere, equitable, true; minister of justice and priest of toleration. . . . [cf. Hebrews 7:17]
> TOKEN.
> Each places the palm of his right hand on the other's forehead; one says, Alleluia, the other answers, Praise the Lord; the first then says, Emanuel [*sic*], the other, God speed you. Both say Amen.
> BATTERY: Twelve equi-timed strokes.
> TO OPEN: It is the predicted hour.
> TO CLOSE: The hour is accomplished.
> PASS WORD: Emanuel.[16]

Masons even have the name *Jaweh* on the Masonic jewel in the 27th Degree.[17]

In all these rituals Masons have cited God's name, requested His blessing, and quoted His words. They have blasphemed God because they have used His name, and all that His name represents, in rituals that deny, distort, and repudiate the very God whose name they use. Once again, *to blaspheme* is defined as "to speak irreverently," or "to speak profanely of or to God," or as "contempt for God," or as "the act of claiming the attributes or prerogatives of deity."[18] What could be more irreverent or contemptible than using the name of God in rituals that deny everything God teaches and represents in the Bible? What is more profane than using the name of God in pagan ritual and applying that name to oneself? The Jews in the Old Testament would not go so far as to *pronounce* God's name, but Masons use it in their profane skits, appropriating it to unbelievers, who mock God by citing His name in approval of doctrines He abhors and condemns.

THE THINGS GOD HATES

One of the most appalling statements found in the ritual is where Masonry claims that Jehovah God created Masonry. Each candidate is taught this in the 30th Degree of the Scottish Rite:

> When the spirit of God moved upon the face of the waters; when the Great Jehovah ordained the creation of the world; when the first Sun rose to greet with its beams, the new morning and the august command was uttered: "Let there be light." *The lips of deity breathed Masonry into existence* and it must live forevermore; for truth is eternal, and the principles of truth are the foundation of Masonry. (Italics added)[19]

To claim that God Himself is the originator of the doctrines found in the Masonic rituals is both a lie and blasphemy. It is absolutely impossible that God could be the author of what He condemns in the Bible:

GOD HATES FALSE TEACHING AND EVERY FALSE WAY

> Yet I sent you all My servants the prophets, again and again, saying, "Oh, do not do this abominable thing [i.e., idolatry] which I hate." But they did not listen to or incline their ears to turn from their wickedness. (Jeremiah 44:4-5)

> Therefore I esteem right all Thy precepts concerning everything. I hate every false way. (Psalm 119:128)[20]

We have seen that Masonry teaches false doctrines that lead men astray. Therefore, if God hates false teaching, He must hate the Masonic doctrines that lead men astray.

GOD HATES FALSE GOSPELS

The apostle Paul knew what God thought about false gospels:

> I am astonished that you are so quickly deserting the one who called you by the grace of Christ and are turning to a different gospel—which is really no gospel at all. Evidently some people are throwing you into confusion and are trying to pervert the gospel of Christ. *But even if we or an angel from heaven should preach a gospel other than the one we preached to you, let him be eternally condemned!*" (Galatians 1:6-8; italics added; NIV)

Chapter 1 demonstrated that Masonry teaches a false gospel of works salvation. Therefore, if God hates false gospels, He must hate the Masonic teachings that cause men to adopt a false gospel.

GOD HATES PRIDE AND LIES

> There are six things which the Lord hates, yes, seven which are an abomination to Him: haughty eyes, a lying tongue, and hands that shed innocent blood, a heart that devises wicked plans, feet that run rapidly to evil, a false witness who utters lies, and one who spreads strife among brothers. (Proverbs 6:16-19)

> A righteous man hates falsehood. (Proverbs 13:5)

Because Masonry teaches salvation by personal righteousness, it fosters pride. Furthermore, Masonry lies about what it really believes by saying it is compatible with Christianity when it is not. If God hates that which fosters pride and lying, then He must hate the Masonic doctrines that encourage such things.

GOD HATES FALSE GODS AND IDOLATROUS PRACTICES

> Thus says the Lord of hosts, the God of Israel, " . . . I sent you all My servants the prophets, again and again, saying, 'O, do

not do this abominable thing which I hate.' But they did not listen or incline their ears to turn from their wickedness, so as not to burn sacrifices to other gods. Therefore My wrath and My anger were poured out and burned in the cities of Judah and in the streets of Jerusalem, so they have become a ruin and a desolation as it is this day."... Thus says the Lord God of hosts,... "Why are you... provoking Me to anger with the works of your hands, burning sacrifices to other gods?" (Jeremiah 44:2-8; cf. Exodus 20:3-5)

Because Masonry leads men to worship a false god (G.A.O.T.U., Jah-Bul-On), it is guilty of the sin of idolatry. If God hates false gods and idolatrous practices, then He must hate the Masonry that promotes them.

GOD HATES ALL WORKERS OF INIQUITY

"For Thou art not a God who takes pleasure in wickedness; no evil dwells with thee. The boastful shall not stand before Thine eyes; Thou dost hate all who do iniquity. Thou dost destroy those who speak falsehood; the Lord abhors the man of bloodshed and deceit" (Psalm 5:4-6). Masonry boasts that men in the Lodge are able to earn and merit God's favor (apart from Christ). In this, Masonry "speaks falsehood" and is deceitful. The entire system of Masonry perpetuates false doctrines, and therefore all who participate in it and support it are purveyors of iniquity. If God hates iniquity, He must hate the system that perpetuates it.

GOD HATES FALSE OATHS

"'These are the things which you should do: speak the truth to one another; judge with truth.... Also let none of you devise evil in your heart against another, and do not love perjury [literally, false oath], for all these are what I hate,' declares the Lord" (Zechariah 8:16,17). Masonry requires every candidate to swear an oath to God that he will be true to Masonic beliefs. Christians should not swear by God to uphold that which God condemns.

In our next chapter we will see how extensive are the false oaths of Masonry—and why God surely hates them. As we have seen in this chapter, what is most significant is that the things God hates are *exactly what Masonry practices.* Jesus warns those who reject Him and still think they can worship God that "he who hates Me hates My Father also" (John 15:23). By opposing everything Jesus has taught, by denying His nature and mission, Masonry proves it hates God, no matter how much it claims to honor God.

In the Old Testament, a righteous man by the name of Jehu once rebuked Jehoshaphat, the king of Judah, and asked, "Should you help the wicked and love those who hate the Lord and so bring wrath on yourself from the Lord?" (2 Chronicles 19:2). The same question could be asked of Christian Masons. Should they help the wicked and love those who hate the Lord? Should they continue to support Masonry and its many false teachings? Christian Masons should not continue to blaspheme God. Christian pastors should not support a religion that teaches men to blaspheme both the God who loves them and His Son, whom He sent to die for their sins.

[The Mason should] prefer death rather than divulge the mysteries of the order.
From the Eighth Degree of the Scottish Rite
J. Blanchard, *Scottish Rite Masonry Illustrated*, 1:141

14

Swearing Oaths

If you are a Christian Mason, did you know that the oaths you swore to uphold Masonry violated and denied your Christian faith? Were you aware that the Masonic oaths you took were not Christian? Maybe you did not realize that they were meant to bind you so strongly to Masonry that you would never be able to extricate yourself. Are you still a Mason today because of your fear of the oaths you took? One secular researcher of Masonry has reported on such fears:

> It has been said that these issues [swearing the Masonic oaths] are of no concern to Freemasons, but hundreds of members of the Brotherhood have spoken to me of the turmoil they experience in attempting to reconcile their religious views with the demands of masonic ritual. . . . The average Christian man who has not studied the theological implications of the oaths, rituals and lectures usually experiences a certain initial moral and religious disquiet about what he has done in joining. Many have admitted to being somewhat ashamed by the initiation ceremony they have undergone.[1]

THE INTENT OF MASONIC OATHS

It is generally accepted in Masonry that the oaths a man takes are to be binding throughout one's entire life, indeed, "for all time."[2] As the 30th Degree of Masonry declares, "Most Enlightened Brethren, the obligations of [Masonic] duty are eternal to the good Mason."[3] The presentation volume for Masonry in the state of Virginia promises that "the penalties incurred for willful violation of your Masonic obligation will not be of a physical nature" but they are "to impress upon the mind of each brother how serious a violation [of one's Masonic oath] will be regarded by the members of the fraternity."[4]

Carl H. Claudy was a Master Mason, a former Grand Master of Masons in the District of Columbia, and a member of all coordinate rites of Masonry. He was awarded many additional Masonic honors and distinctions.[5] Claudy admits that those who framed the Masonic penalties "intended to inspire terror" in the candidate[6] so that anyone who would break his oath would experience

> the loss of my self-respect. [Including] the self-abasement any true man feels who has broken a solemn pledge. *The wrath of a God blasphemed.* The horror of a sin in which there is none greater. . . . These, then, are what the penalties really mean; these are the real consequences to me, if I violate my solemn obligations, *these are what will be done to me* if I fail in living up, so far as I am able, to the covenants I made with my brethren. (Italics added)[7]

It would appear that the "intent to inspire terror" has been effectively used by the Lodge. In 1912, Martin L. Wagner candidly expressed his observations about the penalties of Masonry:

> That Masons believe that these penalties will be mercilessly inflicted upon them, should they betray its secrets, we know to be true in many cases. The convictions of those who have exposed the ritualism of the order, that they took their lives into their hands in doing so is proof. The numerous confessions made to the writer, on the part of both Masons and ex-Masons, is further proof.[8]

In our own conversations with contemporary Masons, we have found that they, too, have fear in their hearts. Right or wrong, they fear breaking the oaths they have taken; they fear the penalties of publicly betraying Masonic secrets. In fact, 33d Degree Mason Manly Hall refers to the literal consequences of breaking Masonic vows in this way:

> The average Mason, as well as the modern student of Masonic ideals, little realizes the cosmic obligation he takes upon himself when he begins his search for the sacred truths of Nature as they are concealed in the ancient and modern rituals. He must not lightly regard his vows, and if he would not bring upon himself *years and ages of suffering* he must cease to consider Freemasonry solely as a social order only a few centuries old. (Italics added)

> Every Mason knows that *a broken vow brings with it a terrible penalty.* . . . When a Mason swears that he will devote his life to [Masonry] . . . and then defiles his living temple . . . he is breaking a vow which imposes not hours but ages *of misery.* (Italics added)

Both Manly Hall and Albert Pike warn the Mason who breaks his vows. Hall believed breaking one's vows "unfailingly invokes the retributive agencies of Nature."[9]

According to Wagner, there is evidence (on rare occasions in the past) that Masons have taken the oaths of revenge literally. He tells what happened to William Morgan, a man who broke his vows: "That William Morgan was murdered in obedience to a Masonic decree, is in the opinion of all non-Masons who have carefully and impartially examined the evidence, proven beyond a doubt, and that his murderers were protected from summary justice, by the institution, is equally proven." Judge Whitney of the Belvidere Lodge in Illinois allegedly "escaped assassination at the hands of Master Masons." Wagner also claims that the murder of Ellen Slade in Boone County, Illinois, "was tacitly approved by the action of the Belvidere Lodge, and of the Grand Lodge of Illinois."[10]

THE CONTENT OF MASONIC OATHS

Is there anything in Masonic oaths today that suggests to men in the Lodge that they too should take vengeance on those who violate their oaths? The evidence of what men must promise in order to enter the Lodge and progress through the different degrees of Masonry prompts an affirmative answer. Ladies, if your husband is a Mason, the following are twelve selected oaths, some or all of which, he swore to obey and do.

FROM THE OATH FOR THE ENTERED APPRENTICE DEGREE

> I, _____, of my own free will and accord, in the presence of almighty God, and this worshipful Lodge, erected to him, . . . most solemnly and sincerely promise and swear, that I will always hail, ever conceal, and never reveal, any of the arts, parts or points of the hidden mysteries of ancient Freemasonry. . . . All this I most solemnly, sincerely promise and swear, . . . binding myself under no less penalty than that of having my throat cut across, my tongue torn out from its roots, and my body buried in the rough sands of the sea . . . should I ever knowingly violate this my Entered Apprentice obligation. So help me God. . . .[11]

FROM THE OATH FOR THE THIRD DEGREE, THE MASTER MASON DEGREE

> [I am] binding myself, under no less penalty than that of having my body severed in two, my bowels taken from thence and burned to ashes, the ashes scattered before the four winds of heaven, that no more remembrance might be had of so vile and wicked a wretch as I would be, should I ever, knowingly, violate this my Master Mason's obligation. So help me God. . . .[12]

FROM THE OATH OF THE PAST MASTER DEGREE OF THE YORK RITE

> I promise and swear, that the secrets of a brother of this degree, delivered to me in charge as such, shall remain as secure and inviolable in my breast, as they were in his own before communicated to me, *murder and treason excepted, and those left to my own election.* (Italics added)[13]

The Mason continues in this oath, saying he is "binding myself under no less penalty than (in addition to all my former penalties) to have my tongue split from tip to root."[14]

FROM THE ROYAL ARCH DEGREE OF THE YORK RITE

[I swear] That I would sooner have my skull struck off than divulge any of the secrets of this degree unlawfully... and have my brain exposed to the scorching rays of the noonday sun. . . .

I furthermore promise and swear, that I will assist a Companion Royal Arch Mason when I see him engaged in any difficulty, and will espouse his cause so far as to extricate him from the same, *whether he be right or wrong*. . . . To all [of this] which I do most solemnly and sincerely promise and swear, with a firm and steadfast resolution to keep and perform the same, without any equivocation, mental reservation, or self evasion of mind in me whatever; binding myself under no less penalty, than to have my skull smote off, and my brains exposed to the scorching rays of the Meridian sun, should I knowingly or willfully violate or transgress any part of this my solemn oath or obligation of a Royal Arch Mason. So help me God, and keep me steadfast in the due performance of the same. (Italics added)[15]

FROM THE INITIATION OF THE TENTH DEGREE
OF THE SCOTTISH RITE

I do promise and swear upon the Holy Bible . . . To keep exactly in my heart all the secrets that shall be revealed to me. And in failure of this my obligation, I consent to have my body opened perpendicularly, and to be exposed for eight hours in the open air, that the venomous flies may eat of my entrails, my head to be cut off and put on the highest pinnacle of the world, and *I will always be ready to inflict the same punishment* on those who shall disclose this degree and break this obligation. So may God help and maintain me. Amen. [The sign of this oath is to "place the point of the poniard under the chin, and draw it downward to the waist, as if in the act of ripping open the abdomen."][16]

FROM THE INITIATION OATH OF THE THIRTEENTH DEGREE
OF THE SCOTTISH RITE

I, _____, do promise before the Great Architect of the Universe . . . never to reveal the secrets which are to be entrusted to me, especially what is to be revealed to me of the

sacred mysteries. I promise to renew my zeal for masonry.
. . . And if I fail in this, my present engagement, I consent to
suffer all the pains of all my former obligations, my body to
be exposed as food to the ferocity of the wild beasts. [This
degree also teaches, "You are now bound by your word of
honor, and you may still retire. But one step more, and you
are bound to us forever and *at the peril of your life.*"] (Italics
added)[17]

**FROM THE INITIATION OF THE FOURTEENTH DEGREE
OF THE SCOTTISH RITE**

I do most solemnly and sincerely swear on the Holy Bible,
and in the presence of the Grand Architect of the Universe
. . . Never to reveal . . . the mysteries of this our Sacred and
High Degree. . . . In failure of this, my obligation, I consent to
have my belly cut open, my bowels torn from thence and giv-
en to the hungry vultures. [The initiation discourse by the
Grand Orator also states, "*to inflict vengeance* on traitors and
to punish perfidy and injustice."] (Italics added)[18]

FROM THE SEVENTEENTH DEGREE OF THE SCOTTISH RITE

I, _____, do promise and solemnly swear and declare in
the awful presence of the Only One Most Holy Puissant Almighty and Most Merciful Grand Architect of Heaven and
Earth . . . that I will never reveal to any person whomsoever
below me . . . the secrets of this degree which is now about to
be communicated to me, under the penalty of not only being
dishonored, but to *consider my life as the immediate forfei-
ture*, and that to be taken from me with all the torture and
pains to be inflicted in manner as I have consented to in the
preceding degrees. [During this ritual the All Puissant teaches, "The skull is the image of a brother who is excluded from
a Lodge or Council. The cloth stained with blood, that we
should not hesitate to spill ours for the good of masonry."]
(Italics added)[19]

FROM THE EIGHTEENTH DEGREE OF THE SCOTTISH RITE

Master—7 raps . . . all rise and candidate is conducted to and
caused to kneel on the step to the altar with his right hand on
the Bible:

I, _____, do solemnly and sincerely promise and swear under the penalty of all my former obligations which I have taken in the preceding degrees, never to reveal directly or indirectly, the secrets or mysteries of [this degree], . . . under the penalty of being forever deprived of the true word, to be perpetually in darkness, my blood continually running from my body, to suffer without intermission the cruel remorse of soul; that the bitterest gall, mixed with vinegar, be my constant drink; the sharpest thorns for my pillow and that the death of the cross may complete my punishment should I ever infringe or violate in any manner or form the laws and rules which have been, are now, or may be hereafter made known or prescribed to me.

And I do furthermore swear, promise and engage on my sacred word of honor, to observe and obey all the decrees which may be transmitted to me by the Grand Inspectors General in Supreme Council of the thirty-third degree. . . . So help me God and keep me steadfast in this my solemn obligation. Amen. (Candidate kisses the Bible.)[20]

FROM THE TWENTY-FIFTH DEGREE OF THE SCOTTISH RITE

I do most solemnly promise and swear, before the most high God, that I will never reveal the secrets of this degree. . . . Binding myself under no less a penalty than that of having my heart eaten by the most venomous of serpents and left thus to perish most miserably, from which may the almighty creator of the universe guide and defend me.[21]

FROM THE TWENTY-EIGHTH DEGREE OF THE SCOTTISH RITE

I, _____, promise and swear, in the presence of the Great Architect of the Universe . . . Never to reveal any of the secrets of the degree of the Knights of the Sun. . . . And should I willfully violate this my obligation, may *my brethren seize me* and thrust my tongue through with a red hot iron, to pluck out my eyes and deprive me of smelling and seeing, to cut off my hands and expose me in that condition in the field to be devoured by the voracious animals, and if none can be found, may the lightning of heaven execute on me the same vengeance. (Italics added)[22]

FROM THE THIRTIETH DEGREE OF THE SCOTTISH RITE

> [During the taking of this oath the Grand Provost of Justice holds the point of his sword to the heart of the candidate.] I, _____, of my own free will and accord, do hereby solemnly and sincerely promise and swear to keep faithful the secrets of the sublime degree of Knights Kadosh and strictly to obey the statutes of the order. . . . All of which I promise to do, *under the penalty of death*. So help me God.
>
> When your rashness prompted you to enter this awful Sanctuary, you were no doubt informed of the danger which threatened you, and of the trials which still await you. Swear therefore, upon your word of honor, never to reveal what you have seen or heard hitherto. . . . Forget not that the slightest indiscretion will *cost you your life*. Are you still willing to proceed? (Italics added)[23]

How can any Christian say that such oaths truly honor God? The Bible commands, "Finally, brothers, whatever is true, whatever is noble, whatever is right, whatever is pure, whatever is lovely, whatever is admirable—if anything is excellent or praiseworthy—think about such things" (Philippians 4:8; NIV).

THE BONDAGE OF MASONIC OATHS

The question remains whether or not the penalties sworn during the oaths are "only symbolic." It is a fact that no candidate entering into Masonry is told during the ritual that the penalties of the oaths he is swearing to are merely symbolic. In his mind, there is no reason for him not to believe that every Masonic obligation deals with vows of literal life and death. Disobedience to Masonic vows is often stated to bring a fatal penalty. Those who violate their Masonic vows clearly admit in their oath that they are worthy of death.

Candidates swear in God's name to have these penalties inflicted upon them. God, not Masonry, is to take responsibility for inflicting punishment upon the violators of these oaths. In his *Encyclopedia* Albert Mackey confirms that the Mason who disobeys his oaths is worthy of death and that it is up to God, not men, to inflict the penalty:

We may say of what are called Masonic *penalties*, that they refer in no case to any kind of human punishment; that is to say, to any kind of punishment which is to be inflicted by human hand or instrumentality. The true punishments of Freemasonry affect neither life nor limb. They are expulsion and suspension only. But those persons are wrong, be they mistaken friends or malignant enemies, who suppose or assert that there is any other sort of penalty which a Freemason recreant to his vows is subjected to by the laws of the Order, or that it is either the right or duty of any Freemason to inflict such penalty on an offending Brother. The obsecration [sacred prayer, entreaty, or oath] of a Freemason simply means that if he violates his vows or betrays his trust *he is worthy of such penalty*, and that if such penalty were inflicted on him it would be just and proper. "May I die," said the ancient, "if this be not true, or if I keep not this vow." Not may any man put me to death, nor is any man required to put me to death, but only, if I so act, then would I *be worthy of death*. The ritualistic penalties of Freemasonry, supposing such to be, are in the hands not of men, but of God, *and are to be inflicted by God*, and not by men.[24] (All but first italics added)

The above Masonic oaths, coupled with the teaching that God Himself is to literally inflict the penalties, are likely to strike fear into the heart of the most stalwart Masonic initiate. Is this not a form of cultic intimidation—using threats of divine retribution to force compliance to a false religion? And, of course, can anyone deny that men sometimes feel urged to wield this sword of justice on God's behalf? In the beginning, most Masons take the oaths literally and fear literal consequences for denying them. Is this not why so many Christian Masons have refused to deny Masonry—because they are fearful of the consequences of denying their oaths? Masons themselves have admitted that the Lodge would probably dissolve were it not for the secrecy of the organization and the fear of the penalties inflicted by the oaths.[25] But is this any way to promote and advance a brotherhood?

The Masonic oaths do bind the Mason to the teachings of Masonry. The oaths of Masonry do protect, reinforce, and perpetuate the unbiblical teachings of Masonry. And here we must ask, How can Christians "swear" to these things in the Lodge when the God of the Bible tells us to shun and turn away from them? Scripture says, "But examine everything carefully; hold fast to that which is good; abstain from every form of evil" (1 Thessalonians 5:21-22; see Romans 14:22). It also says, "And we pray this in order that you may live a life worthy of the Lord and may please him in every way: bearing fruit in every good work, growing in the knowledge of God" (Colossians 1:10; NIV).

It's not uncommon for a man to swear an oath of loyalty and allegiance to the Lodge and get so wrapped up in its activities that his family is placed in a secondary position of importance. Not only that, church attendance may also be greatly reduced. Over the years this can result in family problems—problems for the wife and problems among the children. It also leads men to trust the teachings of the Lodge more than the things taught to them at their church. Here is the experience of former leading Mason Jim Shaw:

> Through the years I must have heard hundreds of men say, "I don't need to go to church—the Lodge is good enough religion for me." So very many such men never attended a church, except with the Lodge once a year to hear Masonry exalted. They were trusting Lodge membership and their own "virtuous life" to assure them acceptance in the "Celestial Lodge Above."[26]

Many Christians do not recognize how the vows of Masonry logically cause them slowly to abandon their commitment to Christ. If the vows "morally" force them to uphold Masonry and yet Masonry itself rejects everything Christian, then Masonry can be upheld only by sacrificing one's Christian commitment. The end result is well illustrated by a former Mason:

> In countless individual cases I have met it. . . . [Masons] insist continually that if they live up to the obligations of the lodge, or if they live moral and virtuous lives, they will get to Heaven. . . . The lodges themselves are the most potent influence to teach people to depend upon their own righteousness and character instead of the blood of Christ. . . . This doctrine largely neutralizes the preaching of the gospel everywhere.[27]

Evangelist John R. Rice describes how his own father abandoned biblical doctrines he once preached as the pastor of a Christian church—as a result of his involvement with the Lodge:

> As his interest in the lodges grew, something happened to his spiritual life. . . . He ceased preaching altogether. . . . And his doctrine changed likewise. . . . He said that he believed sincere heathen people who had a religion and earnestly tried to live up to their light were saved and did not need to be born again. . . . Then his interest in missions and evangelism waned. . . . He absorbed the lodge teaching. It led him away from the Bible, away from the ministry and soul winning, away from the church.[28]

Yet Masonry claims there is nothing in its vows that will interfere with a Christian's beliefs.[29] In the 14th Degree the "Thrice Puissant" asks the candidate, expecting a negative answer, "Did you ever find anything in your obligations which was contrary to and against your religion?"[30] Mackey states that "the solemnity of an oath, is not in itself forbidden by any Divine or human law."[31] Nevertheless, oaths that make a man swear to disobey God are forbidden in the Bible.

ESCAPE FROM MASONIC OATHS

Is the Mason, especially the Christian Mason, bound to keep such oaths? Remember, Masons are not warned beforehand about the contents of these oaths. Here is what the Bible advises him to do:

> If a person swears, speaking thoughtlessly with his lips to do evil or to do good, whatever it is that a man may pronounce by an oath, and it is hidden from him—when he realizes it, then he shall be guilty in any of these matters. And it shall be, when he is guilty in any of these matters, that he shall confess that he has sinned in that thing; and he shall bring his trespass offering to the Lord for his sin which he has sinned. . . . So the priest shall make atonement on his behalf for his sin which he has sinned, and it shall be forgiven him. (Leviticus 5:4-6*a*, 10*b*; NKJV)

The Bible provides a way of escape for those who swear an oath in ignorance. If they have transgressed God's moral law, they are to immediately confess that sin and repent. In the Old Testament a person was to go to the priest, confess that he had sinned, and offer a sacrifice for atonement. Today, a Christian is to come to his eternal High Priest—the Lord Jesus Christ —who has died on the cross for his sin. He is to acknowledge that he is guilty of swearing wrongly and repent of his oath, asking for forgiveness and acknowledging that he will obey God.

The Bible says, "If we confess our sins, he is faithful and just and will forgive us our sins and purify us from all unrighteousness" (1 John 1:9; NIV). It is the duty of every Christian to break and renounce any evil oath that binds him to disobeying God. Swearing to uphold Masonic doctrines is sinful and unscriptural, and should not be a part of the Christian's life for the following reasons.

First, Masonry makes a Christian man swear, in God's name, to doctrines that God has pronounced false and sinful. For example, the Lodge teaches the false doctrine of "the Fatherhood of God." On the other hand, Jesus teaches that only those who receive him, who believe in his name, will he give the right to become children of God (John 1:12).

Second, Masonry makes Christian men swear to accept the lie that salvation can be gained by man's good works. But the Bible contradicts Masonry: "Not by works of righteousness which we have done, but according to his mercy he saved us" (Titus 3:5*a*; KJV).

Third, Masonry makes Christian men swear to accept and promote the lie that Jesus is just one of many equally revered prophets. Each candidate does this when he agrees that all religions can lead a man to God. But the Bible records Jesus' words in contradiction to Masonry: "I am the way and the truth and the life. No one comes to the Father except through me" (John 14:6; NIV).

Fourth, Masonry makes Christian men swear they will remain silent in the Lodge and not talk of Christ, whereas Jesus commanded every Christian to go into all the world and be a witness for Him. Jesus said, "And ye shall be witnesses unto me both in Jerusalem, and in all Judaea, and in Samaria, and unto the uttermost part of the earth" (Acts 1:8; KJV).

Fifth, Masonry makes Christians swear that they are approaching the Lodge in spiritual darkness and ignorance,[32] when the Bible says Christians are already in the light, children of light, and are indwelt by the Light of the world—Jesus Christ. The Bible says, "For you were once darkness, but now [the moment you received Christ as Savior and Lord] you are light in the Lord" (Ephesians 5:8; NIV).

Sixth, by demanding that Christians take the Masonic oath, Masonry leads Christians into committing blasphemy and taking the name of the Lord in vain. As a Christian he has sworn unlawfully to things God has forbidden him to swear to. God says He will not leave such a one unpunished (Exodus 20:7), unless he repents (see Leviticus 5:5; 1 John 1:9).

Seventh, Masonry makes Christians falsely swear that the G.A.O.T.U., whom Masonry claims is the true God of the universe, is present in all other religions. But the Bible says, "I am the Lord; that is my name! I will not give my glory to another or my praise to idols" (Isaiah 42:8; NIV).

> I am the Lord, and there is no other. I have not spoken in secret, from somewhere in a land of darkness; I have not said to Jacob's descendants, "Seek me in vain." I, the Lord, speak the truth; I declare what is right. Gather together and come; assemble, you fugitives from the nations. Ignorant are those who carry about idols of wood, who pray to gods that cannot save. Declare what is to be, present it—let them take counsel together. Who foretold this long ago, who declared it from the distant past? Was it not I, the Lord? And there is no God apart from me, a righteous God and a Savior; there is none but me. Turn to me and be saved, all you ends of the earth; for I am God, and there is no other. (Isaiah 45:18b-22; NIV)

Eighth, Masonry makes Christians falsely swear to the teaching that true worship can be offered in the Lodge to God without the mediatorship of Jesus (Hebrews 9:15). But the Bible says, "For there is one God and one mediator between God and men, the man Christ Jesus, who gave himself as a ransom for all men—the testimony given in its proper time" (1 Timothy 2:5-6; NIV).

Ninth, by swearing the Masonic oath and participating in the doctrines of the Lodge, Christians are perpetuating a false gospel to other Lodge members, who look only to Masonry's plan of salvation to get them to heaven. But the Bible says, "Even if we or an angel from heaven should preach a gospel other than the one we preached to you, let him be eternally condemned" (Galatians 1:8; NIV).

Tenth, according to the Bible, the Christian's spirit, mind, and body are the temple of the Holy Spirit, "bought with a price" (1 Corinthians 6:19-20). By taking the Masonic obligations he is agreeing to allow the pollution of his mind, spirit, and body by those who serve false gods and believe false doctrines. The Scripture warns,

> Do not be yoked together with unbelievers. For what do righteousness and wickedness have in common? Or what fellowship can light have with darkness? What harmony is there between Christ and Belial? What does a believer have in common with an unbeliever? What agreement is there between the temple of God and idols? For we are the temple of the living God. (2 Corinthians 6:14-16*a*; NIV)

God's Word instructs every Christian to break and renounce any evil oath that binds him in sin: "Have nothing to do with the fruitless deeds of darkness, but rather expose them" (Ephesians 5:11; NIV). Every Christian Lodge member should renounce his Masonic oath and confess it as a sin to his Lord. The Lord promises to forgive each one who will do so: "If we confess our sins, he is faithful and just to forgive us our sins" (1 John 1:9; NIV). In this way the Christian will stop adding his support to the sins of the Lodge, whose false religion results in the damnation of so many souls (John 3:18, 36; 8:24; 12:48).

Masonry teaches, and has preserved in their purity,
the cardinal tenets of the old primitive faith, which
underlie and are the foundation of all religions.
Albert Pike
Morals and Dogma

15

Uniting All Religions

Masonry claims that it unites all religions under the umbrella of its teachings. But a simple comparison of different religious beliefs about God demonstrates that this is impossible. Nevertheless, Masonry teaches that it alone is the one true religion of all mankind.

MASONRY CLAIMS TO UNITE ALL RELIGIONS

The Masonic Grand Chaplain of Pennsylvania has declared the Lodge's support of religious freedom: "Freemasonry has always been a bulwark for religious liberty. It is a supporter of all religions. Freemasonry is not a permit for a Mason to replace his church, but to enforce it. It does not supplant, but supplements. It does not subvert, but supports."[1] Masonry is allegedly the genuine friend of all the religions of the world. As Joseph Fort Newton asserts, "Masonry is . . . a worship, in which men of all religions may unite. . . . It is not the rival of any religion, but the friend of all, laying emphasis upon those truths which underlie all religions and are the basis and consecration of each."[2]

One of the major attractions of Masonry is its appeal to human brotherhood and unity among men of all faiths. Masonry wants people to believe that it opens the door to a universal brotherhood of all faiths. Sovereign Grand Commander Francis

G. Paul says, "Universal brotherhood is our aim."[3] Masonic authority H. L. Haywood claims, "In Freemasonry world brotherhood is an actuality, not a remote ideal."[4]

The initiation ritual of the 30th Degree of the Scottish Rite teaches the same goal:

> If then we wish order and peace to prevail on earth, we must be united; we must have but one will, but one mind. Both we find in the teachings of Masonry only, and against that compact of unity, tyranny and usurpation, whether religious or political, must fall subdued and powerless.

> Masonry, victorious over all adverse circumstances, will become the honored medium of uniting all mankind in one vast brotherhood.[5]

This is why many Masonic authorities believe that Masonry will bring about a new world order:

> [Masonry] is a world law destined to change the earth into conformity with itself, and as a world power it is something superb, awe-inspiring, godlike.

> The doctrines of Masonry will ultimately rule the intellectual world.[6]

Albert Pike stated that the hope of the Mason is to destroy all evil in the universe and bring "the final triumph of Masonry, that shall make of all men one family and household."[7] Thirty-second Degree Mason Foster Bailey asserts that Masonry "has a world mission in aid of all men everywhere in the world, and . . . this mission is spiritual."[8] *Mackey's Revised Encyclopedia of Freemasonry* argues that "the mission of Masonry is . . . to banish from the world every source of enmity and hostility," and to extend the principles of Masonry to all nations.[9] Newton adds that the objective of Masonry is "to bring about a universal league of mankind."[10] Clearly then, Masonry claims to truly unite all religions and will eventually unite the world in brotherhood.

A COMMON RELIGIOUS BROTHERHOOD IS IMPOSSIBLE

But at best, Masonry can only trick her members into believing that the "true teachings" of every religion are actually the same as Masonic doctrine. Given the actual teachings of the world's religions, it would be impossible for Masonry ever to unite them. The reason for this is that the deities of Buddhism, Hinduism, Islam, Judaism, Christianity, animism, and the other religions of the world are not the same.

Jehovah (the God of Christianity) is infinite, personal, triune, loving, and holy. Allah (the deity of the Muslims) is unitarian (not triune); he is merciful, but he is not necessarily loving or holy. Brahman, a major deity of the Hindus, is impersonal and monistic (neither unitarian nor triune). Most all Hindus are *polytheistic* (believing in thousands of finite gods, both good and evil). Buddhism is either polytheistic, believing in Buddha and in hundreds of other good and evil gods, or completely *nontheistic*, claiming there is no God. As such, it replaces an absolute God with a confusing state of being called Nirvana. Mormonism is different from all the above in that it is *henotheistic*, accepting worship of one central deity (Elohim) for this world, yet also accepting endless similar gods for other worlds.

Masonry is completely wrong in teaching that all religions ultimately have the same concept of God.[11] The gods of the world religions are simply not the same. All religions have widely divergent concepts of God: he is either (1) personal or impersonal, (2) holy or evil, (3) unitarian, trinitarian, or monistic, (4) infinite or finite, (5) loving or not loving, (6) existent or nonexistent, to name just a few. These are not superficial distinctions. In fact, in many cases they are exact opposites. When Masonry claims that all men worship the same Masonic god within the Lodge, in actuality Masonry has a distinct concept of God that disagrees with all other religions' concepts of God (see chapters 2, 7-9).

The different religions also have different concepts of the nature of man. What's more, they disagree on the nature of salvation and what man can expect at death. When Masonry claims otherwise, it is teaching religious absurdities. One such example is Masonry's pronouncement that Mithra (an evil and finite god) is omnipotent and beneficent and that the "Tao" (an impersonal concept) is really a "loving creator."[12] Think of all the hundreds of millions of secularists in the world who are atheists and do not believe in any religion. How will Masonry unite them?

It would seem that Masonry's claim to be able to form a religious brotherhood in Masonry is doomed from the beginning. Quite the contrary, it can be said that Masonry has only further splintered mankind by adding one more competing religious sect to those that currently exist.

Masonry's distinctive religious beliefs are attractive only to those who are nominal members of their particular religious faith.[13] Knowledgeable believers of every religion will immediately recognize that Masonry denies their deity and beliefs. For the Lodge to claim that Buddha was an early Mason will not endear knowledgeable Buddhists to Masonry.[14] Buddha rejected and repudiated belief in a supreme being, a belief that is a requirement in Masonry. Whatever Buddha believed, he was clearly not a Mason.

Further evidence that Masonry will never be able to unite the different religions in brotherhood can be found in the history of the Lodge itself. Masonry has not even united its own brotherhood in harmony, let alone the vastly competing religions of the world.

The disputes among Masons are well documented. In 1858 Albert Pike wrote an article titled "The Evil Consequences of Schisms and Disputes for Power in Masonry, and of Jealousies and Dissensions Between Masonic Rites." In that article, Pike referred to the problems and errors within Masonry that tended to justify Masonry's critics. He felt that this was accomplished "more than all, in the angry disputes which rend the bosom of the Order, accompanied with bitter words, harsh epithets and loud denunciations, that give the lie to the combatants' claim of brotherhood."[15]

A century later little has changed. An article that appeared in *Masonic Square* entitled "Freemasonry International" in December 1976 carefully noted that

> each Grand Lodge makes its own judgment in the light of its
> own approach to what Freemasonry means. . . . So, of course,
> many opinions differ on what is considered basic Masonry.
> . . . All this goes to demonstrate that one must be very careful
> before applying the practices of one Grand Lodge in the
> lodges of another, for they may be based on quite different
> esoteric [hidden] thinking to an extent where one can be a
> complete contradiction of the meaning behind another. This
> can apply even within one jurisdiction.[16]

Another Mason goes so far as to say that Masonry must
change its "evil activities":

> Certain undesirable aspects of the Masonic work and organi-
> zation must inevitably disappear. The appetite of the curiosity
> seekers, the private political machinations of certain Masonic
> groups, and the purely social and commercial incentives
> which govern much of the Masonic politics in many lands
> must end. . . . Old and evil activities will come to an end. . . .
> Selfishness, ambition, separativeness, wrong motives and po-
> litical propaganda must fade out all together. They have no
> place in Masonry. They run counter to the plans of the Divine
> Design.[17]

The problem with Masonry is that it denies the sinful nature of man and subscribes to a naive idealism that romanti-
cizes and fantasizes a world brotherhood. Masons in today's
Lodge seem unable to agree even on major issues, such as who
God is and whether or not He is relevant:

> We see scarcely any two of our ablest Masonic scholars agree-
> ing on [the nature of God].

> British, Irish, Colonial, American, and other Grand Lodges
> have broken off communication and the right of inter-visita-
> tions with lodges and members of Latin Freemasonry who do
> not insist upon subscription to a belief in the existence of a
> Supreme Being and the doctrine of immortality.[18]

Therefore, it goes without saying that Masons cannot agree
on *minor* issues either. In one of the most damning indict-
ments ever written about Masonry's claim to brotherhood, Masonic scholar Oliver D. Street confessed the following:

We read in our Monitors and in the effusions of Masonic ora-
tors of the "Universality of Masonry," and how that Masonry
"unites men of every country, sect and opinion." . . . We stare
and our bosoms heave with pride that we belong to so bene-
ficial and so universal a brotherhood. It is a beautiful fiction
which it is a pity to destroy, but the lamentable fact is there is
not a word of truth in it. . . . There is not and never has been
and, if many of our most estimable brethren can have their
way, *there never will be universal Masonry.* . . . The Masonries
which exist among many others are repudiated and denied
by one another and by the Masonry of the English-speaking
countries in particular. . . .

The most trivial and absurd difference in either doctrine or practice is seized upon by some Grand Lodge, which
imagines it is the conservator of pure and unadulterated
Freemasonry, to erect impassible barriers between the Masonic bodies of the world. *Among the most rancorous disputes that the world has ever witnessed are those that have
raged among Masons* during the last 200 years over questions of minor or no importance. . . . The intolerance on the
part of many Masons and Masonic bodies towards others
claiming to be Masonic are so extreme that they frown even
on any suggestion of getting acquainted or of even conferring
together. . . . Self sufficient in our own conceit, we will not admit that we can learn anything of value from the Masons of
other countries and in our smug complacence we say that
they are "impossible" as Masons. It is precisely the same
mental attitude of Greek toward Barbarian, ancient Hebrew
toward Gentile, Pharisee toward Samaritan which we so un-
sparingly condemn in others, but which we, like them, cannot see in ourselves. . . . This ignorant and narrow provincia-
lism *will forever prevent the Masons of the world getting
together.* . . .

Yet, 200 years after that liberal and fraternal declaration,
and in spite of it, we see "good men and true, men of honor
and honesty," those who "obey the moral law" still being
kept at a distance from each other by "their particular opinions," by their "denominations or persuasions" concerning
God and religion. Shall this keeping them at a distance be
made perpetual? If so, one of the great objects of our Institution will be defeated. (Italics added)[19]

If Masons cannot achieve brotherhood *inside* the Lodge,
how will they achieve it among the rest of the world that dis-

agrees with them? The answer is that not only can Masonry not unite the world's religions, it does not intend to. For Masonry believes that it alone is really the one true religion.

MASONRY TEACHES THAT IT IS THE ONE TRUE RELIGION

Masonry teaches that all non-Masons are living in spiritual darkness[20] and that only the Lodge leads men into spiritual light. In the first Degree of Masonry, the candidate is told he "has long been in darkness, and now seeks to be brought to light."[21] Mackey himself refers to the candidate in these words:

> There he stands without [outside] our portals, on the threshold of his new Masonic life, in darkness, helplessness and ignorance. Having been wandering amid the errors and covered over with the pollutions of the outer and profane world, he comes inquiringly to our door, seeking the new birth, and asking a withdrawal of the veil which conceals divine truth from his uninitiated sight.[22]

The 28th Degree teaches that "the first degree represents man, when he had sunken from his original lofty estate. . . . He is emphatically a profane, enveloped in darkness, poor and destitute of spiritual knowledge, and emblematically naked. The material darkness which is produced by the bandage over his eyes, is an emblem of the darkness of his soul."[23] In the 30th Degree it is revealed to the initiate that his earlier religious beliefs are "superstition" and that the claim of religious compatibility was only a ruse to get him started in Masonry:

> In all the preceding degrees you must have observed that *the object of Scotch Masonry is to overthrow all kinds of superstition*, and that by admitting in her bosom on the terms of the strictest equality, the members of all religions, of all creeds and of all countries, without any distinction whatever, she has, and indeed can have, but *one single object* and that is *to restore to the Grand Architect of the Universe; to the common father of the human race those who are lost in the maze of impostures, invented for the sole purpose of enslaving them.* The Knights Kadosh recognize no particular religion, and for that reason we demand of you nothing more than to worship God. And whatever may be the religious forms *imposed upon*

you by superstition at a period of your life when you were incapable of discerning truth from falsehood, we do not even require you to relinquish them. *Time and study alone can enlighten you. But remember that you will never be a true mason unless you repudiate forever all superstitions and prejudices.* (Italics added)[24]

From this it can be seen that Masonry teaches that of all the faiths in the world it alone is the true faith and that ultimately all other religions are false superstition. With such a belief, Masonry can hardly claim that it seeks to unite all religions into a common brotherhood. The only way Masonry really seeks to unite all men is to have them abandon their beliefs. As Joseph Fort Newton states, "Masonry seeks to free men from a limiting conception of religion, and thus to remove one of the chief causes of sectarianism." Newton hopes that as Masonry expands around the world, all religious dogmas will "cease to be." All individual creeds and doctrines will be done away with, and what remains will be what is termed "the one eternal religion—the Fatherhood of God, the brotherhood of man, the moral law, the golden rule, and the hope of a life everlasting!"[25]

Masonry believes itself to be a "Holy Empire" whose mission is "to dispel darkness." Thus, it is the mission and "duty of its initiates to diffuse among men its ideals, without which error, superstition and spiritual subjugation must be eternal."[26] Thirty-third Degree Mason Manly P. Hall says that the Mason, because he is "freed of limitation of creed and sect, stands as master of all faiths."[27] This is also the reason Albert Pike argued that "humanity has never really had but one religion and one worship."[28]

Differentiating the god of Masonry from the God of other faiths, Albert Mackey could confidently say, "Freemasons have always been worshippers of the one *true* God."[29] Thus, once Masons are aware that Masonry is the one true religion, they can help "strip from all religions their orthodox tenets, legends, allegories and dogmas."[30]

The following statements by respected Masonic authors and leaders demonstrate conclusively that Masonry presents itself as a religion superior to all other faiths. Former Freemason Edmond Ronayne has stated: "Freemasonry claims to be the only true religion now in the world." He cites McClenachan's *Book of the Ancient and Accepted Scottish Rite*, as promising, "Masonry at last shall conquer, and its altar be the world."[31] Masonic scholar Albert Pike taught that

> [Masonry] is the universal, eternal, immutable religion, such as God planted it in the heart of universal humanity.
>
> Masonry teaches, and has preserved in their purity, the cardinal tenets of the old primitive [universal] faith, which underlie and are the foundation of all religions. All [religions] that ever existed have had a basis of truth; and all have overlaid that truth with errors. [For example,] the primitive truths taught by the Redeemer [Jesus] were sooner corrupted, and intermingled and alloyed with fictions than when taught to the first of our race. Masonry is thus the universal morality which is suitable to the inhabitants of every clime, to the man of every creed.[32]

For Masons, "in all ages, the golden threads of Truth have gleamed in the woof of Error" and only the initiate in the Lodge with his "True Masonic Light" can see the golden threads and "read them aright."[33] In other words, only Masonry knows, and can point out, the true thread of truth in another religion even though that truth lies in a massive wool of errors. Only Masonry has retained the core truth God intended for humanity in its entirety.[34]

Masonic authors have believed and taught that

> There is under all creeds one universal religion.
>
> This one true religion . . . is the very soul of Masonry.
>
> The true disciple of ancient Masonry has given up forever the worship of personalities. . . . As a Mason his religion must be universal: Christ, Buddha or Mohammed, the names mean little, for he recognizes only the Light and not the bearer [i.e., the person].
>
> It is true that Masonry is not a religion, but it is Religion. . . . Religions are many; Religion is one. . . . It brings together men of all creeds in behalf of those truths which are greater than all sects, deeper than all doctrines.

Scarcely a Masonic discourse is pronounced, or a Masonic lesson read, by the highest officer or the humblest lecturer, *that does not earnestly teach this one true religion which is the very soul of Masonry*, its basis and apex, its light and power. Upon that faith it rests; and in that faith it lives and labors; and by that faith it will conquer at last. (Italics added)[35]

Time and again it can be documented in Masonic literature that the teachings of Masonry are considered to be the new faith for the outmoded dogmas and tenets of the world's religions. Whatever religious belief a man brings to Masonry, he is, even with those beliefs, "in a state of darkness" and only through Masonry will he be "brought to the light."[36] All doctrinal beliefs of non-Masonic religion are considered subsidiary and secondary beliefs, teachings that are relatively unimportant compared with the vital truths of Masonry.[37] This is why former Masons have testified that while in the Lodge they generally felt superior in their beliefs to members of other religions.[38]

From all of this we can see that the Masonic claim to tolerance and respect for other religions is a lie. Masonry respects the beliefs of other religions only when those religions agree with it. Masonry says it tolerates and respects the religious beliefs of others, but it really intends to change and replace them. What other conclusion is possible if Masonry hopes to rid the world of all its unenlightened "dogmas," and other "superstitious beliefs"?

Extensive reading in Masonic literature makes clear that Masonry is a substitute religion, however sincerely and emphatically it may attempt to deny this. The more one reads in Masonry, the more obvious and undeniable is the fact that Masonry believes and claims that it alone is the One True Religion.[39] Christian Masons who realize that the goal of Masonry is to replace Christianity with its own religion should not continue to support it.

Many... [Bible] classes are being led by enlightened Masons.... These laymen are bringing to the interpretation of the Bible many of Masonry's great revelations.

The Educational and Historical Commission
of the Grand Lodge of Georgia

16

Influencing the Church

Masonry unflinchingly teaches its members that it is a "handmaiden to religion" and was really intended by God to assist and support the church.[1] Charles Lacquement, the Masonic Grand Chaplain, writes, "Freemasonry... is a supporter of all religions. Freemasonry is not a permit for a Mason to replace his church, but to enforce it. It does not supplant, but supplements. It does not subvert, but supports."[2] In spite of assertions to the contrary, however, Masonry functions like a church and actually replaces the church in the life of the Mason. Carl H. Claudy confesses, "When all else fails a man's spirit, he yet has his Mother Lodge and her Altar to go to; be his spiritual ills what they may be—aye, be his spiritual sins what they may be— he may gather with his brethren around that sacred Altar and find comfort in the love of his Mother Lodge, *such comfort as may come in no other way*" (italics added).[3]

But, as we have seen in recent chapters, the Masonic Lodge teaches Masons to unknowingly blaspheme God's name in its rituals. The Masonic oaths are evil because they cement the initiate's loyalty to false Masonic doctrine through fear. Masonry has deliberately lied to its members when it promises them there is nothing in Masonry that will conflict with their religion or with their duties to God. Masonry is not being honest when it claims it can truly unite all religions in the Lodge.

Rather, the real goal of Masonry is to replace all other religions with the teachings of Masonry. Masonry also wants to infiltrate the church with these teachings and has encouraged Masons to be church leaders. Such are some of the secret practices of the Masonic Lodge.

WHY MASONS SHOULD NOT BE CHURCH LEADERS

This raises an important question. Can the church in good conscience allow members who are Masons to be leaders? It is undeniable that today's Masons hold positions of leadership within the church. Masons are pastors, Sunday school teachers, elders, and members of church boards. Masons wield power and influence in many congregations and have made substantial inroads into the Christian church. Neither can anyone deny that the majority of Christians have been timid in response. Most have not said so much as a word in reply to this situation. Pastors everywhere seem to fear confronting this issue, fearful of hurting people's feelings, fearful of losing financial support, fearful of splitting their church.[*]

Jesus spoke of those who were afraid of offending people for the sake of principle, saying that they "loved the approval of men rather than the approval of God" (John 12:43). Jesus set the example of how Christians should respond to Masonry. He confronted the religiously minded of His own generation who felt that they stood in God's favor solely because of their good works and were proud of it. (This is how Masons feel.) Jesus did not commend, accept, or appoint these people to be leaders in the church. In fact, He condemned these men as hypocrites and deceivers: "You hypocrites! Isaiah was right when he prophesied about you: 'These people honor me with their lips, but their hearts are far from me. They worship me in vain; their teachings are but rules taught by men'" (Matthew 15:7-9; NIV).

Jesus spoke of those, like many Masons today, "who trusted in themselves and thought they were righteous while all the time viewing others with contempt" (Luke 18:9; NASB). He said such persons were not justified before God, no matter how many good works they did:

> To some who were confident of their own righteousness and looked down on everybody else, Jesus told this parable: "Two men went up to the temple to pray, one a Pharisee and the other a tax collector. The Pharisee stood up and prayed about himself: "God, I thank you that I am not like other men—robbers, evildoers, adulterers—or even like this tax collector. I fast twice a week and give a tenth of all I get." But the tax collector stood at a distance. He would not even look up to heaven, but beat his breast and said, "God, have mercy on me, a sinner." I tell you that this man, rather than the other, went home justified before God. For everyone who exalts himself will be humbled, and he who humbles himself will be exalted. (Luke 18:9-14; NIV)

Allowing Masons to govern and teach in the church is like putting leaven into dough. Jesus said that a little leaven leavens the whole lump of dough (Matthew 16:6, 11-12; cf. 1 Corinthians 5:6; Galatians 5:9). In the same way, the teaching and influence of Masonic church leaders permeate the whole church and detrimentally affect the spiritual condition of God's people.

Can any church long remain true to Scripture when it permits men to compromise God's truth? Can a church be blessed of God, filled and directed by the Holy Spirit, and strong and vital when it compromises its own doctrines? Can it uphold the gospel when it permits those who teach "another gospel" of works salvation to maintain positions of church leadership?

In the first century, the apostles would have none of it. In his own day, Paul and others faced a group of people similar to what the church faces today in Christian Masons: "certain ones of the sect of the Pharisees who had believed [in Jesus]" (Acts 15:5). Such men were believers, but they were teaching that good works were necessary to get them to heaven. What was the apostle's response?

> Some men came down from Judea to Antioch and were teaching the brothers: "Unless you are circumcised, according to the custom taught by Moses, you cannot be saved." This brought Paul and Barnabas into sharp dispute and debate with them. So Paul and Barnabas were appointed, along with some other believers, to go up to Jerusalem to see the apostles and elders about this question. . . . Then some of the

believers who belonged to the party of the Pharisees stood up and said, "The Gentiles must be circumcised and required to obey the law of Moses." The apostles and elders met to consider this question. After much discussion, Peter got up and addressed them: "Brothers, you know that some time ago God made a choice among you that the Gentiles might hear from my lips the message of the gospel and believe. . . . Now then, why do you try to test God by putting on the necks of the disciples a yoke that neither we nor our fathers have been able to bear? No! We believe it is through the grace of our Lord Jesus that we are saved, just as they are." (Acts 15:1-2, 5-7, 10-11; NIV)

These "Judaizers" brought the church much trouble. Wherever the doctrine of God's grace is not clearly and uncompromisingly taught, legalism and a trust in works salvation will infect Christians. As was true for the early church and the Pharisees who claimed they were believers, Masons today are powerful; they hold influential positions, and sometimes give significant amounts of money to their churches. But, where is their heart? What comes first in their lives?

Opposing Masonic Leadership in the Church

As a pastor, there may be a significant cost you will face if you preach the truth in this area. If worse comes to worst, you could lose members or even your job.[5] Some members of your flock may criticize you. But is it not more important to honor God's interests than the interests of those who have sworn their allegiance to doctrines and deeds that are opposed to God and His truth?

Would your church not become more spiritual if it were confronted with its worldly attitude and actions? This is what evangelist D. L. Moody said more than a hundred years ago concerning Masonry within the church:

> I do not see how any Christian, most of all a Christian minister, can go into these secret lodges with unbelievers. They say they can have more influence for good, but I say they can have more influence for good by staying out of them and then reproving their evil deeds. You can never reform anything by unequally yoking yourself with ungodly men. True

reformers separate themselves from the world. But, some say to me, if you talk that way you will drive all the members of secret societies out of your meetings and out of your churches. But what if I did? Better men will take their places. Give them the truth anyway and if they would rather leave their churches than their lodges, the sooner they get out of the churches the better. I would rather have ten members who are separated from the world than a thousand such members. Come out from the lodge. Better one with God than a thousand without Him. We must walk with God and if only one or two go with us, it is all right. Do not let down the standard to suit men who love their secret lodges or have some darling sin they will not give up.[6]

What every Christian pastor and leader needs to remember is that when a stand for truth is made, God promises to bless His people for standing up for Him. Perhaps your stand for the truth will encourage other Christian pastors and leaders to do the same. Possibly your actions will lead Christian Masons to repent of their involvement in the Masonic Lodge and so honor God and the truth.

God's Hatred of False Teaching and Idolatry

Consider for a moment what may happen if the church, collectively, does not act in this area. Think of what God would have done if the Israelites had worshiped Him as the Canaanite god Baal and the Egyptian god Osiris? What if God's chosen people had engaged in rites and practices that denied God's instructions? What if Israel's leaders had taught as sacred doctrine the very things that God hated? What if they had blasphemed His name in their sacred rituals?

We know what God did when the Israelites abandoned His truth and worshiped the golden calf ("copied from the Egyptian *Apis*"[7]). The *Apis* was a sacred Egyptian bull to whom divine honors were paid because of its close association with the leading Egyptian deity *Ptah*, the Egyptian creator of the universe. The bull was held up to be special because it was believed to be the mediator between Ptah and the people.[8]

When the Israelites apostatized and worshiped Jehovah as though he were a mediatorial bull, "they said, 'This is your god,

O Israel, who brought you up from the land of Egypt'" (Exodus 32:4). For equating Him with a pagan deity, God brought punishment to His people who should have known better (Exodus 32:10).

God had already shown Israel His hatred of the Egyptian deities. He had pronounced and executed severe judgment upon these false gods and the people who worshiped them (Exodus 7-14; see 12:12; Deuteronomy 11:3-4). Yet Masonry unites God with an Egyptian and a Canaanite deity in claiming that the true name of God is Ja (Jehovah)-Bul (Baal)-On (Osiris).

When Israel disobeyed God and went after false and evil gods and engaged in all kinds of idolatry, God judged them with punishments so severe that few people in all of human history have ever experienced them. They indeed became as God had warned, "a thing of horror to all the kingdoms on earth" (Deuteronomy 28:25; NIV). "I will make them abhorrent and an offense to all the kingdoms of the earth, a reproach and a byword, an object of ridicule and cursing, wherever I banish them. I will send the sword, famine and plague against them until they are destroyed from the land I gave to them and their fathers" (Jeremiah 24:9-10; NIV; see 25:4-11; Deuteronomy 7:1-5, 16; 20:18).

How is what God did to Israel relevant to Masonry within the church today? It is relevant because Masonry engages in similar kinds of beliefs and practices (though not identical) that brought God's final judgment on Egypt, Canaan, and Israel.[9] One former Mason has observed that "the very religious philosophy and false worship which caused Jehovah to destroy his own temple, and banish into captivity his ancient people, are precisely the same philosophy and worship which modern Masons profess shall fit them for the glories of heaven"[10] (cf. Jeremiah 15:6).

Will the church refuse to deal with the sin in her midst? Christian Masons today are "swearing" by Baal, literally and figuratively. In light of how God viewed such things in the past, should this not be of concern to the Christian church today? God says that He will forgive our sin if there is repentance, but if not, we can expect discipline (see Jeremiah 12:16-17).

GOD'S STANDARDS FOR CHRISTIAN LEADERS

The truth of the matter is clear: Masons within the Christian church can exert a corrupting influence and inhibit the collective growth of the church. Scripture emphasizes that one of the primary responsibilities of the church is to see to its own spiritual growth. We are to "grow in the grace and knowledge of our Lord and Savior Jesus Christ" (2 Peter 3:18; NIV). God Himself has placed apostles, prophets, evangelists, pastors, and teachers within the church for the following purpose:

> To prepare God's people for works of service, so that the body of Christ may be built up until we all reach unity in the faith and in the knowledge of the Son of God and become mature, attaining to the whole measure of the fullness of Christ. Then we will no longer be infants, tossed back and forth by the waves, and blown here and there by every wind of teaching and by the cunning and craftiness of men in their deceitful scheming. Instead, speaking the truth in love, we will in all things grow up into him who is the Head, that is, Christ. From him the whole body, joined and held together by every supporting ligament, grows and builds itself up in love." (Ephesians 4:12-16; NIV)

The apostles warned all those in the church of their responsibility to God. They warned pastors, elders, teachers and all those in positions of authority to shepherd the church, and to "be on your guard" because there are enemies both without and within:

> Keep watch over yourselves and all the flock of which the Holy Spirit has made you overseers. Be shepherds of the church of God, which he bought with his own blood. I know that after I leave, savage wolves will come in among you and will not spare the flock. Even from your own number men will arise and distort the truth in order to draw away disciples after them. So be on your guard! (Acts 20:28-31*a*; NIV)

If that which we have documented in this book is the truth actually contained and taught in the Masonic rituals, then pastors cannot permit Masons to be on their boards and exercise positions of influence and leadership in the church: "Since an overseer is entrusted with God's work . . . he must hold firmly to the trustworthy message as it has been taught, so that he can encourage others by sound doctrine and refute those who oppose it" (Titus 1:7, 9; NIV).

God warns that those who teach His Word will receive stricter judgment: "Not many of you should presume to be teachers, my brothers, because you know that we who teach will be judged more strictly" (James 3:1; NIV). Masons should not be permitted to teach the Bible in the church: "You must teach what is in accord with sound doctrine" (Titus 2:1; NIV). Masons should not be allowed to distort the Scriptures by reinterpreting them according to Masonic doctrines. The Educational and Historical Commission of the Grand Lodge of Georgia freely admits this when it discusses the influence of Masonry in the church: "Let us take a look at the number of great Bible classes for men which have been organized by the Church. Many of these classes are being led by enlightened Masons. . . . *These laymen are bringing to the interpretation of the Bible many of Masonry's great revelations*" (italics added).[11]

God also demands that church leaders are to "keep hold of the deep truths of the faith with a clear conscience," to be doctrinally sound, and to first be tested before they are placed in positions of leadership (1 Timothy 3:2-3, 8-10; NIV).

How then can Masons ever be appointed to positions of church leadership? They certainly are not doctrinally sound. If they were doctrinally sound, they would not be Masons. If they are not sound, then the Bible forbids them from being elders in the church. Church leaders are specifically commanded not to have anything to do with "godless myths"—an apt description of modern Masonry (1 Timothy 4:7; NIV). God specifically instructs leaders of the church to watch their "life and doctrine closely" (1 Timothy 4:16; NIV).

Some Masons are important in the community and very personable. But the church is not to elect such men to positions of leadership. This would be favoritism. Paul told Timothy, "I charge you, in the sight of God and Christ Jesus and the elect angels, to keep these instructions without partiality, and to do nothing out of favoritism" (1 Timothy 5:21; NIV).

In contrast, Masons swear an oath in the Lodge that they *will* practice favoritism or show partiality to other Masons. What is worse, Christian Masons swear they will show partiality to other Masons over Christian brothers. As former Mason John R. Rice confesses: "The Mason swears to show partiality to Masons over those not Masons and binds himself to show a preference to his lodge 'brother' that he is not to show to his Christian brother in Christ if that Christian brother be not a Mason."[12] Favoritism is condemned in the Bible (James 2:1-7): "If you show partiality, you are committing sin" (James 2:9).

Pastors, elders, and teachers in the church must be strong in God's grace, in the knowledge of His Word, and in sound doctrine. They must be willing to correct error and to rebuke false teaching:

> An elder must be blameless.... He must hold firmly to the trustworthy message as it has been taught, so that he can encourage others by sound doctrine and refute those who oppose it. For there are many rebellious people. (Titus 1:6, 9-10; NIV)

> Preach the Word; be prepared in season and out of season; correct, rebuke and encourage—with great patience and careful instruction. For the time will come when men will not put up with sound doctrine. Instead, to suit their own desires, they will gather around them a great number of teachers to say what their itching ears want to hear. (2 Timothy 4:2-3; NIV)

How is it then that Christian leaders, with few exceptions, refuse to correct Masonic error and confront the issue of the Lodge's influence within the church? Does not God Himself command pastors to rebuke false teachings, and is Masonry not a false teaching? Today we have many "followers of Baal" in the church. Pastors, elders, and Christian teachers everywhere need to decide if they will stand for God's truth as Elijah did. All Christians call Jesus their Lord. We say, "Lord, help us to live for you. Lord, bless our church." But at the same time we give positions of leadership in the church to those who have split their allegiance, even though this hinders our prayers. Jesus specifi-

cally instructed us how to counsel with Christian Masons who
are in the church:

> If your brother sins against you, go and show him his fault,
> just between the two of you. If he listens to you, you have
> won your brother over. But if he will not listen, take one or
> two others along, so that "every matter may be established by
> the testimony of two or three witnesses." If he refuses to lis-
> ten to them, tell it to the church; and if he refuses to listen
> even to the church, treat him as you would a pagan or a tax
> collector. (Matthew 18:15-17; NIV)

> My brethren, if any among you strays from the truth, and one
> turns him back, let him know that he who turns a sinner from
> the error of his way will save his soul from death, and will
> cover a multitude of sins. (James 5:19-20)

We must be willing to suffer the consequences of "speaking the truth in love" (Ephesians 4:15). If Elijah were to stand
before a lodge full of Masons, do you think his message would
have changed? "Elijah went before the people and said, 'How
long will you waver between two opinions? If the Lord is God,
follow him; but if Baal is God, follow him'" (1 Kings 18:21;
NIV). Remember, "no one who denies the Son has the Father;
whoever acknowledges the Son has the Father also" (1 John
2:23; NIV). Masons also must choose: are they the Lord's—or
are they Baal's? Those who are the Lord's will repent: "Nevertheless, God's solid foundation stands firm, sealed with this in-
scription: 'The Lord knows those who are his,' and, 'Everyone
who confesses the name of the Lord must turn away from wickedness'" (2 Timothy 2:19; NIV).

Those who do not understand, who think they cannot be
so "intolerant" as to embrace only Jesus and His way of salvation, will leave the church: "They went out from us, but they did
not really belong to us. For if they had belonged to us, they
would have remained with us; but their going showed that
none of them belonged to us" (1 John 2:19; NIV).

Freemasonry is a religious mysticism.
H. L. Haywood
The Great Teachings of Masonry

Part 4

Mystical Secrets

Since the 1960s the United States has experienced a major revival of the occult. Channeling and other forms of spiritism, astrology, parapsychology, Eastern religions, witchcraft, Satanism, psychic healing, holistic health practices, occult games, magic, endless cults, the "New Age" movement, and many other practices and philosophies have captured the attention of tens of millions—including some very influential people.[1]

Our culture is in the process of changing its prevailing philosophy from materialism to that of a fragmented world view encompassing various forms of pantheism, spiritism, religious humanism, and Eastern-occult spirituality. In many ways this paradigm shift constitutes a return to what are merely updated versions of very ancient occultic practices and beliefs. Masonry has certainly played a role in all of this.

But what tens of millions of people do not realize is that these occultic practices and philosophies are amoral, irrational, individually dangerous, and socially consequential. Contrary to claims, such practices do not indicate a culture's advancement but signal the beginning of its demise and destruction. As a result of their activities, occult practitioners may suffer serious psychological, spiritual, emotional, and physical problems. Even demon possession and death may result. The writings of Kurt Koch, Merrill Unger, Carl Raschke, John Warwick Montgomery, Malachi Martin, Gary North, John Weldon, plus former occultists document this.[2]

Why is the occult so destructive? According to the Bible, the world of the occult is dominated by Satan and his demons,[3] whose primary goal is the spiritual deception and destruction of mankind (John 8:44; 1 Peter 5:8). When a culture turns to the occult, it turns to the father of lies himself (John 8:44).

In this section, we document the following: how Masonry can encourage the pursuit of the occult (chapter 17); that the spirit world is interested in promoting Masonry (chapter 18); that Masonry is related to ancient pagan religion (chapter 19); and that the Lodge attempts to reserve these "higher" occult truths for those it deems sufficiently worthy (chapter 20). This principally involves those who seek, and attain, the higher degrees and who logically pursue the results of their Masonic instruction on their own through additional studies.

It is one of your great duties as a Most Excellent Master to dispense light to the uninformed Mason.
Charge to the Most Excellent Master upon his initiation
The Manual of Ritual for Royal Arch Masons, p. 81

17

The Occult

In Deuteronomy 18:9-12, God warns men against occult activity, declaring that it is an "abomination" to pursue such practices. Most Masons scoff at the idea that Masonry is occultic. Coil speaks for most Masons when he says, "Freemasonry is no more occult than the Golden Rule; no more mysterious than Morality."[1] Of course, many people say the same about astrology or the Ouija board, yet these are occult activities nevertheless.[2]

Most Masons who participate in the rituals do not understand their occult significance. If they pursue Masonry no further than unthinking participation in the rituals, it may be true for them that Masonry is not occultic. Such Masons are unaware of the occult meaning of many of the Masonic symbols and ritual and have chosen not to pursue the issue. But this is not true for all Masons. Others do pursue the occult significance of Masonry. This is why Knight says,

> Those that have a feeling for the occult—the true adepts—
> recognize each other: they appreciate the real significance
> behind the deliberate Masonic ambiguities. They develop a
> confidence in drawing their own deductions, making their
> own interpretations of symbolism and ritual. Such people

come slowly to be accepted into the inner sanctum of the Brotherhood.[3]

The fact that many Masons choose not to pursue the hidden meaning of Masonry is lamented by most Masonic authorities. Steinmetz points out Mackey's opinion:

> Most of the truly great Masonic writers have deplored the lack of esoteric Masonic knowledge among the craft in general. Mackey speaks of the "Parrot Mason," describing him as: "One who commits to memory questions and answers of the catechetical lectures, and the formulas of the ritual, but pays no attention to the history and philosophy of the institution; [he is] called a Parrot Mason because he repeats what he has learned without any conception of its true meaning."[4]

But for those with eyes to see, Masonry is full of the occult. As one researcher has said, "Behind all Masonic symbolism there is an undisclosed occult interpretation of which most Freemasons are ignorant."[5] One spiritist, commenting on the significance of the Scottish Rite, says, "From the Nineteenth to the Twenty-eighth [Degree] the work is most deeply occult."[6] In fact, one official ecclesiastical inquiry into Masonry concluded, "The whole complex of ideas inherent in Masonry bears close similarities to occultism."[7]

Masonry is a potentially occultic religion and opens the doors to the world of the occult. Masonry encourages the pursuit of the occult in five different ways: (1) Masonry accepts the premise of the New Age and modern parapsychology concerning latent human potential—the development of allegedly "natural" psychic abilities; (2) Masonry bears a striking similarity to many other occult arts; (3) Masonry encourages the individual Mason to pursue its "esoteric truths"; (4) Masonry is related to mysticism and may encourage the development of altered states of consciousness; and (5) many Masons are working for an awakening of what can only be termed "occult Masonry."

BELIEF IN UNLIMITED HUMAN POTENTIAL

Masonry accepts the premise of the New Age movement and modern parapsychology of "unlimited" power within man.

The modern New Age movement believes that man is in some sense divine, a "god" of sorts. The modern discipline of parapsychology (the scientific study of the occult) claims to have found evidence for the idea that man has hidden latent powers.

New Age leader Shirley MacLaine is a well-known promoter of this idea. This is why she endorses psychic development and spirit guides, and why she once chanted, "I am God, I am God," in meditation before the Pacific Ocean (as shown in her televised 1987 mini-series "Out on a Limb").

In *Natural ESP*, New Age writer and psychic pioneer Ingo Swann refers to "the new age of applied ESP" that he believes will emerge when people begin to use these powers. He believes they are part of a higher universal reality. In all people, he "assumes the existence of a kind of psychic nucleus possessing unsuspected capabilities and powers of comprehension hidden somewhere in the recesses of the total self." He asserts, "The capabilities of this deeper self are quite astonishing," and he emphasizes that the "trend of the New Age is toward a self-enlightenment and a deeper communion with the energies and forces that underlie the individual." All people need do is learn to unleash these allegedly "divine" powers.[8]

A number of prominent Masons share the same beliefs. For example, former Sovereign Grand Commander Henry C. Clausen refers to achieving "a true New Age" and asserts that potentially

> we have within us an infinite, unlimited source of power. ... Perhaps the stars in transition have a message for us, as the world plunges through space into the Age of Aquarius. ... Our altar is in the East. ... We know that the new division we are entering will bring new energies. These may have tremendous effects upon us, our civilization and our earth.[9]

In Clausen's commentary on the 28th Degree of the Scottish Rite, he has written of the spiritual world:

> This is a Kabalistic and Hermetic Degree of the greatest antiquity, dealing with the primal matter of all things. ... There are seven stations representing planets that anciently explained the passage of souls between heaven and earth. ... What we

see in this life are reflections of things that exist in the invisible spiritual world. . . . Faith is taught as the miraculous lever that can move humanity . . . [and] senses an *underlying divinity in all things*. (Italics added)[10]

In his discussion of the 32d Degree, Clausen reveals the secret nature of Masonry, which promises occult knowledge and power by revealing the true laws of nature:

> As we progress toward the end of this Degree and seek seriously the Royal Secret which is concealed like the occult science of the ancients, we remember, "Faith begins where reason sinks exhausted." Magic, after all, is but the absolute science of nature and its laws. . . . You will seek the Holy Doctrine—the Blazing Star of Truth, the Royal Secret—of creation. So do we slowly climb toward the final goal, the state of perfection. . . . Some modern scientists concede that in the search for enlightenment, recourse must be made to the mystic. . . . William James . . . harmonized religion and mysticism, concluding that "personal religious experience has its roots and center in mystical states of consciousness." . . . *Telepathy and esoteric psychology can work within us* and release energy, insight and imagination. . . . The Holy Doctrine—the Royal Secret—heretofore has been concealed. . . . But the veil now has been lifted for you. . . . The Scottish Rite symbology and teachings and studies have made the creative law of the universe susceptible of discovery. . . . *Nature's secrets are those of the supernatural [occult] sciences.* . . . Man has an immortal soul, imprisoned for a time within a mortal body, which is capable of improvement and of spiritual development. It is released when death occurs, thus mingling the divine with the human. . . . So, if you will seek and discover, you can travel beyond the material, you can grasp the supersensual, *you can touch the Divine.* You will be carried toward total truth and to that rare and ultimate mystic understanding of self and the universe. You then will know why we are here, what we are doing, and where we are going. (Italics added)[11]

Clausen's teachings are in a number of important respects indistinguishable from the teachings of the New Age movement and human potential parapsychology. But it can be documented that the development of altered states of consciousness and psychic ability is dangerous and ultimately connected to spirit-istic (demonic) powers.[12]

OCCULTLIKE SYMBOLISM AND PHILOSOPHY

Masonry is an introduction to the occult in that its symbolism and philosophy is similar to many other occult arts. That Masonry is related to other occult arts is acknowledged even by Masonic authorities such as Pike, Mackey, Waite, and Wilmshurst. It is more than a coincidental or contrived relationship. This linkage has led some Masons into the occult. Given the nature of the similarities, it would be natural for them to do so.

KABBALISM

Kabbalism* is a complex, symbolical occult art that began among the Jewish people in the first century A.D. and eventually flowered in the Middle Ages. Albert Pike confesses that "the Kabalah is the key of the occult sciences."[13] He sees kabbalism in Masonry at every turn, which is why he encourages the Mason to familiarize himself with kabbalistic doctrine. In fact, he claims that "all the Masonic associations owe to it [kabbalism] their Secrets and their Symbols." Pike explains: "Masonry is a search after Light. That search leads us directly back, as you see, to the Kabalah. . . . [There] the Initiate will find the source of many [Masonic] doctrines; and may in time come to understand the Hermetic philosophers, the Alchemists, . . . and [spiritist] Emanuel Swedenborg."[14]

In the *Liturgy of the Ancient and Accepted Scottish Rite* regarding the 13th Degree can be read the following: "There are profounder meanings concealed in the symbols of this degree, connected with the philosophical system of the Hebrew Kabalists which you will learn hereafter, if you should be so fortunate as to advance. *They are unfolded in the higher degrees*" (italics added).[15]

Albert Mackey also confesses that kabbalism is "intimately connected with the symbolic science of Freemasonry."[16] In his *Encyclopedia* he says,

---

*Also spelled kabalism, cabolism, qabbalism, etc.

The Cabala may be defined to be a system of philosophy which *embraces certain mystical interpretations of Scripture, and metaphysical and spiritual beings....* Much use is made of it in the advanced degrees, and entire Rites have been constructed on its principles. Hence [discussion of] it demands a place in any general work on Freemasonry. (Italics added)[17]

Masonic author Manly Hall observes that "the theories of Qabbalism are inextricably interwoven with the tenets of alchemy, Hermeticism, Rosicrucianism, and Freemasonry."[18]

Any study of kabbalism will quickly reveal that kabbalism was used in the past and is still used today for all kinds of magic, conjuring spirits, divination, and developing psychic powers. God warns the Christian Mason: "Let no one be found among you who ... practices divination or sorcery, interprets omens, engages in witchcraft, or casts spells, or who is a medium or spiritist or who consults the dead. Anyone who does these things is detestable to the Lord" (Deuteronomy 18:10-12; NIV).

ROSICRUCIANISM

There is no doubt as to the connection between Rosicrucianism and Freemasonry. Even a review of W. B. Crow's book *Witchcraft, Magic and Occultism* in the March 1975 issue of *Masonic Square* admitted such a connection between English Masons and Rosicrucianism. Rosicrucianism is a mystical brotherhood stressing personal development of occult powers, spirit contact, and the cultivation of altered states of consciousness. Their name derives from the order's symbol, a combination of a rose and a cross.[19] The observations of Hall will suffice in proving the connections between the Masons and the Rosicrucians:

Many of those connected with development of Freemasonry were suspected of being Rosicrucians.... Frank C. Higgins, a modern Masonic symbolist, writes: "Dr. Ashmole, a member of this fraternity [Rosicrucianism], is revered by Masons as one of the founders of the first Grand Lodge in London." ... Elias Ashmole is but one of many intellectual links connecting Rosicrucianism with the genesis of Freemasonry. The *Encyclopedia Britannica* notes that Elias Ashmole was initiated into the Freemasonic order in 1646.... Speculators have gone so far as to state that, in their opinion, modern Freemasonry has completely absorbed Rosicrucianism and succeeded it as the world's greatest secret society. Other minds of equal learning declare that the Rosicrucian brotherhood still exists, preserving its individuality as a result of having withdrawn from the Masonic Order. . . . One thing is certain: with the rise of Freemasonry, the Rosicrucian Order in Europe practically disappeared, and notwithstanding existing statements to the contrary, it is certain that the Eighteenth degree (commonly known as the Rose-Croix) perpetuates many of the symbols of the Rosicrucian Fire Alchemist.[20]

HERMETIC PHILOSOPHY

Hermetic philosophy (also known as "alchemy") is also a pillar of ancient and modern occultism. In fact, the Egyptian god Thoth (in Greek, "Hermes Trismegistas") was held to be the originator of many of the occult arts. Albert Mackey tells us, "In all the old manuscript records which contain the legend of the Craft, mention is made of *Hermes* as one of the founders of Freemasonry."[21] Henry Wilson Coil seems somewhat embarrassed by the Masonic connection to the occult and yet is forced to admit that it is part of the higher degrees:

> There has been a tendency for two centuries among imaginative and sensational writers to corrupt Freemasonry by coating it with all sorts of mystical and occult veneers, of which Alchemy is but one. So successful have they been that many within and many without the Society assume that there is some affiliation of Freemasonry with theosophy, astrology, spiritualism, occultism, magism, or even fortune telling and sleight of hand. There has never been any association between Freemasonry and the mystical arts, especially Alchemy, though, doubtless, the formulators of the numerous *Hauts Grades* and other higher degrees around the middle of the Eighteenth Century resorted to many such sources for interesting and impressive material, which was valuable in promotion as it was supernatural. Accordingly, the twenty-eighth degree of the Scottish Rite, called Knight of the Sun is partly Hermetic, just as the twenty-first or Prussian knight furnishes an example of sorcery.[22]

Albert Mackey agrees with Coil: "There is a very great similarity between their [the alchemists] doctrines and those of the Freemasons; so much so that the two associations have sometimes been confused."[23] In his *Encyclopedia* he states, "In the Eighteenth Century, and perhaps before, we find an incorporation of much of the science of Alchemy into that of Freemasonry."[24] Clearly then, Masonry has also incorporated alchemy into its rituals and teachings.

The connections of Masonry to various occult arts is one reason many Masons have also become occultists and why many occultists have chosen to pursue the path of esoteric [occult] Masonry. The adaptation of Masonry to this or that form of the occult has occurred regularly throughout its history.[25] Martin L. Wagner reveals that at the end of the eighteenth century "many Freemasons went to Tibet and were initiated in unknown crypts of Central Asia and returned with a rich store of information as could not be secured elsewhere in Europe."[26]

Mason Arthur Edward Waite is acknowledged by all as a consummate occultist.[27] He is the author of *The Occult Sciences*, *The Book of Ceremonial Magic, Doctrine and Literature of the Cabalah*, and other occult texts. Joseph Fort Newton refers to one of his texts, *Mysteries of Magic*, as an apparent digest of the writings of the famous occultist Eliphas Levi. Newton also admits that Masonic authority "Albert Pike was more indebted [to Levi] than he let us know."[28] In this matter, Masonic critic Paul Fisher observes:

> The official historian of the Scottish Rite of the Southern Jurisdiction, Charles Lobinger, said Pike's book "swarms with citations from Eliphas Levi," author of *Dogme et Rituel*, and that *Morals and Dogma* "is shown to be literal and verbatim extractions from those of the French Magus."
>
> Arthur Waite, a Masonic authority on, and translator of Levi's works, has written: "No person who is acquainted with *Morals and Dogma* can fail to trace the hand of the occultist therein and it is to be especially observed that, passing from grade to grade in the direction of the highest, this institution [Freemasonry] becomes more and more Kabbalistic."
>
> Another Masonic writer . . . urged the study of gnosticism and the kabbalah as collateral reading. . . . Freemasonry

is not fundamentally a fraternal insurance organization. It is an occult religion of kabbalistic gnosticism, and Pike's book is the basic source document for . . . [indoctrinating] men in all degrees of Scottish Rite Masonry.[29]

Both Pike and Waite were leading occultists, and both were leading Masons. The Masonic writings of these men reveal many connections between Masonry and the occult. For example, Masonic writer Alphonse Cerza calls Waite "the leading occultist of his day." He cites Silas H. Shepherd as noting that Waite's *Encyclopedia on Freemasonry* "contains much material respecting the mystic and occult phases of Freemasonry."[30] Waite himself wrote, "The development of Freemasonry in France of the eighteenth century may be said truly to have exhausted all branches of . . . occult science."

> They were all . . . represented: Alchemy, Astrology, Kabalism, Ceremonial Magic and even Animal Magnetism [hypnotism], all claiming on one or another pretext a connection with Masonry . . . [and] although requiring Masonic qualifications from their Candidates and possessing a Masonic complexion in their symbols and ceremonial procedure—they were more properly institutions arising out of the Craft, technically connected but actually independent thereof.[31]

Though an occultist, Pike was nevertheless revered by modern Masons. Pike has put it as clear as anyone: "the Occult Science" of the ancients "is found enveloped . . . in the Rites of the Highest Masonry."[32] Many other occultists have used Freemasonry as a means to pursue their occult goals. Spiritist Corinne Heline has written *Mystic Masonry and the Bible.*[33] Occultist Manly P. Hall acknowledges that "Masonry is an abstract science of spiritual [occult] unfoldment."[34]

Hall's text, *An Encyclopedic Outline of Masonic, Hermetic, Qabbalistic and Rosicrucian Symbolical Philosophy*, is something of an occult classic in metaphysical circles. In this large and illustrated text, he purports to reveal the secret teachings underlying some of the major symbolical and mystical occult traditions of the West, what he terms "transcendental philosophy." Only two copies of the first edition were specially prepared. One was presented to the Crown Prince of Sweden and the other was presented to the Scottish Rite Bodies of Oakland, California.[35] In his text, Hall argues that "the Gnostic sects, the Arabs, Alchemists, Templars, Rosicrucians and lastly the Freemasons form the Western chain in the transmission of occult science."[36]

THE "ESOTERIC TRUTHS"

Masonry is an introduction to the occult in that it actively encourages the Mason to pursue its "esoteric truths." Masonic author Allen E. Roberts informs new candidates, "You will be urged to learn more about the Craft than what is revealed in its ritual. You will find that the ritual is but the beginning of what can be a tremendous spiritual and philosophical experience."[37]

The official Masonic manual of the degrees concerning the Rose Croix (degrees fifteen through eighteen of the Scottish Rite) commands, "Teach the Knights to learn something more than the mere formulas and phrases of the ceremonial; persuade them to read the history and study the philosophy of Masonry; induce them to seek to learn the meaning of the symbols."[38]

The Mason is always taught to search for more and more "light" within the context of his Masonic history, philosophy, symbolism, and ritual. Those who earnestly pursue such a path, sooner or later cannot help being led to the study of the occult. The Mason's search for more spiritual meaning logically leads to mysticism, paganism, and the occult.[39]

This is why numerous texts reveal how Masonry can become the means toward the pursuit of "higher" occult truths. Masonic authority Silas H. Shepherd comments on J. D. Buck's *Symbolism or Mystic Masonry*: "Those desiring to study the connection between the occult philosophies and Freemasonry may read this work to advantage."[40] And it seems only natural for those who wish to pursue the connection between Masonry and occultism to read such a book. As Carl H. Claudy has said, even mediums and spiritists can become good Masons: "The Spiritualist [medium] who feels that unseen friends are waiting to receive him and carry him forward can be a good Master Mason."[41]

In an age where occult pursuits have been redefined as divine activities and painted in a benign light, we should expect that many Masons will find their way into the occult. In Masonry the Masonic candidate is forever promised that he will be brought to "the Light." But in each degree he only receives a little bit more of the Light, never quite arriving at the final "Light." Even after the 32d Degree, the Mason "is told that he has still not reached "the Light." He is told that he has only reached the top of the mountain. But the mountaintop is covered with clouds and mists. The light is still obscured, still "out there somewhere, beyond him." He is told, in effect, "You will have to press on and find additional light for yourself."[42]

Former leading Mason Jim Shaw supplies the actual words given in the 32d degree lecture to the Masonic candidate. After a brief statement about the Hindu gods Brahma, Vishnu, and Shiva, and the Hindu mantra (magical sound) AUM, the candidate is told, "All these things which you can learn by study, concentration, and contemplation, have come down to us from our ancient ancestors through Zaranthustra [sic (an early Iranian prophet)] and Pythagoras [a philosopher and occultist, c. 500 B.C]." Then he is told, "You have reached the mountain peak of Masonic instruction, a peak covered by a mist, which YOU in search for further light can penetrate only by your own efforts. Now we hope you will study diligently the lessons of all our degrees so that there will be nurtured within you a consuming desire to pierce the pure white light of Masonic wisdom."[43]

At the end of the Masonic ladder, the candidate is taught to pursue additional light. But where is he to find that additional light? He is to find it in his own search for the real meaning of Masonry. The "hint" is that the true light is found in a higher consciousness that is able to harmonize all opposites. This hint is termed "the Royal Secret." It refers to the belief that man finds the purpose of his being only when his dual nature—of good and evil, spirit and matter, death and life—are finally and perfectly harmonized.[44] This is the typical "enlightenment" of the occult and of Eastern religions.

The Mason learns that all his degree work has only been an initiation, or an introduction to the "higher" occult realities and powers. He is encouraged to find it and told he will if he chooses the path of "wisdom" and pursues it. As Joseph Fort Newton states, "Many mystical influences entered into the making of Masonry. . . . Traces of Gnosticism, of Mithraism, are found, remnants of rites long forgotten; and the impress of the Kabalah is unmistakable. . . . The student [is] free to follow further as his inclination and studies may direct."[45]

It is not surprising to find in the Texas *Monitor* the emphasis put on the importance of additional study and meditation:

> Every candidate for the Mysteries of Masonry, at the proper time and in an appropriate manner, should be taught the truth that the rite of initiation means much more than a formal ceremonial progress through the Degrees. In fact one may receive the entire work, conferred under the most favorable circumstances, and by competent officers, and yet not perceive the true Masonic light, which the symbols and allegories are designed to conceal, as well as to reveal. Initiation is to be attained only after real labor, deep study, profound meditation, extensive research and a constant practice of those virtues which will open a true path to moral, intellectual, and spiritual illumination.
>
> Masonry does not expound the truths concealed in her emblems. It displays the symbol and may give a hint here and there concerning some characteristic of its several meanings, but it must remain for the Neophite to search out for himself its more hidden significations.[46]

H. V. B. Voorhis, a true Masonic giant, is a 33d degree Mason who holds almost unparalleled distinction within Masonry. He holds membership in eighty Masonic bodies and seventy-nine Masonic organizations. In over sixty years as a Mason, he was the presiding officer in thirty-four of those eighty Masonic bodies, as well as vice president of Macoy Publishing and Masonic Supply Company. He holds more Masonic honors than any other Mason—eight special Masonic Medals and five Grand Crosses. For more than twenty-six years he held the office of "Supreme Magus of the Masonic Societas Rosicruciana Civitatibus Foederatis," the longest tenure on record. He has written twenty-six books (and a hundred brochures), including *Masonic Rosicrucian Societies.* Among other honors he is also Grand Representative in the U.S. for four European Masonic bodies.[47]

This leading Mason acknowledged that there were Masonic ties to Egyptian religion, the Rosicrucians, the druids, and other ancient mystery religions. He taught that Masonry reveres Pythagoras because of the attention he paid to occult science "whose mysteries are found in the *Kabbalah* and in all of the occult Masonic studies." He acknowledged that a more profound Masonry exists, and he calls it "occult Masonry."[48]

In his glossary, Voorhis defines occult Masonry as "Masonic philosophies, or degrees, which are more profound than the membership at large comprehends." He defines "occult sciences" as "sciences which are hidden from the vulgar" because such "less educated" persons would neither understand nor appreciate them.[49] The implication is that those better educated through Masonry are among those with the ability to understand and appreciate the occult sciences.

So then, this eminent Mason freely confesses that Masonry and the occult go hand in hand—and he encourages others to pursue the study of the occult arts. It is easy to understand how Masonry is capable of encouraging occult studies. It constantly urges the Masonic student to seek out its ancient and hidden "wisdom."

ALTERED STATES OF CONSCIOUSNESS

Masonry is an introduction to the occult in that it is a system of mysticism that accepts the development of altered states of consciousness. Dozens of books have been published on the mystical side of Masonry, such as Arthur Ward's *Masonic Symbolism and the Mystic Way* or J. D. Buck's *Mystic Masonry.* Many of these Masonic writers hope to inspire other Masons to look to Eastern[50] or Western mysticism and the occult as a means of spiritual development.

For these authors the meaning of Masonry is hidden in the mystical quest: "He who hears but the words of Freemasonry misses their meaning entirely."[51] This premise led Carl H. Claudy to refer to Masonic scholar Albert Pike as the "greatest of Masons as he was [the] greatest of mystics"[52]—and because he did as much as anyone to promote the mystical side of Masonry. Masonic authorities H. L. Haywood and A. E. Waite both agree that "there is a class of religious practices (or experiences) called mysticism; Freemasonry is a religious mysticism; whatever may be the place belonging to religious mysticism in the world is the place belonging to Freemasonry."[53]

Anyone who studies mysticism realizes that a large part of that "place belonging to religious mysticism" deals with altered states of consciousness.[54] This is why mystical Masons stress the importance of developing altered states of consciousness.[55] For example, 32d Degree Mason Foster Bailey refers to "the necessity . . . for complete self-mastery and expansion of consciousness before the achieving of the degree of Master [Mason]."[56]

Masonic authority Wilmshurst[57] and other mystic Masons allege that each degree of the Blue Lodge is able to open one's consciousness to progressively higher levels of being. The Second Degree of Masonry (The Fellowcraft) involves "the use of the psychic and higher intellectual nature," and the Third Degree (Master Mason) may involve "an opening up of consciousness to the very center and depths of one's being"—i.e., to the divinity within.[58]

> The second purpose of the Craft doctrine is to declare the way by which that [divine] centre may be found within ourselves, and this teaching is embodied in the discipline and ordeals delineated in the three degrees. . . .No higher level of attainment is possible than that in which the human merges in the divine consciousness and knows as God knows.[59]

In noting the connection between the initiations of ancient pagans and modern Masonry, Wilmshurst describes how both had a common goal:

> Initiation, therefore, meant a process whereby natural man became transformed into spiritual or ultra-natural man, and to effect this it was necessary to change his consciousness, to gear it to a new and higher principle, and so, as it were, make

of him a new man in the sense of attaining a new method of life and a new outlook upon the universe.[60]

Why is Masonry's cultivation of mystical, altered states of consciousness of concern? Such altered states are open doors to establishing contact with the spirit (demon) world. Cambridge-educated John Ferguson asserts that a state of voluntary spirit possession is "the core of mystical experience."[61] He is correct, as documented by Tal Brooke in *Riders of the Cosmic Circuit: Gods of the New Age* (with research assistance by John Weldon).

An Awakening of Occult Masonry

Masonry is an introduction to the occult because many Masons are working for an awakening of occult Masonry. No one doubts that we live in an age of occult revival.[62] But many people will be surprised to learn that some Masons believe that Masonry plays an important part in maintaining and nurturing this revival. Indeed, these Masons see Masonry as a vehicle for significantly expanding the influence of occultism in the Western world. They hope that their "unenlightened" Masonic members will wake up to their own tradition and recognize its occult power.[63] To permit the secular trivialization of Masonry in disregard of its occult heritage and future potential is seen as a mockery of God.[64]

Because the occult is now socially "out of the closet" and into the open, many Masons believe the time is "ripe" to return Masonry to its occult heritage. The curator and librarian of the Grand Lodge of Free and Accepted Masons of New York is on record as saying, "In this new Aquarian age, when many individuals and groups are working in various ways for the eventual restoration of the [ancient] mysteries, an increasing number of aspirants are beginning to recognize that Freemasonry may well be the vehicle for this achievement."[65] Manly Hall argues that there is more than sufficient precedent within the halls of Masonic scholarship for the modern Mason to return to the ancient meanings of the Craft.[66] Wilmshurst can see "a higher Masonic consciousness awakening in the Craft. Members of the Order are gradually, here and there, becoming alive to the fact that much more than meets the eye and ear lies beneath the surface of Masonic doctrine and symbols."[67] In fact, if Masonry as a whole ever returns to its ancient roots, it could play a significant part in the further expansion of the occult in the Western World.

These five points reveal that Masonry encourages its members to pursue the "secret" side of Masonry, possibly to accept the utilization of altered states of consciousness, and develop "higher" (psychic) powers and other occult practices. Many Masons are not ashamed to admit that they are working for a revival of "occult Masonry." The search for "Masonic light" leads many Masons to the dead end of the occult. The spirit world is indeed interested in promoting Masonry.

The Master Mason, if he be truly a Master, is in com-
munication with the unseen powers.
Manly P. Hall
The Lost Keys of Freemasonry

18

Spiritism

For some people the idea of a spiritistic connection to Masonry would seem ludicrous. But we have already documented that Masonry is related to the occult—and the occult is
the particular domain of the spirit world.[1] Is the spirit world interested in promoting Masonry, and if so, why? One could ask
the same question of many other activities that appear innocent
enough but mask or promote the world of the psychic and the
occult nonetheless. Some examples would be water dowsing
(and radionics), the "Therapeutic Touch" of holistic nursing,
the Ouija board, parapsychology (the scientific study of the occult), astrology, the I Ching, and fantasy role-playing games
such as Dungeons and Dragons®. All of these may seem innocent enough on the surface, but a deeper investigation into
their real nature makes clear that we are dealing with something occultic.[2]

Judging from the nature of Satan and his demons as revealed in the Bible, their proclivity to appear as "angels of
light" (2 Corinthians 11:14), and the history of spiritual deception within the church and among men, it becomes obvious
that the spirit world is interested in advancing anything that
would detract from the cause of Christ and promote spiritual
falsehood. Demons would especially be interested in something that would fulfill these goals while it also appears to be

moral, socially responsible, and spiritually innocent. Thus, there are at least three reasons the spirit world would be interested in promoting Masonry.

The first reason is because of *the cultic characteristics of Freemasonry*, several of which we have already discussed. For example, the religious repudiation of the Christian God, Christ, and salvation qualifies Masonry as "another gospel" (Galatians 1:6-8), and Scripture tells us that false gospels are the product of spiritual warfare and the devil's trickery:

> But I am afraid, lest as the serpent deceived Eve by his crafti-ness, your minds should be led astray from the simplicity and purity of devotion to Christ. For if one comes and preaches another Jesus whom we have not preached, or you receive a different spirit which you have not received, or a different gospel which you have not accepted, you bear this beautiful-ly.... For even Satan disguises himself as an angel of light. Therefore it is not surprising if his servants also disguise themselves as servants of righteousness; whose end shall be according to their deeds." (2 Corinthians 11:3-4, 14-15)

The second reason the spirits would be interested in pro-moting Masonry is because of *its ability to intrude into the church* and the resulting spiritual neutralization of Christian commitment (as discussed in chapter 16). The Scriptures in-form us that the devil and his angels seek to oppose the church and to deceive, defeat, or otherwise destroy Christians' commit-ments to their faith and harm them spiritually (Acts 20:28-31; Ephesians 6:12; 1 Peter 5:8). If Masonry is a substitute religion that replaces the church and opposes Christianity, why wouldn't the devil be interested in supporting something that has infiltrated the church and harmed its cause for more than 270 years? Scripture is clear that Christians live in the midst of spiritual warfare and must take notice of this fact.

> Be of sober spirit, be on the alert. Your adversary, the devil, prowls about like a roaring lion, seeking someone to devour. (1 Peter 5:8)

> Put on the whole armor of God, that you may be able to stand firm against the schemes of the devil. For our struggle is not

against flesh and blood, but against the rulers, against the powers, against the world forces of this darkness, against the spiritual forces of wickedness in the heavenly places. (Ephesians 6:11-12)

Many other Scriptures indicate the reality of the devil's attempts to deceive the people of God and all people in general (Matthew 13:39; Luke 8:12; Acts 26:18; 2 Corinthians 2:11; Ephesians 4:27; 1 Thessalonians 2:18; 1 Timothy 5:15; 2 Timothy 2:26; James 4:7).

The third reason the spirit world would be interested in Masonry is because *Masonry offers both an introduction to, and a furthering of, the cause of paganism, mysticism, the psychic, and the occult.* For these three reasons, it is logical to suppose that the spirit world is interested in promoting and advancing the cause of Masonry. Many Masons may prefer to disbelieve that evidence for this exists. But it can be documented.

In the world of the occult, various spirits are often associated with specific methods of occult development—such as levels of initiation, various spiritual planes, spiritual "rays," and the planets in astrology. But historically this has also been true for certain degrees of Masonry. It is relevant that an acknowledged authority on magic, A. E. Waite, discusses the connection between Masonry and "angelology," that is, the spirit world. In *A New Encyclopedia of Freemasonry*, he discusses the corresponding spirits and alleged angels connected to various Masonic degrees. Among his selected list of sixteen major spirits are the following: "Adarel," an angel associated with the 28th Degree of the Scottish Rite; "Hamaliel," the spirit who governs the planet Venus; "Ariel," the spirit of the air; "Azrael," who is the "angel of death"; and "Casmaran" and "Taljahad," who are associated with the 29th Degree of the Scottish Rite.[3]

The Initiatory Rites of Ancient Pagan Religion

The kinds of initiation found in the ancient mystery religions were more than mere "initiations." They were also introductions to the gods and deities—the spirits who functioned behind the cults and rituals into which the person was being initiated. Perhaps the most influential cult of ancient times was the Dionysian Mysteries (see next chapter). They were named after the Greek Dionysus (the Roman Bacchus) to whom the aspirant was in some fashion dedicated. The initiation and the festivals could involve gross immorality.[4]

Yet even Masonic authority Mackey admits that modern Masonry is related to the Dionysian Mysteries, which are "intimately connected with the history of Freemasonry, and whose influence is, to this day, most evidently felt in its organization." He also observes, "Of all the ancient mysteries, they are the most interesting to the Masonic student."[5]

Mackey even refers to those initiated into this and other ancient cults as "the Freemasons, so to speak—of Asia Minor." In addition, he quotes Albert Pike, who observes of the Dionysian initiate, "One of the most precious advantages promised by their initiation was to put man in communion with the gods."[6]

But how does all of this relate to modern Masonry? Where occult rituals are found, the spirit world is found. By this, we do not mean to imply that the rites of Masonry introduce Masons directly to the spirit world. But neither can we say this never occurs. Can we assume that the modern vestiges of ancient rites—so useful to the spirit world in the past—would never command that world's attention today?

In Alice Bailey's occult text, *The Reappearance of the Christ*,[7] we see that the spirits *are* interested. What of those Masons who are predisposed to occult influences[8] or who are even seeking to contact the ancient spirits? If a Mason were to go through the rites of the Blue Lodge and subsequently pursue a study of the ancient mysteries, noting their connection to the gods, is it not possible that he could utilize the rites of Scottish or York Masonry in an occult context to contact the spirit world—as can occur in any magic ritual? To the extent that Masonry as an institution returns to its past, to that extent it can assimilate the goals and methods of the past.

To understand the potential of modern Masonry for promoting the ancient occult initiations, one need only read the texts by mystics or occultists who are also leading Masons, such as Walter Leslie Wilmshurst's *The Masonic Initiation* and *The Meaning of Masonry*. Wilmshurst sees within Masonry the very means to return to the earlier wisdom of the pagans when "men were once in conscious conversation with the unseen world and were shepherded, taught and guided by the 'gods' or discarnate superintendents [spirits] . . . who imparted to them the sure and indefeasible principles upon which their spiritual welfare and evolution depended."[9] In other words, Masonry can become a means to spirit contact.

But the modern Mason will still ask, "Is there any evidence that the spirit world of *today* is interested in promoting Masonry?" The answer to that is again, Yes.

THE SPIRITS SPEAK

Djwhal Khul was one of the principal spirit guides of occultist Alice Bailey. This spirit guide taught that there are three principal instruments for preparing the earth for the coming universal one-world religion. These three instruments are the field of education, the Christian church, and Masonry. In each field, the spirit claims that committed occultists are working to transform the respective institutions so that it might become a channel for New Age ideals and goals. Of Masonry the spirit teaches, "The Masonic movement . . . is the home of the Mysteries and the seat of initiation. . . . It is a far more occult organization than can be realized, and is intended to be the training school for the coming advanced occultists."[10]

Again, remember that it is a spirit who is speaking these words through a possessed medium. This entity proceeds to reveal that the spirit Hierarchy directs specific persons within each field to perform the will of the spirits.

> In all these bodies there are to be found esoteric groups. . . . These inner groups consist of occult students and of those who are in direct or occasional touch with the Masters [spirits] and of those whose souls are in sufficient control so that the will of the Hierarchy [the governing spirit hierarchy] may be communicated and gradually filtered down to the channel of the physical brain.[11]

In other words, this spirit claims that such individuals are under the guidance and control of the spirit world.

These teachings conform to the idea expressed by some occultists that Masonry and related bodies are the intentional product of the spirit world. Put in another way, such groups are instituted by the spirit world to secure its goals. For example, the Theosophical Society of Helena P. Blavatsky was clearly founded by the spirit world, and yet the spirits who dictated Blavatsky's works also had high praise for Masonry.[12] Few modern societies have done as much to promote the occult in the modern era as theosophy. Yet theosophist and occultist Isabel Cooper-Oakley observes this of Masonry:

> To the student of Theosophy who is also a student of Masonry it becomes more and more apparent that the movement which is generally termed Masonic had its roots in that true mysticism which originated, as an ideal effort, from the spiritual Hierarchy [the spirit world] which guides the evolution of the world.[13]

One of the spirits who inspired Blavatsky noted approvingly, "The Kabalah is indeed of the essence of Masonry."[14]

Masonic author Lynn F. Perkins wrote *Masonry in the New Age*, in which he thoroughly integrates Masonry with occultic and New Age philosophy. Yet he too claims his ideas were inspired by the spirits.[15] Another illustration of the spirits' interests in Masonry is the writings of Harold Waldwin Percival.

Percival was a mystic and spiritist. While he was functioning as a channel for the spirits, they generated through him an influential occultic text called *Thinking and Destiny*. What was later published separately as *Masonry and Its Symbols in the Light of "Thinking and Destiny"* was originally part of the manuscript of *Thinking and Destiny*. In other words, the material on Masonry was also the result of the spirits' inspiration through Percival. According to Percival it was later published separately with the approval of Masons. The goal of this text is to awaken Masons to "true Masonry" and to show how the spirits or "intelligences in the earth's sphere" work through Masonry behind the scenes.[16] The spirits reveal that

> the Brotherhood of Freemasons is the largest of the bodies in the world which are outposts to prepare possible candidates

for an inward [mystical] life.... Intelligences in the earth's
sphere [spirits] are behind Masonry, though the lodges are
not aware of this in the present age. The spirit [philosophy]
that runs through the system of the Masonic teachings connects these Intelligences with every Mason, from the greatest
to the least, who practices them.[17]

So again we see that the spirits claim their involvement
with Masonry. In a similar fashion, Manly P. Hall also notes the
interest of the spirit world in Masonry. He teaches that this spirit world ("celestial intelligences") operates invisibly and imperceptibly behind the man who becomes a Mason and also recognizes its true meaning.[18]

The goal of the spirits is to enlighten Masons and initiate
them into the spiritual hierarchy of the Brotherhood.[19] Presumably, the spirits work through the enlightened Master Mason
because of his spiritual ability; he is said to be the "beloved
Son" of God. For example, consider the following description
that Hall applies to the Master Mason:

> The Master Mason embodies the power of the human mind.
> ...His spiritual light is greater because he has evolved a
> higher vehicle for its expression.... For him the Heavens
> have opened and the Great Light has bathed him in its radi-
> ance.... The voice speaks from the Heavens, its power thrill-
> ing the Master until his own being seems filled with its divin-
> ity, saying, "This is my beloved Son, in whom I am well
> pleased."... The Master Mason is in truth a sun, a great re-
> flector of light.... He, in truth, has become the spokesman of
> the Most High.... Through him passes Hydra, the great
> snake, and from its mouth there pours to man the light of
> God.[20]

Hall describes the Master Mason as a medium through
which the "Most High" and spiritual powers can speak. Thus,
he teaches that the spirits can work through the enlightened
Mason:

> The Master Mason, if he be truly a Master, is in communica-
> tion with the unseen powers.... He is the spokesman for the
> spiritual hierarchies [spirits] of his Craft ...a Priest-King after
> the Order of Melchizedek, who is above the law.... He wears

the triple crown of the ancient Magus, for he is in truth the King of heaven, earth, and hell. . . . He seeks to be worthy to pass behind that veil and join that band [of spirits] who, un-honored and unsung, carry the responsibilities of human growth. . . . It is then, and then only, that a true Mason is born. Only behind this veil does the mystic student come into his own.[21]

For Hall and others, the "true" Mason is the Mason who recognizes his duties to the spirit world.

For our final illustration of the spirits' interests in Masonry we refer to Foster Bailey, a 32d Degree Mason and husband of Alice Bailey, the prominent New Age occultist and founder of Lucius Trust. Bailey also seeks to tie Masonry to occult philosophy and to a spirit hierarchy of Ascended Masters who guide Masonry behind the scenes. These spirits intend to use Masonry as a vehicle toward the globalization of the ancient mystery teachings and the coming occultic New Age. Again, this is why the spirits claim to support Masonry—they see it as a vehicle for the expansion of their purposes on earth.[22]

Along with many other Masons, Bailey believes that there is an awakening within Masonry:

> The time has now arrived for a further spiritualizing of the Masonic movement. . . . Masonry . . . is moving forward be-cause it is frustrated by its apparent emptiness of deeper life values now increasingly craved by intelligent men. . . . The hopeful thing about Masonry today is that it also, like all world groups, is being stirred within itself. Unrest in the Ma-sonic membership is emerging and increasingly large num-bers of the craft are searching for its deeper meanings.[23]

Bailey confesses to necromantic contacts in Masonry. He reveals that the "Grand Lodge" of dead Master Masons guides Masonry and even all humanity "in the way of light." He speaks of the revelations of the higher degrees "for which the so-called Blue Lodge has prepared the candidate."[24] He further states that "subtle and elusive indications are given also of that organized and intelligent activity which is carried on by that Grand Lodge of [dead] Master Masons who have for ages watched over humanity and guided men steadily in the way of light."

> Little as it may be realized by the unthinking Mason who is interested only in the outer aspects of the Craft work, the whole fabric of Masonry may be regarded as an externaliza-tion of that inner spiritual group whose members, down through the ages have been the custodians of the Plan [for the spiritual advance of humanity].[25]

Bailey proceeds to explain that Masonry "was created by the Most High as an instrument in His hands by which to raise humanity."

> Masonry is not man-made; it is God-made. . . . Masonry has survived the ages because in truth and fact we have been guided by inspiration and by intuition, by [spirits of the] Grand Lodge on High, whose members are not dead Masons, but a living Society of Illumined Minds, the Knowers of God's Plan.[26]

In other words, Bailey is teaching that Masonry has been guided by the spirits of the dead who are in tune with God and able to use the Society to fulfill God's will. (Mediums by the thousands teach the same belief concerning their own philoso-phy and practices, yet all such activity is condemned by God in Deuteronomy 18:9-12.) Bailey calls such spirits "the Builders of the occult tradition," the "Illuminati," and other names. Step by step these spirits guide the Masonic candidate:

> They prepare the candidate for those great revelations and expansions of consciousness. . . . Step by step They guide the candidate until he has gained the right to stand in the East before the Presence. . . . Stage by stage They assist at the un-folding of the consciousness of the candidate until the time comes when he can "enter into light" and, in his turn be-come a light-bearer, one of the Illuminati who can assist the Lodge on High in bringing humanity to light.[27]

Here Bailey teaches that the enlightened Mason can actually be-come a partner with the spirit world and can assist the spirits (the "Lodge on High") in their goals for humanity.

But where did Bailey get such an idea? Perhaps in part he derived the idea from the rituals of Masonry itself. For example, some Masonic rituals and vows assume the presence of the Masonic dead. Whether this is taken literally or figuratively is probably up to the individual Mason. Nevertheless, the Commander of the Council of Kadosh takes his vows in "the presence of God the Father Almighty, and of the immortal Spirits of the Great and Good who have died."[28]

According to Bailey this Masonic "Lodge on High" is composed of a hierarchy of spirits who will not only help produce the coming New Age but will also "eventually save the world."

> This world Order, sometimes spoken of as "the Great White Lodge," has existed from the beginning of human life. . . . Also recognized in Masonry as "The Grand Lodge on High" [the Lodge has] existed and worked ceaselessly, as was its destiny, for the expansion of human consciousness. That Lodge is the mother lodge of all Masonic Lodges. . . . He whom we in the west call the Christ, known also in other religions by other names, is the head of the Great White Lodge, and is spoken of in Masonic writings as "the Grand Master of the Lodge on High." He sits, symbolically, in the East and guides "God's higher Masonry." He is the greatest Master Mason of us all.[29]

In other words, for Foster Bailey it is Jesus Christ Himself who is guiding the spirit entities that work through Masonry.

Some teach that the spirit world uses the Masonic rituals themselves (at least in the lives of the "prepared candidates") in order to control or otherwise influence them. This phenomenon is reinterpreted as control by the "higher" Self or the "indwelling" of Light, but in some Lodges at least, it could become the means to spirit influence or even possession:

> The Light of the Intelligence descends into the candidate and fills his body. . . . The mortal body has been transformed into an immortal body. This culmination of the Masonic purpose is sometimes represented by the fire coming down from heaven and by a temple in the Lodge being filled with effulgent light.[30]

The making of a Master Mason is a deeply spiritual event and can only truly take place when the lower nature which we call *the personality is, in fact, under control by the higher man or soul.* Then what is symbolically termed the death of the personality is welcomed and the whole man can be raised. This is part of the inner significance of the third degree of Masonry. . . . Even in its merely exoteric formalism it is dramatic and can be epoch making in the life of the candidate. (Italics added)[31]

Is it conceivable that some Lodges could, through their rituals, become the means for the spiritual possession of certain candidates? We cannot rule out the possibility. Manly Hall, W. L. Wilmshurst, and other mystical Masons actually find in Masonry a secret method of instruction for kundalini* arousal.[32] And this is not the conclusion of the uninformed. According to the *Encyclopedia Britannica*, Wilmshurst is one of the foremost authorities in Masonry, especially British Masonry,[33] and Hall is a respected authority on the occult. But the standard literature on kundalini arousal indicates three things about this practice: its capacity to produce psychic abilities; its universally acknowledged dangers to the mind; and in manifestations, its similarity to spirit possession.[34]

In conclusion, the problem is that we live in an age of occult revival. Thus, the trend in Masonry will probably be in the direction of recognizing more and more of its occult potential. Henry Wilson Coil observes, "Freemasonry is, to a large extent, shaped by developments in the larger society about it and of which it is a part."[35] As we noted earlier, this is why Wilmshurst states that, "A higher Masonic consciousness is awakening in the craft."[36]

In a debate with a professed Christian Mason on "The John Ankerberg Show," the late Walter R. Martin, an acknowledged authority on comparative religion, referred to Masonry as "metaphysical Satanism. . . . That's exactly what it is."[37] That such a designation is not entirely out of place can be seen in the following:

---

*The supposed cosmic consciousness awakened by Tantric Yoga.

- The Masonic connection to ancient paganism and the mystery religions (chapter 19)

- The Masonic connection to the kabbalah, alchemy, Rosicrucianism, and other forms of the occult (chapter 17)

- The imagery of death and blood in the Masonic rites (chapter 14)

- The use in ritual of "sacred" words like *Abaddon* and *Jahbulon*, which are appellations of the devil, as even Albert Pike admitted (chapters 9, 13)[38]

In the aforementioned debate, Walter Martin also stated of Masonry,

> I would object strenuously to the paganism that is in there. For instance, in the temple in Los Angeles, which I took the trouble to visit, there is a statue of Moses, and then there is a statue of Zoroaster, and then there is one of Osiris, and then there are statues of Egyptian gods and goddesses. Now, my objection would be based on this, that when you put a representative of the God of the Bible in the midst of the pagan world, which God judged for its evil, condemned them as vile, depraved, and wicked, then I think that you would have gone over the borderline of just symbol. You're playing with the very dangerous spiritual fire. . . . As a Christian, this to me is totally incongruent with Second Corinthians: "'Come out from among them and be separate,' saith the Lord, 'and I will be your God and you will be my people.'"[39]

When Christians or Masons embrace "metaphysical Satanism" and all of the ancient paganism that God hates, should we expect that to be entirely without spiritual consequence? Perhaps this is one reason many Christian Masons are spiritually neutralized, why others abandon the faith, and why still others suffer spiritual problems.

The point here is simple: paganism and the occult are dangerous—culturally, spiritually, and psychologically. They promote spiritual evil, immorality, and social decay. If a Mason in good conscience, Christian or non-Christian, cannot support the occult in any way, then how can he continue to support Masonry? Given the documentation that the occult is dangerous, how can a person support something that even indirectly promotes paganism and the occult?

Given the fact of spiritual warfare (Ephesians 6:10-18), given the reality of Satan and his demons (Matthew 4:1-10), can we really say that merely partaking of the Masonic Ritual alone will never be without consequence? Consider one real life illustration:

> A young man in his early 40's confided in me recently about obscene sexual images that he was having during his times of spiritual communion, as well as disturbing feelings about blood and killing loved ones. This man is stable, mature, and has no history of mental illness. After counseling it was discovered that the sexual imagery was linked to Freemasonry symbols, the blood and the knife which he was tempted to use to kill a loved one were linked with the Oaths in Freemasonry. When this man was cut free from all of his links with Freemasonry in the name of Jesus those very disturbing feelings and images went and he has not been troubled since.[40]

One can only wonder at the cumulative impact of Masonry in the life of Christian Masons and in the church: the spiritual problems resulting from Masonry that cause depression or lack of trust in God; the intellectual doubts fostered by Masonic syncretism; the millions of man hours of lost evangelism; the distorted reading of the Bible through the eyes of Masonry; the keeping of the Christian in a state of spiritual immaturity or compromise; the robbing of God of the glory due Him alone; the insulting and mocking of God by the adoption of pagan rites that fuse His name to demonic gods. If the spirits are not interested in Masonry, what would they be interested in?

Masonry . . . is their spiritual descendant, and renders much the same ministry to our age which the mysteries rendered to the olden world. . . . This at least is true: the Greater Ancient Mysteries were prophetic of Masonry.

Joseph Fort Newton
The Builders

19

Mystery Religions

Is modern Masonry related to the ancient mystery religions? Some Masons might think this is an unimportant or irrelevant topic. But the mystery religions of the ancient world taught and promoted a number of things that should be of concern to any Mason. These ancient mystery religions, with their secret initiations and rites, were the "engines" of ancient paganism. They existed in most cultures of the day—Persia, Rome, Greece, Egypt, China—and in all their worldly glory and depravity, they nurtured the pagan faith of millions of people.

PRACTICES OF THE MYSTERY RELIGIONS

Allegedly, the teachings of the mystery religions were revealed by the Egyptian god Thoth. They were eclectic religious cults that stressed oaths of secrecy, brotherhood, religious quest, and immortality. They offered secret rites of initiation that were associated with or dedicated to various gods and goddesses of the ancient world. The mysteries usually taught an occultic philosophy of life, such as reincarnation, and some used ritual or other methods to attain "higher" consciousness. They could be ascetic or licentious.[1]

In addition, they often inculcated contact, or union, with the "gods" (spirits) and hoped to attain occult knowledge, power, and immortality from their practices, worship, and contact with these gods. In essence, the mystery religions were part and parcel of the world of the occult in ancient Europe and Asia. They were idolatrous, opposed Christian teachings, and often engaged in immoral rites. By way of illustration, the following are descriptions of the Cybelene, Egyptian, Persian, and Dionysian mysteries:

> In the wild orgies of worship associated with that mystery religion, some devotees voluntarily wounded themselves and, becoming intoxicated with the view of blood [cf. 1 Kings 18:28], with which they sprinkled their altars, they believed they were uniting themselves with their divinity. Others sacrificed their virility to the gods.
>
> St. Augustine wrote that, as a young man, he "took pleasure in the shameful games which were celebrated in honor of the gods and goddesses," including Cybele. On the day consecrated to her purification, "here were sung before her couch productions so obscene and filthy for the ear ... so impure, that not even the mother of the foulmouthed players themselves could have formed one of the audience." ...
>
> During the ceremonial rites dedicated to the Great Mother, a young man stood beneath a platform upon which a steer was slaughtered and showered himself with the animal's blood. After the blood bath, the gore-covered mystic offered himself to the veneration of the crowd. The ceremony was known as the taurobolia. ...
>
> The Egyptian goddess Isis was honored especially by "women with whom love was a profession." ... The morals of the cult of Isis and Osiris were viewed by the Roman community at large as very loose, and the mystery surrounding it excited the worst suspicions.

> Persia introduced dualism as a fundamental principle of religion, and deified the evil principle. It was taught that both evil and the supreme deity must be worshiped. ... The Persian Mazdeans brought the dimension of magic to their rites and made their "mysteries" a reversed religion with a liturgy focused on the infernal powers. "There was no miracle the experienced magician might not expect to perform with the aid of demons. ... Hence the number of impious practices performed in the dark, practices the horror of which is equaled only by their absurdity: preparing beverages that disturbed the senses and impaired the intellect; mixing subtle

poisons extracted from demonic plants and corpses already in the state of putridity; immolating children in order to read the future in their quivering entrails or to conjure up ghosts...." These were some of the "Ancient Mysteries" about which Freemasons boast of being the modern successors.[2]

The initiation ceremonies usually mimed death and resurrection [cf. the Masonic "Hiram Abiff" legend]. This was done in the most extravagant manner. In some ceremonies, candidates were buried or shut up in a sarcophagus; they were even symbolically deprived of their entrails and mummified (an animal's belly with entrails was prepared for ceremony). Alternately, the candidates were symbolically drowned or decapitated. In imitation of the Orphic myth of Dionysus Zagreus, a rite held in which the heart of a victim, supposedly a human child, was roasted and distributed among the participants to be eaten.... In the Dionysus and Isis mysteries, the initiation was sometimes accomplished by a "sacred marriage," a sacral copulation.[3]

CONNECTIONS BETWEEN MASONRY AND THE MYSTERY RELIGIONS

All in all the Mysteries exerted a considerable influence in the ancient world, and this influence was anything but benign. If modern Masonry is related to such paganism, it should be of concern. Had we space, we could show that these religions were truly evil and, in their interaction with the church, functioned as a spiritual counterfeit that deceived many. This should be of concern to the Christian Mason. Does he wish to promote the spiritual "descendant" of a particular form of religion that was pagan and occult?

But most Masons are not aware that Masonry is related to the ancient mystery religions. Still, those who have studied this question, whether Mason or not, have concluded that there is a strong relationship between the ancient mysteries and modern Masonry. For example, Martin L. Wagner spent years of diligent research into Masonry and wrote a voluminous text documenting the connection. He concludes that

> Freemasonry is the religion of the mysteries translated into a new and more modern ceremonial, and expressed by a new system of glyphs and ideographs. It is couched in terms of operative [stone craft] Masonry and explained by legendary

narratives of King Solomon and his architect. But the religion is the same. That has remained unchanged. The form and manner of expressing it have changed.[4]

That is why he concludes, "Modern Masonry is . . . a transposition or transference of the ancient mystery religion into and under the symbols of the work tools, figures of a builder's craft."[5]

In fact, over half of Wagner's text is devoted to thoroughly documenting the veiled relationship between Masonry and ancient phallic religion: "Freemasonry is [ultimately] a sex cult, in which the generative powers are adored and worshipped under disguised phallic rites and symbols. Phallicism is the essence of the religion of the mysteries [Mackey admits this as well] and phallicism is the essence of the religion of Freemasonry." Even Masonic scholars such as Mackey and Pike and some former Masons have admitted the phallic origin of certain Masonic symbols. In addition, few can logically doubt the close relationship between the Masonic Great Architect of the Universe and the generative principle of Nature.[6]

In a similar fashion, after fourteen years of research, Mason[7] J. S. M. Ward wrote *Freemasonry and the Ancient Gods*, a large work that traces Masonry to the mystery religions, and the cults and rites of primitive people in ancient India, Mexico, Egypt, and Rome. So many Masonic authorities and researchers have documented the connection of Masonry to the ancient mysteries that it is a wonder so many Masons are ignorant of the fact.

Part of the reason for this is the many Masons who do not like to acknowledge the Craft's ties to paganism. Coil claimed that "Freemasonry is not and never was connected with Ancient Mysteries in any way."[8] On reflection, it is amazing that a Mason would make such a statement. And it is statements like these that reveal why some Masons are uninformed on the issue. Unfortunately, in an age of occultic revival, the ancient pagan connections to Masonry are likely to become more prominent within Masonry.[9]

It is relatively simple to prove that Masonry is related to the ancient mystery religions of Persia, Rome, and Greece. One need only to study the ancient mystery religions, the books purporting to show a relationship between Masonry and the mysteries, and modern Masonry. Anyone who does this will prove to himself that Masonry is deeply related to ancient paganism. Even the Texas *Monitor* confesses:

> These [Masonic teachings were] practiced from remote ages, in the ancient temples of many nations. Such ceremonies and their correlated teachings have sometimes been referred to as the *Mysteries of Masonry*, with the same signification employed when one speaks of the *"Mysteries of the Magi,"* the *"Mysteries of Osiris,"* the *"Grecian Mysteries of Eleusis,"* and other kindred rites, practiced in the temples of initiation throughout the ancient world....
>
> The presence in the modern Masonic system, of many of the emblems, symbols and allegories of the ancient Temples of Initiation, as well as certain rites performed therein, has persuaded the most learned among Masonic scholars, to conclude that Masonry is of very ancient origin, and is, in some aspects, the modern successor of, and heir to, the sublime Mysteries of the Temple of Solomon, and of the Temples of India, Chaldea, Egypt, Greece, and Rome, as well as the basic doctrine of the Essenes, Gnostics and other mystic Orders.[10]

The Masonic literature documenting this connection to the Mysteries is impressive. Many books were written by Masons who are noted occultists and who admit the connection. Albert Pike's *Morals and Dogma*, Manly Hall's *Masonic Hermetic Quabbalistic and Rosicrucian Symbolical Philosophy*, and Foster Bailey's *The Spirit of Masonry* to name a few. Other Masonic works include George H. Steinmetz's *Freemasonry—Its Hidden Meaning*, Albert Mackey's *The Symbolism of Freemasonry*, W. L. Wilmshurst's *The Meaning of Masonry*, and A. T. C. Pierson's *Traditions, Origin and Early History of Masonry*.[11]

But many other authorities assert their conviction that Masonry is rooted in ancient pagan ritual and belief. In *A Masonic Reader's Guide*, Masonic historian Alphonse Cerza cites two full pages of texts claiming that Masonry is related to ancient paganism.[12] Masonic reviewers of these books often acknowledge that the authors have made their case. This is true of the following books: Charles H. Vail, *Ancient Mysteries and Modern Masonry* (1909); C. L. Arnold, *Philosophical History of Freemasonry and Other Secret Societies* (1854); J. N. Casavis, *The Greek Origin of*

Freemasonry (1955); Albert Churchward, *The Arcana of Free-masonry* (1915).

Cerza cites a number of articles in Masonic literature relating to this theme: for example, "Masonry and the Mysteries"; "The Mysteries of Isis and Osiris and Modern Masonry"; "Freemasonry and the Ancient Mysteries"; "The Resemblance of Freemasonry to the Cult of Mithra"; "The Druses of Syria and their Relation to Freemasonry"; and "Stonehenge: An Ancient Masonic Temple."[13]

All of these texts demonstrate beyond doubt that Masonry is related to and was influenced by the ancient Mystery religions. This is precisely why some modern Masons claim that Masonry has become dedicated only to the "outer form" of its ritual and forsaken its real meaning and power, a meaning close in heart to the Mysteries.

No one knows exactly how Masonry assimilated the ancient Mystery rites. One probable theory is through the influence of the mystical societies and the occult during the Middle Ages.[14] According to this theory, different lodges in different periods of time were variously influenced by alchemy, illuminism, Rosicrucianism, kabbalism, gnosticism, druidism, and theosophy.[15] Fisher observes that

> Jacques De Molay, Grand Master of the Knights Templar, was executed in 1314. However, before he died, according to Pike, he instituted what came to be called the occult Hermetic or Scottish Masonry, the Lodges of which were established in four metropolitan areas, Naples, Edinburgh, Stockholm, and Paris. Those Lodges, Pike asserted, were the initial Lodges of modern Freemasonry.[16]

Thus, it is significant that H. L. Haywood reveals that almost all the historians of Masonry agree that the Lodge was greatly influenced by the occultism of the Middle Ages: "All our historians, at least nearly all of them, agree that Freemasonry owes very much to certain occult societies of groups that flourished—often in secret—during the late Middle Ages, and even into the after-Reformation times. Chief among these were the Rosicrucians and the Knights Templar [and kabbalism]."[17] In his treatment of Rosicrucianism, Mackey admits, "There are sufficient coincidences of character between the two to render the history of Rosicrucianism highly interesting to the Masonic student."[18]

In Mackey's article on medieval theosophy, he admits connections between Masonry and spiritistic influence. First, he observes that "those with whom the history of Freemasonry has most to do were the mystical religious thinkers of the Eighteenth Century." Next, he acknowledges that they claimed supernatural inspiration for their beliefs. Among those mentioned are Emanuel Swedenborg, a spiritist and highly influential occultist, "who, if not himself a Masonic reformer, has supplied the materials of many [Masonic] Degrees." Finally, he states that "theosophic Freemasonry was, in fact, nothing else than an application of the speculative ideas of Jacob Bohme, of Swedenborg, and other mystical [i.e., mystical/occult] philosophers of the same class." And he admits that they were devout believers in the kabbalah and in spirit contact.[19] In other words, even the great Masonic authority Mackey acknowledges a relationship between Masonry, and theosophic and Swedenborgian occultism and spiritism of the eighteenth century:

> The name [occult sciences] is given to the sciences of alchemy, magic, and astrology, which existed in the Middle Ages. Many of the speculations of these so called sciences were in the Eighteenth Century made use of in the construction of the higher Degrees. We have even a Hermetic Rite which is based on the dogmas of alchemy.[20]

Such influence is also why occult authority Manly Hall concludes in his *Masonic Hermetic Cabalistic and Rosicrucian Symbolical Philosophy* that "no reasonable doubt remains that the Masonic Order is the direct outgrowth of the secret societies of the Middle Ages, nor can it be denied that Freemasonry is permeated by the symbolism and mysticism of the ancient and medieval worlds."[21]

Many other Masonic writers and authorities acknowledge the deep ties of Masonry to the ancient pagan mystery religions.[22] In his discussion of the definition of Masonry, Masonic authority Albert Mackey agrees that "its ceremonials were practiced in ancient mysteries."[23] W. Ravenscroft states that Masonry "has striking resemblances to the mysteries of Egypt, Greece and even China."[24] Albert Pike taught that "Masonry, [is the] successor of the Mysteries, [and] still follows the ancient manner of teaching." He went on to maintain that "Masonry is identical with the ancient mysteries"—but only in that Masonry presents "an imperfect image of their brilliancy."[25] Foster Bailey, a 32d Degree Mason and spiritist, concludes that "Study of the spiritual realities found in Masonry reveals that we have perpetrated and increasingly activated the essential principles of the ancient Mystery Schools."[26]

According to Joseph Fort Newton, perhaps the most popular of all Masonic writers, "Masonry stands in this tradition [the ancient mystery religions]. . . . It is their spiritual descendant, and renders much the same ministry to our age which the mysteries rendered to the olden world. . . . This at least is true: the Greater Ancient Mysteries were prophetic of Masonry."[27] In his discussion of the ancient Mystery religions, Albert Mackey acknowledges concerning the rites of Masonry that "they bear in many respects so remarkable a resemblance, that some connections seem necessarily implied."

> For all the antique strangeness of the rituals of the Mysteries, and of their gods and their supernatural machinery, the men who met in their halls were such men as ourselves and are as intelligible, and would be at home with us or we with them could either they or we travel the irreversible paths of time.[28]

What Mackey is saying is that, in spite of their differences, modern Masons would feel at home with those who participated in the ancient pagan rites. Perhaps then it is not surprising that in various Masonic rituals, the "old gods" are honored while the Christians who rejected them are held up to derision: the modern ritual for dedication of the Scottish Rite Hall or Temple confesses, "Our ancient brethren made their libations of wine to propitiate the gods."[29]

Sovereign Grand Commander Henry C. Clausen acknowledges that the 31st and 32d Degrees of the Scottish Rite are based in part upon the *Egyptian Book of the Dead.* Manly Hall confesses that "the [Egyptian] book of the dead is a treasure house of Masonic lore."[30]

Even the Masonic publisher, Macoy Publishing and Masonic Supply Co., admits that "Freemasonry . . . can be regarded as a perpetuation of the philosophical mysteries and initiations of the ancients. This is in keeping with the inner tradition of the Craft."[31] The Holy Bible—Masonic Edition confesses, "It is admitted that Masonry is descended from the ancient mysteries."[32] What many Masons do not seem to comprehend is the extent to which modern Masonry is also a promotion of paganism. How does a modern Mason, let alone a Christian Mason, feel about promoting a system based on ancient paganism?

Clausen, after citing the mystery religions for many cultures, admits, "We [Masons] reveal truly the wisdom of the Lesser [basic] and the Greater [advanced] Mysteries" and "our Scottish Rite is a lineal descendant of these teachings and has maintained the knowledge and the wisdom of these ancient fraternities."[33] But these fraternities were dedicated to the pagan gods of the ancient world—what the Bible calls demons (1 Corinthians 10:20). Perhaps modern Masons should listen carefully to the words of Albert Mackey:

> Almost every country of the ancient world had its peculiar Mysteries dedicated to the occult worship of some especial and favored god, and to the inculcation of a secret doctrine. . . . Thus in Persia the mysteries were dedicated to Mithras, or the Sun; in Egypt to Isis and Osiris; in Greece to Demeter and Samothracia, to the gods Cabiri, the mighty ones; in Syria, to Dionysus; while in the more northern nations of Europe, such as Gaul and Britain, the initiations were dedicated to their peculiar deities, and were celebrated under the general name of the Druidical rites. . . . I need scarcely here advert to the great similarity in design and conformation which existed between these ancient rites and [e. g.] the third or Masters degree of Masonry.[34]

Even the lower rites of Masonry are related to paganism. But if these ancient gods were, in fact, demons and if they had clearly vested interests in such ancient rites, can we be assured that they would not be interested in similar rites today? Because of this, every Mason should be concerned.

In conclusion, Masonry is related to the ancient occultism of the mystery religions. This is why Manly Hall correctly states,

"The true Masonic Lodge is a Mystery School."[35] Does the modern Mason really want to be part of a descendant of an ancient mystery school? Whatever else can be said of the mystery religions, five propositions are clear:

- They worshiped pagan (false) gods and therefore engaged in the grievous sin of idolatry (Acts 17:16; see chapters 6-9).[36]

- They opposed the teachings of the biblical God, Christ, and the church (Acts 13:8; 19:24-29; see Parts 2 and 3).

- They promoted the occult in various forms and therefore supported the work of the devil (Acts 19:19; see chapters 17-18).

- They infiltrated the church and did damage to it (Acts 20:29; see chapters 5, 16, 20).

- They lacked moral content and often engaged in perverse, evil, and immoral rites such as ritual prostitution, bathing in animal blood, homosexuality, and the like (Ephesians 5:12; see chapters 4, 14, 20).[37]

When a Mason consciously participates in rites and beliefs that are similar to the ancient mysteries, does he realize the potential spiritual consequences of what he is doing? Some Masons may claim, "The ancient mystery religions have nothing to do with *modern* Masonry—whatever the mystery religions were, Masonry engages in none of the above." They will say that such criticism is simply not relevant to the Masonry they know. But all five concluding assertions are true. Masonry does not necessarily practice them in the same manner or degree, but we cannot deny the similar functions exercised by the mystery religions and modern Masonry.

For example, Masonry does lack any absolute basis for upholding morality and does promote a sanitized version of those pagan rituals. Masonry advocates an outer form of morality, but for most Masons it is either the morality of nature—which is no morality at all—or that of a "situation ethic."[38] The Masonic rites that blaspheme God, use words of violence, and bind a Mason by terrible oaths to support falsehoods cannot be considered moral rites. In essence then, Masonry is producing the same fruit as its ancient ancestors. Masonry remains the daughter of the mystery religions, even in ways that most Masons do not suspect.

If you have been disappointed in the first three Degrees, as you have received them, . . . remember
that . . . those Degrees . . . have come to us from an
age when symbols were used, not to reveal but to
conceal.
Albert Pike
Morals and Dogma

20

Deception

In much cultism, and often in the world of the occult, the deception of the profane—the outsider—is a noble endeavor.
Such an approach keeps the "sacred" truths, which these cults
consider "pure," hidden from the "unworthy." Deception and
secrecy also protect certain cults from criticism of those particular unethical, unspiritual, antisocial, or even criminal teachings that outsiders would find offensive and perhaps hinder the
growth and influence of the cult.

WHY MASONRY USES DECEPTION

Masonry, too, is a religion of deception and secrecy. As Albert Pike observes, "Secrecy is indispensable in a Mason of
whatever Degree."

> Masonry, like all the Religions, all the Mysteries, Hermeticism
> and Alchemy, conceals its secrets from all except Adepts and
> Sages, or the Elect, and uses false explanations and misinter-
> pretations of its symbols to mislead those who deserve only
> to be misled; to conceal the Truth, which it calls Light, from
> them, and to draw them away from it. Truth is not for those
> who would pervert it. . . . So Masonry jealously conceals its
> secrets, and intentionally leads conceited interpreters astray.[1]

The *Pocket Lexicon of Freemasonry* contains the following similar sentiment: "Our traditions and esoteric work, coming down from a very remote age, are too sacred and too valuable to become the topic of every vain babbler, and have been preserved as relics of the past, as they will be, and handed down for ages to come 'to the worthy and the worthy alone.'"[2]

In Masonry are two basic categories of profane individuals. The first category is the general public. The second category is the Masonic initiate himself at a lower level of Masonic "enlightenment." Both categories of people are by definition profane (unworthy); hence the true nature of Masonry is purposely kept hidden from them. Since the non-Mason, by virtue of his not being a Mason, can never be worthy of the secrets of Masonry, it is only the Masonic initiate who may, if he chooses to pursue Masonry, one day comprehend Masonry as it truly is—and not merely as he currently thinks it is. Thus, "a wide and essential difference may therefore exist between what an individual Mason may think and believe to be Freemasonry, and the official objective doctrines expressed in esoteric terms."[3]

As mentioned earlier, Albert Pike confesses in the standard Scottish Rite text that the first three degrees are only a frail entrance into true Masonry. Speaking to Masons, he says,

> If you have been disappointed in the first three Degrees, as you have received them, . . . remember that . . . those Degrees . . . have come to us from an age when symbols were used, not to reveal but to conceal; when the commonest learning was confined to a select few. . . . These antique and simple Degrees now stand [in modern Masonry] like the broken columns of a roofless Druidic temple, in their rude and mutilated greatness; and many parts, also corrupted by time, and disfigured by modern additions and absurd interpretations. They are but the entrance to the great Masonic Temple, the triple columns of the portico. . . .
>
> Imagine not that you will become indeed a Mason by learning what is commonly called the "work," or even by becoming familiar with our traditions. Masonry has a history, a literature, a philosophy. Its allegories and traditions will teach you much; but much is to be sought elsewhere. The streams of learning that now flow full and broad must be fol-

lowed to their heads in the springs that well up in the remote past, and you will there find the origin and meaning of Masonry.[4]

Thus, according to Pike, the average Blue Lodge Mason has a great deal of work ahead of him.

This esoteric, occult, or hidden aspect of Masonry—which deliberately conceals the truth from and deceives even its own initiates—is documented in great detail in Martin L. Wagner's *Freemasonry: An Interpretation*: "The theism of Freemasonry is peculiar and every precaution is taken by the institution to preserve it incorrupted and concealed from the knowledge of the profane, and from its own disciples until they give adequate evidence that they can be entrusted with this secret."[5]

As Pike readily admits in his discussion of the 30th Degree of the Scottish Rite, those in Blue Lodge Masonry have been intentionally deceived and misled:

> The symbols of the wise always become the idols of the ignorant multitude. What the Chiefs of the Order really believed and taught, is indicated to the Adepts by the hints contained in the high Degrees of Free-Masonry, and by the symbols which only the Adepts understand.
>
> The Blue Degrees are but the outer court or portico of the Temple. Part of the symbols are displayed there to the Initiate, but he is intentionally misled by false interpretations. It is not intended that he shall understand them; but it is intended that he shall imagine he understands them. Their true explication is reserved for the Adepts, the Princes of Masonry. The whole body of the Royal and Sacerdotal Art was hidden so carefully, centuries since, in the High Degrees, as that it is even yet impossible to solve many of the enigmas which they contain. It is well enough for the mass of those called Masons, to imagine that all is contained in the Blue Degrees; and whoso attempted to undeceive them will labor in vain, and without any true reward violate his obligation as an Adept.[6]

HOW MASONRY USES DECEPTION ON THE PUBLIC

Masonry deceives the public on an outer level and on an inner level.

The outer level. To repeat from previous chapters, Masonry claims that it is not a religion, that it is not a substitute for religion, that it is not opposed to Christianity, or any religion, but is tolerant and friendly toward all religious faiths, that it has no distinct concept of God, and that it is not occultic in any manner. But we have seen that none of these claims are true. Masonry, like scores of cults, presents a false view of itself to the world.

Masonry claims that it is only a fraternal fellowship working for the good of all men, but this idea only serves as a disguise to deceive those who are unaware of the more universal and global goals that many Masons are working for—namely, to conform the world to the specific doctrines of Masonry.

All this is why investigators of Masonry must be cautious. Knight refers to the "disinformation tactic which several Freemasons attempted to practice upon me." He also refers to the United Grand Lodge of England's Quarterly Communication to Lodges for June 10, 1981, which encourages the following common Masonic tactic: "You shall be cautious in your words and carriage, that the most penetrating stranger shall not be able to discover or find out what is not proper to be intimated; and sometimes you shall divert a discourse, and manage it prudently for the honour of the worshipful fraternity."[7]

The inner level. Masonry not only publicly denies its true "outer" teachings, it also secretly keeps hidden from the public certain of its esoteric or occult teachings. For example, concerning its correlation to ancient Phallicism,[8] such teachings would be so offensive to both the public and even the majority of Masons that

> were the secret religious doctrines of Freemasonry generally known, the institution would surely fall, for such doctrines as we apprehended them, and institutions founded upon them, can not exist except under the cover of absolute secrecy, and a disguise impenetrable to the uninitiated.... Very few Masons know what Freemasonry is, especially in its fundamental [phallic] religious aspect.[9]

As noted earlier, even Masonic authorities and Landmark no. 23 have admitted that were it not for the Masonic emphasis on secrecy, the Lodge would probably not survive.[10] Masonry therefore deceives the public at two levels. But the Lodge deceives its own members as well, as Pike admitted above.

ON ITS OWN INITIATES

First, Masonry demands that the initiate make lifelong oaths of allegiance to Masonry *before* he understands all that he is swearing to. As one critic of Masonry objected, a Christian especially "has no right to pledge himself in advance to keep secret something the bearing of which on questions of justice and morals he cannot know."[11] When Masonic oaths cause a person to swear upon his own Scriptures to uphold that which denies them or to come to another Mason's aid "right or wrong,"[12] this is deceitfully using a person merely to further the goals of Masonry.

Second, Masonry keeps its "higher" truths hidden from the initiate until he is prepared to receive them. The "Blue Lodge" is only the first step along the Masonic path, and "in the first three degrees nothing but the exoteric [outer] doctrines are revealed." As a result of this

> the neophyte [initiate] comes to the lodge ignorant of its nature, religious character and methods of instruction, and therefore disqualifed to discern the Masonic ideas conveyed by the mimic rites, symbols and art speech. He does not know that a double meaning is attached to these symbols and art speech, so that the most ordinary language is made to carry a deep religious and ethical meaning, which very few apprehend.[13]

This deception of Blue Lodge Masons is why the majority of Masons are ignorant of what real Masonry constitutes and represents. Many leading Masons themselves have admitted that "Masonry jealously conceals its secrets and intentionally leads conceited interpreters astray. Part of the symbols are displayed to the initiated, but he is intentionally misled by false interpretations. . . . The meaning of the symbols is not unfolded at once. We give you hints only in general."[14]

Thus, unless they pursue Masonry to its logical conclusion, the majority of Masons never come to know what true Masonry is. Wagner claims that "not one Mason in ten thousand perceives" what the Lodge really involves:

> Its real secrets lie concealed and . . . these are as densely veiled to the Mason as to any other, unless he has studied the science of symbolism in general, and Masonic symbolism is particular. . . . The real hoodwink* is never completely removed from the eyes of a large majority of the members of the craft. They are never brought to the true light of Masonry. . . . They see the garment, but not the thing the garment conceals."[15]

In other words, as 33d Degree Mason Manly Hall reveals,

> Yet if the so-called secrets of Freemasonry were shouted from the housetops, the Fraternity would be absolutely safe; for certain spiritual qualities are necessary before the real Masonic secrets can be understood by the brethren themselves. Hence it is that the alleged "exposures" of Freemasonry, printed by thousands and tens of thousands since 1730 down to the present hour, cannot injure the Fraternity. They reveal merely the outward forms and ceremonies of Freemasonry. Only those who have been weighed in the balance and found to be true, upright and square have prepared themselves by their own growth to appreciate the inner meanings of their Craft. To the rest of their brethren within or without the lodge their sacred rituals must remain, as Shakespeare might have said, "words, words, words."[16]

Who then is the "true Mason"? The true Mason is the one wholly assimilated by paganism and, ultimately, by an evil form of religion. The writings of Masonic authorities such as Pike, Waite, Mackey, Manly Hall, and others, and also non-Masonic researchers such as Wagner and Fisher lead us to no other conclusion, no matter how many denials uninformed Masons may make. In fact, Wagner's, Fisher's, Knight's, and Pike's volumes alone are adequate for this purpose.[17]

---

* A reference to placing a hood over the candidate's head in Masonic ritual.

ON CHRISTIANS AND MEMBERS OF OTHER RELIGIOUS FAITHS

Many Masons profess faith in another religion besides Masonry. But Masonry conceals from these members the "truth" that Masonry alone is the true religion. This is concealed until they are "found worthy" to accept this and will either willfully abandon their former faith or are gradually assimilated into Masonry.[18] Other Masons remain contentedly ignorant with an illogical syncretism. Nevertheless, "while it [Masonry] tacitly admits the existence of other gods in allowing its disciples to hold their private views, it does so on the theory that these god-ideas are perversions and corruptions of its own theistic conceptions and which it aims to correct."[19]

This is particularly true for Christianity. Of all the religions that Masonry attempts to assimilate, it appears to have been most successful with Christianity. In fact, the methods of Masonry seem almost designed to infiltrate and dismantle Christianity:

> The peculiar theological and religious ideas which Freemasonry holds and aims to inculcate while positively non-Christian, are expressed in terms of Christian theology, not to express the Christian ideas or to show their harmony with Christian thought, but to give them a Christian coloring the more effectually to deceive, mislead and hoodwink the neophyte, the conscientious member, and the non-Mason into whose hands Masonic literature may come, and also to intensify the task of the Mason to learn the real sentiments. . . . It employs the terms regeneration, illumination, resurrection, justification, and other terms of Christian theology to express not the Christian ideas, but under which to hide the Masonic religious operation. These terms have a peculiar and a specific Masonic meaning, and in studying this institution we must not permit ourselves to be misled by this use of Christian theological terms, as many a Mason is misled by them to believe that Freemasonry is a Christian institution.[20]

How is it that the Christian Mason is misled and deceived into thinking Masonry is Christian?

> Because the peculiar Masonic religious doctrines are not taught in a dogmatic manner in the lodge, but by symbols, emblems and mimic rites; because the religious offices of the

officials are veiled ... because of the poor blind candidate continually searching for light, and for more light, ... the candidate can not and does not catch the thought intended to be set forth. Outwardly these things are a medley of contradictions, a confusing series of substitutions, so that he does not discern the hidden religious ideas which are esoterically expressed and unfolded in an orderly and systematic manner. He does not perceive the peculiar religion set forth by the entire symbolism of the lodge, a religion that astonishes us with the sublimity of its conceptions, but shocks us with its grossness, rudeness and obscenity.[21]

Through many methods Masonry claims or implies that its God is the same God that Christians worship. But according to Wagner, "these attempts are simply cunning devices for misleading and deceiving both the Mason and the profane. They are examples of clever sophistry, of skillful syncretism, of cunningly devised fables and delusive fictions, which have a semblance of truth and fact, but which in reality are only veils and disguises for its refined idolatry. They are skillful professions of adherence to the first commandment while in fact they are palpable violations of it."[22]

BY DELIBERATELY ENGAGING IN SEMANTIC DISTORTION

Semantic distortion (an unfair or dishonest use of words) is a common characteristic found in modern cultism. It is an effective means for securing intended deceptions, including those of Masonry. As noted by Wagner above, specific words may be used in an ambiguous or deceptive manner in order to *appear* to teach one thing but *actually* teach something else. Masonry employs specific terms used by the church, but the meaning intended is Masonic, not Christian.[23]

For example, Masonry employs the terms *God, Jehovah, justification, monotheism, unity of God, resurrection*, and *regeneration*, but not in a Christian sense. In Masonry, the true identity of these expressions is not determined by the biblical or Christian definition of the words themselves but by the thought Masonry intends to be conveyed. In other words, to understand what Masonry means by these terms one must first understand their Masonic intent: "This Masonic meaning must therefore be determined in order to understand the Masonic doctrines and sentiments."[24]

Thus, Masonry only presents to men the *appearance* of Christianity. In order to win Christians, Masons must appear friendly to the church. As Knight observes, "there is no doubt that Freemasonry is extremely anxious to have—or to appear to have—good relations with all Christian churches."[25] And Martin Wagner observes, "Freemasons endeavor to prove it is in harmony with biblical monotheism. This is important in order to commend the institution to the favorable consideration of Christians."[26]

But the goal is the deception of the Christian: "Freemasonry, like a pirate ship, floats with a friendly banner inscribed with Jehovah's name that the unsuspecting may become an easy prey."[27] The end result is a classic and cunningly devised duping of both Mason and non-Mason alike:

> This method for the communication and promulgation of the Masonic doctrines is so cunningly devised that it baffles on the one hand those who have professed to expose it and give[s] a rational explanation of its symbols and ceremonies, and on the other, the majority of those who are loyal to the institution, in catching its real sentiments.[28]

In fact, the very sins and deceptions that God's people in ancient Israel fell prey to involve some of the same reasons modern Christians become Masons. These include three dynamics: lack of commitment to God and ignorance of who God really is; lack of spiritual discernment, with the resulting confusion between the true God and a false god; leading to idolatry, blasphemy, and apostasy even while thinking that it is the one true God who is being honored and served.

Thus, for the ancient Israelites (and modern Christian Masons) the first problem was a lack of commitment to God and ignorance of Him:

> The mass of the people found the greatest difficulty in keeping their national religion distinct from that of the surrounding nations. Those who had not a grasp of spiritual principles and knew the religion of Jehovah only as a matter of inherit-

ed usage, or looked upon him as a tribal god for Israel as Baal was of the Canaanites, were not conscious of the great difference between themselves and their heathen neighbors, and fell into Canaanite and other foreign practices with the greatest facility.[29]

The second problem was lack of spiritual discernment and a resulting confusion between the one true God and a false and pagan god: "the Israelites spoke of Jehovah as Baal, and this double use of the term Baal for the generative principle [phallic worship] and for Jehovah, tended to produce confusion between them."[30]

The third problem was the horrible result: idolatry, blasphemy, and apostasy from the true faith, leading, for Israel, to God's judgment:

> By this syncretism the conception of Jehovah was debased by elements borrowed from nature worship. The introduction of these noxious elements not only degraded Jehovah, but they enthroned in his place the symbols of reproduction, and ministered to licentiousness which this sycretism encouraged and legalized. . . . Jehovah himself became regarded as one of the Baals, and the chief of them. Thus through this doctrine of the unity and identity of Jehovah and Baal, the name and the honor of Jehovah was degraded to a sensual deity whose most acceptable worship was the indulgence of lust.[31]

Thus do we find that in a similar fashion Christian Masons achieve similar results as their ancient brethren. Christian Masons

> debase the conception of Jehovah by elements borrowed from this modern nature worship, but disguised in terms of a builder's craft. There are many, both among Masons and non-Masons, who have little or no grasp of spiritual principles and who are not conscious of any great difference between Freemasonry and Christianity, and hence fall into this modern nature worship and its attendant practices with the greatest facility, and see no inconsistency in doing so. By this syncretism of names, Freemasonry keeps the hoodwink on the eyes of its disciples so that they fail to perceive this sophism [a deceptive argument] concerning the deity.[32]

Many brethren, misled by the predominantly Scriptural cast of the Work, and misunderstanding a few scattered references here and there, assume that in some sense Freemasonry is specifically a Christian institution.

H. L. Haywood
The Great Teachings of Masonry

Epilogue:

The Legacy of Christian Masonry

Masonry repeatedly claims that it is an enlightened brotherhood seeking to better the world. From a Christian perspective, this claim cannot be substantiated. Masonry offers its members only a false religion that prevents men from encountering the one true God. And yet Masonic influence continues to be felt within the church. Christian Masons are everywhere.

This influence of Masonry in the church constitutes a spiritual scandal. Jesus said, "Beware of the false prophets" (Matthew 7:15). The apostle Paul warned, "See to it that no one takes you captive through philosophy and empty deception, according to the tradition of men, according to the elementary principles of the world, rather that according to Christ" (Colossians 2:8). He exhorted us to "examine everything carefully; hold fast to that which is good; abstain from every form of evil" (1 Thessalonians 5:21-23).

This is why the church must stand for what is true regardless of the consequences. As the apostle John observed, "No lie is of the truth" (1 John 2:21). This is why Christians need to take a stand against Masonic influence in the church. Individual Masons need to be confronted with the errors of Masonry and the claims of Christ upon their lives. Christian Masons need to be shown the logical impossibility of their position, not to mention the harmful consequences of Masonic influence in their Christian life. The church in general needs to offer more doctrinal content and apologetic instruction in its pulpits.

Jesus said, "And this is eternal life, that they may know thee the only true God, and Jesus Christ whom thou has sent" (John 17:3); and He warned, "Unless you repent, you will all likewise perish" (Luke 13:3). The teaching of the Bible is clear; only Jesus Christ is the mediator between man and God (1 Timothy 2:5-6); He alone is the propitiation (atoning sacrifice) for our sins (1 John 2:2); hence, faith in Him alone can deliver a person from the eternal consequences of his sin (John 3:16; 14:6). Indeed, there is no other name under heaven given among men by which a man will ever find peace with God (Acts 4:12).

Masonry may claim that it can fit a person for heaven, but the Word of God teaches otherwise: "Whoever believes in the Son has eternal life, but whoever rejects the Son will not see life, for God's wrath remains on him" (John 3:36).

Christianity bears an odd relationship to historic Masonry. Christians who would never think of joining a group like the Mormon church or promoting the cult of the Jehovah's Witnesses will nevertheless join Masonry by the thousands. Why is this? It is largely because the religious nature of Masonry is more skillfully concealed. Christian Masons also tend to view Masonry through Christian eyes and fail to see it as it really is.

CHRISTIAN JUSTIFICATIONS OF MASONRY

No one can deny that Masonry unites the Christian believer with unbelievers in *spiritual* fellowship and that this is a direct violation of God's command in 2 Corinthians 6:14-17. "Freemasonry does not permit its members to stay at a distance from each other. As I write and as you read each of us is 'near' to a Chinese brother Mason, or an Argentine brother Mason, or a Zoroastrian brother Mason as we are to each other, or as either of us is to the members of his own lodge."[1] Yet Christian Masons typically attempt to justify their membership in the Lodge.

In spite of the evidence, some claim that the two faiths are compatible. Others claim that there are genuine Christian lodges. But how such a lodge could be truly Masonic and Christian at the same time is never explained. In fact, there are no truly Christian lodges. There are only lodges with a large Christian membership, as the following three propositions attest:

Having a lodge of *any* specific non-Masonic religion is a denial of the principles of Masonry. A *truly* Christian lodge (as opposed to a nominally Christian lodge) is a contradiction of terms and would hardly be permitted by most Masonic authorities.

Christians must still have gone through the Masonic rites, and this involves them in sin.

Masonry and Christianity are mutually exclusive. One is either a good Mason or a hypocrite. To say there are Christian lodges is to say there are Christian "Kingdom Halls" or Christian "Mormon Temples."

A History of Entanglement

How then did Masonry and Christianity ever become entangled in the first place? Masonry began as primarily an organization of working stone masons who banded together for common causes like our modern unions. This Masonry was not of the religious character of Masonry today. Thus, a "Christian Mason" was no more a contradiction of terms than is a Christian lumberer or realtor. In each country, the Mason was free to worship the God of that nation actively. For example, the Regius Manuscript (circa 1390) stated: "Those who would be Masons and practice Masonic art are required to love God and his holy church, the Master for whom they labor, and their Masonic brethren; for this is the true spirit of Masonry."[2]

It was not until 1723 that adherence to a particular sectarian God was officially prohibited and Masonry attempted to become a "universal" religion. That new Masonic charge read, "But though in ancient Times Masons were charged in every country to be of the Religion of that Country or Nation, whatever it was, yet 'tis now thought more expedient only to oblige them to that Religion in which all Men agree, leaving their particular Opinions to themselves."[3]

In the process of transition from operative to speculative Masonry, various lodges retained a more distinctly Christian flavor than others. In 1756 the Christian sentiment of part of Irish Masonry is described by Joseph Fort Newton:

> For example, a prayer "to be said at the Opening of the lodge or making of the Brother," includes these words: "Endow him with a Competency of Thy Divine Wisdom, that he may, with the secrets of Freemasonry, be able to unfold the Mysteries of Godliness and Christianity. This we most humbly beg in the Name, and for the Sake, of Jesus Christ our Lord and Savior. Amen. . . . A Mason is obliged by his tenure to believe firmly in the true Worship of the eternal God, as well as in all those sacred Records which *the dignitaries and fathers of the church have compiled* and published for the use of all good men. . . ." In short, the "Ancient" Grand Lodge was an orthodox trinitarian Christian body.[4]

The Early Masonic Catechisms gives the following opening prayer for 1730:

> Most holy and glorious Lord God . . . give us thy Holy Spirit, to enlighten our Minds with Wisdom and Understanding . . . that all our Doings may tend to thy Glory, and the Salvation of our Souls and we beseech thee O Lord God . . . grant that this, our new Brother . . . may, with the Secrets of Masonry, be able to unfold the Mysteries of Godliness and Christianity. This we humbly beg in the name and for the sake of JESUS CHRIST our LORD and SAVIOR.[5]

But even in the early eighteenth century pagan elements existed in Masonry. A tract published in 1731 in London called "A Defense of Masonry" associates Masonry with Egyptian religion and Pythagoras, the Essenes and Cabbalists, Druids and other pagan beliefs.[6] With the official rejection of Christianity, Christian influences nevertheless remained, and in places a process of "Christianization" set in:

> As time went on it came to pass that Freemasonry began to grow at a great rate, and it was inevitable, owing to the serious and religious character of the ritual, that many of the men drawn to it should be churchmen, or otherwise devout. A trend toward Christianization of the Order set in. In 1760 the Holy Bible was made a Great Light. In 1813, at the time of

the famous Union of the two grand Lodges, the Ancient and the Modern, Freemasonry was specifically declared to be consecrated to the glory of God. After this a tide toward Christianization set in with new power until it at last culminated in the work of Dr. George Oliver, whose name should be held in everlasting remembrance among Masons. To Oliver the whole Masonic system was essentially biblical and wholly Christian. He was so fruitful in influence, his books were so many, and his followers so numerous, that for decades men entirely lost sight of the original principles of Speculative Masonry— . . . indeed, that impulse has not yet by any means spent itself; many brethren, misled by the predominantly Scriptural cast of the Work, and misunderstanding a few scattered references here and there, assume that in some sense Freemasonry is specifically a Christian institution.[7]

Many lodges permitted the Great Architect of the Universe to be described in general Christian terms—as, for example, the "Grand Geometrician of the Universe whose Son died for us and rose again."[8] Because Masonry tends to reflect the culture surrounding it—regardless of its official doctrine—the institution was more outwardly Christian in the Christian Europe and America of the eighteenth century. But even with its Christian language, was Masonry ever Christian? The answer can only be no.

Even in its "Christian" form, Masonry is only reminiscent (at least in its use of Christianity) of the Unitarians and Universalists of the same period. In many ways these organizations appeared Christian, they sounded Christian, but they also denied and opposed fundamental Christian doctrine. For example, the Unitarians denied the Trinity (and therefore Jesus' deity), whereas the Universalists denied eternal punishment (and therefore any need for salvation in a biblical sense). Both taught salvation by good works. Eventually the Unitarians and Universalists apostatized entirely and gave up any semblance of relations to biblical Christianity. In 1961 the two groups merged and became the Unitarian Universalist Association. In the same way, Masonry eventually repudiated its association with Christianity.

In the constitutions of 1723 Masonry deliberately rejected an association with Christianity—an association that even Coil admits was in name only. In his standard historical work, *Free-*

masonry Through Six Centuries, Coil observes, "Lastly, but by no means last in importance, the Society abandoned its nominal adherence to Christianity and became non-sectarian."[9] Having said this, it must be admitted that some lodges retained a Christian veneer.

Even so, knowledgeable Christians of that time still rejected Masonry. For example, evangelist Charles Finney wrote a highly critical book on Masonry.[10] D. L. Moody once said, "I do not see how any Christian, most of all a Christian minister, can go to these secret lodges with unbelievers. They say they can have more influence for good, but I say they can have more influence for good by staying out of them and then reproving their evil deeds. You can never reform anything by unequally yoking yourself with ungodly men."[11] Similarly, according to James Putts's *Masonry*, R. A. Torrey and many other Christians also opposed the Masonry of their time.[12] Over the decades different Christian denominations, Christian researchers, and official inquiries concerning the relationship between the two religions have stressed their diametrical opposition:

Orthodox Presbyterian Church, 1942	"Masonry is a religious institution and as such is definitely anti-Christian ... Membership in the Masonic fraternity is inconsistent with Christianity."[13]
The Lutheran Church— Missouri Synod	"[Masonry] amounts to the practice of idolatry."[14]
Eastern Orthodox Church, 1933	"Masonry trespasses the bounds of the church by interfering with ethical and religious truths."[15]
Catholic German bishops, 1980	"'Masonry has not changed' and can in no way be reconciled with Christianity."[16]
Former Mason	"Freemasonry ... presents a tremendous spiritual obstacle to individual Christian growth."[17]
The Dictionary of Secret and Other Societies, 1924	"Freemasonry ... is a religious sect diametrically opposed to Christianity."[18]

Reformed Presbyterian Church	"Such a society is contrary to the spirit and letter of the religion of Jesus Christ."[19]
British Methodist Church, 1985	"On the most generous reading of the evidence, there remains serious question for Christians about Freemasonry.... There is a great danger that the Christian who becomes a Freemason will find himself compromising his Christian beliefs or his allegiance to Christ, perhaps without realizing what he is doing. Consequently, our guidance to Methodist people is that Methodists should not become Freemasons."[20]
The Baptist Unions of Scotland, Great Britain, and Ireland, 1987	"The clear conclusion we have reached from our inquiry is that there is an inherent incompatibility between Freemasonry and the Christian faith."[21]
The Church of Scotland, 1965	"In our view total obedience to Christ precludes joining any organization such as the Masonic movement which seems to demand a wholehearted allegiance to itself. ... The initiate is required to commit himself to Masonry in a way that a Christian should only commit himself to Christ."[22]
The Free Church of Scotland	"Membership [in] Freemasonry ... is inconsistent with a profession of the Christian faith."[23]
The Church of England, 1985	"[This] report points to a number of very fundamental reasons to question the compatibility of Freemasonry with Christianity."[24]
Russian Orthodox Church	"Any orthodox Catholic Christian [who joins Masonry]... loses all the rights, honors, and privileges of his membership and of his office in the church."[25]

Former Mason	"The religion of the lodge is not only un-Christian, but it is definitely *antiChristian*.... It dishonors Christ. ...Lodge membership is a contradiction of Christianity. It is a compromise for Christians.[26]"
Former Mason	"Everything that I had done in Masonry was at variance with the Holy Scriptures."[27]

The General Association of Regular Baptist Churches, the Association of Christian Reformed Churches, the Independent Fundamental Churches of America, and the Wisconsin Evangelical Lutheran Synod have all rejected Masonry.[28] Even in the nineteenth century, a time when America was largely Christian and did not have to face competition from endless cults and competing religions, former Past Master Ronayne could state that "the Masonic system [has become] the greatest enemy that Christianity has."[29]

In other words, whatever its outward resemblance to, or compromise with, Christianity, Masonry was never truly Christian. It simply took on Christian elements because Christians compromised their faith, joined the Lodge and—perhaps feeling guilt over swearing eternal oaths to Masonry and now realizing it was not Christian—attempted to Christianize it. But in doing so, they betrayed both Masonry and Christianity and left a legacy of compromise, error, and sin that has haunted the church ever since. Thus, there is one way in which Masonry is unlike any other religion or cult that sometimes lures Christians: Masonry has probably lured more Christians to its halls than any other false teaching.

Ten Consequences of Christian Masonry

What have Christians accomplished by accepting Masonry and encouraging other Christians to join the Craft? What is the legacy of Christian Masonry? If a Christian has truly accepted Masonry, then directly or indirectly, to one degree or another, he has taken part in the following ten consequences of Christian Masonry.

CHRISTIANS WHO ACCEPT MASONRY HAVE REJECTED
THEIR CHRISTIAN FAITH

The doctrines of Masonry are opposed to those of Christianity. Christians who have accepted Masonic teachings have denied the faith. Jude 3 tells us that all Christians are to "contend earnestly for the faith which was once for all delivered to the saints."

CHRISTIANS WHO ARE MASONS HAVE DISHONORED GOD AND CHRIST

The Westminster Catechism has correctly stated the emphasis of the Scriptures when it asserts that the chief end of man is to glorify God. But Christian Masons cannot honor God or glorify Him when they support an organization that distorts His nature, denies His Son, and rejects His Word. A Christian Mason once concluded a prayer during a Lodge meeting "in Jesus' name." The response? "The Secretary of the Scottish Rite . . . told me that I was *never* to end a prayer 'in Jesus' name' or 'in Christ's name.' He said, 'Make your prayers *universal.*'"[30] Masonry also deliberately removes the name of Jesus Christ from the Scriptures quoted in its rituals so as to not "offend" non-Christians.[31]

CHRISTIANS WHO ARE MASONS HAVE CONFUSED BOTH MASONS AND
NON-MASONS AS TO THE TRUE NATURE OF CHRISTIANITY

As even Masons have admitted, Christian Masons often "identify the Craft with Christianity"[32]—but to do so is to malign the cause of Christ, to distort the doctrine of salvation and the Scriptures, and to repudiate everything Christian. Mackey observes, "A Christian element has been almost imperceptibly infused into the Masonic system, at least among Christian Freemasons."[33] But this only confuses people. Masons, Christians, and non-Christians conclude that Christianity and Masonry are compatible. If Christian Masons claim to live and speak for God, many people conclude that God must be pleased with Masonry. For example: "Truly God is in Masonry—in its faith, in its ideals, its labor—and without Him it has no meaning, no mission, no ministry among men."[34]

This is one reason Masons are accepted in the church far more than they are in cults. As a former Master Mason observed, "Ministers and other good men are in the Lodge. They help to make it a delusion and snare."[35] When liberal ministers and Masons agree that Christianity and Masonry can coexist, they only mask their "necessarily antagonistic" natures.[36] Sooner or later, the fusion of Masonry and Christianity at the local level results in either the compromise of truth, the split of a church, or both. One pastor recounts his experience when he politely declined the request of Masons to hold their once a year service in the church:

> Over a period of time, I became aware of a gathering storm. . . . In the end the PCC [Parish Community Council] passed a resolution asking me to consider writing to the Masons inviting them back again. If I did not do this, I was told that they would all resign, and one person warned me that I might become "a vicar without Parish." Then they decided to have a further meeting two weeks later. . . . I felt that for many decades the PCC had been badly let down by the clergy who have been Masons and believed that it was compatible with their allegiance to Christ. . . . I felt very puzzled by all that had happened. . . . Why had they been so angry and upset? What puzzled me most of all was that none of them were Masons! . . . I just did not appreciate the spiritual implications of Freemasonry.[37]

In another case the pastor was removed from his church against his will because he would not compromise with Masonry:

> Another clergyman was sacked from his church and ordered to leave. . . . He later claimed before an industrial tribunal that the Presbyterian Church of Wales had dismissed him purely because he had preached against Freemasonry. . . . [Rev. William Colin] Davies said that the Presbyterian Church of Wales was particularly strongly influenced by members of the Brotherhood among its own members and administration. He explained, " . . . I had two churches. In one of them I encountered some Freemasons. I did not know then what I know now. I researched into Masonry and found it entirely incompatible with faith in Jesus Christ. . . . By this

time I had been reported to the local church governing body —the Presbytery—and a committee of seven men came to see me. I now know that some of them were Freemasons. They accused me of being an evangelical Christian, which I am, 'intolerant of unbiblical teaching and in particular Freemasonry.' They accused me of being uncompassionate, which presumably meant I had upset Masons' and their relatives' feelings. . . . Charges had been trumped up by Masons determined to end my opposition to Masonry. I was not allowed to answer the charges. . . . In March . . . it was decided that pressure had to be brought to bear to have me removed. . . . I was dismissed from the pastorate, not from my ministry. These are technically different, in practice the same. I then appealed to the highest body in the church. . . . They said that a period of twelve months should be allowed to see if a reconciliation could be achieved. I agreed to this but they [the Masons] made no attempt at reconciliation. . . . I won my appeal but it was not implemented because my local church would not accept it. I was sacked and told to leave my house within six weeks.[38]

CHRISTIANS WHO ARE MASONS HAVE ENCOURAGED THE CAUSE OF LIBERAL RELIGION

Anyone familiar with liberal religion and Masonry will note many similarities between the two.[39] (E.g., the universal fatherhood of God and brotherhood of man have long been hallmarks of liberal religion.) Both reject the major historic Christian doctrines, the deity of Christ, salvation by grace, the doctrine of hell, and the Bible as the literal Word of God. Both accept a humanistic and rationalistic approach to life and religion (for example, the use of higher critical approaches to Scripture,[40] the idea that Christianity was the product of earlier pagan belief,[41] and that all religions are the religion of God).

> Probably much that is going on today in the Indian [Hindu] and other mission fields among professed Christian teachers who are pressing for an amalgamation of Christianity with all that is best in Hinduism, etc., may be influenced by the fact that these men, though probably not all Masons by initiation, have drunk deeply into the spirit of the craft, and are carrying out its exact program of combining "the best elements in all religions" to form the Universal Religion.[42]

Joseph Fort Newton demonstrates the similarity of beliefs between Masonry and liberal religion:

> Obviously we must draw a line between Religion and theology. . . . Many a man who has only a dim idea of what it means to love God is really doing it all the time. . . . For, according to Jesus, with whom our best instincts agree, we are saved not by what we think but by what we are. Our theology ought to be as revisable as are all other human ideas. . . . Religion . . . is life itself . . . how to join our fleeting lives with "one vast Life that moves and cannot die," which Jesus called the Eternal Life. . . . Where love is there God is. . . . Religion . . . is the life of God and the life of man whereby, as Dante said, we learn to make our lives eternal.[43]

Liberal religionists have long opposed, scoffed at, and ridiculed conservative Christianity as a remnant of an antiquated, medieval faith. The perspective of liberal religion to conservative Christianity is well illustrated by the view of leading Mason W. L. Wilmshurst. In *The Masonic Initiation* he stated:

> It is well for a man to be born in a church, but terrible for him to die in one; for in religion there must be growth. A young man is to be censored who fails to attend the church of his nation; the elderly man is equally to be censored if he does attend—he ought to have outgrown what the church offers and to have attained a higher order of religious life.[44]

This kind of sentiment is why Wagner concludes of Masonry:

> The whole system is a giant evil. We firmly believe that it is the greatest foe that the church has to contend against. It insidiously undermines and overthrows the very foundations of evangelical Christianity. Its tendency is to make men indifferent to doctrine and hostile to the positive teachings of Revelation as embodied in the church's creeds and catechisms.[45]

Unitarian minister E. A. Coil wrote, "The liberal churches, from their beginning, have been developing in thought and sentiment, along the same lines as those followed by most of our great modern fraternities. They have championed and advocated the Fatherhood of God, the Brotherhood of Man, immortality, and salvation by character, and these are the very principles for which nearly all the great fraternities stand." He also chides Christian Masons for attempting to hold to both Masonry and conservative Christianity: "A little child, once its attention is called to the matter, ought to be able to see that it is impossible to harmonize [them]. . . . Men cannot consistently subscribe to both."[46]

CHRISTIANS WHO SUPPORT MASONRY HAVE HELPED ENCOURAGE MYSTICISM AND OCCULTISM

See chapters 17 and 18 for a discussion of this.

CHRISTIANS WHO SUPPORT MASONRY HAVE WASTED TIME AND MONEY BETTER USED IN SUPPORT OF THE CHURCH

No one can determine how many millions of man-hours have been diverted from Christian service to Masonry in the last three hundred years. The office of installation for the Chapter of Rose Croix emphasizes that "The work of Masonry, like the work of God, cannot be done negligently and idly. In this work, one must put forth all his strength."[47] Leading Mason Jim Shaw once commented, "Through the years I must have heard hundreds of men say, 'I don't need to go to church—the Lodge is good enough religion for me.' So very many such men never attend a church except with the Lodge once a year to hear Masonry exalted. They trust Lodge membership and their own 'virtuous life' to assure them acceptance in the 'Celestial Lodge Above.'"[48]

CHRISTIANS WHO ACCEPT MASONIC DOCTRINE HAVE HINDERED THE GOSPEL

Shaw further observes, "Never in all my years of dedicated service to Masonry did anyone in the Lodge witness to me about the love and saving grace of Jesus."[49] Witnessing is forbidden in the Lodge. The offices of installation of the Chapter of Rose Croix demands the promise that the Mason "will never allow . . . religious differences of opinion to govern you in matters affecting your brethren."[50] Nor is the Mason permitted to judge in any sense or manner another person's level of commitment to Christ.[51]

This influence against Christian priorities extends beyond the Lodge. Joseph Fort Newton rejoices when he says of Masonry, "It lays down no dogma about God, it speaks His name rarely.... The life of man with God is a thing so intimate, so inward, so utterly individual, that to violate its privacy, or to invade its sanctity, is a sacrilege, if not a blasphemy.... If only the Church had learned this simple wisdom...."[52]

Masonry teaches that because the Christian faith is exclusive it is an allegedly intolerant faith. Masonry warns its members against intolerance. But being exclusive in one's religious claims is hardly the same as being an intolerant person. Jesus Himself was exclusivistic (John 14:6) and yet tolerant and kind to all people but hypocrites. One former Mason, now a pastor, reveals the great degree to which Masonry inhibits evangelism and sows the leaven of apathy within Christian churches:

> The men who were best informed, most influential, the men with best business judgment, the men most looked up to in the church, moral, kindly, intelligent, sincere men, I found, never did win souls.... Nearly all these principled men... were lodge members! And everywhere I have found it so.
>
> In countless individual cases I have met it. [Masons] insist continually that if they live up to the obligations of the lodge, or if they live moral and virtuous lives, they will get to heaven.... I charge that the lodges themselves are the most potent influence to teach people to depend upon their own righteouensss.... This doctrine largely neutralizes the preaching of the gospel everywhere.[53]

CHRISTIAN MASONS HAVE HELPED KEEP MASONIC INFLUENCE WITHIN THE CHURCH

The doctrines and practices of Masonry are devised to support and protect Masonry. But this works in three ways to intimidate, "force," or otherwise influence Christians to retain and support the goals of Masonry, even within the church.

Each Mason swears oaths of loyalty to protect Masonry (see chapter 14).

Once a Christian becomes a Mason, it is difficult to sway his loyalties. Many Christians join Masonry out of ignorance, not knowing it is opposed to Christianity. But once in Masonry they find it very difficult to extricate themselves:

> First, the deception of the person was skillfully performed. ... Second, after taking the oath, paying the dues, and enjoying a fraternal atmosphere, the person will hardly admit to his error. To admit it will take repentance and humility—and human nature is not inclined toward either. Third, pressure applied by the lodge brothers is often intense. The consequences of leaving the lodge may have lifelong significance.[54]

The Christian Mason's commitment to a brother Mason has priority. One former Mason observes, "A Mason swears to show partiality to Masons over those not Masons and binds himself to show a preference to his lodge 'brother' that he is not to show to this Christian brother in Christ if that Christian brother be not a Mason."[55]

A Mason is never to betray a brother's secrets and is to seek to help him escape from any difficulty, even if he is wrong.[56] What this means is that it can be difficult to detect the un-Christian influence of Masonry within the church by a brother Mason—whatever such influence may be. The logical conclusion to Masonic teaching is that a Christian Mason's loyalty should be to the cause and influence of Masonry, even when it is in opposition to the cause of Christ and the church.

In January 1951 the Anglican clergyman Rev. Walton Hannah wrote a critical article on Masonry in the journal *Theology*. This article touched off a major controversy: "The furor led to a debate in the church Assembly and it began to look as if the whole subject of Freemasonry and the church might be brought before the Convocation of Canterbury. But as the Archbishop of Canterbury himself (Fisher) was a powerful Freemason, the Brotherhood had little trouble in blocking the attempt, and it was ruled out of order on a technicality."[57]

In 1951 another attempt to inquire into the influence of Masonry within the Church of England failed. "Due largely," Hannah says, "to the persuasive influence of the Masonic Bishop of Reading, Dr. A. Groom Parham, this was never debated."[58] Similar results occurred in 1952:

> Hannah records that the "critics of Masonry were frankly out maneuvered by the unexpectedness and speed with which Masons acted": the motion for an enquiry was overwhelmingly rejected. The Church of England has still never considered the matter officially. Hannah's conclusion, echoed today by several deeply concerned Church of England clergy and bishops in private conversation, is that "the church . . . dares not offend or provoke thousands of influential and often financially substantial laymen by enquiring into the religious implications of Freemasonry."

> Effectively, then, the true position of the Roman Catholic Church is not unlike that of the Church of England. Faced with the prestige, influence, and prevalence of Freemasonry in British society, both are similarly paralyzed.[59]

CHRISTIAN MASONS HAVE HELPED DISTORT THE TEACHINGS OF CHRISTIANITY AND OTHER RELIGIONS

Buddhism   Buddha was the first Masonic legislator.[60]

Judaism   Adam was a Grand Master Mason.

"We know from the Bible that Moses was an initiate of the Egyptian mysteries. . . . He became in a real sense a Master Mason."

"Samarian-Babylonian knowledge . . . was the source of the stories in Genesis, the laws of Moses and the concepts of the Kabbalah."[61]

Christianity   "The Gospels themselves [teach Masonic initiation and illumination]. . . . To clear vision, Christian and Masonic doctrine are identical in intention though different in method. . . . Originally membership of the Christian church involved a sequence of three initiatory rites identical in intention with the craft today."

"To teach and persuade, to direct and guide, those who need instruction. . . . The founder of the Christian faith, and his immediate disciples claimed for themselves no higher power."

"The basic principles of Freemasonry are the Fatherhood of God and the Brotherhood of man. Are these not also the basic principles of Christianity?"[62]

CHRISTIAN MASONS HAVE HELPED MASONRY REPLACE THE CHURCH IN THE LIVES OF MEN

Mackey speaks for all Masons when he claims that "Freemasonry is not Christianity or a substitute for it. It is not intended to supersede it nor any other form of worship or system of faith."[63] But this is not the experience of Masons. Christians who encourage Masons to receive Christ typically discover that "the Mason answers that he does not need salvation because he is a Mason, that the Masonic lodge is as good as the church, and that if a Mason lives up to his obligations he will get to Heaven alright without Christ."[64]

This is exactly what the Mason has been taught by the Lodge in its ritual and doctrines. The Lodge is the Masons' *true* church. It is his "Temple," and he gives "worship at this Holy Altar." He is to "realize that each member is a living stone in this Holy House." God Himself is beseeched to "illuminate this Temple, which we now dedicate and consecrate, and make it verily a Holy House and place of Light. Strengthen the hearts and enlighten the souls of those who are of its household, and the household of the Holy Empire everywhere. . . . Permit this Building to be indeed what these Brethren have, in reverence and thankfulness to Thee, called it, 'Thy Holy House'!"[65] Is this not why Masons visit *their* temple weekly and the church but once a year?

The British Methodist church concluded that "Freemasonry thus provides ceremony which on some Masonic interpretations are equivalent to essential parts of Christian practice and offer alternatives to important elements of the Christian faith. . . . It is clear that Freemasonry may compete strongly with Christianity."[66] Ronayne refers to the "common declaration among the fraternity that 'Freemasonry is a good enough religion for me.'"[67] Perhaps no better statement of how Masonry replaces the church can be made than the following by leading Mason Carl H. Claudy:

> The initiate comes in to a Lodge divested of all that marks his consequence among men. He comes blind and helpless.... The Lodge protects him, puts him in the hands of friends, binds him not to fear. His footsteps are guided, he is taught to pray as Masons pray.... A Lodge gives to the Fellowcrafts all the wisdom she may impart to such, prays for them and loves them. The Lodge forgives them their failures and tries them anew, and will fight for them if need be.... When all else fails a man's spirit, he yet has his Mother Lodge and her Altar to go to; be his spiritual ills what they may be—Aye, be his spiritual sins what they may be—he may gather with his brethren around that sacred Altar and find comfort in the love of his Mother Lodge, such comfort as may come in no other way.[68]

The reservations often felt by conscientious Christians are quelled by an appeal to the "Christian tradition" of Masonry:

> The average Christian man who has not studied the theological implications of the oaths, rituals and lectures usually experiences a certain initial moral and religious disquiet about what he has done in joining. Many have admitted to being somewhat ashamed by the initiation ceremony they have undergone. But all this is allayed by the reassurance that so many of the eminent and reputable have for centuries done the same and that the masonic system somehow enjoys an immunity in these matters sanctioned by tradition.[69]

And so Christian Masonry perpetuates Christian Masonry. Perhaps Christian Masons need to hear once more the rebuke of an Anglican vicar, their Masonic "brother": "I for one can never understand how anyone who takes an exclusive view of Christ as the only complete revelation of God's truth can become a Freemason without suffering from spiritual schizophrenia."[70]

Notes

Chapter 1: Masonic Nature and Influence

1. Henry Wilson Coil, *Freemasonry Through Six Centuries* (Richmond: Macoy, 1967), 1:131, 152; John Ankerberg, William Mankin, and Walter Martin, *Christianity and the Masonic Lodge: Are They Compatible?* "The John Ankerberg Show," transcript, 1985, The John Ankerberg Evangelistic Association, Chattanooga, Tennessee: 3; Shildes Johnson, *Is Masonry a Religion?* (Oakland, N.J.: Institute for Contemporary Christianity, 1978), p. 12.

2. H. L. Haywood, *The Great Teachings of Masonry* (Richmond: Macoy, 1971), p. 90; Foster Bailey, *The Spirit of Masonry* (Hampstead, London: Lucius, 1972), p. 125; *Legenda 32 (Part 1)*, a Masonic source apparently used for instruction, c. 1920-30 (n.p., n.d.), p. 33; Albert Mackey, *Mackey's Revised Encyclopedia of Freemasonry*, rev. and enl. by Robert I. Clegg (Richmond: Macoy, 1966), 1:269; Joseph Fort Newton, *The Builders: A Story and Study of Freemasonry* (Richmond: Macoy, 1951), pp. 233, 243, 275.

3. *Mackey's Revised Encyclopedia of Freemasonry*, 1:269.

4. Joseph Fort Newton, *The Religion of Masonry: An Interpretation* (Richmond: Macoy, 1969), p. 116.

5. *Mackey's Revised Encyclopedia of Freemasonry*, 1:269.

6. Ibid.

7. Henry Wilson Coil, *A Comprehensive View of Freemasonry* (Richmond: Macoy, 1973), p. 234.

8. Mackey, *Mackey's Revised Encyclopedia of Freemasonry*, 1:378.

9. Coil, *A Comprehensive View of Freemasonry*, pp. 214-15.

10. Ibid., p. 216.

11. Alphonse Cerza, *Let There Be Light: A Study in Anti-Masonry* (Silver Spring, Md.: The Masonic Service Association, 1983), p. 1.

12. *Mackey's Revised Encyclopedia of Freemasonry*, 2:859.

13. H. L. Haywood, *The Newly-Made Mason: What He and Every Mason Should Know About Masonry* (Richmond: Macoy, 1973), pp. v-vi.

14. Committee on Secret Societies of the Ninth General Assembly of the Orthodox Presbyterian Church (meeting at Rochester, N.Y., June 2-5, 1942), *Christ or the Lodge?* (Philadelphia: Great Commission, n.d.), p. 3.

15. Ankerberg, et al., *Christianity and the Masonic Lodge*, p. 3, cf. p. 5.

16. Henry Wilson Coil, *Coil's Masonic Encyclopedia* (New York: Macoy, 1961), p. 569.

17. Ibid., p. 369.

18. John Ankerberg, Jack Harris, William Mankin, Walter Martin, and Paul Pantzer, *The Masonic Lodge: What Goes On Behind Closed Doors?* "The John Ankerberg Show," transcript, 1986, The John Ankerberg Evangelistic Association, Chattanooga, Tennessee, p. 29.

19. *Mackey's Revised Encyclopedia of Freemasonry*, 2:859.

20. Alphonse Cerza, *A Masonic Reader's Guide*, ed. Thomas C. Warden, Transactions of the Missouri Lodge of Research, vol. 34 (1978-1979), 1980, p. ix; *Coil's Masonic Encyclopedia*, p. 376; Richard Cavendish, ed., *Man, Myth and Magic: An Illustrated Encyclopedia of the Supernatural* (New York: Marshall Cavendish, 1970), s.v. "Freemasonry."

21. The twenty-five lodges responding represented Washington, D.C., Arizona, Colorado, Connecticut, Delaware, Idaho, Illinois, Indiana, Iowa, Kansas, Louisiana, Maine, Massachusetts, Michigan, Missouri, New Mexico, New York, Ohio, Pennsylvania, South Carolina, Texas, Utah, Virginia, Wisconsin, New Jersey.

22. H. V. B. Voorhis, *Facts for Freemasons: A Storehouse of Masonic Knowledge in Question and Answer Form*, rev. (Richmond: Macoy, 1979), p. 172; Cerza, *A Masonic Reader's Guide*, p. 8; *Little Masonic Library* (Richmond: Macoy, 1977), 1:130; Cerza, *A Masonic Reader's Guide*, p. 148.

23. *Little Masonic Library*, 1:130.

24. C. Fred Kleinknecht, *The House of the Temple of the Supreme Council* (Washington, D.C.: The Supreme Council, 33d Degree, 1988), p. 23.

25. H. L. Haywood, *The Newly-Made Mason*, pp. ii, 74; cf. Henry Pirtle, *Kentucky Monitor: Complete Monitorial Ceremonies of the Blue Lodge* (Louisville, Ky.: Standard Printing, 1921). Usually, only the Scottish Rite cites its degrees by number; the York Rite designates its degrees by name. For example, the Fourth Degree of the York Rite is termed "Mark Master" whereas in the Scottish Rite the degree is simply called the Fourth Degree.

26. Henry C. Clausen, *Clausen's Commentaries on Morals and Dogma* (The Supreme Council, 33d Degree, Ancient and Accepted Scottish Rite of Freemasonry, Southern Jurisdiction of the U.S.A., 1976), p. 148.

27. Albert Pike, *Morals and Dogma of the Ancient and Accepted Scottish Rite of Freemasonry* (Charleston, S.C.: The Supreme Council of the 33d Degree for the Southern Jurisdiction of the United States, 1906), pp. 106-7.

28. Ibid., pp. 104-7, 819; see chapter 20.

29. Ibid., pp. 104-5.

30. Kent Henderson, *Masonic World Guide* (Richmond: Macoy, 1984).

31. *Encyclopaedia Britannica, Micropaedia*, 15th ed., s.v. "Freemasonry."

32. Voorhis, *Facts for Freemasons*, p. 190.

33. Henderson, *Masonic World Guide*, pp. 106, 118, 165, 188, 202, 230-46, 271. Masonry's occasional connection with Communism and Facism is briefly explored in Paul A. Fisher, *Behind the Lodge Door: Church, State & Freemasonry* (Washington, D.C.: Shield Press, 1987), pp. 218-25.

34. Fisher, *Behind the Lodge Door*, p. 248.

35. Martin L. Wagner, *Freemasonry: An Interpretation* (n.p., n.d.), distributed by Missionary Service and Supply, Route 2, Columbiana, OH, 44408, p. 23.

36. Fisher, *Behind the Lodge Door*, pp. 242-44.

37. E. L. Hawkins, "Freemasonry," in *Encyclopedia of Religion and Ethics*, ed. James Hastings (New York: Charles Schribner's Sons, nd.), 6:120.

38. Fisher, *Behind the Lodge Door*, pp. 260-68.

39. Ibid., pp. 1-17.

40. J. Blanchard, *Scottish Rite Masonry Illustrated (The Complete Ritual of the Ancient and Accepted Scottish Rite)* (Chicago: Charles T. Powner, 1979), 2:284.

41. Voorhis, *Facts for Freemasons*, p. 191; cf. James Royal Case, *The Case Collection: Biographies of Masonic Notables* (The Missouri Lodge of Research, 1984), p. 117.

42. *Congressional Record*, Senate, 9 September 1987: S11868-70.

43. Voorhis, *Facts for Freemasons*, p. 157. Peale was once featured on the cover of *The New Age* magazine as a 33d Degree Mason. In that issue, he wrote the article "What Freemasonry Means to Me"; cf. *The New Age* (September 1989).

44. Voorhis, *Facts for Freemasons*, p. 125.

45. Fisher, *Behind the Lodge Door*, p. 246.

46. Voorhis, *Facts for Freemasons*, pp. 128-70; cf. *The Case Collection*.

47. Committee on Secret Societies of the Ninth General Assembly of the Orthodox Presbyterian Church (meeting at Rochester, N.Y., June 2-5, 1942), *Christ or the Lodge?* (Philadelphia: Great Commission, n.d.), p. 2; L. James Rongstad, *How to Respond to the Lodge* (St. Louis: Concordia, 1977), p. 10.

48. Wagner, *Freemasonry: An Interpretation*, p. 23.

49. J. W. Acker, *Strange Altars: A Scriptural Appraisal of the Lodge* (St. Louis: Concordia, 1959), pp. 47-48.

50. The General Grand Chapter Order of the Eastern Star, *Ritual of the Order of the Eastern Star*, Washington, D.C., International Eastern Star Temple, 1956, 1970, pp. 56, 161.

51. Ibid., pp. 7-10.

52. Ibid., pp. 77, 57.

53. Ibid.

54. Ibid., p. 51.

55. Ibid., pp. 57-58.

56. Ibid., pp. 162-63.

57. Ibid., pp. 51, 69.

58. Ibid., pp. 125, 72, 80.

59. Ibid., p. 84.

60. Ibid., pp. 153-56.

61. Ibid., p. 158. On one occasion (p. 159), John 11:25-26 is cited. However, there is no reason to believe that this is interpreted in a Christian, rather than a Masonic, sense.

62. Acker, *Strange Altars*, pp. 18-22, 48-58; Rongstad, *How to Respond to the Lodge*, p. 13; Committee on Secret Societies of the Ninth General Assembly of the Orthodox Presbyterian Church, *Christ or the Lodge?*, p. 2; Haywood, *The Newly-Made Mason*, p. ii.

63. Jerald and Sandra Tanner, *Mormonism: Shadow or Reality* (Salt Lake City, Utah: Modern Microfilm Co., 1972), pp. 484-92.

64. Fisher, *Behind the Lodge Door*, pp. 1-15, 187; Rongstad, *How to Respond to the Lodge*, p. 10.

65. Acker, *Strange Altars*, pp. 71-83.

66. John Sheville and James Gould, *Guide to the Royal Arch Chapter: A Complete Monitor with Full Instructions in the Degrees of Mark Master, Past Master, Most Excellent Master and Royal Arch Together with the Order of High Priesthood* (Richmond: Macoy, 1981), p. 145.

67. Cerza, *Let There Be Light*, p. 39.

68. Pike, *Morals and Dogma*, p. 109.

69. Fisher, *Behind the Lodge Door*, p. 206.

70. Ibid., pp. 206-30; cf. Sheville and Gould, *Guide to the Royal Arch Chapter*, p. 245; Cerza, *Let There Be Light*, p. 55; The Baptist Union of Scotland (endorsed by the Baptist Union of Great Britain and Ireland), *Baptists and Freemasonry* (Baptist Church House, 1987), p. 7; Stephen Knight, *The Brotherhood: The Explosive Exposé of the Secret World of the Freemasons* (London: Grenada/Panther, 1983), pp. 85, 269-307; John R. Rice, *Lodges Examined by the Bible* (Murfreesboro, Tenn.: Sword of the Lord, 1943), p. 27; Wagner, *Freemasonry: An Interpretation*, p. 555.

71. Haywood, *The Newly-Made Mason*, pp. 215-16.

72. Haywood, *The Great Teachings of Masonry*, p. 90.

73. *Legenda 32 (Part 1)*, a Masonic source apparently used for instruction, c. 1920-30 (n.p., n.d.), p. 33.

74. Albert Pike, "The Meaning of Masonry," in *Little Masonic Library*, 5:35.

75. *Mackey's Revised Encyclopedia of Freemasonry*, 1:269.

76. Newton, *The Builders*, pp. 233, 275, 246, 247, 241, 241.

77. Malcom C. Duncan, *Masonic Ritual and Monitor* (New York: David Mckay, n.d.), p. 29; cf. Ankerberg, et al., *The Masonic Lodge*, p. 4.

78. *Ceremonies of Installation and Dedication*, rev. (The Ancient and Accepted Scottish Rite of Freemasonry, Southern Jurisdiction U.S.A., 1954), p. 119.

79. Ibid., p. 123.

80. Ibid.

81. Ibid., p. 29.

Chapter 2: Masonic Religion

1. Henry Wilson Coil, *Freemasonry Through Six Centuries* (Richmond: Macoy, 1967), 1:5.

2. Shildes Johnson, *Is Masonry a Religion?* (Oakland, N.J.: Institute for Contemporary Christianity, 1978), p. 12.

3. Edmond Ronayne, *The Master's Carpet or Masonry and Baal-Worship—Identical* (n.p., n.d., distributed by Missionary Service and Supply, Route 2, Columbiana, OH 44408), p. 210.

4. Henry Wilson Coil, *Coil's Masonic Encyclopedia* (New York: Macoy, 1961), p. 600.

5. H. L. Haywood, *The Great Teachings of Masonry* (Richmond: Macoy, 1971), p. 94.

6. Ibid., p. 95.

7. Johnson, *Is Masonry a Religion?*, pp. 12-13.

8. *Little Masonic Library* (Richmond: Macoy, 1977), 1:138.

9. Charles H. Lacquement, "Freemasonry and Organized Religions," *The Pennsylvania Freemason* (February 1989): 7.

10. Paul Edwards, ed., *The Encyclopedia of Philosophy* (New York: Collier Macmillan, 1972), s.v., "Religion."

11. *Webster's New World Dictionary, Second Collegate Edition* (New York: Simon & Schuster, 1984).

12. *Little Masonic Library*, 1:12-13.

13. Raymond Lee Allen, et al., *Tennessee Craftsmen or Masonic Textbook*, 14th edition (Nashville: Tennessee Board of Custodians Members, 1963), p. 6.

14. Grand Lodge of Texas, A. F. and A. M., *Monitor of the Lodge: Monitorial Instructions in the Three Degrees of Symbolic Masonry* (Grand Lodge of Texas, 1982), p. 13. The Masonic origin of the phrase is unknown. It is, however, a common phrase used in occult ritual to signify expected confirmation of ritualistic goals.

15. Malcom C. Duncan, *Masonic Ritual and Monitor* (New York: David Mckay, n.d.), p. 46.

16. Harris Bullock, et al., *Masonic Manual of the Grand Lodge of Georgia* (Free and Accepted Masons, The Grand Lodge of Georgia, 1983), p. 36; Duncan, *Masonic Ritual and Monitor*, p. 72.

17. Duncan, *Masonic Ritual and Monitor*, p. 127.

18. Ibid., p. 183.

19. *Masonic Monitor of the Degrees of Entered Apprentice, Fellow Craft and Master Mason*, 7th ed. (Free and Accepted Masons of Arkansas, 1983), p. 9.

20. *Webster's New Twentieth Century Dictionary, Second Edition Unabridged* (Collins-World, 1978).

21. Allen E. Roberts, *The Craft and Its Symbols: Opening the Door to Masonic Symbolism* (Richmond: Macoy, 1974), pp. 57, 64.

22. George Simmons and Robert Macoy, *Standard Masonic Monitor of the Degrees of Entered Apprentice, Fellow Craft and Master Mason* (Richmond: Macoy, 1984), p. 17.

23. Carl H. Claudy, *Foreign Countries: A Gateway to the Interpretation and Development of Certain Symbols of Freemasonry* (Richmond: Macoy, 1971), p. 23.

24. Allen, et al., *Tennessee Craftsmen or Masonic Textbook*, p. 13.

25. J. Blanchard, *Scottish Rite Masonry Illustrated (The Complete Ritual of the Ancient and Accepted Scottish Rite)* (Chicago: Charles T. Powner, 1979), 1:259-60.

26. Ibid., 1:453.

27. Joseph Fort Newton, *The Religion of Masonry: An Interpretation* (Richmond: Macoy, 1969), pp. 58-59.

28. Henry Wilson Coil, *A Comprehensive View of Freemasonry* (Richmond: Macoy, 1973), p. 186.

29. *Coil's Masonic Encyclopedia*, p. 158.

30. Albert Mackey, *Mackey's Revised Encyclopedia of Freemasonry*, rev. and enl. by Robert I. Clegg (Richmond: Macoy, 1966), 2:847.

31. *Liturgy of the Ancient and Accepted Scottish Rite of Freemasonry for the Southern Jurisdiction of the United States, Part Two* (Washington, D.C.: The Supreme Council, 33d Degree of the Ancient and Accepted Scottish Rite of Freemasonry of the Southern Jurisdiction of the U.S.A., 1982), pp. 167, 198-99.

32. Carl H. Claudy, *Introduction to Freemasonry* (Washington, D.C.: The Temple, 1984), 2:109.

33. E.g., E. M. Storms, *Should a Christian Be a Mason?* (Fletcher, N.C.: New Puritan Library, 1980); Johnson, *Is Masonry a Religion?*; Martin L. Wagner, *Freemasonry: An Interpretation* (n.p., n.d.), distributed by Missionary Service and Supply, Route 2, Columbiana, OH 44408; Stephen Knight, *The Brotherhood: The Explosive Exposé of the Secret World of the Freemasons* (London: Grenada/Panther, 1983), p. 310; *Encyclopaedia Britannica, Micropaedia,* 15th ed., s.v. "Freemasonry"; The Working Group established by the Standing Committee of the General Synod of the Church of England, *Freemasonry and Christianity: Are They Compatible?* (London: Church House, 1987); The Baptist Union of Scotland (endorsed by the Baptist Union of Great Britain and Ireland), *Baptists and Freemasonry* (Baptist Church House, 1987); Report of the Faith and Order Committee of the British Methodist Church, *Freemasonry and Methodism,* presented to the General Assembly of the British Methodist Church and adopted by them 3 July 1985; cf. Committee on Secret Societies of the Ninth General Assembly of the Orthodox Presbyterian Church (meeting at Rochester, N.Y., June 2-5, 1942), *Christ or the Lodge?* (Philadelphia: Great Commission, n.d.), pp. 6-7; *Little Masonic Library,* 1:153; *Ceremonies of Installation and Dedication,* rev. (The Ancient and Accepted Scottish Rite of Freemasonry, Southern Jurisdiction U.S.A., 1954), p. 121; Alphonse Cerza, *A Masonic Reader's Guide,* ed. Thomas C. Warden, Transactions of the Missouri Lodge of Research, vol. 34 (1978-1979), 1980, pp. 89-90.

34. As quoted in H. L. Haywood, *The Newly-Made Mason: What He and Every Mason Should Know About Masonry* (Richmond: Macoy, 1973), p. 211.

35. Lacquement, "Freemasonry and Organized Religions," p. 7.

36. Albert Pike, *Morals and Dogma of the Ancient and Accepted Scottish Rite of Freemasonry* (Charleston, S.C.: The Supreme Council of the 33d Degree for the Southern Jurisdiction of the United States, 1906), p. 524.

37. Allen, et al., *Tennessee Craftsmen or Masonic Textbook,* p. 39.

38. Ibid., p. 58.

39. *Mackey's Revised Encyclopedia of Freemasonry,* 2:847.

40. Duncan, *Masonic Ritual and Monitor,* p. 206.

41. The Baptist Union of Scotland, *Baptists and Freemasonry,* pp. 7-8.

42. Report of the Faith and Order Committee of the British Methodist Church, *Freemasonry and Methodism,* §§21-22.

43. The Working Group established by the Standing Committee of the General Synod of the Church of England, *Freemasonry and Christianity: Are They Compatible?,* p. 40.

44. Knight, *The Brotherhood,* p. 241.

45. Committee on Secret Societies of the Ninth General Assembly of the Orthodox Presbyterian Church, *Christ or the Lodge?,* pp. 22-23; Report of the Ad-Interim Committee to the 15th General Assembly of the Presbyterian Church in America (meeting in Grand Rapids, Michigan, in June 1987), Appendix R, Minutes of the General Assembly.

46. L. James Rongstad, *How to Respond to the Lodge* (St. Louis: Concordia, 1977), p. 24.

47. Ibid., p. 28.

48. Jack Harris, *Freemasonry: The Invisible Cult in Our Midst* (Chattanooga: Global, 1983), p. x.

49. John R. Rice, *Lodges Examined by the Bible* (Murfreesboro, Tenn.: Sword of the Lord, 1943), p. 6; cf. Wagner, *Freemasonry: An Interpretation,* p. 20.

50. *Leaves from Georgia Masonry* (Educational and Historical Commission of the Grand Lodge of Georgia, 1947), pp. 74-75.

51. Alphonse Cerza, *Let There Be Light: A Study in Anti-Masonry* (Silver Spring, Md.: The Masonic Service Association, 1983), p. 28.

52. Knight, *The Brotherhood*, pp. 254, 246.

53. Ibid., pp. 263, 233, 240.

54. Ibid., pp. 244, 242. According to *The Lodestar Review* (January 1989), p. 6, 90 percent of the ministers of a large liberal Protestant denomination are Masons. This is a charge we often hear but, as yet, have been unable to document.

55. Duncan, *Masonic Ritual and Monitor*, p. 57.

56. Haywood, *The Newly-Made Mason*, p. 211.

57. Roberts, *The Craft and Its Symbols*, p. ix.

58. Albert G. Mackey, *The Symbolism of Freemasonry: Illustrating and Explaining Its Science and Philosophy, Its Legends, Myths, and Symbols* (Chicago: Charles T. Powner, 1975), p. 10.

59. Roberts, *The Craft and Its Symbols*, p. 24.

60. Ibid., pp. 23, 13-14, 16, 31, 32, 76, 20, 80.

61. Mackey, *The Symbolism of Freemasonry*, pp. 3-5.

62. Roberts, *The Craft and Its Symbols*, pp. 10, 82, 84.

63. Grand Lodge of Texas, *Monitor of the Lodge: Monitorial Instructions in the Three Degrees of Symbolic Masonry*, p. 63.

64. Duncan, *Masonic Ritual and Monitor*, 1:455.

65. Foster Bailey, *The Spirit of Masonry* (Hampstead, London: Lucius, 1972), p. 12.

66. Roberts, *The Craft and Its Symbols*, p. 36.

67. Claudy, *Introduction to Freemasonry*, 2:92.

68. Bailey, *The Spirit of Masonry*, p. 12.

Chapter 3: Masonic World View

1. W. L. Wilmshurst, *The Meaning of Masonry* (New York: Bell, 1980), p. 74.

2. Allen E. Roberts, *Key to Freemasonry's Growth* (Richmond: Macoy, 1969), p. 18.

3. Carl H. Claudy, *Introduction to Freemasonry* (Washington, D.C.: The Temple, 1984), 2:92.

4. Allen E. Roberts, *The Craft and Its Symbols: Opening the Door to Masonic Symbolism* (Richmond: Macoy, 1974), p. X.

5. *Little Masonic Library* (Richmond: Macoy, 1977), 1:305.

6. *Ceremonies of Installation and Dedication*, rev. (The Ancient and Accepted Scottish Rite of Freemasonry, Southern Jurisdiction U.S.A., 1954), p. 10.

7. *Little Masonic Library*, 1:6-7.

8. Henry Wilson Coil, *Coil's Masonic Encyclopedia* (New York: Macoy, 1961), pp. 352-65; Albert Mackey, *Mackey's Revised Encyclopedia of Freemasonry*, rev. and enl. by Robert I. Clegg (Richmond: Macoy, 1966), 1:559-64; *Little Masonic Library*, 1:1-158.

9. *Little Masonic Library*, 1:2-3.

10. Joseph Fort Newton, *The Religion of Masonry: An Interpretation* (Richmond: Macoy, 1969), p. 41.

11. Claudy, *Introduction to Freemasonry*, 1:63.

12. H. L. Haywood, *The Great Teachings of Masonry* (Richmond: Macoy, 1971), p. 99.

13. Cf. Committee on Secret Societies of the Ninth General Assembly of the Orthodox Presbyterian Church (meeting at Rochester, N.Y., June 2-5, 1942), *Christ or the*

Lodge? (Philadelphia: Great Commission, n.d.), pp. 10-11, 19-20; L. James Rongstad, *How to Respond to the Lodge* (St. Louis: Concordia, 1977), p. 24; Manly P. Hall, *The Lost Keys of Freemasonry or the Secret of Hiram Abiff* (Richmond: Macoy, 1976), p. 93; Foster Bailey, *The Spirit of Masonry* (Hampstead, London: Lucius, 1972), p. 110; John R. Rice, *Lodges Examined by the Bible* (Murfreesboro, Tenn.: Sword of the Lord, 1943), pp. 53-54; Carl H. Claudy, *Foreign Countries: A Gateway to the Interpretation and Development of Certain Symbols of Freemasonry* (Richmond: Macoy, 1971), pp. 24, 121; *Little Masonic Library*, 5:183; Roberts, *Key to Freemasonry's Growth*, p. 8.

14. Rongstad, *How to Respond to the Lodge*, p. 16, citing the *Bulletin* (April 1917), p. 54.

15. *Liturgy of the Ancient and Accepted Scottish Rite of Freemasonry for the Southern Jurisdiction of the United States, Part Two* (Washington, D.C.: The Supreme Council, 33d Degree of the Ancient and Accepted Scottish Rite of Freemasonry of the Southern Jurisdiction of the U.S.A., 1982), pp. 202-3.

16. J. W. Acker, *Strange Altars: A Scriptural Appraisal of the Lodge* (St. Louis: Concordia, 1959), p. 32.

17. The Baptist Union of Scotland (endorsed by the Baptist Union of Great Britain and Ireland), *Baptists and Freemasonry* (Baptist Church House, 1987), pp. 4-5.

18. Wilmshurst, *The Meaning of Masonry*, p. 121.

19. Henry C. Clausen, *Clausen's Commentaries on Morals and Dogma* (The Supreme Council, 33d Degree, Ancient and Accepted Scottish Rite of Freemasonry, Southern Jurisdiction of the U.S.A., 1976), p. xviii.

20. Albert Pike, *Morals and Dogma of the Ancient and Accepted Scottish Rite of Freemasonry* (Charleston, S.C.: The Supreme Council of the 33d Degree for the Southern Jurisdiction of the United States, 1906), pp. 104-7; Martin L. Wagner, *Freemasonry: An Interpretation* (n.p., n.d.), distributed by Missionary Service and Supply, Route 2, Columbiana, OH 44408, pp. 142-49.

21. John Ankerberg, William Mankin, and Walter Martin, *Christianity and the Masonic Lodge: Are They Compatible?* "The John Ankerberg Show," transcript, 1985, The John Ankerberg Evangelistic Association, Chattanooga, Tennessee, p. 14.

22. Roberts, *The Craft and Its Symbols*, p. 6.

23. Rollin C. Blackmer, *The Lodge and the Craft* (Richmond: Macoy, 1976), p. 1.

24. *Leaves from Georgia Masonry* (Educational and Historical Commission of the Grand Lodge of Georgia, 1947), p. 65.

25. Edmond Ronayne, *The Master's Carpet or Masonry and Baal-Worship—Identical* (n.p., n.d., distributed by Missionary Service and Supply, Route 2, Columbiana, OH 44408), p. 242.

26. William H. Russell, *Masonic Facts for Masons* (Chicago: Charles T. Powner, 1968), p. 7.

27. George H. Steinmetz, *Freemasonry—Its Hidden Meaning* (Chicago: Charles T. Powner, 1976), pp. 2, 5.

28. Haywood, *The Great Teachings of Masonry*, p. 99.

29. Joseph Fort Newton, *The Builders: A Story and Study of Freemasonry* (Richmond: Macoy, 1951), p. 258.

30. Hall, *The Lost Keys of Freemasonry*, pp. 64-65.

31. Joseph Fort Newton, *The Religion of Masonry: An Interpretation* (Richmond: Macoy, 1969), pp. 11-12.

32. Newton, *The Builders*, p. 243.

33. Ibid., pp. 246-47.

34. *Clausen's Commentaries on Morals and Dogma*, p. 157.

35. Ibid., pp. 156-58, 210.

36. Manly P. Hall, *An Encyclopedic Outline of Masonic Hermetic Qabbalistic and Rosicrucian Symbolical Philosophy* (Los Angeles: Philosophical Research Society, 1977), p. 176.

37. Albert G. Mackey, *The Symbolism of Freemasonry: Illustrating and Explaining Its Science and Philosophy, Its Legends, Myths, and Symbols* (Chicago: Charles T. Powner, 1975), p. 354; cf. Claudy, *Introduction to Freemasonry*, 3:154.

38. Allen E. Roberts, *The Craft and Its Symbols: Opening the Door to Masonic Symbolism* (Richmond: Macoy, 1974), p. 6.

39. Bailey, *The Spirit of Masonry*, p. 125.

Chapter 4: Masonic Morality

1. John R. Rice, *Lodges Examined by the Bible* (Murfreesboro, Tenn.: Sword of the Lord, 1943), pp. 13-14, 25-27; cf. Paul A. Fisher, *Behind the Lodge Door: Church, State & Freemasonry* (Washington, D.C.: Shield Press, 1987).

2. John Dove, comp., *Virginia Textbook (containing "The Book of Constitutions," Illustrations of the Work, Forms and Ceremonies of the Grand Lodge of Virginia)* (Grand Lodge of Virginia, n.d.), 2:21.

3. Martin L. Wagner, *Freemasonry: An Interpretation* (n.p., n.d.), distributed by Missionary Service and Supply, Route 2, Columbiana, OH 44408, p. 513.

4. Edmond Ronayne, *The Master's Carpet or Masonry and Baal-Worship—Identical* (n.p., n.d., distributed by Missionary Service and Supply, Route 2, Columbiana, OH 44408), p. 72.

5. J. Blanchard, *Scottish Rite Masonry Illustrated (The Complete Ritual of the Ancient and Accepted Scottish Rite)* (Chicago: Charles T. Powner, 1979), 1:454.

6. Ibid., 1:457.

7. William W. Daniel, et al., *Masonic Manual of the Grand Lodge of Georgia,* 9th edition (Free and Accepted Masons, Grand Lodge of Georgia, 1973), p. 190.

8. Raymond Lee Allen, et al., *Tennessee Craftsmen or Masonic Textbook,* 14th edition (Nashville: Tennessee Board of Custodians Members, 1963), p. 88.

9. Rice, *Lodges Examined by the Bible*, p. 26.

10. John Sheville and James Gould, *Guide to the Royal Arch Chapter: A Complete Monitor with Full Instructions in the Degrees of Mark Master, Past Master, Most Excellent Master and Royal Arch Together with the Order of High Priesthood* (Richmond: Macoy, 1981), P. 26.

11. Malcom C. Duncan, *Masonic Ritual and Monitor* (New York: David Mckay, n.d.), p. 230.

12. Ronayne, *The Master's Carpet*, pp. 105-6.

13. Alphonse Cerza, *Let There Be Light: A Study in Anti-Masonry* (Silver Spring, Md.: The Masonic Service Association, 1983), p. 55.

14. The Baptist Union of Scotland (endorsed by the Baptist Union of Great Britain and Ireland), *Baptists and Freemasonry* (Baptist Church House, 1987), p. 7.

15. Rice, *Lodges Examined by the Bible*, p. 27.

16. Ibid., p. 25.

17. Fisher, *Behind the Lodge Door*, pp. 244-45.

18. Stephen Knight, *The Brotherhood: The Explosive Exposé of the Secret World of the Freemasons* (London: Grenada/Panther, 1983), p. 5.

19. Ibid., pp. 6-8.
20. Ibid., p. 4.
21. Ibid., p. 85; cf. pp. 269-77, 298-307.
22. Blanchard, *Scottish Rite Masonry Illustrated*, 1:455.
23. Sheville and Gould, *Guide to the Royal Arch Chapter*, p. 245.
24. Rice, *Lodges Examined by the Bible*, p. 27.
25. Wagner, *Freemasonry: An Interpretation*, p. 555.
26. Ibid., p. 514.
27. Cerza, *Let There Be Light*, p. 55.
28. Allen E. Roberts, *The Craft and Its Symbols: Opening the Door to Masonic Symbolism* (Richmond: Macoy, 1974), p. 43; see Wagner, *Freemasonry*, p. 428.
29. H. L. Haywood, *The Great Teachings of Masonry* (Richmond: Macoy, 1971), pp. 38-39.
30. H. V. B. Voorhis, *Facts for Freemasons: A Storehouse of Masonic Knowledge in Question and Answer Form*, rev. (Richmond: Macoy, 1979), p. 193; Wagner, *Freemasonry: An Interpretation*, pp. 550-56.
31. Haywood, *The Great Teachings of Masonry*, p. 40.
32. Albert Mackey, *Mackey's Revised Encyclopedia of Freemasonry*, rev. and enl. by Robert I. Clegg (Richmond: Macoy, 1966), 2:680.
33. Committee on Secret Societies of the Ninth General Assembly of the Orthodox Presbyterian Church (meeting at Rochester, N.Y., June 2-5, 1942), *Christ or the Lodge?* (Philadelphia: Great Commission, n.d.), p. 14, citing *Jurisprudence*, p. 502.
34. Wagner, *Freemasonry: An Interpretation*, pp. 495-96.
35. Ibid., p. 493.
36. Ibid., p. 536.
37. *Encyclopaedia Britannica, Micropaedia*, 15th ed., s.v. "Freemasonry."
38. L. James Rongstad, *How to Respond to the Lodge* (St. Louis: Concordia, 1977), p. 14.
39. Fisher, *Behind the Lodge Door*, pp. 50-52.
40. *Ceremonies of Installation and Dedication*, rev. (The Ancient and Accepted Scottish Rite of Freemasonry, Southern Jurisdiction U.S.A., 1954), p. 12; Carl H. Claudy, *Introduction to Freemasonry* (Washington, D.C.: The Temple, 1984), 3:161.
41. Rongstad, *How to Respond to the Lodge*, p. 22; cf. W. J. McCormick, *Christ, the Christian, and Freemasonry*, rev. (Belfast, Ireland: Great Joy, 1984/Issaquah, Wash.: Saints Alive in Jesus), p. 54.
42. Knight, *The Brotherhood*, p. 253.
43. Haywood, *The Great Teachings of Masonry*, p. 116.
44. Wagner, *Freemasonry: An Interpretation*, pp. 482-83.
45. Fisher, *Behind the Lodge Door*, pp. 17, 233-36.
46. Ibid., p. 16.
47. Ibid., p. 40; cf. p. 43.

Chapter 5: The Plan of Salvation

1. Raymond Lee Allen, et al., *Tennessee Craftsmen or Masonic Textbook*, 14th edition (Nashville: Tennessee Board of Custodians Members, 1963), p. 17.
2. Ibid., p. 41.

3. Ibid., p. 60.

4. John Ankerberg, Jack Harris, William Mankin, Walter Martin, and Paul Pantzer, *The Masonic Lodge: What Goes On Behind Closed Doors?* "The John Ankerberg Show," transcript, 1986, The John Ankerberg Evangelistic Association, Chattanooga, Tennessee, pp. 30-31.

5. Philippians 3:9; cf. J. I. Packer, *God's Words: Studies of Key Bible Themes* (Downers Grove, Ill.: InterVarsity, 1981), pp. 139-48.

6. George Simmons and Robert Macoy, *Standard Masonic Monitor of the Degrees of Entered Apprentice, Fellow Craft and Master Mason* (Richmond: Macoy, 1984), p. 111.

7. Ibid., p. 125.

8. J. Blanchard, *Scottish Rite Masonry Illustrated (The Complete Ritual of the Ancient and Accepted Scottish Rite)* (Chicago: Charles T. Powner, 1979), 2:32.

9. Ibid., 2:212.

10. Ibid., 2:209.

11. Ibid., 1:85.

12. Ibid., 1:146.

13. Ibid., 1:249.

14. Ibid., 1:318.

15. Ibid., 2:134.

16. Ibid., 1:453.

17. Henry C. Clausen, *Clausen's Commentaries on Morals and Dogma* (The Supreme Council, 33d Degree, Ancient and Accepted Scottish Rite of Freemasonry, Southern Jurisdiction of the U.S.A., 1976), p. 156.

18. Albert Pike, *Morals and Dogma of the Ancient and Accepted Scottish Rite of Freemasonry* (Charleston, S.C.: The Supreme Council of the 33d Degree for the Southern Jurisdiction of the United States, 1906), p. 136.

19. John Sheville and James Gould, *Guide to the Royal Arch Chapter: A Complete Monitor with Full Instructions in the Degrees of Mark Master, Past Master, Most Excellent Master and Royal Arch Together with the Order of High Priesthood* (Richmond: Macoy, 1981), p. 165.

20. Ibid., p. 80.

21. Ibid., p. 72.

22. *Leaves from Georgia Masonry* (Educational and Historical Commission of the Grand Lodge of Georgia, 1947), p. 140; cf. *Funeral Ceremony and Offices of a Lodge of Sorrow of the Ancient and Accepted Scottish Rite of Freemasonry*, reprint (Charleston, S.C.: Southern Jurisdiction of the United States of America, 1946), p. 76.

23. *Ceremonies of Installation and Dedication*, rev. (The Ancient and Accepted Scottish Rite of Freemasonry, Southern Jurisdiction U.S.A., 1954), p. 85.

24. John Dove, comp., *Virginia Textbook (containing "The Book of Constitutions," Illustrations of the Work, Forms and Ceremonies of the Grand Lodge of Virginia)* (Grand Lodge of Virginia, n.d.), 2:38.

25. Jim Shaw and Tom McKenney, *The Deadly Deception: Freemasonry Exposed by One of Its Top Leaders* (Lafayette, La.: Huntington House, 1988), p. 125.

26. John Sheville and James Gould, *Guide to the Royal Arch Chapter*, p. 258.

27. *Holy Bible (Temple Illustrated Edition)* (Nashville: A. J. Holman, 1968), p. 3.

28. Albert Mackey, *Mackey's Revised Encyclopedia of Freemasonry*, revised and enlarged by Robert I. Clegg (Richmond: Macoy, 1966), p. 1:499.

29. Charles H. Lacquement, "Freemasonry and Organized Religions," *The Pennsylvania Freemason* (February 1989): 7.

30. Henry C. Clausen, *Beyond the Ordinary: Toward a Better, Wiser and Happier World* (Washington, D.C.: The Supreme Council, 33d Degree, Ancient and Accepted Scottish Rite of Freemasonry, 1983), p. 254.

31. Malcom C. Duncan, *Masonic Ritual and Monitor* (New York: David McKay, n.d.), p. 132.

32. Henry Wilson Coil, *Coil's Masonic Encyclopedia* (New York: Macoy, 1961), p. 512.

33. John Ankerberg, William Mankin, and Walter Martin, *Christianity and the Masonic Lodge: Are They Compatible?* "The John Ankerberg Show," transcript, 1985, The John Ankerberg Evangelistic Association, Chattanooga, Tennessee, p. 2.

34. The Working Group established by the Standing Committee of the General Synod of the Church of England, *Freemasonry and Christianity: Are They Compatible?* (London: Church House, 1987), pp. 20, 34.

35. Ankerberg, et al., *The Masonic Lodge*, p. 35.

36. John R. Rice, *Lodges Examined by the Bible* (Murfreesboro, Tenn.: Sword of the Lord, 1943), p. 55.

37. Ibid.

38. Ibid.

Chapter 6: The Rule of Faith and Practice

1. George Simmons and Robert Macoy, *Standard Masonic Monitor of the Degrees of Entered Apprentice, Fellow Craft and Master Mason* (Richmond: Macoy, 1984), p. 21.

2. *Masonic Monitor of the Degrees of Entered Apprentice, Fellow Craft and Master Mason*, 7th ed. (Free and Accepted Masons of Arkansas, 1983), p. 15.

3. *Little Masonic Library* (Richmond: Macoy, 1977), 4:218.

4. *Holy Bible (Temple Illustrated Edition)* (Nashville: A. J. Holman, 1968), pp. 3-4.

5. In Newton's quotation (note 4), reference is made to the revelation of God in every religion. In chapter 14, we will prove that Masonry teaches that its own doctrines constitute the "core truths" of all religions. That is why Newton says, "religions are many but Religion [the truth of Masonry] is One." Included here is the idea that universal Masonic doctrines have been overlaid with much error by the individual religions. Thus, Masonry will admit that in all the different scriptures of the world the "revelation of God" can be found, but they understand that it is only fully and perfectly revealed in Masonry. In this manner they can "accept" all men's scriptures and yet hold that they are but dim reflections (or symbolic teachings) of the complete truth revealed in Masonry.

6. Albert Pike, *Morals and Dogma of the Ancient and Accepted Scottish Rite of Freemasonry* (Charleston, S.C.: The Supreme Council of the 33d Degree for the Southern Jurisdiction of the United States, 1906), p. 11.

7. J. Blanchard, *Scottish Rite Masonry Illustrated (The Complete Ritual of the Ancient and Accepted Scottish Rite)* (Chicago: Charles T. Powner, 1979), 1:196.

8. Ibid., 1:316.

9. Albert Mackey, *Mackey's Revised Encyclopedia of Freemasonry*, rev. and enl. by Robert I. Clegg (Richmond: Macoy, 1966), 1:133; *Little Masonic Library*, 1:132.

10. Henry Wilson Coil, *Coil's Masonic Encyclopedia* (New York: Macoy, 1961), p. 520.

11. *Little Masonic Library*, 1:129, 130.

12. *Mackey's Revised Encyclopedia of Freemasonry*, 1:133.

13. *Little Masonic Library*, 1:129; cf. *Coil's Masonic Encyclopedia*, p. 520.

14. Martin L. Wagner, *Freemasonry: An Interpretation* (n.p., n.d.), distributed by Missionary Service and Supply, Route 2, Columbiana, OH 44408, pp. 335-36; cf. pp. 341-42.

15. Pike, *Morals and Dogma*, pp. 744-45.

16. Wagner, *Freemasonry: An Interpretation*, p. 29.

17. J. W. Acker, *Strange Altars: A Scriptural Appraisal of the Lodge* (St. Louis: Concordia, 1959), citing *Digest*, pp. 207-8.

18. *Little Masonic Library*, 1:132.

19. Rollin C. Blackmer, *The Lodge and the Craft* (Richmond: Macoy, 1976), p. 22.

Chapter 7: The Fatherhood of God

1. *Liturgy of the Ancient and Accepted Scottish Rite of Freemasonry for the Southern Jurisdiction of the United States, Part Two* (Washington, D.C.: The Supreme Council, 33d Degree of the Ancient and Accepted Scottish Rite of Freemasonry of the Southern Jurisdiction of the U.S.A., 1982), p. 137.

2. Carl H. Claudy, *Foreign Countries: A Gateway to the Interpretation and Development of Certain Symbols of Freemasonry* (Richmond: Macoy, 1971), p. 24.

3. J. Sidlow Baxter, *Majesty: The God You Should Know* (San Bernardino, Calif.: Here's Life, 1984), p. 196.

4. Ibid., pp. 167-200.

5. George Simmons and Robert Macoy, *Standard Masonic Monitor of the Degrees of Entered Apprentice, Fellow Craft and Master Mason* (Richmond: Macoy, 1984), p. 17.

6. Raymond Lee Allen, et al., *Tennessee Craftsmen or Masonic Textbook*, 14th edition (Nashville: Tennessee Board of Custodians Members, 1963), p. 26.

7. J. Blanchard, *Scottish Rite Masonry Illustrated (The Complete Ritual of the Ancient and Accepted Scottish Rite)* (Chicago: Charles T. Powner, 1979), 1:148, 264; 2:282; cf. 1:229.

8. Ibid., 2:263-64.

9. Ibid., 2:264, 277, 299.

10. Allen, et al., *Tennessee Craftsmen or Masonic Textbook*, p. 13.

Chapter 8: The Nature of God

1. Malcom C. Duncan, *Masonic Ritual and Monitor* (New York: David McKay, n.d.), p. 30.

2. Ibid., p. 78.

3. Ibid., pp. 93-96, 129, 131; cf. Allen, et al., *Tennessee Craftsmen or Masonic Textbook*, pp. 39, 58.

4. Allen, et al., *Tennessee Craftsmen or Masonic Textbook*, p. 16.

5. George Simmons and Robert Macoy, *Standard Masonic Monitor of the Degrees of Entered Apprentice, Fellow Craft and Master Mason* (Richmond: Macoy, 1984), pp. 58, 82.

6. Alphonse Cerza, *A Masonic Reader's Guide*, ed. Thomas C. Warden, Transactions of the Missouri Lodge of Research, vol. 34 (1978-1979), 1980, pp. 106-8.

7. Allen, et al., *Tennessee Craftsmen or Masonic Textbook*, p. 1.

8. Ibid., p. 7.

9. Ibid., p. 180.

10. Martin L. Wagner, *Freemasonry: An Interpretation* (n.p., n.d.), distributed by Missionary Service and Supply, Route 2, Columbiana, OH 44408, pp. 292-93.

11. Allen, et al., *Tennessee Craftsmen or Masonic Textbook*, pp. 13-14.

12. Duncan, *Masonic Ritual and Monitor*, p. 29.

13. Albert Pike, *Morals and Dogma of the Ancient and Accepted Scottish Rite of Freemasonry* (Charleston, S.C.: The Supreme Council of the 33d Degree for the Southern Jurisdiction of the United States, 1906), p. 226.

14. *Little Masonic Library* (Richmond: Macoy, 1977), 5:51-52.

15. Pike, *Morals and Dogma*, p. 516.

16. Albert Mackey, *Mackey's Revised Encyclopedia of Freemasonry*, rev. and enl. by Robert I. Clegg (Richmond: Macoy, 1966), 1:409-10.

17. Carl H. Claudy, *Introduction to Freemasonry* (Washington, D.C.: The Temple, 1984), 2:110.

18. *Little Masonic Library*, 4:32.

19. Carl H. Claudy, *Foreign Countries: A Gateway to the Interpretation and Development of Certain Symbols of Freemasonry* (Richmond: Macoy, 1971), pp. 8-9.

20. Wagner, *Freemasonry: An Interpretation*, pp. 289, 336, cf. p. 330.

21. *Funeral Ceremony and Offices of a Lodge of Sorrow of the Ancient and Accepted Scottish Rite of Freemasonry*, reprint (Charleston, S.C.: Southern Jurisdiction of the United States of America, 1946), p. 77.

22. Charles H. Lacquement, "Freemasonry and Organized Religions," *The Pennsylvania Freemason* (February 1989): 7.

23. Wagner, *Freemasonry: An Interpretation*, p. 285.

24. *Jabulon* has variant spellings in Masonic literature: *Jab-Bel-On, Ja-bul-on, Jabulun*, etc. We use *Jabulon* for the sake of consistency, except in quotations.

25. Henry Wilson Coil, *Coil's Masonic Encyclopedia* (New York: Macoy, 1961), pp. 516-17.

26. *Little Masonic Library*, 5:51.

27. Pike, *Morals and Dogma*, p. 718.

28. Anthony Flew and Alasdair MacIntyre, eds., "Theology and Falsification," in *New Essays in Philosophical Theology* (London: SCM, 1955), p. 96.

29. Wagner, *Freemasonry: An Interpretation*, p. 289.

30. *Coil's Masonic Encyclopedia*, p. 516.

31. Pike, *Morals and Dogma*, p. 516.

32. Wagner, *Freemasonry: An Interpretation*, p. 285.

33. Ibid., pp. 286, 309-10.

34. J. W. Acker, *Strange Altars: A Scriptural Appraisal of the Lodge* (St. Louis: Concordia, 1959), p. 37.

35. Joseph Fort Newton, *The Builders: A Story and Study of Freemasonry* (Richmond: Macoy, 1951), p. 164.

36. Pike, *Morals and Dogma*, p. 552.

37. Newton, *The Builders*, p. 164.

38. Foster Bailey, *The Spirit of Masonry* (Hampstead, London: Lucius, 1972), p. 74.

39. Acker, *Strange Altars*, p. 37.

40. Stephen Knight, *The Brotherhood: The Explosive Exposé of the Secret World of the Freemasons* (London: Grenada/Panther, 1983), p. 234.

41. Pike, *Morals and Dogma*, p. 226; cf. *Little Masonic Library*, 5:51-52.

42. *Coil's Masonic Encyclopedia*, p. 517.

Chapter 9: The Name of God

1. Grand Lodge of Texas, A. F. and A. M., *Monitor of the Lodge: Monitorial Instructions in the Three Degrees of Symbolic Masonry* (Grand Lodge of Texas, 1982), p. XIV; cf. refs. Martin L. Wagner, *Freemasonry: An Interpretation* (n.p., n.d.), distributed by Missionary Service and Supply, Route 2, Columbiana, OH 44408; W. L. Wilmsurst, *The Meaning of Masonry* (New York: Bell, 1980); Alphonse Cerza, *A Masonic Reader's Guide*, ed. Thomas C. Warden, Transactions of the Missouri Lodge of Research, vol. 34 (1978-1979), 1980; Albert G. Mackey, *The Symbolism of Freemasonry: Illustrating and Explaining Its Science and Philosophy, Its Legends, Myths, and Symbols* (Chicago: Charles T. Powner, 1975).

2. Stephen Knight, *The Brotherhood: The Explosive Exposé of the Secret World of the Freemasons* (London: Grenada/Panther, 1983), p. 243; J. W. Acker, *Strange Altars: A Scriptural Appraisal of the Lodge* (St. Louis: Concordia, 1959), p. 32; John Ankerberg, "Is Freemasonry a Religion? and Other Important Questions About 'The Lodge'" (Chattanooga: The John Ankerberg Evangelistic Association, 1986), p. 10.

3. Albert Mackey, *Mackey's Revised Encyclopedia of Freemasonry*, rev. and enl. by Robert I. Clegg (Richmond: Macoy, 1966), 2:735, 746.

4. Martin L. Wagner, *Freemasonry: An Interpretation*, pp. 338-99.

5. Henry Wilson Coil, *Coil's Masonic Encyclopedia* (New York: Macoy, 1961), p. 516. Coil admits that the Royal Arch ritual interprets *On* "to be one of the ancient Egyptian names of Deity," although he notes that this interpretation is disputed by some (*Coil's Masonic Encyclopedia*, p. 456); Mackey asserts that "the word may still be retained as a symbol of the Egyptian god" (*Mackey's Revised Encyclopedia of Freemasonry*), 2:735, 746.

6. See A. E. Cundall, "Baal" in *The Zondervan Pictorial Encyclopedia of the Bible*, ed. Merrill C. Tenney (Grand Rapids: Zondervan, 1975); *Encyclopaedia Britannica, Micropaedia*, 15th ed., s.v. "Baal"; *The New Schaff-Herzog Encyclopedia of Religious Knowledge* (1978), s.v. "Baal"; Lewis Bayles Payton, "Baal, Beel, Bel" in *Encyclopedia of Religion and Ethics*, ed. James Hastings (New York: Charles Schribner's Sons, n.d.); George A. Barton, "Baalzebub and Beelzaboul" in *Encyclopedia of Religion and Ethics*, ed. James Hastings (New York: Charles Schribner's Sons, n.d.); Amihai Mazar, "Bronze Bull Found in Israelite 'High Place' from the Time of the Judges," *Biblical Archeology Review* (September/October, 1983).

7. The Working Group established by the Standing Committee of the General Synod of the Church of England, *Freemasonry and Christianity: Are They Compatible?* (London: Church House, 1987), pp. 27, 29.

8. Cf. Merrill F. Unger, *Archeology and the Old Testament* (Grand Rapids: Zondervan, 1977), pp. 278-79; Lawrence E. Stager and Samuel R. Wolf, "Child Sacrifice at Carthage: Religions Rite or Population Control?" *Biblical Archeology Review* (January/February 1984), pp. 30-51; Cundall, "Baal" *Encyclopaedia Britannica, Micropaedia*, 15th ed., s.v. "Baal"; *The New Schaff-Herzog Encyclopedia of Religious Knowledge*

(1978), s.v. "Baal"; Payton, "Baal, Beel, Bel"; Barton, "Baalzebub and Beelzaboul"; W. L. Liefeld, "Mystery Religions" in *The Zondervan Pictorial Encyclopedia of the Bible,* ed. Merrill C. Tenney (Grand Rapids: Zondervan, 1977); Mazar, "Bronze Bull Found in Israelite 'High Place' from the Time of the Judges."

9. Barton, "Baalzebub and Beelzaboul," p. 298; cf. Luke 11:15-19; Matthew 10:25-27.

10. Cundall, "Baal," p. 433.

11. Wagner, *Freemasonry: An Interpretation*, p. 319; 1 Corinthians 10:20.

12. Wagner, *Freemasonry: An Interpretation*, pp. 319, 343.

13. *Coil's Masonic Encyclopedia*, pp. 516-17.

14. *Freemasonry and Christianity: Are They Compatible?*, p. 30.

Chapter 10: Jesus Christ

1. Grand Lodge of Texas, A. F. and A. M., *Monitor of the Lodge: Monitorial Instructions in the Three Degrees of Symbolic Masonry* (Grand Lodge of Texas, 1982), p. 10.

2. Henry C. Clausen, *Clausen's Commentaries on Morals and Dogma* (The Supreme Council, 33d Degree, Ancient and Accepted Scottish Rite of Freemasonry, Southern Jurisdiction of the U.S.A., 1976), p. 159.

3. Edmond Ronayne, *The Master's Carpet or Masonry and Baal-Worship—Identical* (n.p., n.d., distributed by Missionary Service and Supply, Route 2, Columbiana, OH 44408), pp. 181-184; John Sheville and James Gould, *Guide to the Royal Arch Chapter: A Complete Monitor with Full Instructions in the Degrees of Mark Master, Past Master, Most Excellent Master and Royal Arch Together with the Order of High Priesthood* (Richmond: Macoy, 1981), pp. 139-40; E. Ronayne, *Chapter Masonry* (Chicago: Ezra A. Cook, 1984), p. 206.

4. Jack Harris, *Freemasonry: The Invisible Cult in Our Midst* (Chattanooga: Global, 1983), p. 112.

5. Jim Shaw and Tom McKenney, *The Deadly Deception: Freemasonry Exposed by One of Its Top Leaders* (Lafayette, La.: Huntington House, 1988), p. 72.

6. Albert Mackey, *Mackey's Masonic Ritualist: Monitorial Instructions and the Degrees from Entered Apprentice to Select Masters* (n.p.: Charles E. Merrill, 1867); cf. E. M. Storms, *Should a Christian Be a Mason?* (Fletcher, N.C.: New Puritan Library, 1980), p. 68.

7. Albert Mackey, *Mackey's Revised Encyclopedia of Freemasonry*, rev. and enl. by Robert I. Clegg (Richmond: Macoy, 1966), 1:192.

8. Albert Pike, *Morals and Dogma of the Ancient and Accepted Scottish Rite of Freemasonry* (Charleston, S.C.: The Supreme Council of the 33d Degree for the Southern Jurisdiction of the United States, 1906), p. 167.

9. J. Blanchard, *Scottish Rite Masonry Illustrated (The Complete Ritual of the Ancient and Accepted Scottish Rite)* (Chicago: Charles T. Powner, 1979), 2:47.

10. Grand Lodge of Texas, *Monitor of the Lodge*, p. 89.

11. Blanchard, *Scottish Rite Masonry Illustrated*, 1:81, 83, 92, 103, 107, 225, 245, 265, 268, 285, 324; 2:26, 27, 116, 156, 175, 192.

12. Ibid., 2:35.

13. Shaw and McKenney, *The Deadly Deception*, pp. 126-27.

14. Ibid., p. 127; cf. Henry C. Clausen, *Practice and Procedure for the Scottish Rite* (Washington, D.C.: The Supreme Council, 33d Degree, Ancient and Accepted Scottish Rite of Freemasonry Mother Jurisdiction of the World, 1981), pp. 75-77.

15. *Clausen's Commentaries on Morals and Dogma*, p. 157.

16. Pike, *Morals and Dogma*, p. 525.

17. J. W. Acker, *Strange Altars: A Scriptural Appraisal of the Lodge* (St. Louis: Concordia, 1959), pp. 6, 34; cf. pp. 34-39.

18. Harris, *Freemasonry: The Invisible Cult in Our Midst*, p. 102, citing *Symbolism* (1925), p. 57.

19. Ibid., p. 102, citing *Mysticism* (1900), p. 47.

20. Ronayne, *The Master's Carpet or Masonry and Baal-Worship—Identical*, p. 87.

21. Shaw and McKenney, *The Deadly Deception*, p. 127; Pike, *Morals and Dogma*, pp. 524-77; Harris, *Freemasonry: The Invisible Cult in Our Midst*, pp. 102-3.

22. Corinne Heline, *Mystic Masonry and the Bible* (La Canada, Calif.: New Age, 1975), pp. 19, 33, 47, 90-91.

23. Manly P. Hall, *The Lost Keys of Freemasonry or the Secret of Hiram Abiff* (Richmond: Macoy, 1976), p. 91.

24. Grand Lodge of Texas, *Monitor of the Lodge*, p. 34.

Chapter 11: The Nature of Man

1. Jack Harris, *Freemasonry: The Invisible Cult in Our Midst* (Chattanooga: Global, 1983), p. 132.

2. Grand Lodge of Texas, A. F. and A. M., *Monitor of the Lodge: Monitorial Instructions in the Three Degrees of Symbolic Masonry* (Grand Lodge of Texas, 1982), p. 11.

3. Raymond Lee Allen, et al., *Tennessee Craftsmen or Masonic Textbook*, 14th edition (Nashville: Tennessee Board of Custodians Members, 1963), p. 13.

4. Henry C. Clausen, *Beyond the Ordinary: Toward a Better, Wiser and Happier World* (Washington, D.C.: The Supreme Council, 33d Degree, Ancient and Accepted Scottish Rite of Freemasonry, 1983), p. 254.

5. Grand Lodge of Texas, *Monitor of the Lodge*, pp. 5-6, 13.

6. Allen, et al., *Tennessee Craftsmen or Masonic Textbook*, p. 27.

7. Grand Lodge of Texas, *Monitor of the Lodge*, p. 19.

8. John C. Green, *The Death of Adam: Evolution and Its Impact on Western Thought* (Ames, Iowa: Iowa State U., 1959), p. 338.

9. Cited in David Lack, *Evolutionary Theory and Christian Belief* (London: Methuen, 1957), p. 108.

10. E. K. Simpson and F. F. Bruce, *Commentary on the Epistles to the Ephesians and Colossians*, NICNT (Grand Rapids: Eerdmans, 1975), p. 50.

11. Cited in *Eternity* Magazine (October 1985), p. 24.

12. *The Stockton Herald,* March 13-18, 1960, or March 3-8, 1963.

13. *The Bulletin of the Atomic Scientists* (June 1976): 25.

14. H. L. Haywood, *The Great Teachings of Masonry* (Richmond: Macoy, 1971), p. 139.

15. Ibid., p. 138.

16. M. Scott Peck, *People of the Lie* (New York: Simon & Schuster, 1981), pp. 39-40, 47, 72.

17. The Baptist Union of Scotland (endorsed by the Baptist Union of Great Britain and Ireland), *Baptists and Freemasonry* (Baptist Church House, 1987), pp. 5-6.

18. Allen, et al., *Tennessee Craftsmen or Masonic Textbook*, pp. 61, 126.

19. *Leaves from Georgia Masonry* (Educational and Historical Commission of the Grand Lodge of Georgia, 1947), p. 67.

20. W. L. Wilmshurst, *The Meaning of Masonry* (New York: Bell, 1980), p. 121.

21. *Little Masonic Library* (Richmond: Macoy, 1977), 5:55; Albert Pike, *Morals and Dogma of the Ancient and Accepted Scottish Rite of Freemasonry* (Charleston, S.C.: The Supreme Council of the 33d Degree for the Southern Jurisdiction of the United States, 1906), p. 700; cf. Martin L. Wagner, *Freemasonry: An Interpretation* (n.p., n.d.), distributed by Missionary Service and Supply, Route 2, Columbiana, OH 44408, pp. 16, 349-50.

22. Joseph Fort Newton, *The Builders: A Story and Study of Freemasonry* (Richmond: Macoy, 1951), p. 284; cf. *Little Masonic Library*, 5:55; Albert Mackey, *Mackey's Revised Encyclopedia of Freemasonry*, rev. and enl. by Robert I. Clegg (Richmond: Macoy, 1966), 1:269.

23. Joseph Fort Newton, *The Religion of Masonry: An Interpretation* (Richmond: Macoy, 1969), p. 37.

24. Henry Pirtle, *Kentucky Monitor: Complete Monitorial Ceremonies of the Blue Lodge* (Louisville, Ky.: Standard Printing, 1921), p. xx.

25. Henry C. Clausen, *Clausen's Commentaries on Morals and Dogma* (The Supreme Council, 33d Degree, Ancient and Accepted Scottish Rite of Freemasonry, Southern Jurisdiction of the U.S.A., 1976), p. 157.

26. Manly P. Hall, *The Lost Keys of Freemasonry or the Secret of Hiram Abiff* (Richmond: Macoy, 1976), p. 92; cf. Wilmshurst, *The Meaning of Masonry*, pp. 74-75; Manly P. Hall, *An Encyclopedic Outline of Masonic Hermetic Qabbalistic and Rosicrucian Symbolical Philosophy* (Los Angeles: Philosophical Research Society, 1977), p. 201; Hall, *The Lost Keys of Freemasonry*, p. 110.

27. Hall, *The Lost Keys of Freemasonry*, p. 55.

28. Carl H. Claudy, *Introduction to Freemasonry* (Washington, D.C.: The Temple, 1984), 1:61.

29. Paul Lee Tan, *Encyclopedia of 7700 Illustrations* (Rockville, Md.: Assurance, 1979), p. 395.

30. Ibid., p. 459.

31. Ibid.

Chapter 12: Hell

Some material in this chapter is exerpted from John Weldon and Zola Levitt, *Is There Life After Death?* (Irving, Calif.: Harvest House, 1976).

1. *Masonic Monitor of the Degrees of Entered Apprentice, Fellow Craft and Master Mason*, 7th ed. (Free and Accepted Masons of Arkansas, 1983), p. 15.

2. George Simmons and Robert Macoy, *Standard Masonic Monitor of the Degrees of Entered Apprentice, Fellow Craft and Master Mason* (Richmond: Macoy, 1984), p. 21.

3. *Masonic Monitor of the Degrees of Entered Apprentice, Fellow Craft and Master Mason*, p. 68.

4. William Lane Craig, *The Son Rises* (Chicago: Moody, 1981); Frank Morrison, *Who Moved the Stone?* (Downers Grove, Ill.: InterVarsity, 1969); Gary Habermas and Anthony Flew, *Did Jesus Rise from the Dead? The Resurrection Debate* (San Francisco: Harper & Row, 1987).

5. Donald Barnhouse, *Genesis: A Devotional Exposition* (Grand Rapids: Zondervan, 1970), 1:51-52.

6. Leon Morris, *Christianity Today,* 4 March 1977, pp. 56-57.

7. Lewis Sperry Chafer, *Major Bible Themes* (Grand Rapids: Zondervan, 1926), pp. 298-99.

8. C. S. Lewis, *The Problem of Pain* (New York: Macmillan, 1971), pp. 118-19.

9. Harold O. J. Brown, *The Protest of a Troubled Protestant* (New Rochelle, N.Y.: Arlington House, 1969), p. 213.

10. C. S. Lewis, *The Great Divorce* (New York: Macmillan, 1946), p. 69.

11. Lewis Sperry Chafer, *Systematic Theology* (Dallas: Dallas Theological Seminary, 1971), 4:432-33.

A Christian Response to Part 2

1. E.g., in the 19th Degree, where the Mason is told, "Be thou a Priest forever, after the order of Melchizedek"; cf. Hebrews 7:17, 21-22; J. Blanchard, *Scottish Rite Masonry Illustrated (The Complete Ritual of the Ancient and Accepted Scottish Rite)* (Chicago: Charles T. Powner, 1979), 2:26; Manly P. Hall, *The Lost Keys of Freemasonry or the Secret of Hiram Abiff* (Richmond: Macoy, 1976), p. 59.

2. Martin L. Wagner, *Freemasonry: An Interpretation* (n.p., n.d.), distributed by Missionary Service and Supply, Route 2, Columbiana, OH 44408, p. 24.

3. Dale A. Byers, *I Left the Lodge* (Schaumburg, Ill.: Regular Baptist, 1988), pp. 125-26.

Chapter 13: Blaspheming God's Name

1. *Webster's Collegiate Dictionary*, 5th ed. (Springfield, Mass.: G & C Merriam & Co., 1946).

2. J. Blanchard, *Scottish Rite Masonry Illustrated (The Complete Ritual of the Ancient and Accepted Scottish Rite)* (Chicago: Charles T. Powner, 1979), 1:449-51.

3. Malcom C. Duncan, *Masonic Ritual and Monitor* (New York: David McKay, n.d.), pp. 221-22; cf. p. 252.

4. Ibid., pp. 234-35.

5. Ibid., p. 224; cf. John Sheville and James Gould, *Guide to the Royal Arch Chapter: A Complete Monitor with Full Instructions in the Degrees of Mark Master, Past Master, Most Excellent Master and Royal Arch Together with the Order of High Priesthood* (Richmond: Macoy, 1981), pp. 180, 214.

6. Blanchard, *Scottish Rite Masonry Illustrated*, 1:107.

7. Ibid., 1:81.

8. Ibid., 1:83.

9. Ibid., 1:268; 2:116, 175.

10. Ibid., 1:323-324.

11. Ibid., 1:225.

12. Ibid., 1:245.

13. Ibid., 1:285.

14. Ibid., 1:479-80.

15. Ibid., 2:192.

16. Ibid., 2:26-27.

17. Ibid., 2:184.

18. *Webster's New World Dictionary, Second Collegiate Edition* (New York: Simon & Schuster, 1984), first edition; C. S. Lewis, *The Problem of Pain* (New York: Macmillan, 1971).

19. Blanchard, *Scottish Rite Masonry Illustrated*, 2:290.

20. Cf. Report of the Faith and Order Committee of the British Methodist Church, *Freemasonry and Methodism*, presented to the General Assembly of the British Methodist Church and adopted by them on 3 July 1985. Although King David is speaking in the verse quoted, the sentiment is illustrative of God's love for good and His hatred for all evil; cf. Psalm 31:6; Isaiah 1:14; Ezekiel 11:21; 16:36.

Chapter 14: Swearing Oaths

1. Stephen Knight, *The Brotherhood: The Explosive Exposé of the Secret World of the Freemasons* (London: Grenada/Panther, 1983), pp. 231, 243.

2. Alphonse Cerza, *Let There Be Light: A Study in Anti-Masonry* (Silver Spring, Md.: The Masonic Service Association, 1983), p. 53.

3. J. Blanchard, *Scottish Rite Masonry Illustrated (The Complete Ritual of the Ancient and Accepted Scottish Rite)* (Chicago: Charles T. Powner, 1979), 2:316.

4. John Dove, comp., *Virginia Textbook (containing "The Book of Constitutions," Illustrations of the Work, Forms and Ceremonies of the Grand Lodge of Virginia)* (Grand Lodge of Virginia, n.d.), 2:21.

5. Carl H. Claudy, *The Master's Book* (Washington, D.C.: The Temple, 1985), pp. V-VII.

6. Carl H. Claudy, *Foreign Countries: A Gateway to the Interpretation and Development of Certain Symbols of Freemasonry* (Richmond: Macoy, 1971), p. 90.

7. Ibid., p. 90.

8. Martin L. Wagner, *Freemasonry: An Interpretation* (n.p., n.d.), distributed by Missionary Service and Supply, Route 2, Columbiana, OH 44408, p. 550.

9. Manly P. Hall, *The Lost Keys of Freemasonry or the Secret of Hiram Abiff* (Richmond: Macoy, 1976), pp. 11, 68, 42.

10. Wagner, *Freemasonry: An Interpretation*, pp. 551-53.

11. Malcom C. Duncan, *Masonic Ritual and Monitor* (New York: David McKay, n.d.), pp. 34-35.

12. Ibid., p. 96.

13. Ibid., p. 189.

14. Ibid., p. 190.

15. Ibid., p. 265; cf. Committee on Secret Societies of the Ninth General Assembly of the Orthodox Presbyterian Church (meeting at Rochester, N.Y., June 2-5, 1942), *Christ or the Lodge?* (Philadelphia: Great Commission, n.d.), p. 15; Jim Shaw and Tom McKenney, *The Deadly Deception: Freemasonry Exposed by One of Its Top Leaders* (Lafayette, La.: Huntington House, 1988), pp. 46, 139; Knight, *The Brotherhood*, p. 1; Jack Harris, *Freemasonry: The Invisible Cult in Our Midst* (Chattanooga: Global, 1983), pp. 50-52, 56-57; The General Grand Chapter of Royal Arch Masons International, Committee on Revision of the Ritual, William F. Kuhn, et al. *The Manual of Ritual for Royal Arch Masons,* 45th ed. (1983), pp. 98, 265; Malcom C. Duncan, *Masonic Ritual and Monitor* (New York: David McKay, n.d.), p. 230.

16. Blanchard, *Scottish Rite Masonry Illustrated*, 1:196-97.

17. Ibid., 1:266; 2:261.

18. Ibid., 1:316-17; cf. 1:164.

19. Ibid., 1:448; 2:457.

20. Ibid., 1:473.

21. Ibid., 2:155.

22. Ibid., 2:217.

23. Ibid., 2:269-70, 275.

24. Albert Mackey, *Mackey's Revised Encyclopedia of Freemasonry*, rev. and enl. by Robert I. Clegg (Richmond: Macoy, 1966), 2:760.

25. Paul A. Fisher, *Behind the Lodge Door: Church, State & Freemasonry* (Washington, D.C.: Shield Press, 1987), p. 206.

26. Jim Shaw and Tom McKenney, *The Deadly Deception: Freemasonry Exposed by One of Its Top Leaders* (Lafayette, La.: Huntington House, 1988), p. 77.

27. John R. Rice, *Lodges Examined by the Bible* (Murfreesboro, Tenn.: Sword of the Lord, 1943), p. 57.

28. Ibid., pp. 59-60.

29. Raymond Lee Allen, et al., *Tennessee Craftsmen or Masonic Textbook*, 14th edition (Nashville: Tennessee Board of Custodians Members, 1963), p. 39; Duncan, *Masonic Ritual and Monitor*, p. 206.

30. Blanchard, *Scottish Rite Masonry Illustrated*, 1:313.

31. *Mackey's Revised Encyclopedia of Freemasonry*, 2:723.

32. Duncan, *Masonic Ritual and Monitor*, p. 29; Albert Mackey, *The Manual of the Lodge* (New York: Clark Maynard, 1870), p. 20; John Ankerberg, Jack Harris, William Mankin, Walter Martin, and Paul Pantzer, *The Masonic Lodge: What Goes On Behind Closed Doors?* "The John Ankerberg Show," transcript, 1986, The John Ankerberg Evangelistic Association, Chattanooga, Tennessee, pp. 4-5.

Chapter 15: Uniting All Religions

1. Charles H. Lacquement, "Freemasonry and Organized Religions," *The Pennsylvania Freemason*, February 1989, p. 7.

2. Joseph Fort Newton, *The Religion of Masonry: An Interpretation* (Richmond: Macoy, 1969), pp. 11-12.

3. The Working Group established by the Standing Committee of the General Synod of the Church of England, *Freemasonry and Christianity: Are They Compatible?* (London: Church House, 1987), p. 1.

4. H. L. Haywood, *The Newly-Made Mason: What He and Every Mason Should Know About Masonry* (Richmond: Macoy, 1973), p. 218.

5. J. Blanchard, *Scottish Rite Masonry Illustrated (The Complete Ritual of the Ancient and Accepted Scottish Rite)* (Chicago: Charles T. Powner, 1979), 2:277, 299.

6. H. L. Haywood, *The Great Teachings of Masonry* (Richmond: Macoy, 1971), p. 90; *Legenda 32 (Part 1)*, a Masonic source apparently used for instruction, c. 1920-30 (n.p., n.d.), p. 33.

7. *Little Masonic Library* (Richmond: Macoy, 1977), 5:35.

8. Foster Bailey, *The Spirit of Masonry* (Hampstead, London: Lucius, 1972), p. 125.

9. Albert Mackey, *Mackey's Revised Encyclopedia of Freemasonry*, rev. and enl. by Robert I. Clegg (Richmond: Macoy, 1966), 1:269.

10. Joseph Fort Newton, *The Builders: A Story and Study of Freemasonry* (Richmond: Macoy, 1951), p. 233.

11. Martin L. Wagner, *Freemasonry: An Interpretation* (n.p., n.d.), distributed by Missionary Service and Supply, Route 2, Columbiana, OH 44408, pp. 288-302.

12. Henry C. Clausen, *Beyond the Ordinary: Toward a Better, Wiser and Happier World* (Washington, D.C.: The Supreme Council, 33d Degree, Ancient and Accepted Scottish Rite of Freemasonry, 1983), p. 253.

13. *Little Masonic Library*, 5:102-3.

14. Albert Pike, *Morals and Dogma of the Ancient and Accepted Scottish Rite of Freemasonry* (Charleston, S.C.: The Supreme Council of the 33d Degree for the Southern Jurisdiction of the United States, 1906), p. 277.

15. *Little Masonic Library*, 5:13-14.

16. *Masonic Square for 1975 and 1976*, bound volume (March 1975–December 1975, March 1976–December 1976), 2:122-23.

17. Bailey, *The Spirit of Masonry*, pp. 24-25.

18. *Little Masonic Library*, 1:118; 4:258; cf. Henry Wilson Coil, *A Comprehensive View of Freemasonry* (Richmond: Macoy, 1973), p. 192.

19. *Little Masonic Library*, 1:115-17, 134.

20. Jim Shaw and Tom McKenney, *The Deadly Deception: Freemasonry Exposed by One of Its Top Leaders* (Lafayette, La.: Huntington House, 1988), p. 135.

21. Malcom C. Duncan, *Masonic Ritual and Monitor* (New York: David McKay, n.d.), p. 29; cf. John Ankerberg, Jack Harris, William Mankin, Walter Martin, and Paul Pantzer, *The Masonic Lodge: What Goes On Behind Closed Doors?* "The John Ankerberg Show," transcript, 1986, The John Ankerberg Evangelistic Association, Chattanooga, Tennessee, p. 4.

22. Albert Mackey, *The Manual of the Lodge* (New York: Clark Maynard, 1870), p. 20; cf. Ankerberg, et al., *The Masonic Lodge*, p. 5.

23. Blanchard, *Scottish Rite Masonry Illustrated*, 2:221-22.

24. Ibid., 2:263-64.

25. Newton, *The Builders*, pp. 243, 246, 247.

26. *Ceremonies of Installation and Dedication,* rev. (The Ancient and Accepted Scottish Rite of Freemasonry, Southern Jurisdiction U.S.A., 1954), p. 123.

27. Manly P. Hall, *The Lost Keys of Freemasonry or the Secret of Hiram Abiff* (Richmond: Macoy, 1976), p. 13.

28. Pike, *Morals and Dogma*, p. 102.

29. Wagner, *Freemasonry: An Interpretation*, p. 290.

30. Henry C. Clausen, *Clausen's Commentaries on Morals and Dogma* (The Supreme Council, 33d Degree, Ancient and Accepted Scottish Rite of Freemasonry, Southern Jurisdiction of the U.S.A., 1976), p. 157.

31. Edmond Ronayne, *The Master's Carpet or Masonry and Baal-Worship—Identical* (n.p., n.d., distributed by Missionary Service and Supply, Route 2, Columbiana, OH 44408), pp. 111-12.

32. Pike, *Morals and Dogma*, pp. 219, 161.

33. *Little Masonic Library*, 5:52.

34. Manly P. Hall, *An Encyclopedic Outline of Masonic Hermetic Qabbalistic and Rosicrucian Symbolical Philosophy* (Los Angeles: Philosophical Research Society, 1977), p. 176.

35. Haywood, *The Great Teachings of Masonry*, p. 99; Newton, *The Builders,* p. 258; Hall, *The Lost Keys of Freemasonry*, pp. 64-65; Newton, *The Builders,* pp. 243, 258.

36. Carl H. Claudy, *Foreign Countries: A Gateway to the Interpretation and Development of Certain Symbols of Freemasonry* (Richmond: Macoy, 1971), p. 17.

37. Stephen Knight, *The Brotherhood: The Explosive Exposé of the Secret World of the Freemasons* (London: Grenada/Panther, 1983), p. 234; *Little Masonic Library*, 5:43-44.

38. Shaw and McKenney, *The Deadly Deception*, p. 125.

39. Henry Wilson Coil, *Coil's Masonic Encyclopedia* (New York: Macoy, 1961), p. 512; Allen E. Roberts, *Key to Freemasonry's Growth* (Richmond: Macoy, 1969), p. 18; *Little Masonic Library*, 5:35; Newton, *The Builders*, pp. 62-3, 275.

Chapter 16: Influencing the Church

1. John Sheville and James Gould, *Guide to the Royal Arch Chapter: A Complete Monitor with Full Instructions in the Degrees of Mark Master, Past Master, Most Excellent Master and Royal Arch Together with the Order of High Priesthood* (Richmond: Macoy, 1981), p. 181; H. L. Haywood, *The Newly-Made Mason: What He and Every Mason Should Know About Masonry* (Richmond: Macoy, 1973), p. 211.

2. Charles H. Lacquement, "Freemasonry and Organized Religions," *The Pennsylvania Freemason*, February 1989, p. 7.

3. Carl H. Claudy, *Foreign Countries: A Gateway to the Interpretation and Development of Certain Symbols of Freemasonry* (Richmond: Macoy, 1971), p. 124; cf. pp. 119-26; Report of the Faith and Order Committee of the British Methodist Church, *Freemasonry and Methodism*, presented to the General Assembly of the British Methodist Church and adopted by them 3 July 1985, §§19, 21; Joseph Fort Newton, *The Builders: A Story and Study of Freemasonry* (Richmond: Macoy, 1951), pp. 241-42; Dale A. Byers, *I Left the Lodge* (Schaumburg, Ill.: Regular Baptist, 1988), p. 110.

4. Cf. Stephen Knight, *The Brotherhood: The Explosive Exposé of the Secret World of the Freemasons* (London: Grenada/Panther, 1983), pp. 254-65.

5. E.g., ibid.

6. John Ankerberg, William Mankin, and Walter Martin, *Christianity and the Masonic Lodge: Are They Compatible?* "The John Ankerberg Show," transcript, 1985, The John Ankerberg Evangelistic Association, Chattanooga, Tennessee, p. 34.

7. C. F. Keil and F. Delitzsch, *Commentary on the Old Testament in Ten Volumes* (Grand Rapids: Eerdmans, 1978), p. 222.

8. Cf. Amihai Mazar, "Bronze Bull Found in Israelite 'High Place' from the Time of the Judges," *Biblical Archeology Review* (September/October 1983), pp. 34-40.

9. *Ceremonies of Installation and Dedication,* rev. (The Ancient and Accepted Scottish Rite of Freemasonry, Southern Jurisdiction U.S.A., 1954), p. 69.

10. E. Ronayne, *Chapter Masonry* (Chicago: Ezra A. Cook, 1984), p. 126.

11. *Leaves from Georgia Masonry* (Educational and Historical Commission of the Grand Lodge of Georgia, 1947), p. 74.

12. John R. Rice, *Lodges Examined by the Bible* (Murfreesboro, Tenn.: Sword of the Lord, 1943), pp. 13-14.

Introduction to Part 4

1. John Ankerberg and John Weldon, *The Facts on Spirit Guides; The Facts on the New Age Movement; The Facts on Astrology* (Eugene, Oreg.: Harvest House, 1988); Raphael Gasson, *The Challenging Counterfeit* (Plainfield, N.J.: Logos, 1970); Johanna Michaelsen, *The Beautiful Side of Evil* (Eugene, Oreg.: Harvest House, 1982); Ben Alexander, *Out from Darkness: The True Story of a Medium Who Escaped the Oc-*

cult (Joplin, Mo.: College, 1986); Victor Ernest, *I Talked with Spirits* (Wheaton, Ill.: Tyndale 1971); M. Lamar Keene, *The Psychic Mafia* (New York: St. Martins Press, 1976; John Ankerberg and John Weldon, *Astrology: Do the Heavens Rule Our Destiny?* (Eugene, Oreg.: Harvest House, 1989), chaps. 14-15; J. I. Packer, *God's Words: Studies of Key Bible Themes* (Downers Grove, Ill.: InterVarsity, 1981); Vishal Mangalwadi, *The World of Gurus* (New Delhi, India: Vikas, 1977); Tal Brooke, *Riders of the Cosmic Circuit: Rajneesh, Sai Baba, Muktananda . . . Gods of the New Age* (Batavia, Ill.: Lion, 1986); Ted Schwarz and Duane Empey, *Satanism* (Grand Rapids: Zondervan, 1988); Doreen Irvine, *Freed from Witchcraft* (Nashville: Thomas Nelson, 1973); Mike Warnke, *The Satan Seller* (Danville, Ky.: Warnke Ministries, 1985); Maury Terry, *The Ultimate Evil* (Garden City, N.Y.: Dolplin/Doubleday 1987); Paul Reisser, M.D., Teri Reisser, and John Weldon, *New Age Medicine* (Downers Grove, Ill: InterVarsity, 1988); Samuel Pfeifer, M.D., *Healing at Any Price?* (Milton Keynes, England: Word (UK) Ltd, 1988); John Weldon and Zola Levitt, *Psychic Healing: An Exposé of an Occult Phenomenon* (Chicago: Moody, 1982); John Weldon and James Bjornstad, *Playing with Fire* (Chicago: Moody, 1984); Edmond Gruss, *The Ouija Board: Doorway to the Occult* (Chicago: Moody, 1985); J. Sidlow Baxter, *Majesty: The God You Should Know* (San Bernardino, Calif.: Here's Life, 1984); Ruth A. Tucker, *Another Gospel: Alternative Religions and the New Age Movement* (Grand Rapids: Academie/Zondervan, 1989); John Weldon, *The Encyclopedia of Modern Cults and Religions*, unpublished manuscript, 1989; Elliot Miller, *A Crash Course on the New Age Movement* (Grand Rapids: Baker, 1989); Karne Hoyt, *The New Age Rage* (Old Tappan, N.J.: Fleming H. Revell, 1987).

2. Kurt E. Koch, *Demonology Past and Present* (Grand Rapids: Kregel, 1973); *Occult Bondage and Deliverance* (Grand Rapids: Kregel, 1970); *Christian Counseling and Occultism* (Grand Rapids: Kregel, 1978); *Between Christ and Satan* (Grand Rapids: Kregel, 1962); *Satan's Devices* (Grand Rapids: Kregel, 1978); *The Devil's Alphabet* (Grand Rapids: Kregel, 1969); Merrill Unger, *Biblical Demonology* (Wheaton, Ill: Scripture, 1971); *Demons in the World Today* (Wheaton, Ill: Tyndale, 1972); *The Haunting of Bishop Pike* (Wheaton, Ill: Tyndale, 1971); *What Demons Can Do to Saints* (Chicago: Moody, 1977); Carl A. Raschke, "Satanism and the Devolution of the 'New Religions'," *SCP Newsletter* (Fall 1985); Carl A. Raschke, *The Interruption of Eternity: Modern Gnosticism and the Origins of New Religious Consciousness* (Chicago: Nelson-Hall, 1980); John Warwick Montgomery, *Principalities and Powers* (Minneapolis: Bethany, 1973); John Warwick Montgomery, ed., *Demon Possession* (Minneapolis: Bethany, 1976); Malachi Martin, *Hostage to the Devil: The Possession and Exorcism of Five Living Americans* (New York: Bantam, 1977); Gary North, *Unholy Spirits: Occultism and New Age Humanism* (Ft. Worth: Dominion, 1986); John Weldon, "The Hazards of Psychic Involvement: A Look at Some Consequences" (unpublished manuscript, 1986); Weldon and Levitt, *Psychic Healing*; Johanna Michaelson, *Like Lambs to the Slaughter: Your Child and the Occult* (Eugene, Oreg.: Harvest House, 1989); Schwarz and Empey, *Satanism*; Irvine, *Freed from Witchcraft*; Warnke, *The Satan Seller*; Terry, *The Ultimate Evil*; Gasson, *The Challenging Counterfeit*; Michaelsen, *The Beautiful Side of Evil*; Alexander, *Out from Darkness*; Ernest, *I Talked with Spirits*; Keene, *The Psychic Mafia*.

3. Unger, *Biblical Demonology*; *Demons in the World Today*; *The Haunting of Bishop Pike*; *What Demons Can Do to Saints*.

Chapter 17: The Occult

1. Henry Wilson Coil, *A Comprehensive View of Freemasonry* (Richmond: Macoy, 1973), p. 184.

2. John Ankerberg and John Weldon, *Astrology: Do the Heavens Rule Our Destiny?* (Eugene, Oreg.: Harvest House, 1989), chaps. 14-15; John Weldon and James Bjornstad, *Playing with Fire* (Chicago: Moody, 1984); Edmond Gruss, *The Ouija Board: Doorway to the Occult* (Chicago: Moody, 1985).

3. Stephen Knight, *The Brotherhood: The Explosive Exposé of the Secret World of the Freemasons* (London: Grenada/Panther, 1983), p. 243.

4. George H. Steinmetz, *Freemasonry—Its Hidden Meaning* (Chicago: Charles T. Powner, 1976), p. 2.

5. E. M. Storms, *Should a Christian Be a Mason?* (Fletcher, N.C.: New Puritan Library, 1980), p. 43.

6. Corinne Heline, *Mystic Masonry and the Bible* (La Canada, Calif.: New Age, 1975), p. 91.

7. The Baptist Union of Scotland (endorsed by the Baptist Union of Great Britain and Ireland), *Baptists and Freemasonry* (Baptist Church House, 1987), p. 7.

8. Ingo Swann, *Natural ESP* (New York: Bantam, 1987), pp. xviii, 192, 54-56, 191.

9. Henry C. Clausen, *Clausen's Commentaries on Morals and Dogma* (The Supreme Council, 33d Degree, Ancient and Accepted Scottish Rite of Freemasonry, Southern Jurisdiction of the U.S.A., 1976), pp. 157-58.

10. Ibid., pp. 172, 174.

11. Ibid., pp. 203-4, 210-12.

12. E.g., John Ankerberg and John Weldon, *The Facts on Spirit Guides; The Facts on the New Age Movement; The Facts on Astrology* (Eugene, Oreg.: Harvest House, 1988), pp. 7-48; John Ferguson, *An Illustrated Encyclopedia of Mysticism and the Mystery Religions* (New York: Seabury, 1977), p. 148; Frits Staal, *Exploring Mysticism* (Berkley: Berkeley U. of Calif., 1975); Benjamin B. Wolman, Montague Ullman, eds., *Handbook of States of Consciousness* (New York: Van Nostrand Reinhold, 1986), pp. 286-90.

13. Albert Pike, *Morals and Dogma of the Ancient and Accepted Scottish Rite of Freemasonry* (Charleston, S.C.: The Supreme Council of the 33d Degree for the Southern Jurisdiction of the United States, 1906), pp. 626.

14. Ibid., pp. 745, 744, 741.

15. *Liturgy of the Ancient and Accepted Scottish Rite of Freemasonry for the Southern Jurisdiction of the United States, Part Two* (Washington, D.C.: The Supreme Council, 33d Degree of the Ancient and Accepted Scottish Rite of Freemasonry of the Southern Jurisdiction of the U.S.A., 1982), p. 166.

16. Albert G. Mackey, *The Symbolism of Freemasonry: Illustrating and Explaining Its Science and Philosophy, Its Legends, Myths, and Symbols* (Chicago: Charles T. Powner, 1975), p. 325.

17. Albert Mackey, *Mackey's Revised Encyclopedia of Freemasonry*, rev. and enl. by Robert I. Clegg (Richmond: Macoy, 1966), 1:166.

18. Manly P. Hall, *An Encyclopedic Outline of Masonic Hermetic Qabbalistic and Rosicrucian Symbolical Philosophy* (Los Angeles: Philosophical Research Society, 1977), p. 114.

19. *Encyclopaedia Britannica, Micropaedia*, 15th ed., s.v. "Rosicrucians"; cf. John Weldon, *Encyclopedia* (unpublished), s.v. "Walter Martin, *Kingdom of the Cults*, Appendix"; and Josh McDowell and Don Stewart, *Handbook of Today's Religions* (San Bernardino, Calif.: Here's Life, 1983), chap. 17.

20. Hall, *An Encyclopedic Outline*, p. 139.

21. *Mackey's Revised Encyclopedia of Freemasonry*, 1:449.

22. Henry Wilson Coil, *Coil's Masonic Encyclopedia* (New York: Macoy, 1961), p. 25.

23. Mackey, *The Symbolism of Freemasonry*, p. 338.

24. *Mackey's Revised Encyclopedia of Freemasonry*, 1:49.

25. E.g., Arthur Edward Waite, *A New Encyclopedia of Freemasonry* (New York: Weather Vane, 1970), pp. 201-4.

26. Martin L. Wagner, *Freemasonry: An Interpretation* (n.p., n.d.), distributed by Missionary Service and Supply, Route 2, Columbiana, OH, 44408, pp. 144-45.

27. *Coil's Masonic Encyclopedia*, p. 676.

28. Joseph Fort Newton, *The Builders: A Story and Study of Freemasonry* (Richmond: Macoy, 1951), p. 59.

29. Paul A. Fisher, *Behind the Lodge Door: Church, State & Freemasonry* (Washington, D.C.: Shield Press, 1987), p. 42.

30. Alphonse Cerza, *A Masonic Reader's Guide*, ed. Thomas C. Warden, Transactions of the Missouri Lodge of Research, vol. 34 (1978-1979), 1980, p. 9.

31. Waite, *A New Encyclopedia of Freemasonry*, 2:201-2.

32. Pike, *Morals and Dogma*, p. 839.

33. Heline, *Mystic Masonry and the Bible*.

34. Manly P. Hall, *The Lost Keys of Freemasonry or the Secret of Hiram Abiff* (Richmond: Macoy, 1976), p. 64.

35. Hall, *An Encyclopedic Outline*, p. 3.

36. Ibid., p. 140.

37. Allen E. Roberts, *The Craft and Its Symbols: Opening the Door to Masonic Symbolism* (Richmond: Macoy, 1974), p. 4.

38. *Ceremonies of Installation and Dedication,* rev. (The Ancient and Accepted Scottish Rite of Freemasonry, Southern Jurisdiction U.S.A., 1954), p. 44.

39. H. V. B. Voorhis, *Facts for Freemasons: A Storehouse of Masonic Knowledge in Question and Answer Form*, rev. (Richmond: Macoy, 1979), p. 227.

40. Book review in Cerza, *A Masonic Reader's Guide*, p. 86.

41. Carl H. Claudy, *Foreign Countries: A Gateway to the Interpretation and Development of Certain Symbols of Freemasonry* (Richmond: Macoy, 1971), p. 102.

42. Jim Shaw and Tom McKenney, *The Deadly Deception: Freemasonry Exposed by One of Its Top Leaders* (Lafayette, La.: Huntington House, 1988), pp. 155-56.

43. Ibid., p. 157.

44. Ibid.

45. Newton, *The Builders*, p. 85.

46. Grand Lodge of Texas, A. F. and A. M., *Monitor of the Lodge: Monitorial Instructions in the Three Degrees of Symbolic Masonry* (Grand Lodge of Texas, 1982), pp. xv-xvi.

47. Voorhis, *Facts for Freemasons*, pp. v-vi.

48. Ibid., pp. 6, 227.

49. Ibid., p. 228, cf. *Mackey's Revised Encyclopedia of Freemasonry*, 2:728.

50. Mackey, *The Symbolism of Freemasonry*, p. 333; Hall, *The Lost Keys of Freemasonry*, p.100; Isabel Cooper-Oakley, *Masonry and Medieval Mysticism: Traces of a Hidden Tradition* (Wheaton, Ill.: Theosophical, 1977), p. 34; Claudy, *Foreign Countries*, p. ix; W. L. Wilmshurst, *The Meaning of Masonry* (New York: Bell, 1980), p. 177.

51. Claudy, *Foreign Countries*, p. 5.

52. Ibid., p. ix.

53. H. L. Haywood, *The Newly-Made Mason: What He and Every Mason Should Know About Masonry* (Richmond: Macoy, 1973), p. 211.

54. Staal, *Exploring Mysticism*; Wolman and Ullman, eds., *Handbook of States of Consciousness.*

55. *Clausen's Commentaries on Morals and Dogma*, p. 210.

56. Foster Bailey, *The Spirit of Masonry* (Hampstead, London: Lucius, 1972), p. 127.

57. John Ankerberg, William Mankin, and Walter Martin, *Christianity and the Masonic Lodge: Are They Compatible?* "The John Ankerberg Show," transcript, 1985, The John Ankerberg Evangelistic Association, Chattanooga, Tennessee, p. 29.

58. Wilmshurst, *The Meaning of Masonry*, pp. 11, 112; cf. pp. 74-75, 174-85.

59. Wilmshurst, *The Meaning of Masonry*, pp. 75, 140.

60. Ibid., p. 185.

61. Ferguson, *An Illustrated Encyclopedia of Mysticism and the Mystery Religions*, p. 148.

62. E.g., Ankerberg and Weldon, *The Facts on Spirit Guides*; *The Facts on the New Age Movement*; *The Facts on Astrology.*

63. Bailey, *The Spirit of Masonry*, p. 115.

64. Ibid., p. 124.

65. Wilmshurst, *The Meaning of Masonry*, p. 4.

66. Hall, *The Lost Keys of Freemasonry*, p. 102.

67. Wilmshurst, *The Meaning of Masonry*, p. 54.

Chapter 18: Spiritism

1. E.g., John Ankerberg and John Weldon, *The Facts on Spirit Guides*; *The Facts on the New Age Movement*; *The Facts on Astrology* (Eugene, Oreg.: Harvest House, 1988); Merrill Unger, *Biblical Demonology* (Wheaton, Ill: Scripture, 1971); *Demons in the World Today* (Wheaton, Ill: Tyndale, 1972); *The Haunting of Bishop Pike* (Wheaton, Ill: Tyndale, 1971); *What Demons Can Do to Saints* (Chicago: Moody, 1977).

2. See John Ankerberg and John Weldon, *The Facts on Spirit Guides*; *The Facts on the New Age Movement*; *The Facts on Astrology* (Eugene, Oreg.: Harvest House, 1988); Paul and Teri Reisser, and John Weldon, *New Age Medicine* (Downers Grove, Ill.: InterVarsity, 1988), chap. 6; Ben Hester, *Dowsing: An Exposé of Hidden Occult Forces* (available from author: 4883 Hedrick Ave., Arlington, CA 92505); Clifford Wilson and John Weldon, *Psychic Forces* (Chattanooga: Global, 1988), pp. 331-445; John Weldon and James Bjornstad, *Playing with Fire: Dungeons and Dragons and Other Fantasy Games* (Chicago: Moody, 1984), chap. 5; John Weldon and Zola Levitt, *Psychic Healing* (Chicago: Moody, 1982), chap. 3 (Radionics); Edmond Gruss, *The Ouija Board* (Chicago: Moody, 1975).

3. Arthur Edward Waite, *A New Encyclopedia of Freemasonry* (New York: Weather Vane, 1970), 1:27-29, 55.

4. Albert G. Mackey, *The Symbolism of Freemasonry: Illustrating and Explaining Its Science and Philosophy, Its Legends, Myths, and Symbols* (Chicago: Charles T. Powner, 1975), pp. 45-46.

5. Ibid., pp. 45, 332.

6. Ibid., pp. 45, 331.

7. Alice Bailey, *The Reappearance of the Christ* (London: Lucius Trust, 1974), pp. 120-30.

8. Kurt E. Koch, *Demonology Past and Present* (Grand Rapids: Kregel, 1973); *Occult Bondage and Deliverance* (Grand Rapids: Kregel, 1970); *Christian Counseling and Occultism* (Grand Rapids: Kregel, 1978); *Between Christ and Satan* (Grand Rapids:

Kregel, 1962); *Satan's Devices* (Grand Rapids: Kregel, 1978); *The Devil's Alphabet* (Grand Rapids: Kregel, 1969).

9. W. L. Wilmshurst, *The Meaning of Masonry* (New York: Bell, 1980), p. 173; cf. pp. 175, 185.

10. Djwhal Khul, "The Restoration of the Mysteries," *The Beacon* (May 1963), in Corinne Heline, *Mystic Masonry and the Bible* (La Canada, Calif.: New Age, 1975), pp. xiv-xv; cf. p. xvi.

11. Ibid., p. xv.

12. H. P. Blavatsky, *The Secret Doctrine* (Wheaton, Ill: Theosophical, 1971), 1:14-16, 6:227.

13. Isabel Cooper-Oakley, *Masonry and Medieval Mysticism: Traces of a Hidden Tradition* (Wheaton, Ill.: Theosophical, 1977), pp. 31-32.

14. Blavatsky, *The Secret Doctrine*, 5:90.

15. Lynn F. Perkins, *Masonry in the New Age* (Lakemont, Ga: CSA, 1971), pp. 18-19.

16. Percival rejected the more typical occultic descriptions as to how *Thinking and Destiny* was produced (Harold Waldwin Percival, *Masonry and Its Symbols in the Light of "Thinking and Destiny"* [Forest Hills, N.Y.: The Word Foundation, Inc., 1979], pp. xi-xiii), possibly the result of his allegedly "devout Christian" upbringing (Percival, *Masonry and Its Symbols*, p. xiv). But that it was not a product of his own mind but was rather the result of spiritistic inspiration should be clear to anyone who is familiar with the various forms that spiritistic inspiration takes and who reads Percival's own description of the process of his inspiration (Percival, *Masonry and Its Symbols*, pp. xv-xvi, xi, 47, 53-58).

17. Percival, *Masonry and Its Symbols*, pp. 1, 2.

18. Manly P. Hall, *The Lost Keys of Freemasonry or the Secret of Hiram Abiff* (Richmond: Macoy, 1976), pp. 11-13.

19. Ibid., pp. 16-17, 25.

20. Ibid., pp. 54-55.

21. Ibid., pp. 57, 59-60.

22. Foster Bailey, *The Spirit of Masonry* (Hampstead, London: Lucius, 1972), pp. 20-21, 133-34, 71-79, 125-26, 99-102, 120, 123-132.

23. Ibid., pp. 128-30.

24. Ibid., p. 20.

25. Ibid.

26. Ibid., p. 119.

27. Ibid., p. 21.

28. *Ceremonies of Installation and Dedication*, rev. (The Ancient and Accepted Scottish Rite of Freemasonry, Southern Jurisdiction U.S.A., 1954), p. 66.

29. Bailey, *The Spirit of Masonry*, pp. 120, 134, 79, 134.

30. Percival, *Masonry and Its Symbols*, p. 47; cf. pp. xvi, 33, 42-44, 53-54.

31. Bailey, *The Spirit of Masonry*, p. 127.

32. Manly P. Hall, *An Encyclopedic Outline of Masonic, Hermetic, Qabbalistic and Rosicrucian Symbolical Philosophy* (Los Angeles: Philosophical Research Society, 1977), p. 79; Wilmshurst, *The Meaning of Masonry*, pp. 149, 185.

33. John Ankerberg, William Mankin, and Walter Martin, *Christianity and the Masonic Lodge: Are They Compatible?* "The John Ankerberg Show," transcript, 1985, The John Ankerberg Evangelistic Association, Chattanooga, Tennessee, p. 29.

34. Arthur Avalon, *The Serpent Power* (New York: Dover, 1974); Gopi Krishna, *The Awakening of Kundalini* (New York: Dutton, 1975); Hans-Ulrich Rieker, *The Yoga of Light* (Los Angeles: Dawn Horse, 1974).

35. Henry Wilson Coil, *A Comprehensive View of Freemasonry* (Richmond: Macoy, 1973), p. 218.

36. Wilmshurst, *The Meaning of Masonry*, p. 54.

37. Ankerberg, et al., *Christianity and the Masonic Lodge*, p. 30.

38. J. Blanchard, *Scottish Rite Masonry Illustrated (The Complete Ritual of the Ancient and Accepted Scottish Rite)* (Chicago: Charles T. Powner, 1979), 1:453-57; cf. Ankerberg, et al., "Christianity and the Masonic Lodge," pp. 30-31; Stephen Knight, *The Brotherhood: The Explosive Exposé of the Secret World of the Freemasons* (London: Grenada/Panther, 1983), pp. 236-37; cf. "Baalzebul" (2 Kings 1:2, 16; Matthew 12:24-27; cf. *The New Schaff-Herzog Encyclopedia of Religious Knowledge* (1978), s.v. "Baal"; Lewis Bayles Payton, "Baal, Beel, Bel" in *Encyclopedia of Religion and Ethics,* ed. James Hastings (New York: Charles Schribner's Sons, n.d.); George A. Barton, "Baalzebub and Beelzaboul" in *Encyclopedia of Religion and Ethics,* ed. James Hastings (New York: Charles Schribner's Sons, n.d.).

39. Ankerberg, et al., *Christianity and the Masonic Lodge*, p. 31.

40. The Working Group established by the Standing Committee of the General Synod of the Church of England, *Freemasonry and Christianity: Are They Compatible?* (London: Church House, 1987), p. 55. Most of Martin L. Wagner's text, *Freemasonry: An Interpretation* (n.p., n.d.), distributed by Missionary Service and Supply, Route 2, Columbiana, OH 44408, is devoted to documenting the connection of Masonry and its symbolism to ancient phallicism.

Chapter 19: Mystery Religions

1. *Encyclopaedia Britannica, Macropaedia,* 15th ed., s.v. "Mystery Religions."

2. Paul A. Fisher, *Behind the Lodge Door: Church, State & Freemasonry* (Washington, D.C.: Shield Press, 1987), pp. 273-74.

3. *Encyclopaedia Britannica, Macropaedia,* 15th ed., s.v. "Mystery Religions."

4. Martin L. Wagner, *Freemasonry: An Interpretation* (n.p., n.d.), distributed by Missionary Service and Supply, Route 2, Columbiana, OH 44408, p. 253.

5. Ibid., p. 161.

6. Wagner, *Freemasonry: An Interpretation*, p. 251; Albert G. Mackey, *The Symbolism of Freemasonry: Illustrating and Explaining Its Science and Philosophy, Its Legends, Myths, and Symbols* (Chicago: Charles T. Powner, 1975), pp. 185-86; Jim Shaw and Tom McKenney, *The Deadly Deception: Freemasonry Exposed by One of Its Top Leaders* (Lafayette, La.: Huntington House, 1988), pp. 143-45; Mackey, *The Symbolism of Freemasonry*, pp. 185-86, 352-53; Wagner, *Freemasonry: An Interpretation*, pp. 296-98, 357-58.

7. Alphonse Cerza, *Let There Be Light: A Study in Anti-Masonry* (Silver Spring, Md.: The Masonic Service Association, 1983), p. 1.

8. Henry Wilson Coil, *Coil's Masonic Encyclopedia* (New York: Macoy, 1961), p. 432.

9. W. L. Wilmshurst, *The Meaning of Masonry* (New York: Bell, 1980), pp. 3-4.

10. Grand Lodge of Texas, A. F. and A. M., *Monitor of the Lodge: Monitorial Instructions in the Three Degrees of Symbolic Masonry* (Grand Lodge of Texas, 1982), pp. xiii-xiv.

11. Albert Pike, *Morals and Dogma of the Ancient and Accepted Scottish Rite of Freemasonry* (Charleston, S.C.: The Supreme Council of the 33d Degree for the Southern Jurisdiction of the United States, 1906); Manly P. Hall, *An Encyclopedic Outline of Masonic Hermetic Qabbalistic and Rosicrucian Symbolical Philosophy* (Los Angeles: Philosophical Research Society, 1977); Foster Bailey, *The Spirit of Masonry*

(Hampstead, London: Lucius, 1972); George H. Steinmetz, *Freemasonry—Its Hidden Meaning* (Chicago: Charles T. Powner, 1976); Mackey, *The Symbolism of Freemasonry*. Wilmshurst, *The Meaning of Masonry*; Committee on Secret Societies of the Ninth General Assembly of the Orthodox Presbyterian Church (meeting at Rochester, N.Y., June 2-5, 1942), *Christ or the Lodge?* (Philadelphia: Great Commission, n.d.), p. 9.

12. Alphonse Cerza, *A Masonic Reader's Guide*, ed. Thomas C. Warden, Transactions of the Missouri Lodge of Research, vol. 34 (1978-1979), 1980, pp. 30-33.

13. Ibid., pp. 32-33.

14. E.g. Joseph Fort Newton, *The Religion of Masonry: An Interpretation* (Richmond: Macoy, 1969), p. 173.

15. Arthur Edward Waite, *A New Encyclopedia of Freemasonry* (New York: Weather Vane, 1970), 1:351-64, 421; 2:146, 201; Mackey, *The Symbolism of Freemasonry*, pp. 332, 338, 355; Fisher, *Behind the Lodge Door*, pp. 27, 29, 336-7.

16. Fisher, *Behind the Lodge Door*, p. 45.

17. H. L. Haywood, *The Great Teachings of Masonry* (Richmond: Macoy, 1971), p. 94; cf. p. 95.

18. Albert Mackey, *Mackey's Revised Encyclopedia of Freemasonry*, rev. and enl. by Robert I. Clegg (Richmond: Macoy, 1966), 2:877.

19. Ibid., 2:1035-36.

20. Ibid., 2:728-29.

21. Hall, *An Encyclopedic Outline*, p. 167.

22. Cf. Stephen Knight, *The Brotherhood: The Explosive Exposé of the Secret World of the Freemasons* (London: Grenada/Panther, 1983), p. 233; Wilmshurst, *The Meaning of Masonry*, pp. 3-4; Steinmetz, *Freemasonry—Its Hidden Meaning*, p. 49; *Mackey's Revised Encyclopedia of Freemasonry*, 2:689-92.

23. *Mackey's Revised Encyclopedia of Freemasonry*, 1:269.

24. *Ceremonies of Installation and Dedication,* rev. (The Ancient and Accepted Scottish Rite of Freemasonry, Southern Jurisdiction U.S.A., 1954), 2:5.

25. Pike, *Morals and Dogma*, pp. 22-23.

26. Bailey, *The Spirit of Masonry*, p. 125.

27. Joseph Fort Newton, *The Builders: A Story and Study of Freemasonry* (Richmond: Macoy, 1951), pp. 47-48. Again, the mysteries were divided into categories of "lesser mysteries" and "greater mysteries" depending on the degree of initiation. Some Masons parallel this to the first three degrees of the Blue Lodge (the Lesser Mysteries) and the York and Scottish Rites (the Greater Mysteries); cf. E. Ronayne, *Chapter Masonry* (Chicago: Ezra A. Cook, 1984), p. 125.

28. *Mackey's Revised Encyclopedia of Freemasonry*, 2:690; 3:1429 (cf. p. 1452).

29. *Ceremonies of Installation and Dedication,* pp. 69, 125.

30. Henry C. Clausen, *Clausen's Commentaries on Morals and Dogma* (The Supreme Council, 33d Degree, Ancient and Accepted Scottish Rite of Freemasonry, Southern Jurisdiction of the U.S.A., 1976), pp. 196-97; Manly P. Hall, *The Lost Keys of Freemasonry or the Secret of Hiram Abiff* (Richmond: Macoy, 1976), p. 103.

31. Hall, *The Lost Keys of Freemasonry*, p. V.

32. *Holy Bible—Masonic Edition*, rev. (John A. Hertel Co., 1957), p. 21; L. James Rongstad, *How to Respond to the Lodge* (St. Louis: Concordia, 1977), p. 9.

33. *Clausen's Commentaries on Morals and Dogma*, p. 2; cf. Lewis Sperry Chafer, *Major Bible Themes* (Grand Rapids: Zondervan, 1926); Lewis Sperry Chafer, *Systematic Theology* (Dallas: Dallas Seminary, 1971), vol. IV; Harold O. J. Brown, *The Protest of*

a Troubled Protestant (New Rochelle, N.Y.: Arlington House, 1969); C. S. Lewis, *The Great Divorce* (New York: Macmillan, 1946); C. S. Lewis, *The Problem of Pain* (New York: Macmillan, 1971); M. Scott Peck, *People of the Lie* (New York: Simon & Schuster, 1981); *Chalcedon Report,* Box 158, Vallecito, CA (January 1984); Alice A. Bailey, *The Externalization of the Hierarchy* (New York: Lucis, 1948).

34. Mackey, *The Symbolism of Freemasonry*, pp. 35, 38.

35. Hall, *The Lost Keys of Freemasonry*, p. XXIII.

36. Cf. W. L. Liefeld, "Mystery Religions" in *The Zondervan Pictorial Encyclopedia of the Bible,* ed. Merrill C. Tenney (Grand Rapids: Zondervan, 1977).

37. Cf. Wagner, *Freemasonry: An Interpretation*, p. 332 (see also pp. 137-563). Additional corroborating material on Masonry and morality (pp. 503-63) and detailing the influence of Masonry in the church could not be discussed due to space considerations. But cf. William W. Daniel, et al., *Masonic Manual of the Grand Lodge of Georgia,* 9th edition (Free and Accepted Masons, Grand Lodge of Georgia, 1973), p. 190; Raymond Lee Allen, et al., *Tennessee Craftsmen or Masonic Textbook,* 14th edition (Nashville: Tennessee Board of Custodians Members, 1963), p. 88; Malcom C. Duncan, *Masonic Ritual and Monitor* (New York: David McKay, n.d.), p. 230; Edmond Ronayne, *The Master's Carpet or Masonry and Baal-Worship—Identical* (n.p., n.d., distributed by Missionary Service and Supply, Route 2, Columbiana, OH 44408), pp. 105-6; The Baptist Union of Scotland (endorsed by the Baptist Union of Great Britain and Ireland), *Baptists and Freemasonry* (Baptist Church House, 1987), p. 7; John R. Rice, *Lodges Examined by the Bible* (Murfreesboro, Tenn.: Sword of the Lord, 1943), pp. 25-7; Fisher, *Behind the Lodge Door*, pp. 50-52, 244-45; Knight, *The Brotherhood*, pp. 4, 85, 269-307; Wagner, *Freemasonry: An Interpretation*, p. 555; Allen E. Roberts, *The Craft and Its Symbols: Opening the Door to Masonic Symbolism* (Richmond: Macoy, 1974), p. 43; *Encyclopaedia Britannica, Micropaedia,* 15th ed., s.v. "Freemasonry"; Rongstad, *How to Respond to the Lodge,* pp. 14, 22.

38. Wagner, *Freemasonry: An Interpretation*, pp. 493, 503-63; Roberts, *The Craft and Its Symbols,* p. 43; H. V. B. Voorhis, *Facts for Freemasons: A Storehouse of Masonic Knowledge in Question and Answer Form,* rev. (Richmond: Macoy, 1979), p. 193; Haywood, *The Great Teachings of Masonry,* pp. 38-40; Committee on Secret Societies of the Ninth General Assembly of the Orthodox Presbyterian Church, *Christ or the Lodge?,* p. 14; *Mackey's Revised Encyclopaedia of Freemasonry,* 2:680.

Chapter 20: Deception

1. Albert Pike, *Morals and Dogma of the Ancient and Accepted Scottish Rite of Freemasonry* (Charleston, S.C.: The Supreme Council of the 33d Degree for the Southern Jurisdiction of the United States, 1906), pp. 109, 104-5.

2. W. J. Morris, *Pocket Lexicon of Freemasonry* (Chicago: Ezra A. Cook, n.d.), p. 53.

3. Martin L. Wagner, *Freemasonry: An Interpretation* (n.p., n.d.), distributed by Missionary Service and Supply, Route 2, Columbiana, OH 44408, p. 288.

4. Pike, *Morals and Dogma*, pp. 106-7.

5. Wagner, *Freemasonry: An Interpretation*, pp. 288-89.

6. Pike, *Morals and Dogma*, pp. 818-19.

7. Stephen Knight, *The Brotherhood: The Explosive Exposé of the Secret World of the Freemasons* (London: Grenada/Panther, 1983), pp. 5, 7.

8. Wagner, *Freemasonry: An Interpretation*, pp. 137-503.

9. Ibid., p. 139.

10. Albert Mackey, *Mackey's Revised Encyclopedia of Freemasonry*, rev. and enl. by Robert I. Clegg (Richmond: Macoy, 1966), 1:561.

11. Committee on Secret Societies of the Ninth General Assembly of the Orthodox Presbyterian Church (meeting at Rochester, N.Y., June 2-5, 1942), *Christ or the Lodge?* (Philadelphia: Great Commission, n.d.), p. 16.

12. Malcom C. Duncan, *Masonic Ritual and Monitor* (New York: David McKay, n.d.), p. 230.

13. Wagner, *Freemasonry: An Interpretation*, pp. 142, 150.

14. Ibid., p. 143.

15. Ibid., pp. 162, 141, 147-48.

16. Manly P. Hall, *The Lost Keys of Freemasonry or the Secret of Hiram Abiff* (Richmond: Macoy, 1976), p. 69.

17. Wagner, *Freemasonry: An Interpretation*; Paul A. Fisher, *Behind the Lodge Door: Church, State & Freemasonry* (Washington, D.C.: Shield Press, 1987); Knight, *The Brotherhood*; Pike, *Morals and Dogma*.

18. J. Blanchard, *Scottish Rite Masonry Illustrated (The Complete Ritual of the Ancient and Accepted Scottish Rite)* (Chicago: Charles T. Powner, 1979), 2:263-64; cf. chap. 5.

19. Wagner, *Freemasonry: An Interpretation*, p. 289.

20. Ibid., pp. 153-54.

21. Ibid., p. 154.

22. Ibid., p. 299.

23. Ibid., p. 282.

24. Ibid., p. 323.

25. Knight, *The Brotherhood*, p. 244.

26. Wagner, *Freemasonry: An Interpretation*, p. 329.

27. Ibid., p. 320.

28. Ibid., p. 152.

29. Ibid., pp. 333-34.

30. Ibid., p. 334.

31. Ibid.

32. Ibid., p. 335.

Epilogue: The Legacy of Christian Masonry

1. H. L. Haywood, *The Newly-Made Mason: What He and Every Mason Should Know About Masonry* (Richmond: Macoy, 1973), p. 219.

2. *Little Masonic Library* (Richmond: Macoy, 1977), 1:10.

3. Ibid., 1:14-15.

4. Ibid., 2:113.

5. Douglas Knoop, G. P. Jones, and Douglas Hamer, transcribers and eds., *The Early Masonic Catechisms* (London: Quatuor Coronati Lodge No. 2076, 1975), p. 22.

6. Ibid., pp. 210-25.

7. H. L. Haywood, *The Great Teachings of Masonry* (Richmond: Macoy, 1971), pp. 96-97.

8. Henry Wilson Coil, *Coil's Masonic Encyclopedia* (New York: Macoy, 1961), p. 517.

9. Henry Wilson Coil, *Freemasonry Through Six Centuries* (Richmond: Macoy, 1967), 1:158.

10. Charles G. Finney, *The Character, Claims and Practical Workings of Freemasonry* (Southern District of Ohio: Western Tract and Book Society, 1869).

11. John Ankerberg, William Mankin, and Walter Martin, *Christianity and the Masonic Lodge: Are They Compatible?* "The John Ankerberg Show," transcript, 1985, The John Ankerberg Evangelistic Association, Chattanooga, Tennessee, p. 34; John R. Rice, *Lodges Examined by the Bible* (Murfreesboro, Tenn.: Sword of the Lord, 1943), p. 75.

12. Rice, *Lodges Examined by the Bible*, p. 77.

13. Committee on Secret Societies of the Ninth General Assembly of the Orthodox Presbyterian Church (meeting at Rochester, N.Y., June 2-5, 1942), *Christ or the Lodge?* (Philadelphia: Great Commission, n.d.), pp. 22-23.

14. J. W. Acker, *Strange Altars: A Scriptural Appraisal of the Lodge* (St. Louis: Concordia, 1959), p. 31.

15. Ibid., p. 59.

16. Stephen Knight, *The Brotherhood: The Explosive Exposé of the Secret World of the Freemasons* (London: Grenada/Panther, 1983), p. 253.

17. Jack Harris, *Freemasonry: The Invisible Cult in Our Midst* (Chattanooga: Global, 1983), p. 143.

18. E. M. Storms, *Should a Christian Be a Mason?* (Fletcher, N.C.: New Puritan Library, 1980), p. 78.

19. Ibid., p. 79.

20. Report of the Faith and Order Committee of the British Methodist Church, *Freemasonry and Methodism*, presented to the General Assembly of the British Methodist Church and adopted by them 3 July 1985, §§21-22.

21. The Baptist Union of Scotland (endorsed by the Baptist Union of Great Britain and Ireland), *Baptists and Freemasonry* (Baptist Church House, 1987), p. 8.

22. Ibid., p. 10.

23. Ibid.

24. The Working Group established by the Standing Committee of the General Synod of the Church of England, *Freemasonry and Christianity: Are They Compatible?* (London: Church House, 1987), p. 40.

25. Acker, *Strange Altars*, p. 60.

26. Rice, *Lodges Examined by the Bible*, p. 47.

27. H. J. Rogers, *The Word of God vs. Masonry* (Van Alstyne, Tex: B & R, n.d.), p. 2.

28. Dale A. Byers, *I Left the Lodge* (Schaumburg, Ill.: Regular Baptist, 1988), pp. 116-17.

29. E. Ronayne, *Chapter Masonry* (Chicago: Ezra A. Cook, 1984), p. 127.

30. Jim Shaw and Tom McKenney, *The Deadly Deception: Freemasonry Exposed by One of Its Top Leaders* (Lafayette, La.: Huntington House, 1988), p. 72.

31. Edmond Ronayne, *The Master's Carpet or Masonry and Baal-Worship—Identical* (n.p., n.d., distributed by Missionary Service and Supply, Route 2, Columbiana, OH 44408), pp. 181-86; Ronayne, *Chapter Masonry*, p. 206.

32. Joseph Fort Newton, *The Religion of Masonry: An Interpretation* (Richmond: Macoy, 1969), p. 16.

33. Albert Mackey, *Mackey's Revised Encyclopedia of Freemasonry*, rev. and enl. by Robert I. Clegg (Richmond: Macoy, 1966), 1:201.

34. Newton, *The Religion of Masonry*, p. 61.

35. Rice, *Lodges Examined by the Bible*, p. 55.

36. Haywood, *The Great Teachings of Masonry*, p. 106.

37. Knight, *The Brotherhood*, pp. 258-60.

38. Ibid., pp. 262-64.

39. Cf. L. James Rongstad, *How to Respond to the Lodge* (St. Louis: Concordia, 1977), p. 24; Committee on Secret Societies of the Ninth General Assembly of the Orthodox Presbyterian Church, *Christ or the Lodge?*, pp. 10-20; Acker, *Strange Altars*, p. 42; Manly P. Hall, *The Lost Keys of Freemasonry or the Secret of Hiram Abiff* (Richmond: Macoy, 1976), p. 93; Rice, *Lodges Examined by the Bible*, pp. 53-4; *Little Masonic Library*, 5:183; Carl H. Claudy, *Foreign Countries: A Gateway to the Interpretation and Development of Certain Symbols of Freemasonry* (Richmond: Macoy, 1971), pp. 24, 121; Allen E. Roberts, *Key to Freemasonry's Growth* (Richmond: Macoy, 1969), p. 8.

40. Paul A. Fisher, *Behind the Lodge Door: Church, State & Freemasonry* (Washington, D.C.: Shield Press, 1987), pp. 55-57.

41. Henry C. Clausen, *Clausen's Commentaries on Morals and Dogma* (The Supreme Council, 33d Degree, Ancient and Accepted Scottish Rite of Freemasonry, Southern Jurisdiction of the U.S.A., 1976), p. 173.

42. William C. Irvine, *Heresies Exposed* (Neptune, N.J.: Loizeaux Brothers, 1970), p. 98.

43. Newton, *The Religion of Masonry*, pp. 19-20, 25, 29, 34.

44. Byers, *I Left the Lodge*, p. 74; cf. Irvine, *Heresies Exposed*, p. 96; W. L. Wilmshurst, *The Meaning of Masonry* (New York: Bell, 1980), pp. 5-216.

45. Martin L. Wagner, *Freemasonry: An Interpretation* (n.p., n.d.), distributed by Missionary Service and Supply, Route 2, Columbiana, OH 44408, p. 24.

46. Committee on Secret Societies of the Ninth General Assembly of the Orthodox Presbyterian Church, *Christ or the Lodge?*, pp. 19-20, 19.

47. *Ceremonies of Installation and Dedication,* rev. (The Ancient and Accepted Scottish Rite of Freemasonry, Southern Jurisdiction U.S.A., 1954), p. 44.

48. Shaw and McKenney, *The Deadly Deception*, p. 77.

49. Ibid., p. 125.

50. *Ceremonies of Installation and Dedication . . . of the Ancient and Accepted Scottish Rite of Freemasonry* (The Ancient and Accepted Scottish Rite of Freemasonry, Southern Jurisdiction, U.S.A., 1954), p. 47.

51. Albert Pike, *Morals and Dogma of the Ancient and Accepted Scottish Rite of Freemasonry* (Charleston, S.C.: The Supreme Council of the 33d Degree for the Southern Jurisdiction of the United States, 1906), p. 308.

52. Newton, *The Religion of Masonry*, p. 80.

53. Rice, *Lodges Examined by the Bible*, pp. 57-58.

54. Rongstad, *How to Respond to the Lodge*, p. 28.

55. Rice, *Lodges Examined by the Bible*, p. 13. According to John Dove, comp., *Virginia Textbook* (Grand Lodge of Virginia, n.d.), p. 21, "Obedience, assistance and the protection of one another are pledged by each Mason to all others, binding them by a common tie which should last as long as life itself."

56. Malcom C. Duncan, *Masonic Ritual and Monitor* (New York: David McKay, n.d.), p. 230; Rice, *Lodges Examined by the Bible*, pp. 25-6.

57. Knight, *The Brotherhood*, pp. 240-41.

58. Ibid., p. 241.

59. Ibid., pp. 241-42, 254.

60. Pike, *Morals and Dogma*, p. 277.

61. *Little Masonic Library*, 5:14; Wilmshurst, *The Meaning of Masonry*, p. 179; *Clausen's Commentaries on Morals and Dogma*, p. 174.

62. Wilmshurst, *The Meaning of Masonry*, pp. 207-11; *Legenda 32 (Part 1)*, a Masonic source apparently used for instruction, c. 1920-30 (n.p., n.d.), p. 30; Alphonse Cerza, *Let There Be Light: A Study in Anti-Masonry* (Silver Spring, Md.: The Masonic Service Association, 1983), p. 45.

63. *Mackey's Revised Encyclopedia of Freemasonry*, 2:847.

64. Rice, *Lodges Examined by the Bible*, p. 51.

65. *Ceremonies of Installation and Dedication*, pp. 123, 119, 122-26.

66. Report of the Faith and Order Committee of the British Methodist Church, *Freemasonry and Methodism*, §§19, 21.

67. Ronayne, *Chapter Masonry*, p. 126.

68. Claudy, *Foreign Countries*, pp. 121-24.

69. Knight, *The Brotherhood*, p. 243.

70. Ibid., p. 234.

Selected References

Acker, J. W. *Strange Altars: A Scriptural Appraisal of the Lodge.* St. Louis: Concordia, 1959.

Allen, Raymond Lee, et al. *Tennessee Craftsmen or Masonic Textbook,* 14th edition. Nashville: Tennessee Board of Custodians Members, 1963.

Ankerberg, John, William Mankin, and Walter Martin. *Christianity and the Masonic Lodge: Are They Compatible?* "The John Ankerberg Show." Transcript, 1985, The John Ankerberg Evangelistic Association, Chattanooga, Tennessee.

Ankerberg, John, Jack Harris, William Mankin, Walter Martin, and Paul Pantzer. *The Masonic Lodge: What Goes On Behind Closed Doors?* "The John Ankerberg Show." Transcript, 1986, The John Ankerberg Evangelistic Association, Chattanooga, Tennessee.

Bailey, Foster. *The Spirit of Masonry.* Hampstead, London: Lucius, 1972.

Blackmer, Rollin C. *The Lodge and the Craft.* Richmond: Macoy, 1976.

Blanchard, J. *Scottish Rite Masonry Illustrated (The Complete Ritual of the Ancient and Accepted Scottish Rite).* Chicago: Charles T. Powner, 1979.

Blue Lodge Enlight'ment [sic]: *A Ritual of the Three Masonic Degrees.* Chicago: Ezra A. Cook, 1964.

Bullock, Harris, et al. *Masonic Manual of the Grand Lodge of Georgia.* Free and Accepted Masons, The Grand Lodge of Georgia, 1983.

Byers, Dale A. *I Left the Lodge.* Schaumburg, Ill.: Regular Baptist, 1988.

Ceremonies of Installation and Dedication, rev. The Ancient and Accepted Scottish Rite of Freemasonry, Southern Jurisdiction U.S.A., 1954.

Cerza, Alphonse. *Let There Be Light: A Study in Anti-Masonry.* Silver Spring, Md.: The Masonic Service Association, 1983.

"Checking It Out" (Masonic Affiliates). *News & Views,* The John Ankerberg Evangelistic Association (August 1986).

Claudy, Carl H. *Foreign Countries: A Gateway to the Interpretation and Development of Certain Symbols of Freemasonry.* Richmond: Macoy, 1971.

————. *Introduction to Freemasonry.* Washington, D.C.: The Temple, 1984.

————. *The Master's Book.* Washington, D.C.: The Temple, 1985.

Clausen, Henry C. *Beyond the Ordinary: Toward a Better, Wiser and Happier World.* Washington, D.C.: The Supreme Council, 33d Degree, Ancient and Accepted Scottish Rite of Freemasonry, 1983.

————. *Clausen's Commentaries on Morals and Dogma.* The Supreme Council, 33d Degree, Ancient and Accepted Scottish Rite of Freemasonry, Southern Jurisdiction of the U.S.A., 1976.

————. *Practice and Procedure for the Scottish Rite.* Washington, D.C.: The Supreme Council, 33d Degree, Ancient and Accepted Scottish Rite of Freemasonry Mother Jurisdiction of the World, 1981.

Coil, Henry Wilson. *A Comprehensive View of Freemasonry.* Richmond: Macoy, 1973.

————. *Freemasonry Through Six Centuries.* Richmond: Macoy, 1967.

Committee on Secret Societies of the Ninth General Assembly of the Orthodox Presbyterian Church (meeting at Rochester, N.Y., June 2-5, 1942). *Christ or the Lodge?* Philadelphia: Great Commission, n.d.

Cooper-Oakley, Isabel. *Masonry and Medieval Mysticism: Traces of a Hidden Tradition.* Wheaton, Ill.: Theosophical, 1977.

Craig, William Lane. *The Son Rises.* Chicago: Moody, 1981.

Daniel, William W., et al. *Masonic Manual of the Grand Lodge of Georgia,* 9th edition. Free and Accepted Masons, Grand Lodge of Georgia, 1973.

DeVelde, Everett C., Jr. "A Reformed View of Freemasonry." In *Christianity and Civilization Vol I: The Failure of the American Baptist Culture,* ed. James B. Jordan. Tyler, Tex.: Geneva Divinity School, 1982.

Dove, John, comp. *Virginia Textbook (containing "The Book of Constitutions," Illustrations of the Work, Forms and Ceremonies of the Grand Lodge of Virginia)*. Grand Lodge of Virginia, n.d.

Duncan, Malcom C. *Masonic Ritual and Monitor*. New York: David McKay, n.d.

Finney, Charles G. *The Character, Claims and Practical Workings of Freemasonry*. Southern District of Ohio: Western Tract and Book Society, 1869.

Fisher, Paul A. *Behind the Lodge Door: Church, State & Freemasonry*. Washington, D.C.: Shield Press, 1987.

Funeral Ceremony and Offices of a Lodge of Sorrow of the Ancient and Accepted Scottish Rite of Freemasonry. Reprint. Charleston, S.C.: Southern Jurisdiction of the United States of America, 1946.

Gasson, Raphael. *The Challenging Counterfeit*. Plainfield, N.J.: Logos, 1970.

The General Grand Chapter of Royal Arch Masons International, Committee on Revision of the Ritual, William F. Kuhn, et al. *The Manual of Ritual for Royal Arch Masons,* 45th ed. 1983.

Habermas, Gary, and Anthony Flew. *Did Jesus Rise From the Dead? The Resurrection Debate*. San Francisco: Harper & Row, 1987.

Hall, Manly P. *An Encyclopedic Outline of Masonic Hermetic Qabbalistic and Rosicrucian Symbolical Philosophy*. Los Angeles: Philosophical Research Society, 1977.

_____. *The Lost Keys of Freemasonry or the Secret of Hiram Abiff*. Richmond: Macoy, 1976.

Harris, Jack. *Freemasonry: The Invisible Cult in Our Midst*. Chattanooga: Global, 1983.

Haywood, H. L. *The Great Teachings of Masonry*. Richmond: Macoy, 1971.

_____. *The Newly-Made Mason: What He and Every Mason Should Know about Masonry*. Richmond: Macoy, 1973.

Henderson, Kent. *Masonic World Guide*. Richmond: Macoy, 1984.

Johnson, Shildes. *Is Masonry a Religion?* Oakland, N.J.: Institute for Contemporary Christianity, 1978.

Knight, Stephen. *The Brotherhood: The Explosive Exposé of the Secret World of the Freemasons*. London: Grenada/Panther, 1983.

Koch, Kurt E. *Between Christ and Satan*. Kregel: Grand Rapids, 1962.

_____. *Demonology Past and Present*. Kregel: Grand Rapids, 1973.

_____. *Satan's Devices*. Kregel: Grand Rapids, 1978.

Knoop, Douglas, G. P. Jones, and Douglas Hamer, trans. and eds., *The Early Masonic Catechisms*. London: Quatuor Coronati Lodge No. 2076, 1975.

Leaves from Georgia Masonry. Educational and Historical Commission of the Grand Lodge of Georgia, 1947.

Liturgy of the Ancient and Accepted Scottish Rite of Freemasonry for the Southern Jurisdiction of the United States, Part Two. Washington, D.C.: The Supreme Council, 33d Degree of the Ancient and Accepted Scottish Rite of Freemasonry of the Southern Jurisdiction of the U.S.A., 1982.

Little Masonic Library. Richmond: Macoy, 1977.

McClain, Alva J. *Freemasonry and Christianity.* Winona Lake, Ind.: BMH Books, 1977.

McQuaig, C. F. *The Masonic Report.* Columbiana, Ohio: Missionary Service and Supply, 1976.

Mackey, Albert. *Mackey's Masonic Ritualist: Monitorial Instructions and the Degrees from Entered Apprentice to Select Masters.* n.p.: Charles E. Merrill, 1867.

————. *Mackey's Revised Encyclopedia of Freemasonry.* Rev. and enl. by Robert I. Clegg. 3 vol. Richmond: Macoy, 1966.

————. *The Manual of the Lodge.* New York: Clark Maynard, 1870.

————. *The Symbolism of Freemasonry: Illustrating and Explaining Its Science and Philosophy, Its Legends, Myths, and Symbols.* Chicago: Charles T. Powner, 1975.

Martin, Malachi. *Hostage to the Devil: The Possession and Exorcism of Five Living Americans.* New York: Bantam, 1977.

Masonic Monitor of the Degrees of Entered Apprentice, Fellow Craft and Master Mason, 7th ed. Free and Accepted Masons of Arkansas, 1983.

Michaelsen, Johanna. *The Beautiful Side of Evil.* Eugene, Oreg.: Harvest House, 1982.

Monitor of the Lodge: Monitorial Instructions in the Three Degrees of Symbolic Masonry. Grand Lodge of Texas, 1982.

Montgomery, John Warwick, ed. *Demon Possession.* Minneapolis: Bethany, 1976.

Morgan, Captain William. *Illustrations of Masonry by One of the Fraternity.* n.p., 1827.

————. *Principalities and Powers.* Minneapolis: Bethany, 1973.

Morrison, Frank. *Who Moved the Stone?* Downers Grove, Ill.: InterVarsity, 1969.

Newton, Joseph Fort. *The Builders: A Story and Study of Freemasonry.* Richmond: Macoy, 1951.

————. *The Religion of Masonry: An Interpretation.* Richmond: Macoy, 1969.

North, Gary. *Unholy Spirits: Occultism and New Age Humanism.* Ft. Worth: Dominion, 1986.

Packer, J. I. *God's Words: Studies of Key Bible Themes.* Downers Grove, Ill.: InterVarsity, 1981.

Pike, Albert. *Morals and Dogma of the Ancient and Accepted Scottish Rite of Freemasonry.* Charleston, S.C.: The Supreme Council of the 33d Degree for the Southern Jurisdiction of the United States, 1906.

Pirtle, Henry. *Kentucky Monitor: Complete Monitorial Ceremonies of the Blue Lodge.* Louisville, Ky.: Standard Printing, 1921.

Raschke, Carl A. *The Interruption of Eternity: Modern Gnosticism and the Origins of New Religious Consciousness.* Chicago: Nelson-Hall, 1980.

_____. "Satanism and the Devolution of the 'New Religions'." *SCP Newsletter* (Fall 1985).

Reisser, Paul, M.D., Teri Reisser, and John Weldon. *New Age Medicine.* Downers Grove, Ill: InterVarsity, 1988.

Revised Knight Templarism Illustrated. Chicago: Ezra A. Cook, 1986.

Roberts, Allen E. *The Craft and Its Symbols: Opening the Door to Masonic Symbolism.* Richmond: Macoy, 1974.

Ronayne, Edmond. *Chapter Masonry.* Chicago: Ezra A. Cook, 1984.

_____. *Freemasonry at a Glance.* Chicago: Ezra A. Cook, 1904.

_____. *The Master's Carpet or Masonry and Baal-Worship—Identical.* n.p., n.d., distributed by Missionary Service and Supply, Route 2, Columbiana, OH 44408.

_____. *Ronayne's Handbook of Freemasonry with Appendix (Mahhah-bone).* Chicago: Ezra A. Cook, 1976.

Schnoebelen, William J., and James Spencer. *Mormonism's Temple of Doom: Mormonism, Magick, Masonry.* Idaho Falls: Tripel J., 1987.

Schwarz, Ted, and Duane Empey. *Satanism.* Grand Rapids: Zondervan, 1988.

Shaw, Jim, and Tom McKenney. *The Deadly Deception: Freemasonry Exposed by One of Its Top Leaders.* Lafayette, La.: Huntington House, 1988.

Sheville, John, and James Gould. *Guide to the Royal Arch Chapter: A Complete Monitor with Full Instructions in the Degrees of Mark Master, Past Master, Most Excellent Master and Royal Arch Together with the Order of High Priesthood.* Richmond: Macoy, 1981.

Simmons, George, and Robert Macoy. *Standard Masonic Monitor of the Degrees of Entered Apprentice, Fellow Craft and Master Mason.* Richmond: Macoy, 1984.

Tucker, Ruth A. *Another Gospel: Alternative Religions and the New Age Movement.* Grand Rapids: Academie/Zondervan, 1989.

Unger, Merrill. *Biblical Demonology.* Wheaton, Ill: Scripture, 1971.

————. *Demons in the World Today.* Wheaton, Ill: Tyndale, 1972.

Wagner, Martin L. *Freemasonry: An Interpretation.* n.d., n.p. (distributed by Missionary Service and Supply, Route 2, Columbiana, OH44408).

Waite, Arthur Edward. *A New Encyclopedia of Freemasonry.* New York: Weather Vane, 1970.

Wilmshurst, W. L. *The Meaning of Masonry.* New York: Bell, 1980.

BOOKS BY JOHN ANKERBERG AND JOHN WELDON

When Does Life Begin? And 39 Other Tough Questions about Abortion, Brentwood, Tenn.: Wolgemuth & Hyatt, 1990.

Astrology: Do the Heavens Rule Our Destiny?, Eugene, Oreg.: Harvest House, 1989.

The Case for Jesus the Messiah: Incredible Prophecies that Prove God Exists, Chattanooga, Tenn.: Ankerberg Theological Research Institute.

The Facts on Astrology, Eugene, Oreg.: Harvest House, 1989.

The Facts on False Teachings in the Church, Eugene, Oreg.: Harvest House, 1989.

The Facts on the Jehovah's Witnesses, Eugene, Oreg.: Harvest House, 1989.

The Facts on "The Last Temptation of Christ," Eugene, Oreg.: Harvest House, 1989.

The Facts on the Masonic Lodge, Eugene, Oreg.: Harvest House, 1989.

The Facts on the New Age Movement, Eugene, Oreg.: Harvest House, 1989.

The Facts on Spirit Guides, Eugene, Oreg.: Harvest House, 1989.

Is the Theory of Evolution Supported or Disproved by Today's Scientific Facts?, Chattanooga, Tenn.: Ankerberg Theological Research Institute, 1987.

Masonry at a Glance

GENERAL INFORMATION

Name: The Masonic Lodge

Size: 4,000,000 U.S., 6,000,000 worldwide

Goal: conversion of the world to Masonic ideals

Theology: polytheistic, syncretistic, monistic

Practice: secret ritual, individual spiritual quest

Historic antecedents: ancient pagan Mystery religion, medieval trade unions and occult practices

Spheres of influence: church, education, business, politics, charitable agency

Ethics: subjective, relative, amoral

Levels of initiation: social, religious, mystical

Worldview: humanistic, eclectic, mystical

Occult dynamics: New Age mysticism, potential for developing altered states of consciousness or spiritism

Source of authority: Masonic ritual/doctrine; Grand Lodges; prominent Masonic leaders

Key themes: Universal Fatherhood of God/Brotherhood of man; Immortality of the Soul; religious quest for spiritual enlightenment

Attitude to other religions: condescending

Key literature: Masonic Monitors (texts of ritual); writings of prominent Masons (Mackey, Coil, Pike, etc.)

THEOLOGY

God: unitarian, deistic, pantheistic

Name of God: The Grand (or Great) Architect of the Universe; Jabbulon

Christ: a supremely good man

Man: inwardly divine

Sin: character flaws, ignorance of spiritual reality

Salvation: by good works, character

Bible: a symbol of divine truth

Afterlife: universalistic

FALSE CLAIMS

Masonry is not a religion or substitute for religion

Masonry is not occultic

Masonry does not offer a system of salvation

To be merely a fraternal brotherhood

To constitute the one true religion

To support the church

To be tolerant of all religons; further, to unite all religions

To honor the Bible and all Scriptures

To not interfere with one's religion or politics

Index of Subjects

Index of Persons

This index identifies most pages where authors are named; it does not identify many places these authors are quoted but not named.

MASONS

Major authors recommended by the Grand Lodges (see also pp. 19-20) have asterisks.